Phenomenology and Mysticism

The Verticality of Religious Experience

ANTHONY J. STEINBOCK

Indiana University Press
Bloomington and Indianapolis

Publication of this book is made possible in part with the assistance of a Challenge Grant from the National Endowment for the Humanities, a federal agency that supports research, education, and public programming in the humanities. Any views, findings, conclusions, or recommendations expressed in this publication do not necessarily reflect those of the National Endowment for the Humanities.

This book is a publication of

Indiana University Press
601 North Morton Street
Bloomington, Indiana 47404-3797 USA

www.iupress.indiana.edu

Telephone orders	800-842-6796
Fax orders	812-855-7931
Orders by e-mail	iuporder@indiana.edu

First paperback edition 2009
© 2007 by Anthony J. Steinbock
All rights reserved

The Library of Congress cataloged the cloth edition as follows:

Steinbock, Anthony J.
Phenomenology and mysticism : the verticality of religious experience / Anthony J. Steinbock.
     p.   cm.   — (Indiana series in the philosophy of religion)
Includes bibliographical references and index.
ISBN 978-0-253-34934-7 (cloth : alk. paper) 1. Philosophy and religion.
2. Phenomenology. 3. Mysticism. 4. Experience (Religion) I. Title.
BL51.S64 2007
204'.22—dc22

2007007274

ISBN 978-0-253-22181-0 (pbk.)

2 3 4 5 6 15 14 13 12 11 10

For
Leslie Anne Brown

CONTENTS

ACKNOWLEDGMENTS

This book results from a longstanding concern with the problem and nature of evidence. During various stages of this work, I have benefited from multiple interactions with colleagues, students, and friends.

When this project was just underway, I had the advantage of two enthusiastic readers, Lucian Stone and Christopher Nelson, and discussions with them at the Longbranch Café in Carbondale, Illinois. Their knowledge of Western mysticism and Lucian Stone's expertise in the Islamic mystical tradition, in particular, was a great help. I am indebted to Leslie Brown for her diligent reading of an earlier version of this book and for her encouragement while writing it; her incisive comments and my many discussions with her have improved this work in both content and style. Art Luther has remained throughout this process an enthusiastic and patient listener, a demanding reader willing to take me to task, and a friend exemplary of critical thinking and openness. This work has benefited immensely from his attention. I have also profited from a small reading group of energetic graduate students who judiciously studied and discussed this manuscript with me at Common Grounds Café in Carbondale, Illinois: Christina Gould, John Hartmann, Jason Rickman, Matthew Stapelton, and Mark Tschappe.

The completed project of *Phenomenology and Mysticism* was presented at a special gathering at Stony Brook University. I am especially grateful for my two commentators who took on this task, Peter Manchester and Brady Heiner, and for their generous commentaries. I am also indebted to Ed Casey, Natalie Depraz, Gene Gendlin, Bob Gibbs, Tao Jiang, Edward Linton, O.S.B., Mary Rawlinson, Rebecca Rozelle, and Donn Welton for their discussions with me on various aspects of this work. I also want to acknowledge my debt of thanks, both to Merold Westphal for his "wish list" of suggestions and to Dee Mortensen, sponsoring editor at Indiana University Press, for her support.

This work has benefited from two grants. The American Council of Learned Societies (ACLS), "Contemplative Practice Fellowship," provided me with summer support to develop and teach a course integrating the contemplative traditions into higher educational settings. This course, "Mystical Literature and Meditation," served as an incubator for the initial work on the mystics that I have presented here. I am also grateful to Southern Illinois University at Carbondale for the yearlong Faculty Seed Grant that assisted me in developing this book project.

Finally, thanks are due especially to my mother, Marie, and to my father, Samuel, for their living examples of openness to different religious faiths. I am grateful also to my sister, Teresa, and her husband, Ali, for engaging conversations on Islam and Judaism. The presences of my son, Joseph, and daughter, Samara, remain constant invitations to verticality.

Phenomenology and Mysticism

Vertical Givenness
in Human Experience

Phenomenology and Mysticism gives an account of a specific dimension of human experience and its own evidence that is traditionally expunged from philosophical treatment. To give such an account, we have to operate with a substantially broader view of experience and evidence than we customarily admit into our inventory. For example, we usually think that what counts as evidence or what can be experienced are empirical or even intellectual objects. The spheres of experience and evidence that are more robust than just those of objects, I call vertical givenness, or "verticality." Sensitivity to vertical givenness is not accomplished by constructing a metaphysics or by applying either theological convictions or ethical belief systems to the experiences, but by taking a phenomenological approach to these different kinds of givenness, that is, by evaluating what is actually *given in human experience,* thereby expanding our notion of evidence. This expansion, which is grounded in experience, opens us to the religious, moral, and ecological spheres of existence, even though the quality of these kinds of experiences is fundamentally different from the ways in which objects are presented in perception or in judgments. Because the religious, moral, and ecological dimensions are given (though given in their own unique ways), they are susceptible to critical, philosophical thinking.

In addition to describing phenomenologically the givenness of verticality, I explicate the philosophical implications of vertical givenness. I do this by articulating its evidential force and its modifications in the religious sphere, by contrasting vertical presence with the movement of "withdrawal" and forgetfulness, by suggesting what vertical evidence means for the individuation of the person, and finally, by critically examining the process of de-spiritualization that deforms or reverses verticality, a process I term, here, *idolatry.* This is the task of personal and cultural critique. Ultimately, if our society and ecosystems are in disarray and in turmoil, it is because our relations to the vertical dimensions of experience are in disarray and in turmoil.

In this Introduction, I show how phenomenology as a philosophical approach is appropriate to this task of *Phenomenology and Mysticism* and explain what I mean by vertical givenness as well as the kinds of vertical givenness.

Although there are several forms of verticality, this work concentrates on just one kind of vertical givenness, what I term *epiphany,* and its countervailing movements of idolatry. It is this mode of givenness, epiphany, that articulates the structure of this work, not the presupposition of a being called "God." *Phenomenology and Mysticism* treats the dimension of human experience that is opened up by this kind of givenness and is therefore devoted to a phenomenology of religious experience. While I name other modes of vertical givenness pertaining to the moral and ecological spheres, I reserve them for future work.

Givenness and Experience

By taking experience as a touchstone for reflection, I am concerned not merely with *what* is there in experience, but with *how* this "what" appears to us. Phenomenologists, for example, have traditionally expressed this "how" of the appearance under the general title of "givenness" or "modes of givenness." Experience means the way or mode in which something is *given* to us.

Among all philosophical attitudes, it has been the virtue of phenomenological philosophy to call into question the naïveté that structures our everyday life, our "taking it for granted," by carrying out a shift in perspective. It accomplishes this by holding in abeyance or "bracketing" the assumptions pertaining to life as we live it and by suspending the prejudices concerning the being of things; it does this in an effort to expose how their meanings arise and to understand the structures of those meaningful experiences. The central issue in phenomenology is neither the subject nor the object, but *givenness.*[1] I find "givenness" a particularly suitable expression for describing experience because it takes us beyond a subject-object dichotomy often attributed to Western philosophical thought insofar as givenness is not necessarily attached to the appearing of an object over against a subject.

We are involved in the very course of our experiences. We hardly notice them when they flow on concordantly without disruption or when everything works harmoniously. These concordant experiences are "normal." One lives "normally" in everyday experience in the sense that one survives the disappointments caused by the rupture of meaning, the discordances, the atypicalities and unfamiliar sensible and eidetic landscapes of experience by integrating them into an overarching harmonious set of experiences. Cognitive reflection within these experiences poses no special difficulties because it too is involved in the very movement of these events; it is affected by them, it reflects on them, and it moves within them. Cognitive reflection remains normal in this constitutive sense.

But phenomenological reflection is supposed to be a peculiar kind of attentiveness that radically distinguishes itself from the movement of the natural everyday comportment, whether on the level of passive habituality and anonymous functioning, or on the level of egoic judicative rationality. In one sense, phenomenological reflection becomes radically "abnormal" when it ruptures the concordance of everyday life; it not only reflects on it, but in distinction from everyday "normal" reflection, it no longer yields to the flow of positing meaning, and instead abstains from the presuppositions that it carries out pre-reflectively and reflectively.

In another sense, however, phenomenological reflection is "normal"— "hyper-normal," as Edmund Husserl would say—in the sense that it is optimal; for it institutes a new order of experience that is, contextually speaking, "the best possible" even though it is not "concordant" with the natural attitude; it does this by describing the very ways in which the natural attitude unfolds and how objects and the world are there as in-themselves-for-us. Phenomenology is a peculiar kind of reflective attentiveness that distances itself from everyday life in order to get to the root of that very life.[2]

Inquiring into how something is given, and in order to short-circuit our active and latent prejudices, the phenomenologist holds assertions about being in abeyance, and to this extent he or she is said to be the disinterested observer or spectator.[3] What kind of attentiveness is it that claims not to participate in the world's validities? In what sense is the phenomenologist disinterested?

Phenomenology is a type of reflective attentiveness attuned to givenness that occurs *within* experiencing itself. One describes the experience of the "thing itself" as it is given within the very process of experiencing the matter, while simultaneously glancing at a distance, as it were, through an attentive reflection. It is only when these matters appear outside of the experiencing altogether that the putative descriptions of experience are merely construed or constructed.

In order to accomplish its openness to the matters themselves within experience, the phenomenologist can actively dis-position him- or herself. On the one hand, this entails disposing oneself openly toward the matters in question; on the other, it entails an attempt to "dis-position" him- or herself from the event, that is, to dispose of the "self." The interest at stake in the so-called phenomenological dis-interestedness is precisely *self*-interest, namely, the self's interest in the world that intrudes on the scene and imposes itself on the phenomena; the preconceptions in question concern the preconceptions of the self with which one comes to the phenomena. We leave aside for now to what extent this can be accomplished. My point is that what phenomenology really wants to bracket is a self-imposition so as to let the matters flash forth as they give themselves; what we become dispassionate about is our selves through an attempted dis-position of the self, and by so doing, dispose ourselves to being struck *in which ever way* the given gives itself. This is at least the pretension and the goal.

Of course, this manner of putting it can be misleading. As we will see, generally speaking, it is impossible to dis-pose the self in order then to have the phenomena give themselves, especially where it concerns matters of vertical experience. Dis-position is not idle or random curiosity in things that we generate from ourselves, but an active remaining open; it has a directedness because the open posture is motivated *by the self-givenness* of the matters themselves. Moreover, the individual him- or herself is not the sufficient condition for carrying out such a dis-position. Thus, the "conversion" cited at least nominally by Husserl in the *Crisis* and elsewhere is to be understood most profoundly as a conversion necessary even for the practice of phenomenology, but it is also a conversion that most profoundly is not generated from the self.

What is the phenomenologist to do in order to approach this self-disposition? Husserl advanced an exercise he called generally the *epoché,* or the reduction. This is not the place to explore the details of practicing the reduction.[4] Suffice it to say that either by design or by trial, Husserl did not propound one single intellectual activity accomplished once and for all under the rubric of the reduction but practiced a philosophical activity, sometimes with more clarity, sometimes with more obscurity, that he took up over and over again according to the circumstances and intellectual bearing. The way through psychology, the way through the lifeworld, the way through anthropology, the Cartesian way, the way through the empirical sciences, the way through regional ontologies, and so forth, are just so many ways of attempting to liberate the phenomena and to mitigate the intrusion of the self on the phenomenal field. They constitute rigorous and disciplined exercises aimed at abstaining from the simple assertion of being in favor of witnessing how its meaning is given to us.

Phenomenology can be understood as a methodological attempt to practice such a disposition for a possible dis-position. Such a practice can lead us, perhaps beyond our own efforts, to the forgetfulness of the self as the openness to perceptual and epistemic objects, but also to whatever gives itself in its own manner: to the *epiphany* of the Holy, to the *revelation* of human persons, to the *manifestation* of cultural products, to the *disclosure* of the Earth, and to the *display* of elemental beings. All the givens that phenomenology is trying to track have in some sense been given all along, so that the phenomenologist's activity is just as much a response to such an initiated givenness.

In becoming vulnerable to the givenness of what is giving itself in its self-givenness, the phenomenologist becomes *subject to* the experience in the description. So it may happen that even if we try to describe these givennesses "abstractly" or "theoretically," by opening ourselves implicitly to the direct experience of them, we open ourselves to being "struck" by them, instigating a perceptual, an epistemic, an aesthetic, a moral, or even a religious insight, relation, and transformation. Of course, if there is too much *self*-interest, we can distort the descriptions/experiences to such an extent that the whole process becomes compromised. The danger here is not just that we leave too much out of account but that we become mere academics, mere professionals.

The task in phenomenology is not to become inured to the forces of the given, but to dispose ourselves toward them, realizing that the self-givenness of the given is not simply our own doing. This implies, further, that the given itself is not neutral, and my position in relation to it, or rather, my disposition in relation to it, cannot be neutral, either.

Something counts as a matter of experience to the extent that it can be given; and in principle, one should be open to all kinds of givenness, which is to say, all types of experience, without discrimination, no matter how paradoxical the givens may seem to be. Traditionally, there has been an arbitrary exclusion of areas of experience from philosophical discussion. Because there are certain areas of experience that are conceived in advance as not being able to be described meaningfully since they are putatively not given, many of our reflective enterprises have been dismissed as so much theology, sophistry, or dogmatism.[5]

In my view, this exclusion hides a deep-seated and widespread contemporary prejudice, one so powerful and pervasive that it has dominated nearly all contemporary thinking on these topics, even if it has not been expressed in this way. The prejudice is this: All matters, especially those that concern the Holy, have to conform to *one* type of givenness in order to be given and hence to be experienced. If they do not conform, they are said to remain essentially on the limit of experience and are subject only to theory, speculation, or mere personal belief.

Phenomenology is a style of philosophical reflection, however, that is trained on the given, and, in principle, on however the given gives itself. In its peculiar manner of attentiveness, the givens are susceptible to philosophical description. Since the central issue of phenomenology is givenness that bears on experience, phenomenology is in a privileged position to surmount this arbitrary restriction to one kind of givenness and to inquire into the givens peculiar to verticality.

Verticality

And there is nothing more disastrous for all of epistemology than to establish at the beginning of one's methodological procedure a too narrow, restrictive concept of "experience," to equate the whole of experience with one particular kind of experience and with that mental attitude that is conducive [only] to it, and then to refuse to recognize as "primordially given" anything that cannot be reduced to this one kind of experience.

—MAX SCHELER, 1920[6]

One of the principal theses defended in this work [Totality and Infinity] consists in maintaining that the noesis–noema structure is not the primordial structure of intentionality (which is not equivalent to interpreting intentionality as a logical relation or as causality).

—EMMANUEL LEVINAS, 1961[7]

The Sphere of Presentation

The mode of givenness that has dominated a philosophical (and especially a phenomenological) way of seeing, I call *presentation*. Presentation is a type of givenness that is peculiar to sensible and intellectual objects and is more or less dependent upon my power to usher things into appearance within a context of significance.

When I intend an object, an object gives itself (whether or not it is the object I intended). I lean against the tree, I enjoy the fresh air, I look up and admire the rock cliff, I imagine the contours above that I cannot see, I walk toward the rope; flushed with both excitement and nervousness, I talk about it with a friend, I convey its qualities, I map out my approach. My opening to the thing ushers its appearance to me and for me as bodily or intellectually significant—even if a moment later it does not turn out to be what I initially intended it to be.

Far from the presentation of an object being static, a feature of an object points further on to new features in response to my initiating moves, the subsequent orchestration of my body, and the instigation of my thoughts. Walking toward the rock cliff motivates new appearances; what was presented at first points further on to new ontic themes and new horizons, and I pursue a richer fulfillment; I strive toward an expected situation delineated by what was initially presented; perhaps I will dismiss it later as a hallucination. Moreover, I organize my world according to types and perhaps later, concepts: I walk down a path I have never walked before, I identify this rock formation before me as granite, even though I have never seen this particular formation in "real life," I can categorize it under a particular species of igneous rock.

In many ways, then, the object yields to my perceptual and cognitive powers. If it is dark outside, I can shine my flashlight or lantern on the rock surface and usher it into appearance. If I only see the front side, I not only can anticipate a back side, but I can change positions and in this way provoke its new appearance. I can drill holes into the rock surface and explore "inside" the rock. I can break it down into its chemical and physical properties, and where it resists physical inspection, I can theorize about it and catalogue it.

Belonging to presentation is the *power of provocation*. It is to be contrasted with the process of *evocation*, which belongs to modes of vertical givenness. Briefly, by the power of provocation I understand my ability to induce or to produce an experience; by the process of evocation, I understand the process of "eliciting" so as to let an experience come of its own accord or so that another can "freely" experience this givenness in its own terms.

All this—presentation and provocation—is possible, in part, because of the "depth" structure of my relation to the world.[8] When an object *presents* itself, it does so with a certain prominence and in such a way that it implies new themes that can become salient; there is always a "horizon" or background of significance as a nexus of referential implications that leads me to new presentations. The context is that in which some things come to the fore, and appear, and other things simultaneously recede into the background, becoming provisionally concealed, characterizing the very interplay of perceivers and explicitly or implicitly perceived objects.

Objects that are "presented" are given in both "inner" and "outer" experience, and they are given through functions and acts peculiar to this very order of givenness, namely, through perception, moving, thinking, imagining, believing, remembering, anticipating. In each instance the object or situation is presented in conjunction with the perceiver or thinker who prompts a schema of possible presentations that are, in turn, concordant with these aspects or those objects already presented. The object's identical sense remains identical in and through variations of perspective. The presented object, the Self of the object, endures through time with its temporal horizons. In its genesis, it *becomes* an in-itself-for-us.

The object's sense is understood as my accomplishment, a *Leistung*. Here "accomplishment" is also a broad enough concept to encompass the work done on the part of the object to appear. Although presentation does have the effect of bringing a world *to me,* allowing me to possess a world; although presentation is ultimately instigated by me, this mode of givenness is not at all tied one-sidedly to the subjective aim, since it encompasses the givenness prompted on the side of the object: The objects themselves call us to an encounter; they function as allures and affectively motivate my turning toward them so that they can be ushered into appearance in an explicit way.[9] In fact, in order for something to come into being as prominent, it must be affectively significant and exercise an affective pull on the perceiver or thinker, whether or not it actually comes into being as an explicit theme. This salience and turning toward can be more or less gradual or sudden.[10] I respond to the demands on the part of the object for it to be given in the best possible manner: I tilt my head to adjust to the presentation, I orient myself by a tall building, and so forth. Furthermore, a particular scene may come to the fore purely passively: objects, or aspects of objects, team up with others by transferring their affective significance without any active participation on the ego's part. But even here, through presentation, the things remain relative to my field of possibilities.

Precisely because of this interplay of intentionality, this "constitutive duet," as Husserl called it, the economy of concealment and appearance governs the way things are presented.[11] Certainly, an object can resist my intending, my power to present; my perceptual "I can" can be checked by an "I cannot," a concept may exceed by ability to think it, my "I think" can be guarded by an "I cannot think." But even in these cases, what challenges my ability or freedom to think is still relative *to me,* and thus it remains within the general economy of presentation. Likewise, I can try to stop my intellect or inhibit my perceptual powers, but even this would still be to circumscribe the intellectual or perceptual fields by my "I think" or my "I can."

It is not necessary to describe this structure of presentation any further; it is already well known through the work of the early phenomenologists like Husserl, Heidegger, Merleau-Ponty, and Gurwitsch, just to name a few. All this—the dynamic interplay or "constitutive duet" of my "I can" and the affective pull of the object, the intersubjective orientation to the world, the passive association of sense, the constitution of both simple and categorial objects, the foreground/background structure of the phenomenal field—all this belongs to the province of *presentation* and is governed by its systematic laws and interconnections.

There is nothing intrinsically problematic or illegitimate about this order of givenness.[12] However, the difficulty has been and continues to be that "presentation" is assumed to be the *only* mode of givenness. This has two regrettable consequences. First, if we were not attentive to any difference in the way the matters give themselves, we could attempt to apply presentation to anything that has the potential of being given. Thus, for example, animals other than human, the other person, God, would be described as susceptible to the same kind of intention and fulfillment, verification and disappointment that we find in the case of perceptual or intellectual objects. Kant's First Critique is certainly to the point. We would fall into a philosophical illusion to think, for example, that God can be experienced like an object.

Second, if we were attentive to a difference in givenness, we could concede that there are "matters" that do not conform to this kind of givenness in principle or that there are matters that are in principle not accessible to perception or thought (the person as "Other," for example). In this instance, the matters would be described only paradoxically as being accessible *in the mode of* inaccessibility, given *as not being able* to be given, experienced *as not being able* to be experienced; hence, they would be characterized as on the "limit" of phenomenal givenness.[13] And if one still wanted to speak of these matters, such discourse would be dismissed as so much speculation, theology, dogmatism, essentialist thought, foundationalism, metaphysics of presence, philosophy of origins, and so forth.

While presentation describes a dimension of our experience that concerns the relative givenness of things in the economy of appearance and concealment, and while it describes our relation to the world as one of both immediate and mitigated belief in its being, presentation has become the dominant model of givenness for us and has been allowed to efface other legitimate modes of givenness. But why should phenomenology, in order to reflect *within* the very experiencing itself, not open itself to *all* kinds of "givens" *in the distinctive manner that they give themselves?* Is it not an act of forceful arbitrariness to limit in advance the ways in which givenness takes place?

Precisely because presentation has defined what gets counted exclusively as a matter of experience, vertical relations have been left virtually out of philosophical and, specifically, phenomenological accounts. As a collateral consequence, if and when we do treat God, the other person, or the Earth, we tend to miss the unique style of givenness characteristic of each sphere. Take Kierkegaard to cite just one example among others. While Kierkegaard understood the religious dimension as an absolute relation to an absolute, at least in *Fear and Trembling,* he misses the genuine givenness of the other person, obfuscating the moral dimension of experience.[14] Likewise, the aesthetic dimension of experience is confined to presentation and leaves out any serious consideration of the Earth as the aesthetic ground of spatio-temporal experience. Similar critiques can be made *mutatis mutandis* of Heidegger, Husserl, Henry, Levinas, and Merleau-Ponty. The fact that the unique style of givenness peculiar to each sphere has been missed by so many prominent philosophers should at least cause us to take note of the extent to which the model of presentation has a hold on us and how much it colors what we regard as important.

Although the dominance of presentation and the effacement of other modes of givenness is evident in the vast majority of work from classical phenomenology to postmodern philosophy, the adherence to a monolithic order of givenness—which either covers everything or defines *via negativa* what cannot count as givenness—has been called into question in contemporary thought.

The most inchoate attempts can be seen in the struggle to expand the sphere of evidence to include moral, but especially religious experience—though the presupposition is that one must enlarge the field of *presentation* in order to cover religious or moral themes, and only then possibly brush up against various limits to such an approach. Exemplary of this approach is Adolf Reinach, who writes, "religious experiences, especially sudden ones, cannot be 'understood.' They are not 'motivated.'" For this reason, he calls for us above all to respect the sense that religious experiences have of their own accord, "even if [their sense] leads to enigmas."[15] Under this general style, we also place Jean Hering for his phenomenological study of the unique nature of religious consciousness[16] and Kurt Stavenhagen for his research into the possibility of an absolute personal comportment vis-à-vis an absolute sphere.[17]

These should be distinguished from other attempts that merely describe empirically the variety of religions and religious experiences—whether to catalogue their types or advance a philosophy of religion—because they not only presuppose attributes of the Divine, but they fail to ask how the Holy or the other person is *given*. This is the case, despite the fact that even these approaches can provide a genuine starting point if they yield (or were to yield) an inquiry into modes of givenness. As examples of this kind we would include the likes of William James,[18] G. van der Leeuw,[19] and Friedrich Heiler.[20]

Ultimately, both kinds of attempts are unsatisfactory because of their implicit or explicit adherence to presentation even when they are trying to challenge its bounds. There are, however, other key figures who have been able to mount the challenge to the dominance of presentation in a more forceful and explicit manner. Most notably are Max Scheler, who distinguishes explicitly and systematically between givenness as revelation (*Offenbarung*) from manifestation (*Offenbarkeit*),[21] as well as Michel Henry, whose monumental work *L'essence de la manifestation* criticizes as "ontological monism" this kind of limitation of givenness to one kind of being (=monism) and understands the very essence of manifestation to be revelation.[22] I also have in mind Emmanuel Levinas's work, *Totalité et infini*, which, despite the fact that it seems to qualify the Other as what is not able to be given, makes a clear distinction between givenness as disclosure and absolute givenness or givenness as revelation.[23] Following in this tradition is also Jean-Luc Marion, who draws a similar distinction between manifestation and revelation in his work *Dieu sans l'être*.[24] These works mark an important and fruitful beginning where the openness to the field of evidence is concerned.

Despite the fact that vertical givenness is distinct from presentation, I nonetheless speak of "experience" in both cases. The assumption that experience should be reserved only for object givenness—no matter how broadly or narrowly conceived—was held not only by the great religious thinker and philosopher Martin Buber (who contrasted the I–It word pair ["experience"] with the I–Thou word pair ["relation"]),[25] but also in a more equivocal manner by Levinas—equivocal because at times he asserts that the Other cannot be experienced and at other times he himself writes of an "experience" of an Other as an "absolute experience."[26]

The virtue of such descriptions lies in the attempts to show that there is "something else" going on here, beyond the presentation of objects. But it is a sign of capriciousness to assume that one must equate "experience" and "presence" with the presentation of objects, that is, with a "having" of things, perceptually or epistemically, or with an accomplishment initiated by the self. It is an insidious form of positivism to force vertical experiences into the noesis:noematic logic of appearance and fulfillment under the rubric of being true to "evidence." It only highlights the prejudice that presentation exhausts experience, and that presentation somehow comes first and gets to claim experience for itself. If we take givenness seriously, then it would go against the very grain of the given itself to hold, for example, that God, the other person, the Earth are not "experienced" just because vertical givenness is radically different from what gets experienced in presentation.

Vertical Givenness and the Problem of Idolatry

I use the term "verticality" because of the existential sense it bears—the orientation, the meanings, and the dynamic movement it evokes. Verticality expresses a lived directedness—religiously, morally, and bodily—like when we aspire to reach new heights, when we look up to someone, when we value the life of another above our own, when someone honored or esteemed is held in "high" regard, when we are "upright" both morally and physically, when we are in an elated mood or "uplifted" because of an event or at the sight of a friend. And it also implies the antithetical movement of falling. If we were to look for a meteorological expression to evoke vertical movement, "updraft," would be an appropriate term.

In philosophical literature the concept of verticality has been largely ignored or suppressed. But it has cropped up every now and again, erupting into contemporary thought in poetry and prose. W. H. Auden asks us, where we are able, to honor the person who is "vertical," even though we tend only to value the one who is "horizontal."[27] Bachelard was acutely aware of the significance of verticality when he wrote of the "truly *positive* experience of verticality."[28] Verticality permeates all existence: "At the very heart of psychic phenomena there will be a real *verticality*. This verticality is no empty metaphor; it is a principle of order, a law governing filiation, a scale along which someone can experience the different degrees of sensibility. Finally, the life of the soul, all the delicate and discreet emotions, all the hopes and the fears, all the moral forces that are involved in one's future have a *vertical differential* in the full mathematical sense of the word."[29] Reflecting on the axiomatic character of the vertical, Bachelard sums up: "The positive dynamism of verticality is so clear that we can formulate this aphorism: what does not rise, falls. Human being *qua* human being cannot live horizontally."[30]

For Erwin Strauss the "upright" is a posture, but not merely physiologically; it is an *Einstellung,* an attitude, in the global sense as a specific mode of being in the world. He notes that cultural patterns such as lowering our heads or kneeling in prayer, arms uplifted, bowing, expressions of reverence, asking and granting a request, the fact that one has "leanings," and so forth, despite their divergences in other cultures, are all variations on the theme of verticality.[31]

Verticality is the vector of mystery and reverence; horizontality is what is in principle within reach, graspable, controllable. I prefer verticality to a term like "transcendence" because the latter is encumbered with too many philosophical and religious presuppositions that oppose it to "immanence." In this respect, I also find it illuminating that in his last work, Merleau-Ponty starts to move away from expressions like "transcendence" and even his favored expression, "depth," toward *verti-cality* as the operative ontological characterization. In this way, verticality suggests dynamic orientation/sense, movement, dehiscence, density.

The "rediscovery of vertical Being," Merleau-Ponty writes, is the solution to the problem of the soul and body, the encroachment of the visible and the invisible.[32] As a probable reply to Heidegger, Merleau-Ponty even writes of rediscovering *phusis* and *logos* in terms of "vertical history."[33] And in reply to Sartre, Merleau-Ponty contends that "It is the whole field of the 'vertical' that has to be awakened. Sartre's existence is not 'vertical,' not 'upright' [*debout*]: it certainly cuts across the plane of beings, it is transversal with respect to it, but precisely it is too distinct from it for one to be able to say that it is 'upright.' What is upright is the existence that is threatened by weight, that leaves the plane of objective being, but not without dragging with it all the adversity and favors it brought there."[34] These insights into Being as vertical announce a task as well: "it is a question of creating a new type of intelligibility (intelligibility through the world and Being as they are—'vertical' and not horizontal)."[35]

The unpredictability of the vertical, the dangerous, spontaneous, undomesticable quality of the vertical is incompatible with what we predominantly value and are encouraged to value. If we live in a "horizontal" world that suppresses the vertical, it is nonetheless a world that is susceptible to verticality and beyond its control; it is a world into which the vertical erupts.

It is only when we mistakenly—but for historically understandable reasons—want to reduce the vertical to domination and to control over another that we might be led to think of verticality as something "static." In fact, verticality is antithetical both to the fixed meaning and static hierarchy peculiar to Totalitarianism[36] and to the reactionary nonhierarchical homogeneity of power (which institutes its own power of homogeneity or "invisible ideology") that permits all differences as long as they make no difference.[37]

For me, verticality evokes and signifies those dynamic vectors of experience that have a unique structure of their own, harbor their own kinds of evidence and manners of givenness, and as such are irreducible to the field of experience characterized by what I have called presentation. What is given vertically incites awe, and only as a later consequence, wonder. Modes of givenness are "vertical" in the sense that they take us *beyond* ourselves. These modes of vertical givenness are testimony to the radical presence of "absolutes" *within* the field of human experience.

By "absolute" I mean a presence that is so unique that it can be predicated neither of singularity nor plurality. "Absolute" in this sense is not synonymous with "universal." There are three main spheres of absolute experience: the religious, which pertains to the vertical experience of the Holy; the moral, which pertains to the vertical experience of the other person; and the ecological, which pertains to the vertical experience of the Earth as aesthetic ground.

The general philosophical project with which I begin here is to describe vertical kinds of evidence. Each mode of vertical givenness has its own manner of givenness, its own internal coherence and regularity, and its own essential interconnections that pertain to evidence, modalization, deception, illusion, and so forth. Epiphany, revelation, manifestation, disclosure, and display are distinctive modes of vertical givenness, and each of them is distinctive in kind from presentation.

Epiphany is the mode of givenness that qualifies a dimension of experiencing as religious. For this style of experiencing and evidence, I appeal to the mystics within the Abrahamic tradition: Jewish, Christian, and Islamic mystical experiences. The description and clarification of epiphany is the task of this work.

Revelation is a mode of givenness that qualifies a dimension of experiencing as moral. The movement in and through which the person is *revealed* is interpersonal such that the moral sphere is foundational for political, economic, and social life. Revelatory givenness is the experiential dimension that pertains to exemplarity. By exemplarity, I mean a personal kind of givenness that is both revealing and revealed; it is the "personal" tie between human persons and between human persons and the Holy.

Manifestation designates a vertical givenness that pertains to the ways in which products or cultural artifacts give themselves as "giving" the Holy or human persons. While cultural objects can be "presented," they can also "manifest" vertically. Here they function as "icon." An icon does not represent something, but points beyond itself; and like the movement of exemplarity, it stems from what is other, not from itself. But whereas the person as the locus of epiphany and revelation evokes absolute infinite Person while remaining absolute as person, the icon "evokes" the absolute in its own relativity. Icons cannot be made absolute just because in their manifestation, they evoke absolutes. By remaining relative in manifesting an absolute, an object may lose its efficacy as icon depending upon historical circumstances. For example, the way a work of art is taken can vary according to historical contexts, changes in aesthetic perception, "losses" or "advances" in cultural life, or in the demise or augmentation of religious institutions.

There are two types of iconic givenness where manifestation is concerned. First, a bodily movement like dance, or a cultural artifact like a painting can manifest the Holy in the sense of being the site of the Holy, but when it is fixed merely as an art object, or as a scientific object for carbon dating, it no longer functions in this instance as "icon." Second, an object can manifest the finite absolute human person. A shirt, for example, can manifest persons and vertically give a network of relations, relations that are most profoundly moral (here we see the significance of Marx's critique of capitalism, alienated labor, and surplus value).

In short, whereas the exemplar is a *personal revelation* pertaining to absolute infinite and absolute finite persons, the icon is an *impersonal manifestation* pertaining to absolute persons (infinite or finite).

Disclosure pertains to the way the Earth as ground is given in spatio-temporal experience as absolute. The Earth as such is never *presented* in the perception of an object or as an object; rather, it is *disclosed* as absolute ground (*Boden*) in that perception and not as an object, for example, a "planet." Even though our own body functions as a ground or zero-point of orientation for the perception of things near and far, left or right, it is the Earth that is disclosed as ground for our bodily (aesthetic) orientation toward things and that ultimately gives them meaning. Up and down is the dimensionality that becomes prominent here. It is by virtue of the Earth's function as ground that the lived-body can be self-giving and such that transcendent objects can be given at all.[38]

Finally, even though the Earth is given as absolute in its function as aesthetic ground in terms of *disclosure,* elemental beings can *display* the Holy. Things Earthen (a tree, a grain of sand, a body of water, etc.) can also display absolute Person while themselves remaining relative. It is in this respect that we can speak, for example, of the sacredness of water.

In the strictest sense, idolatry is the destruction of vertical relations. Certainly, one could interpret this destruction or disorientation, experienced as the problems of oppression and objectification, as violence and its resulting personal and social discontents, and the like, in terms of a crisis (Husserl), ideology (Marx), forgetfulness (Heidegger), or even as a problem of drives (Freud). But one could only do so at the expense of arbitrarily dismissing and ignoring actual dimensions of our lives: religious, moral, and ecological. Only when these dimensions are brought back into our account of human experience do we encounter the full wonder, weight, and horror of our contemporary situation. It is from this perspective of the fullness of our experience, which I attempt to recognize without dismissive prejudice, that the experiences and problems disclose themselves in terms of verticality and idolatry.

Idolatry is a way of living that "deforms" or reverses "verticality." I use the term "idolatry" despite the fact that, and precisely because, it does not—and indeed cannot—accommodate itself to a postmodern worldview. Unfortunately, the identification of idolatry as the root of the problems we face can all too easily be read as a call to fundamentalist violence. It is quite understandable that one would want to avoid using "religious" terminology today, given the pervasive stronghold of religious conservatism, the sometimes tyranny of orthodoxy, and the easy association of anything "religious" with spiritually and physically violent movements. But we would eschew the religious dimension of experience as a whole for these reasons only at our own peril and at the hazard of missing a crucial dimension of our lives.

Compromising verticality in the very face of the epiphany of the Holy, the revelation of the person, or the disclosure of the Earth, idolatry has the effect of systemically closing off epiphanic, revelatory, manifest, disclosive, and displaying givenness; it is the deepest way to characterize our de-spiritualizing downspin in all its forms. Living under the sway of idolatry becomes actualized in many ways: injustice, hatred, racism, institutionalized poverty, militarism, misogyny, ecological terrorism, and general earth-alienation.

We see idolatry function not only on macro levels of experience but on micro ones as well: when someone sees a lonely or frightened person on the street but keeps his mind on business affairs; when someone witnesses a friend's joy at good fortune but thinks only of how it affects her; when someone watches images of war on the local news but is troubled about how it will effect tomorrow's stock market; when someone hears the cry of another in emotional or physical distress but is preoccupied with payment for succor; when someone hikes in a forest and sees the trees merely as a renewable resource.

Our habituation to this way of being slips over, often unnoticed, into the way we treat others. We find that the more we invest ourselves in our selves and in things, and the more successful we become in this style of involvement, the less we are able to dispose ourselves to modes of vertical givenness. Vertical relations get reversed. We live in idolatry in such a profound manner that we do not even experience it *as* idolatry; it becomes the "natural" element of our experience, the way our own smells and odors become the background and basis for detecting any other smells or odors. One of the dangers of idolatry is that, persisting too deeply in this way of life, it will dominate our thoughts, actions, and perceptions, with the additional effect that we will lose our power to discern loving from hating in our daily lives.[39]

This reversal of verticality in favor of idolatry has led to the profound de-spiritualization of our times: egotism, materialism, indifference, cruelty; as the film-maker Robert Bresson notes, just plain ugliness and stupidity become ways of life.[40] It has the further consequence of dulling our sensibilities to exemplars and icons that otherwise point us back vertically; exemplars, icons, and elements appear "flat."

Each sphere of vertical experience is susceptible to its own kind of idolatry. In the religious sphere, it arises in terms of pride (before the Holy), idolatry of the world expressed in terms of both secularism and fundamentalism, and delimitation, or the mono-dimensional character of experiences that fail to evoke vertically. In the moral sphere, idolatry takes the form of pride (before others), idolatry of the world expressed in terms of humanism and reification—a form of idolatry I term "evil." In the ecological sphere, idolatry appears as lived-body centeredness, the misplaced absoluteness of the Earth expressed as environmentalism and objectification.

Although there are several forms of vertical givenness, this work is concerned with just one kind of vertical givenness, namely, epiphany and its countervailing movements of idolatry. *Phenomenology and Mysticism* treats the dimension of human experience that is opened up by this kind of givenness and is therefore devoted to a phenomenology of religious experience.

More specifically, in the first chapter, I begin with a general characterization of religious experience. But it is only general. In order to sharpen the meaning of religious experience as the experienced presence of the Holy, I appeal on the whole to the mystical experiences within the Abrahamic religious traditions. As I indicate below in more detail, mystical experiences are not to be equated with all religious experiences, but in their focus and exemplarity, they elucidate the deeper meaning of religious experience as the inter-Personal structure of epiphany. It is in the following three chapters that I focus more specifically on the three principal figures that I employ as exemplary of the Abrahamic religious traditions: St. Teresa of Avila, a Christian mystic (chapter 2); Rabbi Dov Baer of Lubavitch, a Jewish mystic (chapter 3); and Rūzbihān Baqlī, an Islamic mystic or Sufi (chapter 4).

The subsequent chapters are philosophical elaborations of these phenomenological givens. I develop the implications of these givens by describing the unique and irreducible structure of evidence and its modalizations in the religious sphere (chapter 5), by explicating this religious mode of vertical givenness *as* epiphany in distinction to withdrawal (chapter 6), and by expounding upon epiphany as it concerns the issue of personal individuation (chapter 7). Because idolatry is founded in verticality, since it only makes sense within verticality, and because epistemically, we implicitly disclose idolatry by understanding verticality, I develop vertical modes of givenness first and then bring idolatry into sharper focus (chapter 8).

CHAPTER 1

The Religious and
Mystical Shape of Experience

The Indeterminacy of Religious Experience

I operate with a specific sense of religious experience described and clarified by the mystics of the Abrahamic tradition. But before going straightaway to this clarification of religious experience through the mystics, let me acknowledge that it is possible to speak meaningfully about religious experience in a general manner.

Rudolf Otto understands religious experience as the experience of being before "an overpowering, absolute might *of some kind*,"[1] the experience of the presence of that "Something" that Otto calls the "numinous" and that is experienced as *mysterium tremendum* in awe: "It may become the hushed, trembling, and speechless humility of the creature in the presence of—whom or what?" What we gain from such a description is that most generally religious experience can be entirely indeterminate. Human beings can have a religious stirring outside of any established religious tradition; a religious sense may arise out of a striking existential situation; it may come upon one as a vague feeling of "ultimate reality."

Notice that in this respect religious experience can be understood as an indistinct extra-ordinary experience of "sacredness" that can range from the experience of nature as divine, to the daemonic, to, in monotheism, the living, Personal God.[2] However, and this is important, the numinous is not *necessarily* qualified in any personal way in all religious experiences, since in any religious experience this "who or what" may still remain undetermined, latent, unexplored in an individual life, or unexpressed in cult. The "Sacred," the "Holy," moreover, might well be experienced in all things in a unique set of experiences, but without any Personal quality.

This "something," furthermore, is given in a religious context with an experience of dependency. The feeling of dependency that arises through a religious experience is occasioned first and foremost by the "positive" presence of a superior being or superior beings, and not from a negative appraisal of, say, my weakness or out of *"ressentiment."*[3] A sense of inadequacy, religiously speaking, can only arise from the positive experience of the supremacy of the deity or deities in relation to which I then see myself as dependent or as a "creature."[4] The experience of dependency and creaturehood is a response to the self-givenness of an absolute kind, that is, to the "Generative Source," to "Spirit," to the "Almighty," to "the Holy"; other responses to such a givenness include ritual prayer or offerings, and they may be undertaken in cult without such self-evidence, or they may be expressed in the unique order of acts such as awe, giving thanks, worship, supplication, homage, repentance, veneration, acceptance, and obedience.[5]

But where religious experience is concerned, the experience of myself as "dependent" or even "insignificant" is not restricted to myself alone. Such an "individual" experience implicitly and simultaneously includes me as part of the entire collective realm of finitude and creaturehood. The insight of the self-inclusion of human beings in the sphere of the finite is peculiar to nearly all creation accounts. In the *Popol Vul,* for example, after failing in their first three attempts to create human beings, the gods succeed only too well—making humans with perfect vision (i.e., knowledge); the divine beings therefore cloud human vision with a fog, making them lower than the gods and in this respect on a par with all other created beings.[6]

Whatever the content within this range, the religious sphere is determined by its own irreducible self-evidence and is not derived from any other sphere of evidence; it is not motivated by extra-religious or nonreligious acts but is stirred by the religious event itself, whatever that may be. In short, as we will see, the evidence peculiar to the religious sphere cannot be produced from outside of the religious dimension itself.[7] Religious experiences and their norms, therefore, neither *arise from* nor are *reducible to* cultural, ethical, biological, or aesthetic experiences and norms or any combination of them. It has own structure, its own integrity. This is what is meant, in part, by saying that religious experiences have a style, order, "lawful regularity," normativity, or kind of givenness, as well as modalizations *all their own.* In fact, viewed from the position of organic reality merely, religious acts of any kind are unfounded, unwarranted, and generally pointless. Bergson's dynamic religion—contrary to what he would want to maintain—cannot be seen as emergent from the life-force to solve paradoxes or ally fears posed by life. Instead, dynamic religion, which is epitomized by the individuals' experience of the divine as in mystical experiences, becomes the foundation for open morality, for "religion," as well as for static myth-making functions.[8]

I noted above that one can speak meaningfully of religious experience in an indeterminate and general manner. Yet religious experience can also be understood in a more determined manner, for example, as the experience of living in the presence of the Holy. While religious experience may be given in many different ways, there are certain religious experiences that focus on what I consider to be the most profound character of this givenness. These are called "mystical experiences." My attempt at further qualifying religious experience depends upon clarifying it inter-Personally. I appeal to mystical experiences to clarify the inter-Personal nature of religious experience by drawing on selected mystics, not because they exhaust the realm and range of inter-Personal experiences, but because their experiences exemplify them. An explication of mystical experiences, while necessary, cannot alone give specificity to the religious dimension (chapters 2–4); a deeper philosophical clarification of this dimension of experience can be acquired by working through its matters of evidence and by qualifying the nature of epiphany, explicating the tenor of individuation, and treating idolatry (chapters 5–8).

The Specificity of the Religious Sphere through Mystical Experience

I am aware that the application of the "mystical" to special experiences of the Holy is a relatively late development. Bouyer notes, for instance, that the term *mustikos* was originally used in connection with the mystery religions and concerned the secrecies of ritual practices.[9] From Philo of Alexandria through Clement and Origen to Pseudo-Dionysius, the expression was applied to difficult (mysterious) exegetical problems, which in Christianity concerned scriptural exegesis rooted in a profound and ineffable knowledge of God that was mediated by the sacraments. Other earlier uses of the term that bore, synonymously, on sacred or spiritual reality were still in play through the sixteenth and seventeenth centuries, but then began to name the "hidden" or the "essential," and to refer to the silent inner secrets of experience vouchsafed through a predominately contemplative manner of knowing. It is only at this juncture that we see a transition from the adjectival and adverbial uses of *mystery* to the substantive use as a noun, and hence eventually to "mysticism" and to the "mystics."[10] The so-called "mystical tradition" as we refer to it today develops by retroactively appropriating it *as* a tradition about this time. But rather than let the history of the term strictly define the meaning of such an experience (since it is possible for a subsequent expression to reactivate previous or even latent meanings), I use the expression for a special genre of inter-Personal experiences operative within the religious sphere.

Mystical experience is a discrimination of experience within religious experience. It is characterized by *special intimacies* of the presence of the Holy. These special intimacies are not restricted to, but can include intimacies more commonly associated with, experiences like "union." I draw on mystical experience to clarify religious experience (and thus the structure of epiphany) because mystical experience refines the evidence already given in the religious sphere. Mystical experience can do this because it lives the immediate Person-to-person movement that may only be (but not need be) implicit in religious experiencing as such. In this way, the mystics can become exemplary of religious experience by highlighting the "evidence" of epiphany, the "Personal" evidence, as a distinctive vertical mode of givenness. Accordingly, as paradigmatic of religious experience, mystical experiences are always religious experiences, but not all religious experiences are mystical ones. By epiphany being clarified through mystical experience, we can say that religious experiences are so many ways of living out the inter-Personal sphere. Religious experience can be clarified as inter-Personal through lived experiences and practices of various mystics. Admittedly, this makes religious experience less "general" in the sense that it does not pretend to cover every "spiritual" tradition, West or East; but by the same token, it makes it all the more distinctive.

Having sketched by way of introduction the operative meaning of *mystical* experience, I turn now to the meaning of mystical *experience*. Why call it mystical "experience"? In contrast to McGinn, who prefers to use the term "consciousness" as "a more precise and fruitful category,"[11] I privilege the term "experience" for a number of reasons. The language of consciousness too easily restricts matters of experience, whatever they may be, to epistemic objects, suggesting in turn that transformations pertaining to the individual person are merely changes in awareness or knowledge. This would quickly reduce mysticism to psychologism or to altered mental states, whereas the real issue here is living the self-givenness of a presence, a Personal presence. Accordingly, a change or revolution of the "heart," where the Holy is lived dynamically, is not a ratio-cognitive event. On the other hand, experiences that concern the self-givenness of Person do not merely impact the "mind," but get played out spiritually and somatically, for example, in terms of a change in our ways of loving, in terms of tears, ecstasies, pains, and so forth.

By experience, in general I mean the givenness of something (be it an object, a human person, or the Holy) as "it" is lived. As noted above, it is arbitrary to restrict what we count as experience only to the way objects are presented perceptually and epistemically. By mystical experience, I do not mean everything that is nonrational, weird, exotic, occult, or paranormal. I mean the self-givenness of the Holy *qua* Personal presence as this presence is lived. The self-givenness pertaining to the Holy is a vertical mode of givenness, namely, epiphany. Epiphany is the personal presence of the Holy, and mystical experience is precisely the personal givenness of the Holy as lived in an especially intimate manner. Epiphany is not rare, unusual, or exceptional in the sense that it is sometimes added on to mundane affairs. This is a secular interpretation that is rather new and certainly not anymore justified because it is more recent. For the mystics, the Holy runs through everything and everyone; in its everydayness, epiphany is nonetheless optimal, and not average. This is why there can be a sense of the "religious" in the more general indeterminate sense. It is the mystic who lives this optimal character in the everyday experience of the Holy as an inter-Personal gift. This is how the lives of the mystics become exemplary and how mystical experience becomes exemplary of religious experience.

To be sure, this is a delicate point. There are those who maintain that mystical experiences are everywhere; some even go so far as to assert "we are all mystics."[12] Such a claim is understandable; it is based in the insight that epiphany, which qualifies an experience as religious, transpires in everyday experience and that these experiences are open to everyone. I agree that the religious dimension of experience is a fundamental component of human experience—that is my point. I also agree that mystical experience should not be limited to the "spiritual zenith of contemplation."[13] Even if many of the mystics within the Abrahamic tradition, for example, could be called contemplatives, the mystical life is not to be equated with the contemplative life because what qualifies the mystics as such are their experiences, not the fact that they engage in contemplative practices. It is further clear that mystical elements can also be present in ordinary forms of experience, like the experience of nature.[14] Mystical experiences take on various forms, and it would be premature on our part to assert in advance that they are just in the reach of a few privileged individuals. But this does *not* mean that everyone is a mystic. Rather, strictly speaking, it means that mystical experiences are not *within anyone's reach* because they are not correlative to our efforts in the first place, as would be the case in the field of presentation; they are experienced as "gifts." One can always strive to dispose oneself to the Holy, one can always engage in rigorous spiritual exercises and try to live a "religious" life in this way, but it is not a foregone conclusion that mystical experiences will come about.

I would further add that, as we will also see below, mystical experiences are in no way limited to experiences of union, and moreover, union is not even the point of the mystics' lives; rather, it consists in service to God, the redemption of the world, and the participation in establishing loving and justice.

We lose the distinctiveness of mystical experiences when we run all spiritualities, traditions, and religious experiences together; we fail to appreciate the radical nature of self-abandonment, the moral rigor required for spiritual and material nonattachment, the unique demands placed on a life *oriented* in this way (and not just occasionally) that affords little time for squander or pause—and all this without any guarantee that something will come of it.

Not everything is a mystical experience even if mystical experiences reveal what is most characteristic of a religious experience. It is well known that Mother Teresa experienced visions, locutions, and ecstasies for several months until she began her explicit mission to serve the poorest of the poor; yet she reports living out this mission for the rest of her life (50+ years) nourished only by these one-time religious experiences and her love of her fellow human beings, and indeed with the experience of being forsaken by God.[15] This is perhaps an extreme example. I use it only to insist that mystical experiences are a special kind of religious experience and that there is a useful phenomenological distinction to be made between the experience of "awe" or "creaturehood" in relation to the "Creator" in a religious experience (e.g., Otto), and the uniquely personal nature of religious experience clarified in mystical experience with which I operate here.

Givenness in Mystical Experience and Phenomenology

My approach, as mentioned in the Introduction, is a phenomenological one. I take this approach because it is one that bears most directly on the matters *as experienced,* and does not take them merely as matters for speculation. Insofar as the Holy can be said to be experienced, these experiences are open to critical description, even if they do not conform to descriptions with which we *seem* to be most familiar, like the experiences of tables and chairs. This is why it is necessary to be open to a broader field of evidence. Such a task, as undertaken in this work, is *philosophico-phenomenological,* not theological.

The phenomenological style of description generally appeals to *first-person* experiences. It does this in an effort to be faithful to the matters as they are given. As noted above, Edmund Husserl, the so-called father of the phenomenological method, appeals to a special disposition toward the matters (what he calls the "reduction") so as to let the phenomena appear as they give themselves and to describe the phenomena as they give themselves, untainted by accrued prejudices of mind and habit. He also urges those who read his own works to practice this disposition along with him so as to let his descriptions be evocative for us to see too, instead of being taken as academic depictions. Rather than mere conceptual explanation, the phenomenologist's effort is to guide us to the point where the matters can flash forth of themselves, stirring in us the lived experience he or she is trying to awaken. Such a dispositional effort can be witnessed in one of Husserl's early students, Wilhelm Schapp. Faithful to this style of thinking, Schapp prefaces his renowned work *Beiträge zur Phänomenologie der Wahrnehmung* in this way: "My only hope is that I did not write anything that I did not see for myself."[16]

But have I not gone too far in suggesting that an attentive description of spiritual, even mystical matters can rejoin a phenomenological project? Is it correct to say that the mystics gave descriptions of experiences that could in some way be susceptible to a philosophical enterprise? Let us recall in the first place that phenomenology was never just a descriptive, but also a normative enterprise, and that the sense of phenomenological description was to point us further to the radical bases of our lives. It was never merely an academic or neutral project: Consider not only Husserl's investigations into the "lifeworld," but also his earlier investigations into transcendental logic.[17] We are perhaps also familiar with Husserl's conviction that the phenomenological philosopher is to be understood as nothing less than the functionary of humanity.

But far from his position equating phenomenology with a brand of humanism, Husserl himself goes even farther: "I also want what the churches want: to lead humanity to the *Aeternitas*. My task is to try to do this through philosophy. Everything that I have written up to now is only preparatory; it is only a development [*Aufstellen*] of methods. In the course of one's life, one unfortunately does not arrive at the core, at what is essential. It is so important for philosophy to be led out of liberalism and rationalism, and to be led once more to what is essential, to *truth*. The question concerning ultimate reality, truth, must be the object of every true philosophy. This is my life's work."[18] Husserl himself was no mere academic. If the phenomenological enterprise has a role to play in the description of spiritual, religious, and even mystical experiences, it is because it is a shift in perspective that in principle is open to all kinds of givenness and thus is in a position—however modestly—to orient us to them (and not, mistakenly, as a method that "provokes" those givens).

Still, the problem remains that one of the difficulties when writing about mystical experiences concerns this implicit claim to first-person access to such experiences for the descriptions. This is one of the reasons that I appeal to accounts provided by the mystics. It is an appeal to the authority present in the mystics by virtue of their experiences, an authority that is given *in and through* the experiences, and not from a commitment to a philosophical theory or by theorizing about the nature of God.

In this regard, the present work is not alone. Augustin Poulan, for example, in his classic treatise entitled *The Graces of Interior Prayer* (*Des grâces d'oraison*, 1910), distinguishes between a "speculative school," which attempts to systematize all the givens theologically and as a consequence remains basically static, and a "descriptive school." The descriptive school, to which he adheres, takes mysticism as "forward moving" and is able to accommodate itself to this dynamic element by becoming more and more exact, for example, in distinguishing one experience from another as the mystics themselves become more sensitive to the subtle differences in experiences. This method fit his practical aim, which was to address those who are approaching or who do not know how to find their way in mystical graces.[19]

My purpose, however, is not to provide practical advice, but philosophically, to give a broader account of the sphere of evidence in order to do justice to this dimension of human experiencing, and in terms of cultural critique, to confront difficulties we encounter at their root as idolatry. This is done by evoking the significance of vertical experiences.

One should also recognize the pioneering efforts by Gerda Walther. Not wanting to share in the prejudices peculiar to psychologism or empiricism, not wanting to reduce spiritual phenomena to quantifiable facts in the natural sciences, she remained faithful to the early spirit of phenomenology in Husserl and Pfänder. Guided by the experiences of several mystics, she recognized in her *Zur Phänomenologie der Mystik* (1923) "a mode of givenness that is fundamentally different," an irreducible "spiritual givenness" that is peculiar to the "primordial phenomenon" of mystical experience as the primordial source of religious experience. In so doing, she brought to light basic structural features of mystical experience and examined how such experiences are possible.[20]

Another, more contemporary approach in this vein is provided by Nelson Pike in his *Mystic Union: An Essay in the Phenomenology of Mysticism,* a work focusing on Christian mysticism. Despite the use of the term "phenomenology" in the title, he characterizes his approach as "phenomenography" because it is the study of the phenomena (the givens in mystical experience) as they are reported and thus understands what he is doing to be a branch of hermeneutics.[21] (I return to the issue of hermeneutics and phenomenological method below.)

While there are many fine works on mysticism that deal, ultimately, with mystical experiences and evoke a phenomenological discourse,[22] and others that deal with mystical "fact" but are not phenomenological,[23] there are also other lamentably facile approaches that are merely reductive. Treating the mystics as witnesses to a unique sphere of evidence given in the first person should not be construed as a reduction to psychologism. These mystical experiences constitute a witnessing to givenness and therefore do not originate in a subjective mental state. Again, just because the mode of givenness relevant here, epiphany, does not conform to the givenness of presentation or to the way objects are given, which are in principle able to be ratified intersubjectively, does not mean that mystical experiences (be they experiences of rapture, quiet, delight, ecstasy, visions, locutions, etc.) are aberrant mental states.

For a disregard of the integrity of this sphere of evidence, one need only examine the arrogance and simplistic reductionism concerning the experiences, for instance, of the Jewish mystic Joseph Caro by some contemporary "medical experts" (though by no means by all of them). These experiences get reduced to "hysterical manifestations,"[24] "hallucinatory projections of Caro's conscience and of his inner craving for supernatural knowledge and power," "personality disassociation," and a "qualitative suggestion of schizophrenic process."[25] In a different context, one could also consult Deikman's *The Observing Self,* in which he understands mysticism as a science in Western psychological terms.[26] Still other approaches try to understand mysticism in terms of psychodynamics, psychoanalytic object-relations, cognitive psychology, and comparative sociocultural analyses.[27]

What these medical, psychological, psychoanalytic, and sociological diagnoses and analyses miss is that the presence of the Holy is given with its own structure, immediacy, and "order" and as such does not need to conform to a narrow, restrictive view of experience in order to count as a different kind of evidence. Bergson wonders, for instance, how the mystics could ever have been grouped with the mentally ill once we grasp the internal movement of their lives and spirit. Admittedly, we live in a situation of unstable equilibrium whereby the health of mind and body as well as their pathologies are not easily defined. Yet, he continues, there is an exceptional mental healthiness—what Husserl would call "hyper-normality"—that is readily recognizable, a healthiness that is expressed in the penchant for action, in the faculty of adapting and re-adapting oneself to circumstances, and in the spirit of simplicity that triumphs over complications: "And could this not serve as the very definition of intellectual verve?"[28]

This should not suggest that one cannot be deceived or that one cannot suffer from self-delusion; it does not mean that there are not sociological, historical, and cultural matrices in which the mystics live. In fact, the mystics themselves are the first to admit this! Indeed, it is quite legitimate to ask whether or not there is a lived, phenomenological difference between, say, mystical experience and what we understand today as psychopathology. It would be premature on my part simply to give an answer without having to give due consideration to how the mystics themselves handle these and similar questions. This is something I take up in chapter 5, concerning the problem of evidence in the religious sphere. What I can say here, however, is that when the mystics attempt to sort out a genuine experience from a deception or a malady, they appeal to operations *on or within that level of religious experiencing* and do not reduce the religious, say, to the psychological or vital level of experience. The fact that they are able to pose the question concerning a delusion and attempt to distinguish it from a genuine experience of Divine presence and to see these experiences within a religious tradition presupposes epiphany; and most importantly, it calibrates the problems they encounter *in their own terms* and *within that sphere of evidence.*

Drawing on the mystics might seem to be counterproductive in discerning basic structures of religious experience. How can the descriptions of such "elite" persons be taken as descriptive of our relation with the Holy in the religious sense and as sketching, however modestly, the structures of these experiences? It is precisely the refined character of their lives (and not the fact that there are either few or many) that enable us to see more clearly the essential structures of that founding inter-Personal sphere. Thus, quite contrary to the mystical relations being "exclusive," "isolated," or "rare," they are instead *exemplary* of epiphany and of what is always already going on in that inter-Personal sphere for all of us and open in principle to all of us, though for most of us it is lived rather obscurely or in a misdirected manner. This is why someone like Bergson can write: "In reality, for the great mystics it is a matter of radically transforming humanity, to begin with, by setting an example. The goal could be attained only if there existed in the end what should have theoretically existed in the beginning, a divine humanity."[29]

Do we have access to these experiences? Yes and No. Yes, to the extent that epiphany is happening all the time. Richard Kearney, in his recent work, is therefore quite justified in formulating this dimension of experience as "epiphanies of the everyday."[30] The effort required is one of "bracketing" one's self in order to liberate the vertical dimension in the things themselves and in ourselves; the effort is one of disposing oneself (or dis-posing the self, as mentioned in the Introduction to this work) so that we can *perhaps* be struck in ways similar to the ways in which the mystics themselves are struck. This disposition of the self, however, is not merely an intellectual exercise, for such a divestment of self is *lived through,* for example, as humble service, which may entail what the mystics refer to as poverty, obedience, and so forth. No, in the sense that many of these epiphanic experiences that I describe on the basis of the mystics (chapters 2–4) are themselves *beyond* the pale of our own efforts (and their own efforts) and come to the individual as gift or grace. In this sense there is nothing one can do *to provoke* this dimension of experiencing. Indeed, as St. Teresa of Avila instructs, it is prideful to go around wearying ourselves that we do not have these special experiences. And there is certainly no point in diluting the significance and uniqueness of mystical experiences so that we think they are simply at our disposal or within our discretion.

Generative Phenomenology and Hermeneutics

I privilege the first-person accounts of several mystics (even though they are not "my" experiences) because they provide a point of access for phenomenological description. By first-person accounts, I do not necessarily mean autobiographical accounts. It is not the history of the person or facts about the person that are of import, but the description of vertical experiences that differ essentially from the presentation of objects. The focus is not the individual and his or her mental states, but the given, lived vertical experiences. Such accounts, as we will see below, are available in the spirit of the mystics' faithfulness to the self-givenness of the Holy, a faithfulness emphasized by their unrelenting appeals to experience as the condition for everything the respective mystic writes.

In and through such first-person accounts, we can be attentive to the complex texture of givenness (i.e., presence) of the Holy, as well as to modalizations of this unique kind of evidence in possible deceptions and illusions. Though the mystics' primary concern was not with the mere description of "evidence"—since the descriptions of various stages, their evidence, problems of deception, and so forth, were a means to serve others—many of their records are nevertheless there for us and open for us both descriptively and evocatively.

One could still question: Does not the appeal to the first-person accounts provided by the mystics mitigate the integrity of a phenomenological approach? The first-person perspective is essential for phenomenology, so the fact that I appeal to these first-person accounts of the mystics is not the issue. The question concerns the fact that they are not claimed as my own first-person accounts but come to us through the mystics' recorded descriptions. Now one might object that phenomenology reigns over "pure internal experience," while hermeneutics claims for itself the domain of language and texts. To be sure, *if* one takes phenomenology to be restricted to the static phenomenology of consciousness and confines evidence to apodictic intellective objects, then many types of phenomenology could no longer be considered phenomenology at all, including this type here. This, however, is a very truncated conception of phenomenology.[31]

For my part, I do not limit phenomenology to its earliest expression because this is not all that phenomenology can be and has become. In an earlier work on Husserl and phenomenological method,[32] I showed how phenomenology is confined neither to a static method of the Cartesian type, nor to the more "progressive," dynamic method called "genetic" phenomenology. In that work, I extrapolated upon and attempted to elucidate phenomenology's generative dimension, introducing a generative phenomenology. Generative phenomenology is a style of phenomenology that can handle matters that are geo-historical, social, normative, and communicative. The matters that I deal with in the present work can be treated by phenomenology in its generative sense—though the problematic that I deal with here, the meaning of religious experience and its unique style of evidence, was not an explicit theme in that work. Given this understanding, I have no objection to regarding what I am doing as a "hermeneutic phenomenology" if the emphasis is on "phenomenology" as a mode of generative phenomenology.[33]

The fact that these first-person accounts stem from others and not from myself should not be taken as an impediment, but as a privilege of access. It is not clear, in fact, that the description of our own first-person experiences demand any less examination than the description of the first-person description by others. Even my own descriptions of my first-person experiences are distanced reflections on my own experiences, and to this extent they can coincide with others' reflections on my experiences. From the accounts provided by the mystics, we can discern basic structures of experience and relate other descriptions of mystical experiences to them without having "to put myself in the place of the other" (which, by the very structure of the uniqueness of personal experience I am describing here, is impossible). It is true that my descriptions of my bodily movements are distinct from others' descriptions of their bodily movements. But phenomenology, as a cooperative effort, never excluded others' first-person accounts in an effort to clarify the phenomena. Phenomenology, instead, did not wish for third-person, ostensibly objective accounts of our lifeworld to wear the mask of truth, to parade as self-subsistent, and thereby to dominate the field of *lived* experiences. I do not have to have had the experience of a phantom limb, as described in Merleau-Ponty's *Phenomenology of Perception,* in order to give a phenomenological account of it as an ambivalent presence in the global kinesthesis of the lived body and my being in the world.[34]

When we study St. Teresa of Avila, Rabbi Dov Baer, Rūzbihān Baqlī, their distinctive kinds of experiencing, their encounterings of the Holy that are nuanced by their religious backgrounds, their distinctive witnessings preserved for us in writing—all this evokes an open sphere of "spirit" that does not exhaust its uniqueness in the lives of the individuals. Their experiences illuminate what being human can mean, since they are possibilities of experience, essential possibilities as actualized. The fact that their lives elucidate an essential possibility does not mean, on the other hand, "we are all mystics."

Rather than phenomenology being the mere description of "facts," it is trained on *modes of givenness* such that givenness guides the description, not the reverse. The phenomenological effort in description is not only "to describe faithfully" but to attempt *to evoke* the phenomena in such a way that others might more easily see/experience for themselves (with no guarantee that they will), or to read or hear the descriptions so that we might "see"/"experience" for ourselves (with no guarantee that we will). So, while I find Pike keenly sensitive to the nuances and difficulties inherent in such an undertaking, I see no justification for neologisms (like "phenomenography"); rather, it points to a richer and deeper understanding of the phenomenological task.

It is not out of naïveté that I use the expression "presence" of God in this work. I do it with the full understanding that it is in vogue to speak of absence, or of presence as riddled by absence, and to engage in the postmodern critique of the "metaphysics of presence." I reappropriate this term "presence" on the basis of descriptions that point to experiences of the Holy as overabundant, to an "ineffability" grounded in excess or surplus, not in a lack, withdrawal, or absence.

Of course, it could be objected that the mystics resort to imagery and metaphor in order to express this overwhelming presence of God. Ineffability would then seem to hamper any effort to describe such experiences as the mystics record them since the experiences are never represented adequately in language. Let us leave aside the fact that description takes place inadequately even in perceptual experience since the givenness (evidence) is essentially inadequate. As Husserl writes, even external perception is a constant pretension to accomplish what it is not in a position to accomplish, namely, the complete givenness of the object; we are never without a *plus ultra*.[35]

If the mystics speak apophantically, it is because there is qualitatively "too much" to be said; the presence is too ebullient. Noteworthy is the fact that despite the problem of "ineffability," the mystics are never reduced to silence! In fact, if they remained silent, their silence would only reaffirm the hegemony of language as indication and not as evocation. If they sense their discourse is inadequate, it is more profoundly due to their anxiety of standing before the Holy and being called to forgo the demands of the self by doing the "will of God."

We witness, in the mystics that I treat here especially, an uncanny ability to negotiate the "self-deregulating regulation and self-regulating deregulation"[36] of the prohibition of idolatry when speaking the ineffable —though not expressed in these terms. The ineffable here is not merely the more restricted sense of the name of God, *ha-Shem,* but the articulated modes of experiencing.

It is due to a kind of presence that is experienced as overwhelming from their side as finite persons that the mystics are motivated to eloquence and imagery. It is not that there is somewhere an "adequate" language, and imagery and metaphor are a second best. Rather, for the mystics, imagery and metaphor suggest at least an implicit awareness of language's own limits; and to the extent that it (imagery) is aware of its (language's) own *insufficiency at indicating or provoking* the Holy (e.g., "this is God"), imagery becomes for the mystics a "superior" mode of language. Imagery, in this regard, is perhaps less naïve than philosophical discourse. What is particularly interesting is the fact that the mystics, especially those from the Islamic tradition, cite the *necessity* of using *images* and the beauty of it when *evoking* God (*iḥsān*) because beauty is in the manner of God. On the one hand, for them, it is the only way; on the other hand, one cannot take oneself too seriously in doing this "only way." This is the difficulty the mystics encounter when they are tried for heresy, the difficulty they encounter with "ecstatic sayings," which I take up in chapter 8. This points to an interesting hermeneutic, because the sayings could not be "ecstatic" unless the experiences somehow transcended the literal expression.

Certainly, the meaning of the experience is "in" the account in the sense that—as Merleau-Ponty would say—love is "in" the flowers when presented by the lover to the beloved. But there is an *irreducibility* of the experiences to language in the mystics, even though these experiences are evoked for us only through their creative descriptions.[37] This is one reason why the mystics cite an "overflowing" of the experiences over the categories of the understanding that depict the experiences: Because one cannot comprehend what one understands, as St. Teresa writes, "there is an understanding by not understanding." It is not that the descriptions are meaningless or that we cannot get anything out of them because of the depth of the experiences. On the contrary, the descriptions try to say "too much" because at times there is "too much" meaning, "too much" given, because for the mystics, the experiences are *from* God and not only *of* God. Of necessity, their descriptions must be *creative evocations,* even if they use terms others have used; there are no ready-made markers along the spiritual path, and the nature of this inter-Personal encounter is itself creative. This, together with the imperative of serving others, is why we see the necessity for many of the mystics of inventing a new vocabulary and symbolic matrix where a satisfactory one is not available, of using old expressions in an unaccustomed way, stressing conceptualization—all without being attached to a standard of literalism and without recognizing these formulations as satisfactory.

If we understand this methodological approach as a phenomenological one in the sense of a generative phenomenology, which entails a hermeneutic component, it is nevertheless important not to confuse this methodological dimension with religious experience.

Remoteness is predicable of real or ideal objects, and it is they that are susceptible to the kind of hoionic presence peculiar to the dialectic of being present and absent. From the philosophical/mystical anthropology I am tracking here, persons as absolute cannot be given with the relativity of objects. Even though they are inaccessible as objects, persons are immediately and directly given in a way that cannot be subsumed under object-givenness, and this holds above all for the Holy. Meaning on this level cannot be negotiated between the experiencer and the experienced (cf. chapter 5).

One can certainly submit an experienced presence, the givenness of the Holy in the form of "prayer," "ecstasy," or "unveilings" to interpretation. Such religious experiences are embedded in a religious tradition and in the individual's personal relation to the Holy. St. Teresa of Avila, just to give one example, constantly attempts to "test"—after the fact—whether a particular givenness (say, a prayer of quiet, a prayer of spiritual delight, a prayer of rapture) is actually from God or from another source, like self-delusion. One way of testing cited by St. Teresa is what I call looking for the "historical efficacy" of prayer, that is, if it leaves one "calm" rather than frustrated, if the virtues flourish, and so forth. There is also an imperative interpersonal dimension to understanding prayer in St. Teresa's writings, ecstasy in Rabbi Dov Baer, and unveilings in Rūzbihān Baqlī in the form of relating and discussing the experiences with a confessor or master. This can be understood as a hermeneutical endeavor.

The danger, however, is to say that hermeneutics at this level is called forth in ascertaining the evidence of prayer, ecstasy, and unveiling (something that we find constantly at stake in the mystics); to say that religious experience given "at the pleasure of God" is nuanced by the richness of the historical context is to my mind different from saying that the presence of God emerges only from a dialectical interplay or negotiation of meaning, that epiphany is given only through the give and take of the interpretative enterprise (passive or active). One can identify an epistemological feature here for us, insofar as there is a concern with what we would call evidence; but this does not mean that God is experienced as an epistemological object of presentation. I agree that the interpretation of the presence of the Holy is a formidable undertaking. And if one wishes to call the practice of what is known generally as the "discernment of spirits" an interpretative enterprise, then I would concur.[38] I only hedge calling this "hermeneutics" if one identifies the hermeneutics of experience as a process of dealing with perceptual or epistemic objects. If one wants to call the spiritual practice of the "discernment of spirits" hermeneutics, that is fine, but I think it is safer to call it by that name (discernment) rather than risk conflating practices.

What one must take into account in any such designation is that there is an essential difference between the modes in which the Holy is given—the ways the mystics describe—the "authority" of the givenness, the "spontaneity" and the like (cf. chapter 5), and the way in which objects are presented. If we assume that hermeneutics characterizes the field of the latter, namely, presentation, then I think we should be careful in cavalierly applying the term loosely to the former. I want to avoid calling *religious experience* hermeneutics plain and simple because this tends to make the presence of God relative to me and my powers, and this ultimately would be an expression of forcing my will on the presence of God, which is to say, to commit idolatry. The religious experience is "absolute" in the sense described above, not dialectical or hermeneutical. What we must avoid at all costs is a new type of positivism that creeps in under the name of hermeneutics. A hermeneutics of religious experience must itself be situated and relativized *by* religious experience, its unmistakable features made salient by a givenness that it is incapable of producing.[39] At least for the mystics of the Abrahamic tradition—and here I am getting ahead of myself—there is perhaps what one could call a question of God. But this question is not something that I pose initially and that I command; rather, it is a question coming from God to which I can respond, *"hineni,"* "Here I am," which then invites my first question.

The Abrahamic Tradition

One further note that I hope clarifies the scope of my approach and its self-defined limits: I focus here on a core of experience revealed and developed within the Abrahamic tradition that concerns "person" and lived in terms of verticality and idolatry. These are not neutral or universal, but absolute experiences. It is not that there are not other religious traditions that have the notion of person generally speaking, or even spiritual traditions that do not unfold on the basis of person at all—Zen Buddhism in the later case. But it is peculiar to the Abrahamic religious traditions that the *experience* of the absoluteness of the Holy (sometimes expressed as the "Oneness" of God) is expressly cultivated. This, as we will see in chapter 6, is described in a personal manner. Because they live from the experienced Oneness of God, the mystics often share *more with each other,* even though they spring from different religions and religious backgrounds—something we witnessed in the early Middle Ages between the Jewish, Christian, and Islamic mystics—than do the mystics and "believers" who belong to the same confession. Among the mystics, we can see a true ecumenical dialogue taking shape without any attempt to be ecumenical.

My point here is that in the Abrahamic religious traditions the personal dimension—or rather, the inter-Personal dimension—becomes the specific determination of religious experience such that absolute experience can be qualified as vertical. It is precisely from the experience of verticality that we are able to confront our contemporary social ills and acts of violence as, at root, idolatry. Certainly, there are many dimensions to the Abrahamic tradition, and to focus on it is not to reduce Judaism to Christianity to Islam. They are experientially unified, however, by what I am calling here *vertical* experiences in relation to which the acts antithetical to verticality can be criticized as *idolatry*.

Let me emphasize that my investigation into religious experience is not an attempt to give a global narrative of "the sacred." In this respect, this work is self-avowedly not "comparative" in the sense of a work that deals with all religious traditions or various types thereof.[40] It is not an attempt to survey all spiritualities from a putative neutral nowhere. The abstention from a surveying attitude on my part does not arise because I think it would be impossible to do so due to the vast quantity of religions. Rather, my focus on the Abrahamic mystics emerges from the singular integrity of sets of experiences that can be understood as vertical. Moreover, just because there are religious possibilities other than the Abrahamic ones that have been revealed does not mean that the Abrahamic inter-Personal reality is somehow "arbitrary"—a designation that William James would misleadingly give it.[41]

True, the position that I develop is gleaned from *certain* experiences and hence cannot claim to be exhaustive or definitive. By the same token, because these religious possibilities originate from these experiences—and hence are not, or are no longer, mere possibilities but historical realities —they cannot be arbitrary either. Nevertheless, they can be and are *decisive*, even though I am able to recognize that these other possibilities can be decisive for another though I do not experience them in this way.[42] A "way" is given as decisive and lived as "the" way for me, for us; in and through it, experience emerges. It is from this "decisive" way that we encounter other ways that are not lived as decisive for me, for us. We live in and through the "home" toward another that is not lived as home, that is experienced by us as alien. That there are other ways, we know from the testimonies of and encounters with others—Hindus, Zen Buddhists, and so forth.[43] Because of such encounters, our way cannot be lived as exhaustive or *definitive*. A decisive, absolute experience ("absolute" in the sense defined above), is not a universal perspective. It is precisely this irreducible structure that makes experiences like conversion a possible and living reality. Critique, as exercised from the home, is not and cannot be "universal"; it is however intra- and cross-cultural. In the former instance (the universalist, definitive, exhaustive stance), one abstracts from experience, from history, from tradition; in the latter (decisiveness), one lives *through* experience.[44]

Rather than this decisiveness bespeaking relativism, it points to the irreversible character of religious experience, and interpersonal experience in general.[45] It is also what prevents one both from establishing a perspective as a universal meta-narrative and from writing to the lowest common denominator. One winds up doing the latter when one only wants to speak of "spiritual" experiences, rather than "religious" or "inter-Personal" experiences because "spiritual" putatively fits them all and is thereby less selective. The danger here is that one establishes a privileged discourse or set of experiences as ostensibly "neutral," which then insidiously and unwittingly inserts its hegemony over all others in the name of a spurious universal accessibility.[46] Instead, these descriptions are rooted in the Abrahamic tradition and the unity of these experiences as intimated above.

Specifically, the critique of idolatry—in the religious sphere, fundamentalism as well as secularism, and their ramifications ranging from capitalism to misogyny—is only possible from the lived absoluteness of the Holy as Person. It is from such absolute experience (the lived experience of the absoluteness of Person), exemplified by but not restricted to the mystics, that one can and must engage idolatry.

While I focus on the Abrahamic tradition, the Jewish, Christian, and Islamic realities of this tradition are irreducible and historically distinctive. Each has unique insights into the dimension of the Holy, and each has cultivated religious responses that are peculiar to the positive values witnessed and lived within a concrete historical tradition. Jewish experiences that are rooted in God's revelation in the Torah, God's intervention in history, and the promise of Messianic redemption, cannot be equated with Christian experiences that are rooted in God's incarnate presence as the person of Christ, the Messiah and Redeemer; these, in turn, cannot be reduced to Islamic experiences that are unified in God's revelation in the Quran and the exemplary role of the Messenger/Prophet Muhammad.

Although it would be simplistic to lump all spiritual and religious traditions together and to speak of a unified mystical tradition, these three can be regarded as a whole because of their "Abrahamic" character. In this respect, as a whole, they are essentially distinctive from, say, Zen Buddhism, Taoism, Hinduism, or Shamanism—even though we can productively undertake comparative analyses between them and find striking similarities among them. Indeed, the latter have their own dimensions of spiritual practices and directednesses that are irreducible, and there is certainly no point in blurring their differences in the enthusiastic recognition of some common structures.

The Jewish, Christian, and Islamic religious orientations are referred to as "Abrahamic" because from their point of view, God had singled out Abram, later called Abraham, to establish his covenant. This covenant consisted, not in erecting great buildings or tabernacles, constructing towering pyramids, fashioning pompous statues, and the like, but in instructing his children and their children to follow in the ways of the Lord by pursuing justice and doing what is just and right (Genesis 18:18–19, Isaiah 51:1–2, Micah, 6:8).[47] Because of Abraham's absolute faith in this One God of justice and righteousness, he was able to reject other gods as idols. Although there is some variation on the test of faith and marking the covenant where Abraham is concerned—in the Judeo-Christian perspective, it is epitomized in the *akidah,* or the binding of Isaac, son of Sarah; in the Islamic perspective, it involves Ishmael, son of Hagar, and Ishmael's willing self-sacrifice—all three traditions share the basic faith and conviction in the Oneness or absoluteness of God, lived as an historical presence; accordingly, they situate themselves in this trajectory. Though they "originate" this origin differently, all three ultimately share the same root and are guided by the same set of insights. Its essential structures distinguish it from other spiritual experiences, and it is lived as "home" for those who dwell experientially within it.

All three religious orientations, Jewish, Christian, and Islamic, furthermore, confront idolatry by appealing to this One God; and this challenge is expounded upon in the religious founders themselves. Abraham, let us recall, is said to have revolted against the pagan gods that his people and family worshiped, shattering the temple idols.[48] In a like manner, Moses comes down from Mount Sinai, sees the people dancing around the golden calf, and destroys the calf (Exodus 32:7ff). Jesus, after finding that people have desecrated the temple, fashions a whip and drives out the merchants (John 1:13). Muhammad, "the nearest of kin to Abraham" (Quran 3:68) destroys all the idols representing the gods of multiple Arab tribes housed in the Kabba, the "House of God" in Mecca.

As noted above, the mystics from the three Abrahamic traditions often share a great deal *with each other* across these demarcated traditions because their experiences arise from a common source, ultimately, from inter-Personal experiences, even though the springboards to the mystical experiences (i.e., the particular religious practices, rituals, styles of prayer, etc.) are decidedly unique and different. Again, one could even go so far as to say that at this level of experiencing one could find more in common between and among the diverse Abrahamic mystics, since it goes to the core of experiencing, than one could find between the adherents of different Abrahamic religions or even between the mystics of one tradition and believers of that same confession. Those adhering to a certain confession or belief structure, those engaged in a particular cult, may not be practicing *from* the center of these inter-Personal experiences in such a direct manner. This is why it is entirely possible for the mystics to be in conflict at times with the confessions of their own tradition but in concert with other mystics who spring from a different religious tradition.

For the portion of this work that is descriptive of religious experiences via the mystics, I rely on three figures as exemplary within the grand and looming Abrahamic mystical tradition: Rabbi Dov Baer of Lubavitch within the Jewish tradition, St. Teresa of Avila within the Christian tradition, and Rūzbihān Baqlī within the Islamic tradition. I do not take them as "representative" of each tradition in the sense that they are able to speak for all in the same way, or as giving an average view. It is also not my task to categorize all mystical experiences and to create a universal index. This would belie the radically *personal* nature of the experiences in question. I do, however, take these mystics as *exemplary* in the sense that through their concrete, uniquely personal focus they each bring to the fore the epiphanic character of givenness through experiential descriptions and testimonies. One might argue that, in principle, it would be possible to draw upon only one figure within the Abrahamic tradition for these purposes. I use these three figures, each from a different tradition within the Abrahamic orientation, rather than just one, because often what one person or tradition is only able to say implicitly is lived explicitly in another. In this way the three figures mutually enhance one another, are mutually elucidating, and evoke the richness of this

Abrahamic way. This also shows all the more forcefully the inter-Personal nature of the vertical experiences that leads to the common life in the absoluteness of the inter-Personal experience, which in turn becomes the basis for challenging idolatry.

In taking up these religious figures, using their descriptions as a touchstone for phenomenological reflection, I introduce the respective religious and historical background relevant to the particular mystics. Each section in the chapters that introduce the milieu of the mystics will have different emphases and highlights, depending on the religious tradition they inherit and in which they articulate their experiences. For example, Jewish mysticism evolves through several historical permutations, exhibiting different trends or styles in mysticism; Christian mysticism was largely dependent upon monasticism; Islamic mysticism draws heavily upon the experiences of Muhammad. Thus, there is not a one-to-one correspondence of issues or equality of themes treated in this part of the chapters devoted to an historical orientation of the mystics. Finally, for the sake of simplicity, I cannot treat all the variations within a religious tradition.[49] It is neither desirable, nor necessary, nor possible to be exhaustive in this regard.

I develop my exposition of the mystics first by treating St. Teresa of Avila, then Rabbi Dov Baer, and finally Rūzbihān Baqlī. I use this array and not the chronological order of the mystic's respective tradition's foundation or the order of their historical position. I do this with an eye to the character of their descriptions, how the issues introduced in one mystic play out in the others, how some of the problems raised in one person are supplemented by another's experience, and in general how one set of descriptions elucidates the expositions of the others.

All three of the mystics articulate the givenness of the Holy but evoke this presence with different terms and with different modulations of experience. It would not be wrongheaded to say that their experiences motivate their own technical language that has meaning within their particular tradition, but that is nevertheless accessible outside of that tradition. For St. Teresa this presence, which is a dynamic movement, is called "prayer"; for Dov Baer it is termed "ecstasy"; for Baqlī it is "unveiling." I reserve the philosophical elaborations of these experiences for chapters 5–8. I now turn to these Abrahamic mystics and to the phenomenological "givens."

CHAPTER 2

St. Teresa of Avila and Mysticism of Prayer

For it is one grace to receive the Lord's favor; another, to understand which favor and grace it is; and a third, to know how to describe and explain it. And although no more than the first grace seems necessary, it is a great advantage and a gift for the soul that it also understand the favor so as not to go about confused and afraid—and so that it may become more courageous in following the path of the Lord. . . .

—ST. TERESA OF AVILA (OBRAS, 97; VOL. 1, 17.5)

The Monastic Heritage and the Carmelite Order

Within the Christian tradition of mystical experience, I focus primarily on the sixteenth-century Carmelite nun St. Teresa of Avila. While one cannot say that monasticism is essential to the Christian mystical experience, it was so tightly intertwined with mysticism historically that one can hardly conceive of Christian mysticism developing, let alone flourishing, without it. It was nothing less than monasticism itself, McGinn explains, that virtually provided the context for cultivating the knowledge of Scripture, the life of penance, and the practice of prayer that prepared the Christian for intimate contact with God. Combining austere existence and often ascetical self-mastery with the knowledge of God, it was the monastics, both men and women, who became the ideal Christians.[1] The monastic life-style was in fact the religious context for St. Teresa of Avila as a Carmelite nun, and hence it deserves some modest attention here.

Even though small communities of desert ascetics and practices of meditation and prayer were not unique to Christianity, the dawning of third-century Christianity witnessed pervasively emerging forms of ascetic and group life. At first this style of Christian life was exemplified by the Eastern "Desert Fathers," the "solitary ones" or *monachoi* (monks) as they were called in Greek. It was this desert experience and these Desert Fathers who then became exemplary for later Christian mystical experience.

St. Antony (c. 250–356 CE), regarded by Athanasius as "the monk," was taken as the sufficient model of spiritual life and ascetic practice.[2] Yet it was not until the latter part of the fourth century that monks emerged as a distinctive Christian entity and force.[3] Without going into further permutations in the evolution of monasticism, for example with Pachomius (290–346 CE),[4] who is recognized as founding an enclosed, communal hermitage; with Basil of Caesarea (c. 329–379 CE), who provided a model for codes or *Rules* of organized communal life;[5] with Augustine of Hippo (354–430 CE) and John Cassian (c. 360–430 CE), who imported into the West and elaborated upon these programs of Christian perfection, it can be said without much qualification that the model having the most influence on the first millennium of monastic life originated with St. Benedict (c. 480–547 CE) and his "*Rule*." Even though there were approximately thirty rules written between 400 and 700 CE, it was the fifth-century compendium which came to be known much later as the *Rule of St. Benedict* that was decisive for the future of monasticism and indirectly for Western Christian mysticism.[6] One of the reasons for this was the adoption of the Rule by Benedict of Aniane and the promulgation by Charlemagne (desiring uniformity in his realm) that all should conform to *the* Rule of St. Benedict as the norm for all monks.[7]

Monasticism had flourished during the first millennium CE, and Christianity witnessed an increasing number of orders and rules—including, around the time of the Carmelites, the Franciscans, and the Dominicans. The monastic movement of the Carmelites can be traced back approximately to 1155 CE after the Crusaders took hold of Jerusalem in 1099 CE. The original Carmelites were an amalgam of clerics, laypersons, pilgrims, nobles, and former crusaders. But despite their various backgrounds and occupations, they held a common vision, namely, to renew the prophetic vocation of Elijah in a Christian context.[8]

While the movement was multiform, we can stress two elements that distinguished this prophetic vocation and context as a Christian one. First, Jesus is accepted as the Messiah (*mashiyach*), the "anointed one" who fulfilled the prophecies of Scripture. In Jesus, all three messianic roles—the kingly function in the line of David, the priestly function in the line of Aaron, and the role of Suffering Servant in the prophetic lineage—were all embodied in the *person* of Jesus. Jesus is accepted as the Messiah, the Christ, who is the personal center, the Revelation, the Word made flesh, where the Christian encounters the Father in the Spirit.[9]

Second, and related to this point, the Christian experience of the Holy is a Trinitarian one. The Holy Spirit, the third person of the Trinity, is an eschatological reality, not merely the function of a supernal principle of knowledge.[10] Christians share in the Holy Spirit insofar as they share in the Father through Christ, as sharing in the Divine Sonship. The Holy Spirit therefore relates not only to the *eschaton* but to the personal manner of working in the "community of believers" (cf. 1 Corinthians 12:1ff., Galatians 4:6, Romans, 8:14–23). This is not the place to detail the doctrine of the Trinity, the differences in the Eastern Church (represented, for example, by the Cappadocian Fathers) and the Western Church, and how it has evolved.[11] Suffice it to say that for the Christian, the Trinitarian experience of God does not vitiate the Oneness or Absoluteness of God. The three "persons" of the Trinity—the Father, the Son, and the Holy Spirit—constitute internal distinctions within a common life, a relational Oneness of the Godhead. With this brief consideration, let me return to the significance of the Carmelite order.

Mt. Carmel—the location of the cave of the prophet Elijah—was the site of these monastics. Elijah, let us recall, was the tenacious prophet from the ninth century BCE, the admonisher of King Ahab of the Northern Kingdom of Israel, and adversary of the latter's Phoenician Queen Jezebel, worshiper of Baal (see 1 Kings 17–19). Elijah, whose name means, literally, "Yahweh is my God," founded the "school of prophets." Enduring through the fifth century BCE, the school of prophets ceased after the Babylonian exile, but its mission was briefly reappropriated following about a four-hundred-year lapse. Because Elijah had served God so resolutely, even under threat of imminent death, he became known in later years as the harbinger of the messianic age and thus of the Messiah (see Malachi 3:23: "Lo, I will send the prophet Elijah to you before the coming of the awesome, fearful day of the Lord"). Not surprisingly, the early Christian-Jews imputed to John the Baptist, who baptized and thus "announced" Jesus, the spiritual heritage of Elijah ("Because it was towards John that all the prophecies of the prophets and of the Law were leading; and he, if you will believe me, is the Elijah who was to return" [Matt. 11:13–14]).[12]

Appropriating the prophetic vocation within a Christian context was experienced as a call to bear witness to the redemptive presence of Christ. A prophet, a *navi*, witnesses God from the personal experience of God. Following Elijah's style of prayer, the Carmelites committed themselves to a disciplined and eremitical life by retreating into the "cells" of Mt.

Carmel, emulating the prophetic mission of inspiration both to serve and to challenge others from the experience of God. In this way they became apostolic "witnesses," occasionally descending the Holy Mount to be of service to others.[13] (Witnessing, it may be recalled, comes from the Greek *martyrein,* where we get our English term "martyr.") These new Carmelite prophets considered as their founder neither the first prior or superior of their order, St. Berthold, the Calabrian monk, nor a particular Christian saint (compare, for example, the Benedictines, the Franciscans, the Dominicans, etc.), but precisely Elijah.[14] Thus, there is a direct spiritual connection made by the Carmelite Order to the prophetic tradition.

Interestingly, too, the chapel on Mt. Carmel was consecrated to Mary, "Our Lady," the "Mother of Carmel." Generally speaking, in Catholic Mariology, the primary significance of the virgin birth is a testimony to the Christian reality that the old humanity of Eve is transcended through the new humanity of Mary, who is unlike other women in relation to human sin.[15] Accordingly, Mary's virginity has a spiritual significance, not a physiological one, such that Mary herself, who is to become the Mother of God, must also be different vis-à-vis human nature. This is the reason for the doctrine of the Immaculate Conception, which pertains to Mary, not to Jesus. The reason for the Marian devotion of the Carmelites, observes Rohrbach, lay in the early Carmelites' contention that Mary's life was the perfect Christian expression of the prophetic vocation in a Christian context, and that through her they could Christianize and thus realize the ancient prophetic role in their own environment.[16]

The Carmelite Rule was at first an oral one. When it became necessary to have a written Rule due to increased number of adherents and ecclesiastical approbation, the Rule was brief, unlegalistic, and scripturally oriented, with the flavor of Eastern monasticism. Exhibiting the influences of Basil and Cassian, there was an insistence on continual prayer, asceticism, silence, and the simplicity of life, winning the title, the "Rule of Mysticism."[17] Among the *regulae,* the Carmelite Rule included forsaking personal property, abstentions from meat, fasting each year from September 14 to Easter, avoiding idleness, attending daily Mass, and observing silence from the late evening to 9:00 AM. But, as Rohrbach explains, the Carmelites have always regarded one sentence as the core of the Rule: "'Let them remain alone in their own cells, or near them, meditating day and night on the law of the Lord and watching in prayer, unless they are engaged in some other just occupations.' This statement embodies the core of the prophetic vocation: the unremitting life of solitude with God, and a provision whereby the prophet can break his solitude for the inspirational work of the moment."[18] So, while there is ample time devoted to prayer, fasting, and abstinence, it is the presence of God that takes precedence. The life of the Carmelite monk is therefore in the deepest sense a spontaneous one, since he or she must stand open to the call of God in service as did Elijah (1 Kings 18:15), and this cannot be something determined in advance, legislated by precise rules, or regulated by the order of the intellect.

The Personal Milieu and Mysticism of St. Teresa

Paternal granddaughter of a Toledan Jewish cloth merchant who was forced to convert to Christianity, Teresa de Ahumada (1515–1582) was born in Spain during the reign of Ferdinand and Isabella during one of the tumultuous periods of the Inquisition. One can find many striking and obvious similarities in the expression of St. Teresa's spirituality and the outlawed Jewish faith and mystical practices (for example, between the descriptions of her *Interior Castle* and 1,000-year-old Jewish Merkabah mysticism). Rather than concentrate on this aspect of St. Teresa's background, however, I will focus more directly on her role as a Carmelite nun.[19]

The land in which Jews, Muslims, and Christians had lived together in peace and friendship now strove for political and national unity by religious control through a particular understanding of Christianity. Where St. Teresa is concerned, the Inquisition and popular piety took a harsh turn against strains of Christianity that emphasized mental prayer over ceremony, interior inspiration, self-abandonment, recollection, and "illumination" practiced early on by devout women (*beatas*), Franciscans of *converso* origin, and others who gained the repute of *alumbrados* (those who belonged to the illuminist movement), *dejados* (those whose spirituality was characterized by self-abandonment), and *recogidos* (those who emphasized the spiritual practice of recollection).[20] These tendencies in some form, as we will see, are all peculiar to St. Teresa's unique spirituality. Furthermore, rather than forsaking the corporeal for the sake of the spiritual, Christ's *humanity* was never experienced by her as an impediment to mystical practices; rather, her path of mysticism was devoted to Christ in his "most sacred humanity."[21] "I believe I've explained," she writes, "that it is fitting for souls, however spiritual, to take care not to flee from corporal things to the extent of thinking that even the most sacred humanity causes harm. Some quote what the Lord said to His disciples that it was fitting that He go. I can't bear this. I would wager that He didn't say it to His most Blessed Mother."[22] Finally, the fact that St. Teresa was a woman made her all the more suspect in the eyes of some of the Church officials, since it was a growing belief that as a woman, she could be taken by the Devil as his intermediary to lure "men" into evil.[23] It is therefore not surprising that the Inquisition sequestered her work, known today as "The Book of Her Life," for over a decade, though she was never found guilty in any of her appearances before the Inquisition.

Raised in Avila, she entered the austere life of a Carmelite nun in the Carmelite monastery of the Incarnation at the age of twenty. It was St. Teresa's desire to serve God more deeply by forgoing the comfort to which many of the Carmelites had grown accustomed as the order spread to and established itself in the West, drifting little by little from its original ideals. She found the need to revive the emphasis on poverty, asceticism, and apostolic work that had characterized the Carmelite vocation from the outset.[24]

Only wanting to create a single sanctuary for herself and a handful of nuns to follow the unmitigated rule, St. Teresa wound up instigating a reform of the Order of Discalced Carmelites,[25] founding no less than seventeen Carmelite monasteries for women, sometimes with great difficulty and effort. In the end, she inaugurated a renewal within the Carmelite Order.[26]

The Carmelites have known a great number of mystics and saints, some quite popular, like St. John of the Cross (1542–1591) or St. Thérèse of Lisieux (1873–1897); some recent, like Edith Stein (1891–1942), former assistant to the phenomenologist Edmund Husserl, convert from Judaism to Catholicism, and martyr under the hands of the Nazis. I take up the writings of St. Teresa of Avila for the Christian portion of my exposition for several reasons that I briefly mention here.

St. Teresa's writings have the character of being "raw," honest, direct, unpretentious, and expressive of a profound sensitivity to the complexities and nuances of spiritual experience. Because she was not schooled as a theologian in any classical sense, her writings are not immediately informed by ready-made theological concepts. I do not suggest, as Stace does, that the mystics (or most of them), often betray their experiences by conforming their writings (and in turn, their experiences) to church doctrine.[27] In fact, it is more the case that figures in the lineage of the mystical tradition were formative of that very doctrine itself and as a result could not separate their mystical experiences from them. One need only consider the patristic authors like St. Ambrose[28] or St. Augustine and his debates with the Pelagians to see how church doctrine and theological authority emerge along with special spiritual experiences.[29] True, after church doctrine was fairly established, some mystics were either deemed to be heretical or were brought before inquisitional authorities.

Even here, however, these mystics can hardly be said to have compromised their experiences in favor of fixed doctrine. This is especially the case for St. Teresa. Afraid, not of the Inquisition but of compromising her genuine experiences of God, afraid as well of being herself deceived and leading others astray, she replies to the warnings of others about the Inquisition: "This amused me and made me laugh, for I never had any fear of such a possibility. . . . And I said they shouldn't be afraid about these possible accusations; that it would be pretty bad for my soul if there were something in it of the sort that I should have to fear the Inquisition; that I thought that if I did have something to fear I'd go myself to seek out the Inquisitors."[30]

Because the experience of the Holy and service, and not conformity to church doctrine per se, are central for the mystics, almost any of the Christian mystics could have served as an example of the mystical style for my purposes. But what I find particularly compelling in St. Teresa's descriptions is an unparalleled first-person subtlety and attention to experiential detail to which, moreover, she was not particularly attached.[31]

Furthermore, it is common for many mystics to emphasize exclusively the character of union with God as making up a mystical experience. Although union is often understood to be the ultimate phase of mystical experiences (in contrast to someone like Baqlī or 'Aṭṭār in the Islamic tradition),[32] St. Teresa considers a whole range of experiences, which while they can be counted as mystical, either precede the experience of union or are significant and irreducible elaborations upon it.[33]

Finally, one of the reasons that St. Teresa does not focus exclusively on union is that in her first-person descriptions, she is unflaggingly attentive to the many shapes of the presence of God, to a wide range of absolute self-evidence in kind and degree, and accordingly is attuned to the problem concerning whether or not these experiences are really from and of God. Are the visions, locutions, consolations, delights, ecstasies, wounds of love, tears, really givens from and of God, or are they delusions motivated by physical weakness, self-deception due to over-eagerness on the individual's part, or deceptions caused by the devil? These intricate descriptions and attempts at descriptions highlight some of the issues of presence, evidence, and modalizations peculiar to vertical experience.

For St. Teresa, the task of describing the various levels of what I call vertical experience was not understood as a scholarly undertaking. It was motivated by obedience to her superiors and was directed toward persons pursuing a spiritual life so that those who have had similar experiences might be able to mark their way and avoid deceptions and difficulties characteristic of a spiritual path.[34] Her descriptions were filled with praises for the grandeur of God and were given with the hope of evoking a possible way to God.

The difficulty in presenting modes of vertical experience has to do not merely with "accurate" description but with having to conceptualize something that by its nature cannot be constrained by conceptualization and having to invent new expressions by borrowing from old ones, all the while not remaining restricted to or by them. This is all done in an effort to serve others in humility and to help realize the kingdom of God. Her writing is not first and foremost what we might call "indicative speech"; she holds her writing neither to a contemporary standard of literalism nor to an analytic measure of adequation. Not only is her writing as much "evocative" as it is "descriptive," but description necessarily serves for her evocation.

How can one describe and evoke such extraordinary matters? There is a great freedom of imagery found in religious language, where the concrete images can never be taken *too* seriously.[35] The mystics are not exceptions to this use of imagery, but are the rule—as we will see in the cases of St. Teresa, Dov Baer, and Baqlī. Echoed throughout St. Teresa's writings are reflections like this one: "I am laughing to myself over these comparisons for they do not satisfy me, but I don't know any others."[36] The comparisons do not satisfy her because she is constantly attentive to "*nuevas palabras*," or "new words," where there had been no relevant vocabulary. Moreover, because these experiences are always too much for her language to handle—in the sense of overflowing those concepts— even these new words, should they come, are never deemed sufficient. This is why she, like others, continues to enlist a wide variety of imagery and comparisons. For example, in St. Teresa's writings the individual is compared to a worm, a sponge, a tortoise, a broken vessel, a silkworm, a dove, a bride; and God is experienced and described as a king, Majesty, a father, a mother, a lover, a spouse; God's presence is compared to a palace, a font, a spark, a fire, a fragrance, calm, friendliness, a treasure, a precious jewel in a reliquary, wine, sweetness, tenderness, expansion, delightful pain, peaceful, glory, refreshing, power, a gentle whistle.

My interest lies primarily in the ways in which she describes how the Holy is given and thus the ways in which she points to the articulated presence of God. For these descriptions, St. Teresa relies on two major images: an earlier one, water, from *Libro de la Vida* (*The Book of Her Life*), and a later one, the "dwelling places" (*moradas*), from her *Moradas del Castillo Interior* (*The Interior Castle*).

The latter imagery was already well known from Jewish mystical practices understood as the *Hechalot* (palaces) spiritual experience.[37] There are obvious advantages to the latter set of descriptions. Because they were written over a decade after *La Vida* (while the latter was still in the hands of the Inquisition), St. Teresa had gained much more experience in matters that she had not understood previously, especially as this experience pertained to union. In addition, other levels of spiritual and mystical experience received more differentiation in the later work. The main levels number seven, though she confesses that there are many dwelling places within each dwelling place (*Obras*, 583; *Collected Works*, Vol. 2, Epilogue .3), and that in the beginning stages we should think in terms of millions of rooms, since there are many points of entry or ways to engage the spiritual path (*Obras*, 478–79; *Collected Works*, Vol. 2, I.2.12).

Furthermore, the imagery of the interior castle is also helpful to the extent that it portrays the individual moving in an interior, spiral-like fashion toward its center—which is God. It expresses the fact that for St. Teresa, God is really at the core of who we are and that there is never a question of really (i.e., ontologically) being outside the presence of God.

The difficulty I find with the imagery of castle chambers is that it can be interpreted too statically. Here, her descriptions of the presence of God tend to portray an articulation of divine givenness as a "state" or a fixed room (be the doors closed or open). Or again, they might be misleading by suggesting that the articulations of the presence of God receive their differentiation by *our* going somewhere. Yet because for her "everything is movement," and because she really wants to evoke that the dwelling place is an inter-Personal mode of giving and not a fixed "gift," she needs a metaphor that is more dynamic. In this regard it is interesting to note that even while composing *Moradas,* St. Teresa lauds the metaphor of water: "For I don't find anything more appropriate to explain some spiritual experiences than water . . . and [I] am so fond of this element that I have observed it more attentively than other things" (*Obras,* 499; *Collected Works,* Vol. 2, IV:2.2).[38] It is precisely this imagery of water that was the vehicle for her descriptions from "The Book of Her Life."

Despite the fact that her earlier imagery of water only testifies to four main degrees of experience (instead of seven like "The Interior Castle"—the only real disadvantage), I prefer it for the purposes of my explication for several reasons. First, the imagery of water lends itself much more easily to dynamic movement, which she herself says is characteristic of loving; moreover, it evokes a surfeit of givenness, which she tries to express with types of "supernatural" or "infused" prayer. Also, and related to the former, the way St. Teresa compares the presence of God to water emphasizes the *manner of giving: the presence of the Holy is its manner of giving.* Since the descriptions coming from the interior castle imagery are more differentiated, I integrate them where appropriate into my exposition. At any event, it is important for us not to take any of the comparisons too literally, for their purpose is not to denote something with analytic exactitude, but to evoke certain experiences of God that, for her, should attune us to such experiences as much as possible, and to whet our spiritual appetites, especially if we are among those who are not privy to such experiences.

When St. Teresa writes of her experiences of the presence of God, whether in the imagery of the dwelling places or water, she uses the term "prayer." For most of us, prayer usually connotes a petition of some kind, a kind of ritual worship, or an attempt on our part to communicate vocally or interiorly with a Supreme Being. Often prayer tends to be an attempt to bend God's will to our own. While St. Teresa does write of prayer as a kind of discursive activity that can be accompanied by reflection or with an awareness of an interlocutor (e.g., *Obras,* 474; *Collected Works,* Vol. 2, 1:1.7), prayer is understood much more profoundly either as an effort to conform our will to God's will or as a modulation of the presence of God. For these reasons she will include as prayer not only active meditation but experiences like the prayer of quiet, the prayer of spiritual delights, the prayer of recollection, the prayers of union, sleep of the faculties, rapture, and so forth.

Describing various levels or stages of experience, St. Teresa contends that not everyone is led by the same path or in the same measure. There is not a recipe or a step-by-step program; even to proceed in this way would be to attempt to put limits on God.[39] Since God may lead each individual differently, the degrees of prayer that St. Teresa discusses need not necessarily coincide with the progressive stages of inter-Personal intimacy and development (*Obras*, 494; *Collected Works*, Vol. 2, III.2.13). To the extent that this is significant, she is attentive to different kinds of presence and deception, and the discernment of differences between kinds of givenness. Her discernments in general have their basis *in the way the presence is lived*.[40] The degrees of prayer, their intensity and effects, are *experientially discerned,* not theoretically conjectured, and this is one of the aspects that gives them their validity and their force.

Moreover, because the differences discerned are internal to the givenness or the experience itself, among and within each degree, the experience of *this* prayer (say, the prayer of quiet) will be experienced as the fullest possible such that it would be impossible to anticipate, to imagine, or to desire anything else or anything more; in a word, the prayer will be overfull from the start.[41] The "next" prayer given, which could not have been anticipated, is experienced as even more full and as that much more of a "gift." Accordingly, one would have to say *not* that each degree of prayer is somehow incomplete or partial, but that each level of prayer is given as overabundant. It is only from one experience to the other that we could look back and ascertain that this prayer did not exhaust the experience even though it was "complete." The evidence for this evaluation is the givenness of a new, deeper kind of presence. I explicate the phenomenological significance of these modes of presence or prayer (as well as what the Rabbi Dov Baer calls "ecstasy," and Rūzbihān Baqlī, "unveiling") in chapters 5–8. Let me now turn to an exposition of the various degrees of prayer or presence of the Holy as described by St. Teresa.

Modes of Prayer

Four main degrees of prayer typify the imagery of water. More particularly, St. Teresa likens the experience of God to that of cultivating a garden and to the ways it must be watered. First, the water can be drawn from a well, which requires considerable work on our part; second, the water may be procured by our turning the crank of a water wheel so that by means of aqueducts we get more water with less work. Third, water may arrive by the flow of a river or stream, demanding less frequent work on our part but saturating the ground better. Finally, the water may come by rain showers, requiring no work on our part; God explicitly takes over the role of the gardener (*Obras,* 71ff., *Collected Works,* Vol. 1, 11.7).

St. Teresa compares the first degree of prayer to drawing water from a well. Already a special kind of givenness, this prayer is instigated by striving to be in God's presence and rendering God service. This prayer is called "acquired" prayer because there are some things that we can do and a givenness of the Holy that seemingly comes to us through our own efforts.[42] What do "our efforts" or "things we can do" entail? These include, for St. Teresa, doing good deeds, repentance and penance, the discursive work of thinking about our past life, mortification, obedience, determination, the intellect striving to think about God or God's humanity, imagining God within oneself, keeping Christ present, meditation, mental prayer (which she identifies as an intimate sharing between friends), being mindful of God's honor and glory, forgetting ourselves, turning away from what angers God, perseverance, serving with justice and fortitude, being courageous in striving. In the beginning, this can be quite painful and arduous, she explains, because one does not fully understand whether one is really repentant and determined to conform one's will to God's. What our efforts amount to, in other words, is not trying to make God's presence happen, but self-surrender, conforming our style of loving to God's, or again, disposing ourselves to God with disinterest and without being attached to favors that God may bestow upon us.[43] Even though there will be periods of "dryness," like trials and the sense of our own wretchedness, St. Teresa contends that when a person wants to pray, even though it be vocal prayer, he or she will find God.[44]

This acquired prayer, which occupies the first degree of prayer in her *Vida,* is expanded later so that it belongs to the first three dwelling places in *Moradas.* They are depicted as (1) an intense fear of offending God, a mirror for humility so as to praise God, discovering one's lowliness, and the practice of self-knowledge; (2) hearing God in and through the voice of others (which is not to be confused with locutions and visions from God), a vivacity of the intellect where the faculties are more skilled; and (3) great solace. In general, in acquired prayer, one experiences the presence of God in "consolations" (*contentos,* i.e., joy, peace, satisfaction) or feelings of tenderness. These consolations are from God, yet they do exhibit a structure similar to the joyful consolations that one may encounter in other aspects of our lives, for example, seeing a person we love very much, succeeding in large and important ventures, seeing a loved one alive after one has been told that he or she was dead, inheriting a great fortune. In all these instances, consolations are marked by suddenness, are said to be more constraining than expansive, and arise in conjunction with virtuous work we perform (*Obras*, 495–96; *Collected Works*, IV:1.2–6 II; *Obras*, 501–502, *Collected Works*, IV:2.9–10 II).

Staying with her image of watering a garden, the second degree of prayer is compared to turning the crank of a water wheel so that the gardener obtains more water with less labor. The "more" here is not a quantitative, but a qualitative designation, for what is at issue is a different kind of water and a different fount that makes the virtues grow incomparably better (*Obras*, 85–86; *Collected Works*, 14.4–5 I). This second degree of prayer (which corresponds to the fourth dwelling place) admits of more differentiations than one supposes at first blush.

Within the second degree of prayer we find the prayer of "interior recollection," or being recollected in God into which one is drawn, absorbed, so as to recover what one had seemingly lost. As the term "recollection" suggests, this prayer is already within the presence to which we are returning; it is not outside of God. The prayer of recollection is distinguished from spiritual delights (*gustos*), since the former is said to be less intense than the latter, and because the prayer of recollection is experienced as the beginning through which one experiences delights.[45]

Whereas in the first degree of prayer, contentment was said to be constrictive, here spiritual delights are characterized as "expansive," producing "ineffable blessings" (*Obras*, 496; *Collected Works*, Vol. 2, VI:1.4–6; *Obras*, 500–501; *Collected Works*, Vol. 2, VI:2.4–6). These spiritual delights leave a very pleasing interior quiet, peace, and sweetness; and in this prayer the faculties are gathered within so as to enjoy that satisfaction with greater delight.[46] There are far fewer cravings for things, and an awareness of the beginning of a love of God that has much less self-interest (*Obras*, 92; *Collected Works*, Vol. 1, 15.14). In this second degree of prayer, sometimes equated with the "prayer of quiet," St. Teresa further distinguishes between it and the prayer of spiritual sleep, insofar as the latter is "a little more intense" than the former (*Obras*, 506; *Collected Works*, Vol. 2, IV:3.11).

This general degree of prayer (be it recollection, delights, prayer of quiet, or the prayer of spiritual sleep) is depicted as "the beginning of all blessings" (*Obras*, 92; *Collected Works*, Vol. 1, 15.15) because it is the onset of what St. John of the Cross and St. Teresa call "infused" prayer, or what she also calls "supernatural" prayer in distinction to "acquired" prayer.[47] Infused prayer (which, by the way, is a nice aqueous term), suggests a divine givenness, or the presence of God that is in no way contingent upon our efforts, literally a "pouring in" that is not an accomplishment on our part—not just an "inflow," but an over-spilling that is beyond measure or standard. If there were any question of the first prayer being similar to the givenness of what we designated by the term "presentation"—because it correlates in some ways to our efforts—it is clear that this mode of givenness is not. It is "vertical" in a clearer sense: there is no "technology of the self" here, no techné that produces prayer in St. Teresa's sense. St. Teresa writes: "I understood well that I was already experiencing something supernatural because sometimes I was unable to resist; to have it whenever I wanted was out of the question" (*Obras*, 127; *Collected Works*, Vol. 1, 23.5). Accordingly, even if I do want to "do work" and even though I may "work at" prayer, this kind of prayer is not associated with "my" work. It is a different quality of prayer that cannot be induced. There is an incomparable difference between this second prayer in relation to the first, because one is able to rest without having to work constantly or to be active in discursive or mental prayer. In the first prayer, one gets fatigued in trying to recollect the senses, practicing hours of prayer, solitude, and thinking about his or her past life, since one is so used to being distracted. Here it comes on of its own accord as a surplus over such effort.

Once this prayer is experienced, she contends, it will be impossible not to understand that this "little spark" cannot be acquired. Even if we should strive for delight and try everything in our power, we will only be left cold, and one will do more by "putting a little straw there with humility" than piling on cords of wood with words and reflections (*Obras*, 88–90; *Collected Works*, Vol. 1, 15.3–9). "Because the Lord Himself *gives this prayer in a manner very different* [*porque el mesmo Señor la da de manera bien diferente*] from that which we gain through our nice little reasonings," it is better in these times of quiet to proceed gently and noiselessly, responding from love and service, for one does not deal well with God by force (*Obras*, 92; *Collected Works*, Vol. 1, 15.14; my emphasis).

These prayers occur quite despite our efforts, St. Teresa explains; still there is some distraction by the intellect, still some "noise." One need not renounce discursive prayer entirely in this second stage; one can still recite vocal prayers if there is the desire or ability. For independently of our desires and machinations, "if the quiet is great it [will be] difficult to speak without a good deal of effort," and even though we may be distracted or cogitating, we will still experience the delight and joy (*Obras,* 89–90; *Collected Works,* Vol. 1, 15.7–9).

There is an important issue that needs mention at this stage of explication. According to St. Teresa, we cannot try to stop the intellect on our own, for the intellect, and our activity or freedom in general, *cease to work only because God suspends them.* More precisely, the work or effort on our part is stilled because God "*occupies it in another way.*" One cannot use activity to stop activity; one cannot suspend effort through effort as an attempt to procure a more profound degree of prayer, because intellectual activity is called into question only through the *awakening of loving* (i.e., a being occupied in another way), and for St. Teresa this has a Personal form (*Obras,* 503; *Collected Works,* Vol. 2, IV:3.4).[48]

Accordingly, one cannot induce an infused or mystical experience, for example, through mental techniques or medicinal therapies. "Taking it upon ourselves to stop and suspend thought is what I mean should not be done; nor should we cease to work with the intellect, because otherwise we would be left like cold simpletons and be doing neither one thing nor the other" (*Obras,* 76; *Collected Works,* Vol. 1, 12.5). In certain spiritual traditions, attempting to still the mind through meditation and focusing is a valid technique. One could even say that where "acquired prayer" is concerned, this could be a possible beginning spiritual path. However, when St. Teresa describes *acquired* prayer, she is thinking of the efficacy of our activity, so even practicing passivity would still be a form of activity; trying to stop the intellect would be an exercise of our power. Let the mind engage its energies as much as it will in focused meditation; let the self be vigilant in its spiritual exercises. What holds activity in abeyance—"above" or despite my activity in which I must in some sense be engaged—is something of a different order. This "different order" is not just anything. For instance, objects or things, though different, cannot call reason into question. Her insights are instead grounded in a *Personal* "order," or rather an inter-Personal order, that is qualified as such through loving; it is by virtue of an incommensurate inter-Personal intervention that there is such a going-beyond the activity of the self's own efforts. In St. John of the Cross's terms, it is God who brings the spirit from meditation to "contemplation."[49]

Being left "simpletons" by trying to stop the intellect—while undesirable—is not the major concern here, but rather the fact that the attempt to do so would be governed by *pride* and would leave the self-serving impression of our power of disposition. "And I say again, even though it may not be understood, this effort to suspend the intellect is not very humble" (*Obras*, 76; *Collected Works*, Vol. 1, 12.5). Such a practice is considered not to be humble by St. Teresa because it exemplifies an attempt to accomplish infused prayer by one's self and not to surrender to the movement of God: The "I" would be mindful of itself and not of God. Infused prayer demands, not that we desire favors from God, but that we become detached from every kind of satisfaction and enter the path of prayer solely with the determination "to help Christ carry the cross" (*Obras*, 91; *Collected Works*, Vol. 1, 15.11–12).

The more profound the relationship to God, the more progress there must be in virtue, writes St. Teresa, and if there is no progress in humility, everything will be ruined (*Obras*, 76; *Collected Works*, Vol. 1, 12.4–5). The importance of humility is one reason she chides those who desire to provoke the presence of God or complain that "they" have not "acquired" infused prayer! In a very rare passage of expressed discontent, she writes: "But when I see servants of God, men of prominence, learning, and high intelligence make so much fuss because God doesn't give them devotion, it annoys me to hear them. I do not mean that they shouldn't accept it if God gives it, and esteem it, because then His Majesty sees that this is appropriate. But when they don't have devotion, they shouldn't weary themselves. They should understand that since His Majesty doesn't give it, it isn't necessary; and they should be masters of themselves."[50] Thus, St. Teresa does not suggest that we should give up our efforts, or that we should not "master" ourselves; we should on her account. But self-overcoming only takes place if and when God suspends our efforts by occupying us in another way, by giving us prayer that is independent of our mastery.

Although St. Teresa writes that only a very few pass or are taken beyond this second degree of prayer, there is an "incomparably greater" prayer of spiritual delight and sweetness experienced in a third degree of prayer. Here the garden is irrigated; the water flows from a river or spring with much less labor, although some labor is required in directing the flow of water, which is to say, God himself practically takes on the task of the gardener as the one who does everything. However brief the experience, "the water is *given without measure*" (*Obras*, 96; *Collected Works*, Vol. 1, 17.2; my emphasis). In St. Teresa's imagery, it is not the "self" who apportions the water—which at best would be a gradual process executed according to our limitations and at worst an attempt to control the presence of God—but a sudden overabundance whereby our activity is so held in check and bound to God's love that one consents "only" to this giving.

Consenting to this kind of giving is also an "effect" of this prayer and is one reason why St. Teresa speaks frequently here of "service," that is, "works of charity" as conforming our style of loving to God's. This mode of prayer is distinguished experientially from the previous, second degree of prayer through this integrated service, or what we could call the *praxis* of mystical experience: "Although this prayer seems entirely the same as the prayer of quiet I mentioned, it is different—partly because in the prayer of quiet the soul didn't desire to move or stir . . . ; [but] in this prayer . . . it is as though engaged in both the active and contemplative life together. It tends to works of charity and to business affairs that have to do with its state in life and to reading" (*Obras*, 97; *Collected Works*, Vol. 1, 17.4).

The prayer peculiar to the third degree of the presence of the Holy is called the sleep (or later, the suspension) of the faculties, because the faculties do not actually fail and are only able to be completely occupied with God; even if one strained to distract oneself, she does not think that one would be entirely successful (*Obras*, 93; *Collected Works*, Vol. 1, 16. 1ff.). The intellect gives neither much assistance nor little; it sees *so much* that it does not know where to fix its gaze, flitting around like a moth to candlelight, being only bothersome and annoying. Again, the best thing to do is to let it go its way, for only God can stop it (*Obras*, 96–98; *Collected Works*, Vol. 1, 17.3–7). The quality of this prayer is so in excess of what we ourselves could produce that, according to the Carmelite nun, what one could not achieve in about twenty years with its own labors to bring repose to the intellect, God accomplishes in a moment (*Obras*, 96; *Collected Works*, Vol. 1, 17.2).

In the second degree of prayer there is an emergent indifference to things; here in the third degree of prayer, she writes of a nearly complete death to things and to the self. This indifference and this near death to things and to the self, however, are not really a depreciation of the inherent values of self or of things in and of themselves. For example, she explicitly discourages an attempt to negate corporeal existence out of a resentment of corporeal life, and she encourages her Carmelite Daughters to be like the Blessed Mother in seeing these matters as a help rather than a hindrance, on the model of Jesus' Sacred Humanity (*Obras,* 551–52; *Collected Works,* Vol. 2, VI:7.14). She also points to the examples of other saints (like St. Anthony of Padua, St. Francis, St. Bernard), insisting that the "Creator must be sought through creatures," which depends upon the unique relationship God has with the individual person (*Obras,* 122; *Collected Works,* Vol. 1, 22. 7–8). It is on the basis of a new presence that one readjusts the esteem one held for other things; what was held as "natural" is revalued through an implicit comparison to the "enjoyment of God" that outweighs the former and that now seems unnatural (*Obras,* 542–43; *Collected Works,* Vol. 2, VI:5.9): "For since it [the soul] desires to live no longer in itself but in You, it seems that its life is unnatural [*contra natura*]" (*Obras,* 94; *Collected Works,* Vol. 1, 16.4).

Finally, along with the delicate happiness and the heaviness that comes with this prayer, humility is much greater and more profound because one does nothing more than consent to the giving and embrace the gifts (*Obras,* 96; *Collected Works,* Vol. 1, 17.3).

The fourth degree of prayer is likened to watering a garden by a surfeit of rain, where the entire garden is saturated without any effort on our part; this water often comes when the gardener least expects it, though usually after a long period of prayer (*Obras,* 101; *Collected Works,* Vol. 1, 18.9). While in all modes of prayer the "gardener" does some work, this work is accompanied by so much delight that the prayer is not experienced as work but as glory. Moreover, while experiencing this fourth mode of prayer, the "senses" and the "soul" are given no freedom to communicate the joy even though one desires to do so, and even though one rejoices incomparably more. The person is under the power of another, she writes, and it is God who communicates or gives it "in the *manner* of who [He is]."[51] Likewise, the intellect has no power to do anything. "Since it [the soul] cannot comprehend what it understands, there is an understanding by not understanding" (*Obras,* 102; *Collected Works,* Vol. 1, 14.2).

In general, this fourth degree of prayer, which is generally referred to as "divine union," is said to satisfy much more deeply than the prayer of quiet. This level of prayer can be described in terms of the following differentiations: the prayer of union, the prayer of the wound of love, the prayer of rapture, the prayer of transport, the prayer of the flight of the spirit, and the prayer of the great impulses. Space does not permit an extended discussion of each of these modes of prayer. Before giving some general characteristics, let me note that St. Teresa tends to describe the nuances between and within these prayers in terms of more or less intensity, and the metaphor she uses to depict this variation of intensity is a flame. A small fire, she writes, is just as much a fire as a large one, but the latter has higher shooting flames and heats faster (cf. *Obras,* 100–101; *Collected Works,* Vol. 1, 18.7).

In "The Interior Castle," St. Teresa distinguishes more explicitly between three main levels of experienced union (the fifth, sixth, and seventh dwelling places). The fifth dwelling place is likened to a short meeting, and during this time of union, one neither sees, nor hears, nor understands, because the union is always short; the intellect is in awe, one loves more deeply than one understands, and there is a wealth of humility and other virtues (*Obras,* 108–110; *Collected Works,* Vol. 1, 20. 1ff.; *Obras,* 625ff.; *Collected Works,* Vol. 1, "Spiritual Testimonies," 59.5ff.).

Belonging to this fourth kind of watering, or what is distinguished as the sixth dwelling place, is a spiritual betrothal and a conclusion of the betrothal.[52] Although almost identical, these two dimensions of union can be distinguished in terms of the depth of divine presence and its effects. The sixth dwelling place is marked by several kinds of prayer: (1) the prayer of the wounds of love, which is a pain that arises from one's intimate depths, which is experienced as a longing for God; and (2) the prayer of rapture, which is sudden, lasts longer than that of union, and is felt more exteriorily; it is accompanied by a deep awareness of one's inability to do anything and of the misery over every speck of dust or fault that has impeded conforming one's loving to the orientation of God's (*Obras,* 115; *Collected Works,* Vol. 1, 20.23–25; *Obras,* 134–35; *Collected Works,* Vol. 1, 25.3–6). It is further described as an upward movement, a levity of the body, as a detachment from things, and as being absorbed in God (*Obras,* 110, 113, 116; *Collected Works,* Vol. 1, 20.8, 18, 29).

Rapture is further differentiated in terms of (a) being touched by some word it hears about God, even though one is not in prayer; it is deeply intimate in the sense that no one understands it except these two, namely, God and the individual (*Obras,* 536ff.; *Collected Works,* Vol. 2, VI:4.3ff.); and (b) elevation or flight of the spirit, which receives this nomenclature because it is swift and because one is unable to offer any resistance, though it does require great courage to let oneself be taken wherever God may want (*Obras,* 108; *Collected Works,* Vol. 1, 20.1; *Obras,* 627; *Collected Works,* Vol. 1, "Spiritual Testimonies," 59.11). God lets loose the deluge, and one can do no more than receive (*Obras,* 540ff.; *Collected Works,* Vol. 2, 1ff.).

The prayer of the great impulses is yet a further elaboration of union, experienced as a deep pain, occurring much later than visions and usually arriving without any preceding prayer. The pains are similar to the "wounds of love" mentioned above, but here one is overcome with the sudden remembrance that one is distanced from God, and the pains are so intense, she writes, that if they were to be very frequent, one's life would not last long (*Obras,* 628; *Collected Works,* Vol. 1, "Spiritual Testimonies," 59.18).

Service, moreover, is described as essential to the experience of union. Being truly spiritual amounts to being a servant of God, which is to say, to care for, or suffer for, others. The orientation toward others is characteristic of serving God because the more one aligns oneself with God, the more one emulates infinite loving. Service becomes more deeply absolute because it is executed without any thought of glory for what one does (cf. *Obras,* 516ff.; *Collected Works,* Vol. 2, V:3.1ff.; *Obras,* 559–60; *Collected Works,* Vol. 2, VI:9.15–18; *Obras,* 581; *Collected Works,* Vol. 2, VII:4.14).

The experience of the Holy ascribed to the seventh dwelling place is portrayed as an entirely new way of givenness called "spiritual marriage." It is as distinct from the former as marriage is to betrothal. God joins the individual to himself such that even though there is a cross to bear, there is no disquiet. All the faculties are not lost, but they remain as though in amazement (*Obras,* 576; *Collected Works,* Vol. 2, VII:3.11). The senses are at peace in a deep silence, and one experiences a forgetfulness of self (*un olvido de sí*) as one of the first effects (*Obras,* 574; *Collected Works,* Vol. 2, VII:3.2; *Obras,* 577; *Collected Works,* Vol. 2, VII:3.12; *Obras,* 581; *Collected Works,* Vol. 2, VII:4.11). St. Teresa further relates a desire to suffer for God, a love for one's persecutors, and a compassion to take on any burden to free them from their trials; she describes a desire, not to die (and be with God in this way), but to serve God in the world.

Finally, there is reportedly no dryness as before; there are no interior trials, and even if one is occupied with external matters as in conversation, God does not cease to be present (*Obras,* 574–76; *Collected Works,* Vol. 2, VII:3.1–9). The spiritual marriage is so intense that St. Teresa will compare it to rain falling from the sky into a river or fount or like bright light entering into a room through two different windows (*Obras,* 571; *Collected Works,* Vol. 2, VII:2.3–4).

It is from these experiences that we can understand the already over-full quality of the first degree of "acquired" prayer, where the mundane and the sacred seemed to be at odds, as well as the sanctification of what would seem to us at the start to be the most mundane of tasks. Each moment, every task is now lived *as prayer;* all objects and events are mani-festations of the Holy; all elements disclose God. This perspective of life as prayer is exemplified in the instruction St. Teresa gives novices who were disturbed at being drawn away from contemplative prayer in obedience for the sake of menial, mundane tasks: "Know that if it is in the kitchen, the Lord walks among the pots and pans helping you both interiorly and exteriorly" (*Obras,* 690; *Collected Works,* Vol. 3, "Foundations," 5.8).

Through the imagery of watering a garden and the interior castle, St. Teresa of Avila attempted to describe a distinctive kind of presence, the givenness of the Holy as it is lived inter-Personally. Rather than this pres-ence being just another type of object presentation, it has its own internal dynamic. As we will see in chapter 5, the evidence peculiar to this sphere of experience yields a unique set of difficulties, modalizations of religious experience that have the tenor of deceptions, illusions, and so forth that are *peculiar to this sphere.*

Where her portrayal of the richness of this kind of experience is con-cerned, we note in broad outline an important phenomenological distinc-tion between "acquired" prayer and the "infused" or "supernatural" prayer that is given beyond our own efforts. Rather than the presence of the Holy being uniform or simply a matter of "union," it is deeply nuanced, highly personal (in several senses), and articulated in the manner that the Holy gives it. The internal discriminations of four levels (in the case of the water imagery) or seven chambers (in the case of the interior castle metaphor) function more in the vein of helpful demarcations than of exhaustive determinations of this field of experience. Accordingly, what is essential here is not that there are a specific number of levels of what St. Teresa calls "prayer," but that the religious dimension of human experi-ence demands its own set of descriptions because it yields a unique sphere of evidence. We see the same demands for such an undertaking and wit-ness some of the same essential features in Rabbi Dov Baer, but expressed in different terminology and by means of different articulations—not in terms of prayer, but expressed as a mysticism of "ecstasy."

CHAPTER 3

Rabbi Dov Baer
and Mysticism of Ecstasy

*My whole aim from youth, on behalf of my beloved friends, who
seek the words of the living God in truth, is for the light of eternal life to be fixed firmly in their soul to the full extent intended.
This is the matter of revelation of the divine in their soul, each
according to his capacity.*

—RABBI DOV BAER[1]

*For the efflux of anything spiritual is but by means of a mag-
nanimous love.*

—RABBI SCHNEUR ZALMAN[2]

The Jewish Mystical Tradition and the
Prophetic/Ecstatic Character of Chasidism

Rabbi Dov Baer (1773–1827), the Mitteler Rebbe, as he is also known,
is the figure on whom I focus within the variegated and multiform
Jewish mystical heritage. His religious home is located more particularly
within the Chasidic tradition, and even more specifically within Chabad
Chassidism. Dov Baer stands out because of his first-person mystical testimonies, something seldom found within Jewish mystical literature.[3]

The sense of handing down intimate knowledge and practices pertaining to the Divine is maintained in Kabbalah, the very term expressive
of Jewish mysticism. *Kabbalah* means "tradition," both in the sense of
experiential wisdom that is passed down by and hence "received" from
others, and in the sense of experience and intimate knowledge given by
God. The "received," intimate knowledge was originally revealed in and
as the Torah. In the Jewish tradition, *torah*, which literally means "teaching" or "showing," was originally given to Abraham and then to Moses.
Thus, *torah* has both a broad sense of any divine teaching (such as the
Ten Commandments), and a more precise meaning, the Pentateuch, or
the "five books of Moses." Because the Torah encompasses teaching in
this sense, some speak of the Torah as the entire *Tanach*, or Jewish Bible,

which includes the books of the Prophets and the Writings as well as the oral tradition found in the Mishnah and Talmud.

The Torah is regarded as flowing out from the Divine Name, the Tetragrammaton (the four Hebrew letters that make up the name of God, יהוה); even more, the Torah is itself seen as the Holy Name.[4] For the mystic, the Torah does not merely possess an obvious, explicit level of meaning depicted on the order of historical events but harbors deeply layered dimensions of spiritual meanings pertaining to the very movement of the Divine. Let me give just one example.

Rabbi Dov Baer writes of an experience of divine ecstasy in which the effect is expressed as "going out of Egypt," and more generally, as being moved from one's place (hazazah mi-mechomo, literally, ec-stasy). Within the context of Jewish mysticism, his meaning can be explicated. The term for Egypt, מצרים, written as it is in Ancient Hebrew without vowels, is transliterated and pronounced as mitzraim; but this very term, מצרים, is also the term for "limitations," transliterated and pronounced as metzarim. For the mystic, the historical event of the exodus is not just a factual occurrence that happened long ago, or one we remember and recount to our children at Pesach, but an event that concerns each and every person and can be repeated in each and every person.

The event in question is a responding to God with acceptance, hineni ("Here I am"), as did Moses (and Abraham before him), by shedding material limitations through which we are all enslaved. In this way we open ourselves to an encounter with the Divine. "Leaving Egypt" is not a matter of recapitulating ontogenetically what occurred phylogenetically, for it is not a matter of repeating the same mundane facts. Rather, the mystic "encounters" an infinite "point" at the interstices of history such that it is not exhausted at any historical moment but can occur spiritually "in" each historical person. Leaving Egypt is the task of liberating ourselves and others from physical and spiritual materialism, which imprisons us and keeps us estranged from God: hence the process of redemption. Thus, all events in the Torah, no matter how patent they may appear at first glance (Creation, Covenant, Redemption, etc.) take on a "mystical" significance.[5] For the Jewish mystic, to live the exodus spiritually is to live a life of valuing God absolutely, outside of all forms of idolatry, as disposing oneself to God.

It would be overly simplistic to say that there were only two major trends in the long and varied tradition of Jewish mysticism. But if one could say that a third-person discourse, pseudonymous authorship, and an emphasis on the collective person dominated theosophical-theurgical Kabbalah, as is quite clear in the example of the *Zohar,* or "Book of Splendor" of the thirteenth century,[6] then one could also say that there emerged an intensely individual *personal* form of experience and literature that developed with the *ecstatic* or *prophetic* form of Kabbalah—a form that complements, and at times is even at odds with, the theosophical-theurgical Kabbalah.[7]

Against the backdrop of Sabbatianism[8] and the Frankist debacle,[9] emerged the Master of the Good Name, the Baal Shem Tov. Born Israel ben Eleazar (1698 or 1700–1760) in a small town near Podolia and Moldavia, and known by about the age of 36 as the Baal Shem Tov, the "Besht" (as he is referred to by the acrostic) became the founder of the modern form of Jewish piety and mysticism known as Chasidism. The Besht himself left no major written works behind, except for some epistles. Since he communicated primarily through anecdote, parable, and aphorism, all we know about him and his teachings was disseminated by his disciples like the Maggid of Mezerich and passed on through the teachings and living personal examples of the *tzaddikim* (the saintly, righteous persons, exemplars of the Torah) such as Rabbi Nachman of Bratzlav, Rabbi Jacob Joseph of Polonnoye, and Rabbi Schneur Zalman of Liadi.[10]

One of the fundamental notions of the Besht's interpretation of Judaism and Jewish mysticism is not that God is everything, but that God is *in* everything; thus, it is possible to serve God in all things, as it is possible to occlude God's presence (the *shechinah*) by sinning. Our task, through concentrated prayer and *tzedakah,* is to liberate the sparks of holiness in all people, even in the wicked, and in all things.

While asceticism was a Jewish mystical ideal that endured for millennia, the internal sense of asceticism became spiritless during the time of the Besht. The mystical and spiritual practices of these Chasids, therefore, received a different orientation. No stranger to the Talmudic tradition, and studying Lurianic Kabbalah and the *Zohar* in detail and depth as well, the Besht (and early Chasidism) emphasized neither asceticism nor legalism, but rather concentrated prayer as flowing from a joyful heart—not commiserating in sadness and despair, but in repentance and returning to the service of God; not formalism, but *hitlahavut,* enthusiasm in the sense of a "burning" for God; not castigation, but mercy and compassion. In a deep sense, the Chasid or "pious one" was prophetic. A prophet, as the Hebrew term *navi* implies, means precisely to bear witness to God with burning enthusiasm, "ecstatically." In this sense, a prophet puts world history in divine perspective and only derivatively has to do with prediction, even where it concerns the messianic age (e.g., Genesis 20:7, Exodus 7:1, Numbers 12:6). In distinction to the theosophical-theurgical Kabbalah, it is no coincidence that Rabbi Dov Baer will use the term "ecstasy" to describe the personal kinds of experience of the presence of God that we can understand in the deepest sense as prophetic.

For the Chasid, the world is ready to be made divine, and our co-participation with God can elicit such collective and individual redemption. Mystical practices and knowledge were not to be limited to a few but were to be accessible to "all the children of Israel," learned and unlearned. What is required, however, is the performance of acts with *kavannah,* that is, with sincere, focused, directed, concentrated intention toward God and in such a way that one executes a *mitzvah,* or good deed with one's entire being and with *tzedakah:* righteousness, charity, justice.

One strives to cleave to God through *mitzvot* and *tzedakah,* not out of individual satisfaction or to be united with God merely, but to re-unite God with all reality. There are many accounts of the internal separation and exile of God based in the *Zohar* and Lurianic Kabbalah.[11] Suffice it to say that for these Jewish mystics, God requires human beings to participate in restoring the disorder. The reparation of the world (*tikkun olam*), in which God as Divine Presence (*shechinah*) is inextricably involved, is the task of each person. The re-ordering, which is a re-ordering of loving, the restitution of God (as *en sof* and *shechinah*), the reparation of the world, and union of God and God's creation in history is the meaning of messianic redemption for the Jewish mystic. Accordingly, as Heschel puts it, the Jewish mystic does not try to compel the unseen to become visible (which we will interpret later as a process of idolatry), but to assist God in undoing evil and in redeeming the light that became concealed.[12]

Tzedakah and the *Tzaddik*

Expressive of these experiences of God is a particular act central to all of Judaism and not just to the mystic, namely, *tzedakah. Tzedakah* means righteousness, where there is no distinction between love or charity, the performance of kindness and compassion, and justice. Interestingly, Simone Weil recognizes precisely this point when she writes, for example, that we are the ones who have invented the separation between justice and charity, because it removes the one who possesses from the obligation of giving, and if he gives, he thinks himself entitled to be pleased with himself, while the receiver can be exempted from gratitude: "Only the absolute identification of justice and love makes the coexistence possible of compassion and gratitude on the one hand, and on the other, of respect for the dignity of affliction in the afflicted—a respect felt by the sufferer himself and the others."[13]

It is through our *avodah*, or service of *tzedakah* that God's countenance, or the *shechinah* radiates with us in and through our co-participation.[14] Accordingly, *tzedakah* is the flip side, the concrete expression of *teshuvah*, or repentance, which is a returning to God in service and thus a returning to our divine selves. One of the effects of *tzedakah* is therefore "to elicit" or "to evoke" (not, of course, "to cause") the presence of God, for love awakens a loving response. In this sense, there is an arousal from below that elicits an arousal from above: God's presence is given of its own accord, but as solicited, invited through our actions of *tzedakah:* "For the effect [of *tzedakah*] is to elicit the light of God to the world of *Asiyah*" and thus can be seen a process of redemption, a redemption that is ultimately by God but is evoked through our individual and communal concrete acts of *tzedakah*.[15] Whereas the point of emphasis in *teshuvah* is weighted on the individual, the emphasis in the act of *tzedakah* is clearly interpersonal (expressing the precept of "neighborly love").[16] "Each one becomes better through his fellow-being."[17]

Tzedakah is thus seen as the core of all the precepts; it is greater than all the commandments, preferable to sacrifice. Ceremony, solemnity, ritual are insignificant compared to love of others and joy expressed in kindness. (See Hosea 6:6: "I desire loving-kindness [*chesed*] instead of sacrifice, the knowledge [*daat*] of God more than burnt offerings.") Worship, sacrifice, and the like are dependent on moral living; and serving God can only be accomplished perfectly through loving, justice, and righteousness. Whereas sacrifice exists essentially in the mode of quantity, measure, and limit, *tzedakah* can be given without restraint, limit, and measure. Whereas sacrifice can be hollow and is able to cut my relation with God off from others, *tzedakah* is essentially interpersonal and inter-Personal. This does not mean that one can or should give unending "things" (which one could do while harboring an attitude of regret or resentment) or bestow upon another so many "goods" that one fosters dependency in others, and so forth. Rather, in the spirit of generosity there can be no limits, for example, in being compassionate to the poor and to the destitute, in showing mercy to an offender; in true *tzedakah,* one does not set limits to the diffusion of supreme *chesed* or loving-kindness, but performs this act in the mode of the infinite. Thus, writes, Zalman, "it behooves everyone not to be particular in insisting on the law [which exists in the mode of measure], but to set aside his own life and to go far beyond the measure of the law"; for otherwise, even the Torah scholar "has not even the Torah."[18] It is not strict obedience to the law for its own sake that is at issue, but divine justice in human history.

The *tzaddik,* which is etymologically connected to *tzedakah,* is the exemplar of *tzedakah,* the "righteous" or the "saint." According to Rabbi Zalman, the *tzaddik* is characterized by a "great love," which subdues in varying degrees the *sitra achra* or evil; good deeds outweighing those that are bad, the *tzaddik* leads a life of love, fearsome awe, and faith. The *tzaddik* is superior to the extent that this is the person who converts evil and makes it ascend to holiness.[19]

It is no coincidence, for instance, that Rabbi Zalman opens his *Likutei Amarim* by considering the following "oath": "Be righteous [*tzaddik*], and be not wicked [*rasha*]; and even if the whole world tells you that you are righteous, regard yourself as if you were wicked." Why the seemingly redundant injunction, "be not wicked"? Zalman interprets this by asserting that not everyone is privileged to become a *tzaddik;* one does not have the advantage of choosing either experiencing God in the manner of true delight or of truly abhorring all evil (i.e., absolutely loving God absolutely, absolutely abhorring evil absolutely), for this is given as a gift. Furthermore, writes Zalman, even though one's entire aspiration is in God's Torah and one studies assiduously day and night, this does not guarantee that one has dislodged evil. As long as the love of God, and founded on this the hatred of evil, are not absolute, there must still be some vestige of love and pleasure in evil.[20] There is a story of Rabbi Pinhas interrupting a heated discussion among his disciples. "'Rabbi,' they said, 'we were saying how afraid we are that the Evil Urge will pursue us.' 'Don't worry,' he replied. 'You have not gotten high enough for it to pursue you. For the time being, you are still pursuing it.'"[21]

The second clause is accordingly to be interpreted as saying that even if one is not on the level of a *tzaddik,* be as righteous as you can; one's efforts are nonetheless necessary, so at least strive not to be wicked and strain at abhorring evil by performing acts of *teshuvah* and *tzedakah*.[22] Both of these ways, moreover, are seen as positive values: on the one hand, loving God, on the other, abhorring evil, though the latter is still regarded as founded in the former.

Finally, if others were to regard us as a *tzaddik* (and notice Zalman does not say if we ourselves think we are a *tzaddik*, for this would be a pernicious sign of pride), we are to act as if we were wicked, as if we were nothing. For in comparison to the Holy One, all is as if nothing, and so one esteems oneself as if nothing. This is not to say that one *is* nothing, for this would vitiate the very role of creation, which is the spiritualization of matter, or redemption.[23]

Chabad Chassidism

Cleaving to God, enthusiasm, prophetic ecstasy, *kavannah, tzedakah,* and the like, were features of the Chasidic movement founded by the mystic and great thinker, Rabbi Schneur Zalman (1747–1813). Wanting to quell the degeneration of Chasidism a generation or two after the death of the Besht—a degeneration brought on in part through laxity in prayer, mounting pride, superstition, and belief in magic—Rabbi Zalman emphasized study, but without it being merely a scholarly enterprise. Holding that simple and uncomplicated faith is not enough, he introduced into Chasidism the ideal of contemplation on the Holy, insisting—often in the face of harsh criticism—that this ideal and the revelation of divine mysteries should *not* be restricted to the few. The reason this brand of Chasidism gets the appellation of "Chabad" Chasidism concerns the teachings of the Kabbalah, explicitly, with regard to the divine emanations. I mention these briefly here in order to set the appropriate background for Dov Baer's descriptions of ecstasy.

According to the teachings of the Kabbalah, God is *en sof*, Infinite, without limit; the *en sof* is also called *ayin*, Nothingness, the "Primordial Point," since it is absolutely simple and in comparison to all being, cannot be said; it "is" ineffable fullness.[24] From the *Or en Sof*, the Light of the Infinite, and through the process of *tzimtzum* (contraction), various levels of the creative process are emitted—levels that make up the *sefirot* (emanations) of God or the aspects of the Divine Personality. Depending on the scheme, *keter*, or crown, which is associated with Divine Will is the first *sefirah* (emanation). But according to another scheme, *keter* is co-eval with the *en sof* and thus is considered too sublime to be included among the ten *sefirot*. Working from this scheme, and in descending order, *chochmah* (wisdom) is the "first"; *binah* (understanding), the second; and *daat* (knowledge) is interpolated as the third. These are followed by *chesed* (loving-kindness, grace, love, benevolence, associated with greatness and mercy); *gevurah* (power, might, associated with *din* or judgment); *rachamim* (compassion, associated with *tiferet,* or beauty); *netzach* (lasting endurance, victory, associated with prophecy); *hod* (splendor, majesty, also associated with prophecy); *yesod* (foundation, associated with the *tzaddik*); and *shechinah* (Divine Presence or glory) or, as it is also called, *malchut* (sovereignty).

It is written in Genesis 1:26–27 that human beings are made in the image of God. Some Jewish mystics also derive the name for human being, *adam,* from likeness: "I will ascend the back of a cloud—I will match [or be like, *eddameh*] the Most High" (Isaiah 14:14).[25] For this reason not only the Tree of Life but the human being is understood as a likeness of the *sefirot;* they are accordingly depicted very often in this way (see chart 1).

When *keter* is not included in the scheme of emanations, the first three emanations, *chochmah, binah,* and *daat,* form a triad whose acrostic is *ChaBaD.* By calling attention to these three *sefirot,* Chabad Chasidism emphasizes the movement within prophetic/ecstatic Kabbalah that integrates the contemplative process into prayer, study, ethical action, and social praxis.[26] For the Chabad, only when one focuses with one's whole being in heart and mind in contemplation does one become truly attracted to God.

Upon the death of the Rabbi Schneur Zalman, founder of Chabad Chasidism, his son Dov Baer of Lubavitch became the new head and guide of this movement. This did not come free of practical problems. For just as a Mother or Abbot has difficulties with which to contend in monastic communities, a *tzaddik* has his, though the precise nature of these difficulties might be and usually are different. One of the main differences between Christian and Jewish communal forms of mysticism is that while the Christian monastic mystic lives a celibate existence, the Jewish mystic does not. In fact, due to the *mitzvah* of having and raising children, these Jewish mystics lived as family members in communities. And even though these larger communities were not secular, they still had to care for mundane features of everyday existence along with the exigencies of professional and family life.[27]

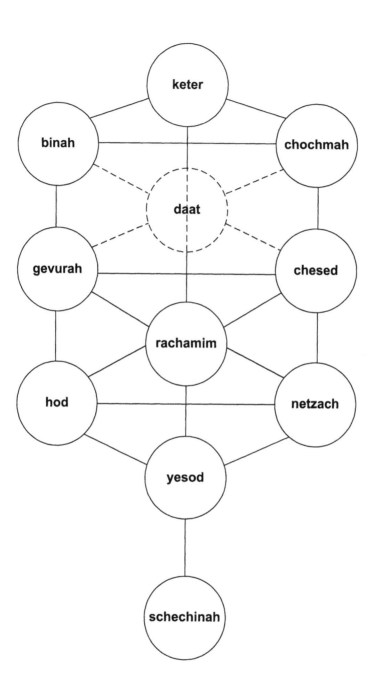

CHART 1. The Sefirot

For his part, Rabbi Dov Baer had to deal with misunderstandings compounded by the spatial dispersion of Chabad members, confusion due to a dilution of Chasidism's spiritual meaning in actual practice, and seekers of "sham" ecstasy, deceptions owing to a growing number of preachers who, having insufficient practice and training, still proclaimed to others that they were guardians of secrets, only to acquire fame or to gain followers.

What makes Dov Baer so attractive, at least for my purposes, is that his work, *Kuntres ha-hitpa'alut*, or "Tract on Ecstasy," was written with a sincerity and a sense of urgency to and for others to clarify mystical experiences and to address numerous problems, not the least of which was negotiating everyday distractions of earning a living, providing food and shelter, and so forth.[28] It was not written from a "propagandist impulse," to borrow Idel's term, like we find in Chayyim Vital or Rabbi Yizak of Komarno,[29] or merely to expound on Kabbalistic doctrine, "for I have no intention of merely expounding theoretically," writes Dov Baer (*Tract*, 72). Instead, Dov Baer writes from experience because he is *compelled* to write for the sake of the Chasidim in order to elucidate the subtleties and nuances of experiences pertaining to the mystic path. Thus, unlike, say, Maimonides, Dov Baer was not concerned with reconciling a Western philosophical worldview and a Jewish one, but with describing the lived experience of the Holy for those persons requiring guidance. It was both necessary and urgent to confront others on the topics of ecstasy, proper burning enthusiasm, and contemplation, not only because these are "the general basis and foundation for acceptance of the words of the living God in prayer etc.," but ultimately for the recuperation of the divine sparks, that is, to co-participate in the sanctification of the world (*Tract*, 78–79).

It is thanks to these compelling circumstances, which obliged Rabbi Dov Baer to write his treatise, that we are privy to a description of variegated dimensions of mystical experience. It is on the basis of such experiences—those living experiences of God that were, writes Dov Baer, "built on my experience from my youth, for these twenty years or more"—that he describes ("with the help of God") various levels of mystical experience and distinguishes them from delusional or false forms of the same (*Tract*, 176, cf. 129, 136.)[30]

Modes of Ecstasy

In contrast to the relatively free variety of imagery employed by St. Teresa and the apparent malleability of levels and degrees governed by the shape and evolution of the experiences, Rabbi Dov Baer utilizes vehicles within his Jewish tradition to communicate with his charges and to articulate such mystical experiences. The primary term here is "ecstasy" (*hitpa'alut*), which in its operative context means the presence of God described from the "perspective" of the individual's experience of this presence.

Although St. Teresa relies on the earlier Kabbalistic imagery of the chambers in her later "mature" descriptions, appropriating the traditional number of seven to help discern the modes of experiential presence, Rabbi Dov Baer deviates from the ancient Jewish pattern of mystical experience in favor of another that becomes expressive of the newer Chasidic style of mysticism. Here the Rabbi discerns ten distinctive types of ecstasy, five pertaining to the "natural" sphere of the human being, and five peculiar to the divine sphere of the human being. More precisely, each kind of ecstasy is unique to an aspect of soul, and although there are only five names with respect to the soul, they have different import, depending on whether they are natural or divine.[31] The "kinds" of soul, as well as their correlative stages or degrees of ecstasy, are mentioned throughout the *Tanach* (being evoked in varying contexts), and they are also mentioned by name in the late-medieval mystical work, *The Bahir*.[32] In paragraph 53, *The Bahir* refers to them as five names of (i.e., belonging to, with regard to) the soul (*shemot le-neshamah*); Dov Baer more explicitly treats them as indicative of five different stages or kinds of experience that get articulated each in their own way, either in terms of their naturalness or their sanctity.

In ascending order, Dov Baer treats the kinds of ecstasy as follows: (1) *nefesh*, (2) *ruach*, (3) *neshamah*, (4) *chayyah*, and (5) *yechidah*. Each level of soul has a unique quality that is also discerned *from the kind of ecstasy to which it belongs*. For example, action and resolve concerning the deed belong to the sphere of *nefesh*, which derives from the quality of acknowledgment. This quality of intention toward the Holy peculiar to *nefesh* can be found scripturally, for example, in the prayer connected to the *Shema*, the *V'ahavta*: "You shall love the Lord your God with all your heart and all your soul [*nafsh'cha*] and with all your might" (Deut. 6:5). Furthermore, *nefesh* belongs to the *sefirah* of *malchut* or *shechinah* and corresponds to the world of *asiyah*, or action.[33] In *ruach*, which is often translated as "spirit," there is greater vitality, and it bears on the integration of thought and deed (as evoked, e.g., by Job). It is associated with the six ascending *sefirot* (from *yesod* to *chesed*) and corresponds to the world of *yetzirah*, or formation. *Neshamah* concerns the illuminations of the "minds" of wisdom and understanding in the heart, where there is greater light and inner vitality. *Neshamah* pertains to the *sefirah* of *binah* and to the world of creation.[34] *Chayyah* concerns wisdom and understanding in themselves and is associated with *kavannah*. It is linked to the *sefirah* of *chochmah* and the world of *atzilut,* or nearness. Finally, *yechidah* is the dimension of the elemental, simple will, higher than reason or intellect; there is literally no "reason" for it (*Tract,* 93–94). It corresponds to the *sefirah* of *keter,* or crown, and to the world of the primordial human, *adam kadmon.*

Having described the various soul levels, I now turn to the Rabbi's descriptions and explanations of ecstasies. I begin with the natural forms of ecstasy, which for Dov Baer pertain to the vital sphere, and then treat the divine forms. I reserve the discussion of false or delusive forms of ecstasy and their motivations for chapter 5 on evidence.

Natural Ecstasy

By "natural," Dov Baer understands two things, one more explicitly, the other more implicitly. On the one hand, by natural, Dov Baer means the dimension of existence that is psycho-physical, or again, that which belongs to the vital sphere in the broad sense, which includes various intellectual functions (*Tract,* 94, 97). Even pleasures derivable from something like fame are still considered natural or vital in comparison to divine ones (*Tract,* 101). On the other hand, he suggests by way of description that natural ecstasy corresponds to that ecstasy which is won by expending effort on my part, that is, which is not overtly given as a gift (as will clearly be the case with divine ecstasy). In either case, even the natural form of ecstasy presupposes some movement along a spiritual path.

Hearing (*shimacha*), in Kabbalist teachings, refers to understanding (*binah*). To say "Oh Lord, I have learned of Your renown" (*Adonai shema'ati shimacha*) as the prophet Habakkuk writes (3:2), means literally, "Oh Lord, I have heard Your Hearing," or again, "Oh Lord, I have understood Your Understanding."[35] According to Dov Baer, there are different ways of hearing. Some hear with great profundity, some hear and are moved to ecstasy quickly, but only superficially (*Tract,* 147). This first degree of ecstasy, pertaining to the natural or vital level of *nefesh,* is what Dov Baer calls "hearing-from-afar."

Hearing-from-afar means the person "hears" and contemplates *only,* without connection to deed; the individual understands until it becomes true and acceptable *to the individual self.* While this qualifies as the "main beginning" for those who seek and inquire for God in truth, it affects only the mind; the heart is not stirred (*Tract*, 80). The Divine is still remote from the individual such that doubt remains as to the benefit the Holy brings; it is of no real *personal* concern.[36] Appreciating and acknowledging the value of contemplation, the individual longs to be moved, but as yet is not actually aroused by the subjects upon which he contemplates. Expending great energy in disposing himself to the Divine, he attains an abbreviated version of ecstasy—not spontaneously, but by dint of his effort at contemplating some divine theme. Still, there is as yet no difference in the individual's behavior (*Tract*, 103–104).

While Dov Baer will distinguish between authentic and false ecstasy, this most inferior form of ecstatic experience is nonetheless not "false." For at least contemplation on the Divine is important to the individual, and the nearness of God is something greatly desired (*Tract*, 83). This desire springs from the weight that God's majesty assumes for the individual and issues in shame when he considers that he is remote from God. Reflecting on the nature of his unworthiness, the individual undergoes a general derogation, a transvaluation of material things, since now they are measured against the Divine (*Tract*, 84–85). Dov Baer writes: "He falls greatly in his own estimation and the world falls greatly in his estimation."[37] Furthermore, at least this intention toward God is precisely an intention toward the Divine and not an intention that is directed explicitly toward oneself or toward things; this is accompanied by a resolve to turn from evil and to do good so that perhaps, by disposing himself to God in this way, he will actually be moved out of himself.

The injunction of the *V'ahavta* expresses such a beginning spiritual path whereby one's eyes, so to speak, are attempting to fix on the absolute value of God absolutely, on God alone, as expressed in the conclusion of the *Shema*, namely, *"Adonai echad."* The individual is ready to value God above all else; his aim is to instigate an absolute relation to the One, the Absolute, and not to be confused by placing absolute worth on things, business affairs, economic prosperity, and so forth.

The second intellectual/vital stage is called "goodly thought joined to the deed." Even though in the first stage the individual's intention is directed toward God alone, whereby the value of God assumes great proportions, it is no more than an acknowledgement; it is not even a "goodly thought" but a "thought without qualification," since there are as yet no consequences that follow in deed (*Tract*, 81). In contrast to the latter "cold thought," there is some attraction of the soul in this second stage, since one is stirred and slightly moved—moved from one's place, moved to do good deeds, moved to a longing for the Divine to be revealed in these good deeds (*Tract,* 84–85). Contemplation on the Divine occurs as a type of hearing in thought through which one is absorbed and engrossed.[38]

The effects of this ecstasy are love and fearsome awe with respect to the deed, whereby one loves with great vitality and likewise shuns evil because it is just to do so. Still, this ecstasy does not yet have the quality of "inwardness" peculiar to the ecstasy of the heart. Thus, writes Dov Baer, "he has been moved only to ecstasy in thought, not, as yet, to ecstasy of heart at all" (*Tract,* 84).

The ecstasy of the heart, the third stage according to Dov Baer, does not follow easily upon mind ecstasy. Only through forceful effort, only when one's thought greatly exerts itself with much vigor and toil and intense concentration, only when one immerses oneself in the contemplation of the greatness of God for a considerable time will there come to the person at least this lower love and fearsome awe.[39] For this reason heart ecstasy is also known as the "labor" of love whereby service is essentially wedded to ecstasy in contemplation. Ecstasy follows upon severe effort because it is not induced explicitly in the heart; the Divine is given in an ambiance that is only indirect, such that great effort is required on the part of the individual to enable this "surrounding" light to be transformed into a more direct light. For all that, this ecstasy is experienced with more lightness and vitality. In Dov Baer's words: "For in worldly matters no sooner does some good thing come to mind, moving the mind to ecstasy, than the heart is touched with ecstasy and is immediately moved with the sparks of fire in longing, or conversely, to bitterness where there is some evil thing which the mind hates etc." (*Tract,* 86).

Within heart ecstasy itself there are a variety of degrees, since some are moved in greater ecstasy of heart than mind, others moved to ecstasy with greater joy. What they all have in common, according to the Rabbi, is not just a love and fearsome awe that pertains to the deed, but "actual" love and fearsome awe. By "actual" Dov Baer means the nearness of God experienced as my good, whereby there is so much ecstasy of the heart that it overflows with experienced inner light and vitality in performing the deed with great desire, or conversely, with an ecstasy of wrath at that which opposes the good. Engaging in good deeds with an emotional engagement and commitment, energetically and with great desire, the person will guard against evil doings and anything that would threaten those good deeds with the same ardor.[40]

Love and service is a deeper form of ecstasy than the love and fearsome awe of mere goodly thought. But still higher and more profound than the heart's ecstasy is the stage of ecstasy enumerated as the fourth, namely, the heart's *kavannah* (or sincere, focused, directed, concentrated intention toward God). In contrasting this stage of ecstasy with the former, Dov Baer maintains that although one is moved to real ecstasy with longing, joy, or bitterness in the third stage, the very divine contemplative matters that had stirred the ecstasy (such as God surrounding and filling all things) are abbreviated, reduced merely to the ecstasy of the heart; and all that remains of it is that part which concerns the heart alone (*Tract*, 88–89). In the heart's focused concentration, however, the whole mind and heart are absorbed in the divine matter alone, and it is "too high" or too deep to be contained in what was previously experienced as the ecstasy of the heart. In distinction to a natural fearsome awe and love in the preceding stage, which is separate from the act of contemplation itself, this is an "intellectual fearsome awe and love" expressive of *chochmah* (wisdom), *binah* (understanding), and *daat* (knowledge)—or *Chabad*—in their exalted form.

In the former case, there is what Dov Baer calls a "thus" or "therefore," which is to say, love and fearsome awe follow upon contemplation. They are truths at which one arrives after or according to contemplation—indicative of a distance between love and fearsome awe on the one hand, and contemplation on the other. In the fourth level of experiencing, however, love and fearsome awe are not separate from contemplation itself, but "come involuntarily and of their own accord by compulsion without any choice or freewill whatsoever" (*Tract*, 89–90). In this case, contemplation and intellectual love and fearsome awe are united spontaneously without having to unite them in the manner of a "therefore."

Rabbi Dov Baer does not give much description of the final stage of natural ecstasy that transcends contemplation. He writes merely and succinctly that it is called the simple will, the elemental will that is higher than any contemplation whatsoever and from which the intellect is derived, concluding simply by adding that "this is sufficient for him who understands" (*Tract*, 92).

The five stages or degrees of ecstatic experience just delineated pertain to the intellectual soul, also known as the natural or vital soul. All this bears on "serving the Lord with the body" and not yet "serving the Lord with the [Divine] soul" (*Tract,* 94). Because we are concerned with the descriptions of the natural in relation to divine ecstasy, the clarification of these orders of experience is imperative. There are four points worthy of both mention and explication before proceeding to the delineation of divine ecstasy.

The first is a rather obvious one. There is a clear hierarchical ordering between the natural and the divine. But what could too easily go unnoticed is the fact that Dov Baer does not negate the natural or the body in favor of the divine; rather, he describes degrees and stages of ecstatic experience *peculiar to* the "natural," bodily, or psycho-physical dimension of existence. Moreover, just because the latter is not as profound as divine experiences—for reasons we will see below—it does not follow that they are of no or little value. The experiences to which he witnesses are testimony to the integrity of this dimension of experiencing, even given its inherent limitations.

Second (and this is at times more implicit than explicit in Dov Baer's exposition), the "natural" is natural precisely because these modes of ecstasy are instigated by our efforts.[41] Although I will take this up later (in chapter 5), what marks the stages of "authentic" divine ecstasy is the fact that our efforts are not in play; instead, ecstasy is given "purely," as a matter of grace (*Tract,* 105).

Third, there is a difference in modes of "self-awareness." In natural ecstasy, one hears, understands, or is still attuned to oneself in some measure. It is in this sense that one is "self-aware" (*er hört sich*), in Dov Baer's terminology, such that I consider myself "something" (i.e., something special or even something not special), making God more remote (*Tract,* 128). Now, ecstasy can become the important matter, which pertains to my pleasure of the experience.

Finally, the natural and divine dimensions of experience, while distinct, are not disconnected. On the contrary, according to Dov Baer, the natural dimension, even the lowest level of natural ecstatic experience, is already informed from the very start by the Divine (cf. *Tract,* 94–95). Ultimately, even the experience pertaining to natural ecstasy in comprehending the Divine is also the result of the Divine (*Tract,* 99). What makes natural ecstatic experience possible, even if we never attain divine ecstatic experience, is that the Divine is always already implicitly present, even if—due to our recalcitrance—in a much removed manner. Could we not say, then, that *nefesh* is *yechidah* in the manner of concealment of *yechidah* (*Tract*, 112)? Understood in this way, that is, from the perspective of Divine givenness, the natural can be said to be divine, but as in the mode of removal. This points, in the final analysis, to a connection and distinction between natural and divine, and not to a separation or dualism. Only from a secularist, merely "natural" perspective would there be a problem of dualism. But—and this cannot be overemphasized—the presupposition of the natural as a "starting point" (which is to say the negation of the Divine) is really a Modern prejudice and a presupposition that cannot go unquestioned and taken for granted; it turns out to be abstract and arbitrary (see esp., chapters 5 and 8).[42]

To sum up, then, we have two levels of distinction between these ecstatic experiences: the one operative between the psycho-physical or bodily dimension of mystical experience and a "spiritual" dimension of mystical experience, each with its own unique stages and degrees; and the other pertaining, respectively, to the natural and divine *qua* effort-laden and grace-ful dimension of mystical experiencing. The one is natural because it requires effort and concerns the psycho-physical dimensions, the body or lived-body; the other is divine because it bears on ourselves as made in the "image and likeness of God," as divine soul or divine dimension of existence received through grace. Having interpreted the difference and interrelation between the natural and divine, I now turn to an elaboration of the degrees of divine ecstasy as elaborated by Dov Baer.

Divine Ecstasy

Where divine ecstasy is concerned, one cannot produce or induce a mystical experience. At times Dov Baer refers to these divine ecstasies as "excessive" or "revealed" because they are beyond what we ourselves could induce; there is no "reason" for them and in this sense they are without cause (*Tract*, 155). Efforts such as contemplating the words of God are only geared toward disposing oneself to the revelation (or in our terms, "epiphany") of the Holy; they do not cause such a givenness, but through them we open ourselves toward a possible "something" that we cannot induce (*Tract*, 96). In whatever form it takes, this "something" is experienced as a kind of *devekut*, a true cleaving to God, which Dov Baer terms essential life (*Tract*, 68, 95). Within the manner of divine mystical ecstatic experience there are various degrees and stages. Specifically, there are five stages of divine ecstasy that in their own way correspond to the five different kinds of soul: some are moved in the manner of *nefesh*, others in the manner of *ruach*, and still others are moved in the manner of *neshamah, chayyah*, and *yechidah* (*Tract*, 111).

Dov Baer terms the lowest stage of divine ecstasy "piety." It is through one's thoughtful will for the Divine to obey God in actual practice that one experiences a resolve to turn from evil and to do good. By means of worship and fearsome awe of God, each according to one's own capacity, the divine soul is strengthened in the process of acting well. But the resolve peculiar to piety is not a near, inner vitality. God's name can be invoked, for example, without deep meaning, allowing one actually to act in opposition to God. For this reason, explains Dov Baer, it is still possible for one to be internally divided in this kind of piety. For instance, one can implore God with all sincerity to help one succeed in doing something that transgresses divine commandments, for example, having devotion to God but neglecting the well-being of others. Even though one's "simple faith" may be strong, one might still pray in piety without making any of these connections (*Tract*, 116–17). This indicates for Dov Baer that such an individual is still at a remove from the Divine.

Whereas the former piety has no inner vitality, since God is still far, the second stage of divine ecstasy (the seventh where the whole range is concerned) is described as a "piety with warmth and vitality." The experience of warmth and vitality in piety is expressive of a new orientation. In distinction to the former kind, now it is like "second nature" not to transgress God's will (*Tract*, 118). Rabbi Zalman writes that it is the Holy One (and not our power) who joins action or the good deed to "revealed" fearsome awe and love.[43] Such instances belong to the experience of the good deed with great inner vitality in which these good deeds are experienced as "being moved from one's place" in the spiritual sense of going out of Egypt.

Dov Baer cites three ways in which this mode of piety comes to expression: in martyrdom, in repentance, and in religious conversion. In the first case, martyrdom, martyrs offer up their life not just in thought but in practice. The power to sacrifice oneself does not stem from oneself but from an "essential" power, that is, from the strength from the divine.[44] "At the moment of martyrdom this force shines forth openly out of concealment"; God "awakens" one as if out of a sleep to withstand such a trial. Not only does the capacity of martyrdom come from God, but it only takes place authentically, as martyrdom, "before" God. It is essentially something that cannot be self-willed or something "I" want to do in order to get closer to God or "to win my place in paradise."[45] One values one's own life, but above this one values God.

Though it is not the only way, in Judaism (like in Christianity, expressed in the Greek *martyrein*), martyrdom is a modality of becoming a witness. Aside from the martyrology and special prayers recited on High Holy days, the call to witness is implicit in the very recitation of the *Shema*, the central prayer in Judaism. As it is penned in the Torah, two letters are written larger than the rest.[46] These two letters, *ayin* and *dalet* spell the word *eyd*, which means "witness," harking back to the expression by Isaiah (43:10, 12): *atem eydai*, "My witnesses are *you*."[47]

Such deeds as true martyrdom, which are done for the glory of God and not for oneself, are accomplished in cleaving and not through self-action. Were this force to shine forth continuously, continues Dov Baer, a person would never sin (*Tract*, 118, 126). But because this presence is not continuous in the same way all the time, we become painfully aware of our remoteness from God. Remoteness is one reason why piety with warmth is also evident in repentance.

In repentance (*teshuvah*), one weeps at transgressions one has committed. Even though one has done certain deeds that, historically speaking, cannot be undone, repentance alters the meaning of the past events such that one's will is more aligned with God's. It is expressive of a change of heart. For Dov Baer, one may strive to be sorry, one can prepare oneself to return to God, but it cannot be equated with pure voluntarism. Rather, it is because the divine spark is attracted "involuntarily" that "it rouses itself in weeping of its own accord." This becomes particularly evident when one is spontaneously filled with remorse and when the remorse is more profound on some days than on others (*Tract*, 123–25).

Finally, religious conversion is another example of piety experienced with warmth and vitality. Conversion of this sort does not amount to picking a new religion, since one is stirred by God and guided along a certain path and is called to it. For the Rabbi, it stems from "the divine spirit in the Community of Israel, the members of which are constantly attracted, as if by actual nature, to the divine Source whence they were hewn" (*Tract*, 122). While Dov Baer does not put it this way, strictly speaking, religious conversion would have to apply to a conversion to one's own "faith." In this respect, conversion may not only issue from an alluring insight won from a different path but could issue from repentance or *teshuvah,* which is a returning to God within one's present path.

Resulting from the actual comprehension of the Divine by the divine soul, wisdom and understanding are moved, in the third stage, to the heart's ecstasy. In distinction to the natural ecstasy of the heart mentioned above, this ecstasy occurs of its own accord, "without any choice or will or effort whatsoever." (*Tract,* 126–27). The heart spontaneously "sings for joy unto the living God." For the Chabad mystic, service (*avodah*) is only truly service when it is done with gladness and a joyful heart and when one does not go around depressed, anxious, and full of self-doubt or sorrow; for these are either expressions of a lack of faith in God's forgiveness or expressions of pride.[48] Being rooted in the love of God, service clothes the commandments and is accomplished, not from some personal motive or even in order to cleave to God, but simply for God.[49] On this score, Rabbi Zalman cites Rabbi Isaac Luria, proclaiming that even worry about sins is only suitable during confession, but not during prayer and Torah study, since the latter should be carried out with joy stemming exclusively from holiness.[50]

Love directed toward God can have two sources. The first is what we saw above as a "natural" love, that is, a love garnered through our own efforts, expressed for example in the desire to cleave to God and often characterized by Jewish mystics as a burning flame. Devoting one's heart and mind to matters that elicit love, this ardent or eternal love (*ahavat olam*) is at the root of service and is a kind of love that everyone can, in principle, attain. One does not desire anything in the world, that is, anything of relative value no matter what it is; one desires absolutely only God, God alone (*echad*); for in comparison to God, all things are as if nothing. This love, an acquired love, is already a vertical movement toward God as absolute.

The other kind of love is characterized as a "great love" (*ahavah rabbah*) or "love with delights" (*ahavah beta'anugim*). It is a love that comes "by itself," of its own accord, in the "manner of a gift." Here we are not occupied with ourselves as the ecstasy is taking place; the ecstasy is "spontaneous," "involuntary," "without contrivance" (i.e., one is not "*self*-aware"). Found in experience of the *tzaddikim,* or saintly persons, it is further characterized as an ecstatic, overabundant love and is depicted sometimes as "very wide" in the sense of being "without limit and end."[51]

Spontaneous, like the third stage of divine ecstasy, but encompassing, it is the fourth level of divine ecstasy, described as the divine ecstasy of the mind. Divine concentration or *kavannah* is the presence of the Divine that is not derived by an understanding of the Divine or generated by a "therefore." Absorbed in the thing itself, the matter comprehended comes about before it can be articulated in detail, similar to the way a melody arrives "only 'as one,' exceedingly spontaneous note" (*Tract,* 132–33). Not found among most people, observes Dov Baer, this mode of ecstasy is at the root of disposing oneself to God in worship and purification.

Demanding a special grace, which enables one to divest oneself of one's self in favor of God, the ecstasy of the sefirah *Keter,* the Crown itself, is the highest level of ecstasy described by Dov Baer. It is called a *hylic* delight, being the source of every kind of delight (*Tract,* 137).[52] Cleaving to God, burning for God, this mode of ecstasy is the simple will, which does not become divided into many contradictory wills as was previously the case: "His whole being is so absorbed that nothing remains and he has no self-consciousness whatsoever" (*Tract,* 139).[53] Here the learned and the ignorant equally experience the limitless love that is expressed absolutely and that is higher than *nefesh, ruach, neshamah,* and even *chayyah,* which itself is higher "altogether than reason and knowledge" (*Tract,* 139–40). It is a love clearly without motivation or cause: "For there is no reason for this simple *hylic* will and delight, not even a hidden reason in the source of *hylic* intellect, etc." (*Tract,* 139). From the perspective of this ecstasy, which is the richest and deepest of them all, in which one cleaves fully to God, *yechidah* can be said to be present in all other kinds of soul and ecstasy, but in the manner of concealment.

Although Dov Baer writes from the perspective of the individual who is undergoing the experiences and likewise portrays the stations as a possible "ascension" toward God, the gradation of progression toward God can also be seen from the perspective of the ultimate stage of divine ecstasy in reverse order, namely, as a self-distancing from God. Distance from God can therefore be interpreted as putting ourselves in the way of actual and possible nearness, so that even though Divine givenness is not our accomplishment, we can—for example, through self-deceptions and delusions—occlude or obscure Divine givenness.

The two main modes of ecstasy described above, each with its own respective differentiations and levels of soul, can be articulated in terms of a difference between that which can be attained ("with the help of

God") through our own efforts, and that which can only be garnered as a matter of grace. The point is not the ecstasy itself, but rather the fulfill-ment or spiritualization of creation, which is to say, it concerns restoring the presence of God, the *shechinah,* from its exile.

Rabbi Dov Baer's descriptions of mystical experience from within the Chasidic Jewish tradition emphasize the "ecstatic," or what is also known as the "prophetic" dimension of mystical experience, in distinction to other types of Jewish mysticism. These levels of experience are articu-lated according to five kinds of natural soul and five kinds of divine soul, varying in dimensions of depth, reliance on one's efforts, ties to the self, and the dimensions of grace and union with God. The ultimate meaning of these vertical experiences is not the individual's elevation to God in union, but righteousness as a way of participating in the re-union of God and creation.

While the different levels of experience delineated by Dov Baer in his *Tract on Ecstasy* welcome further examination, my concern here is not specifically with the number of levels that Dov Baer describes. Admittedly, in some ways they might appear accidental, aligned as they are with a template of five types of soul found in the *Tanach* and *Bahir,* even though one could argue equally that there are these five types of soul and ten levels of givenness because they were precisely given in that way. My overall concern, rather, is with the attempt to elucidate the nuances and distinctiveness in what I am calling vertical experiencing. Let this exposition suffice as a general orientation to the problematic of vertical experience, a problematic to be addressed more explicitly in chapter 5 and the ensuing chapters. Before pressing on to the philosophical explica-tion of evidence, I introduce one further figure, this one from the Islamic mystical tradition.

CHAPTER 4
Rūzbihān Baqlī and
Mysticism of Unveiling

*He appeared to me in the form of divinity, holiness, and tran-
scendence. Everything other than him from the throne to the earth
vanished beneath the assaults of his greatness. . . . He appeared
in the witnessing of the beauty of divine presence—and that is
a strange thing, since he [usually] displays the manifestation of
beauty in the form of greatness. He agitated my conscience, made
my intellect nothing, and tore my heart to bits. I was there for
some time. Then he said, "You are seeking me and I am seeking
you; if you look, you will find me in yourself, without taking the
journeys of the hidden."*

—RŪZBIHĀN BAQLĪ (§196)[1]

Islamic Mysticism and the Prophetic Tradition

What has become known as "Islam" emerged as the third religious
movement within the Abrahamic tradition. On the seventeenth night
of the month of Ramadan in 610 CE, during his month-long spiritual
retreat to a cave on Mt. Hirā, an angel—Gabriel—gave Muhammad a
command "to recite" (*iqra'*). Enveloped by the overpowering presence
of God, Muhammad recited divinely inspired words. The Revelation/
Recitation makes a direct connection to previous revelations given to the
Jews and Christians, and in fact presupposes them. The Quranic revelation finds its uniqueness in the fact that this was the first time in Arabia
that the One God, "the God"—"al-Lāh" or "Allāh," had revealed himself
in the people's own language.[2] Taking the form of verses recited aloud by
Muhammad, they were named *Quran*, meaning "recitation," inaugurat-
ing the first Holy Scripture of Islam. Compiled from a series of revelations
that lasted for over two decades (610–632 CE), the Quran spurred, among
other things, what we would call today the mystical dimension of Islam,
or "Sufism."

According to the research of Carl Ernst, prior to the nineteenth century Islam and Sufism were never dissociated as separate orders, and as

recently as the late eighteenth century, most of the exceptional religious scholars in the centers of the Muslim world were intimately engaged with the mystical dimension of Islam.[3] In fact, it is the mystics who played the decisive role in the interpretation of the Quran. Even on a more common level, Sufi poetry has perhaps done more for shaping the literary sphere of the Muslim world than any other single force, contributing to such languages as Arabic, Persian, Turkish, Sindhi, Panjabi, Urdu, and Pashto.[4]

Before taking up the role of Sufism more explicitly, and the particular Islamic mystic I treat here, Rūzbihān Baqlī, some background to the religious tradition of Islam to which Sufism is inherently wedded is in order.

When we speak of "Islam," we can do so in both a more general and a more specific manner. The term "islām" / اسلام (which is built upon the same root م/ل/س [s/l/m] as "salām" / سلام or peace) means "to submit," namely, to submit to, or to surrender oneself to the One God as Abraham did in his faithfulness to God (4:125).[5]

Islam as a religious practice is a discipline of turning oneself absolutely to God, of abandoning oneself to God, and of striving toward the forgetfulness of self. In a very general sense, "islām" can be understood as the form of any religion before the presence of God (3:19). As submitting oneself to God, and in finding peace in this submission, accordingly, islām must be distinguished from submitting oneself to "things" or associating things with God, that is, idolatry (shirk). In this respect, any of the three revealed religions of the Abrahamic tradition could rightfully be called "islām," whereas the act of submitting oneself to things, or raising things to the level of God would be understood as idolatry. In turn, muslim signifies one who submits or surrenders to God, one who practices the act of "islām."

There is certainly a more specific sense to Islam and to being a Muslim. Islam is more familiarly a particular religion within the Abrahamic tradition, circumscribed by a set of specific religious observances and rituals; and a Muslim is one who adheres to them. One set of practices is known as the five pillars of Islam. The first pillar entails "witnessing," reciting the Shahādah: "lā ilāh illā Allāh," "There is no god but the God," and "Muhammadun rasūl Allāh," "Muhammad is God's messenger." Thus, the first act in becoming a Muslim demands bearing witness to the Oneness of God, as well as accepting Muhammad as God's messenger.[6]

It is written in the Quran that every nation has its own messenger (10:47) and that no messenger has been sent "except (to teach) in the language/ Of his (own) people, in order/ To make (things) clear to them" (14:4). In this regard, we are to make "no distinction among the prophets" —a phrase that is repeated throughout the Quran (see 2:136; see also 2:285 and 3:84). The prophets include all those who are chosen by God to receive and to witness a message. These figures are not restricted to those who are traditionally viewed as prophets in the Judeo-Christian tradition, like Ezekiel, Jeremiah, or Isaiah, but begin with Adam and include Noah, Abraham, Moses, and Jesus, all the way down to Muhammad. On some accounts, there are 124,000 prophets; on others, as many as 224,000.[7]

Despite this similarity in spiritual weight among the prophets, one can still discriminate within the broad notion of "prophet" between a prophet (*nabī*) and a messenger [*rasūl*]. While all those people chosen by God to receive a message can be counted among the prophets, only a small number of those are called to found religions, and for this number is reserved the appellation "messenger." In this respect, Abraham is said to be a messenger, while Isaac, Ishmael, Jacob, and Joseph—who extrapolate from, reform, confirm, or clarify the founding message—are regarded as prophets.[8] Accordingly, while Muhammad is a prophet, the last prophet, according to the Islamic tradition, he is most profoundly a messenger.[9] This is precisely what is echoed in the second portion of the *Shahādah*: "*Muhammadun rasul Allah*," "Muhammad is God's messenger." This second portion expresses for the Muslim, furthermore, that not only is Muhammad a prophet and a founder, but that he has concluded the lineage of prophets.

> Muhammad is not
> The father of any
> Of your men, but (he is)
> The Messenger of Allah,
> And the Seal of the Prophets. (33:40)

For the faithful, Muhammad is holy in the sense that he is completely trustworthy, a *servant* true to the revelation of God. Although holy in this sense, Muhammad is not divine in the sense that Jesus is for Christians. Muhammad is a messenger, but "no more" than a messenger, says the Quran, that is, not a divinity (3:144, 17:93–94). Muhammad is not the message, not the revelation, but he who is entrusted with the revelation. It is instead the Quran that constitutes the revelation, and it is the Quran that constitutes the core of Islam.

Sufism as the Mystical Heritage of Islam

What we know today under the rubric "Sufism" developed spontaneously within Islam as special religious and moral practices. The appellation "Sufism" (*taṣawwuf*) most likely stems from the Arabic term *suf*, meaning "wool," and was applied to those who practiced a life of self-surrender and who donned this coarse woolen attire of humility to set themselves off from a lifestyle of selfishness, comfort, and luxury. This is the generally accepted derivation of the term, though already the fourth/tenth century[10] Sufi al-Qushayrī (376/986–465/1072) entertains other derivations. Some say the name "Sufism" comes from the Arabic word for purity, *ṣafā;* others hold that it comes from the early disciples who, in their devotion, left their homes and surrounded the Prophet on the bench (*ṣuffa*) outside the mosque (garnering the title, the "people of the Bench" [*ashāb-i ṣuffa*]).[11] Perhaps the best response was supplied by Abū Bakr al-Shiblī, who was asked: "Why are the Sufis called by this name?" He replied: "It is because of the traces of the self that remain within them. If this were not the case, there would be no name attached to them!"[12]

Whatever etymology or origin we might ascribe to the term Sufism, it nevertheless depicts a profound religious and moral movement within Islam that internalizes the self-abandon to the One God on the model of the Prophet Muhammad. This mystical path centered on serving God absolutely with the hope of experiencing Allah in a direct and personal manner. Such a practice intrinsically dissociated itself from knowing God through reason, from following ethical prescripts by rote, and from merely taking for granted the messages of the prophets.[13] Beyond the ascetic and devotional practices of early Islam that characterized Sufism in the very beginning, by the third/ninth century, which begins the classical period of Sufism, Sufism was given to creative spiritual introspection and the examination of moral, legal, and philosophical issues inspired by lived experiences.[14]

Taking the shape of loose-knit organizations linked by shared spiritual practices and common devotions, these bonds eventually developed into the schools of mysticism or teaching centers that were handed down from master or guide (*murshid*) of "the Path" to heir or aspirant (*murīd*), forming a continuous chain of succession.[15] But it was not until the beginning of the fifth/eleventh century that teaching lineages and hospices began to spring up around exceptional Sufi masters, institutionalizing a Sufi order.[16] Despite the absence of a monastic ideal, early Sufis nevertheless justified an ascetic connection to Muhammad, in part, by virtue of his spiritual retreat to the cave on Mt. Hirā in the Meccan valley, where he was enveloped by the Divine Presence and first received the Revelation.

The Sufi wants to act like the Prophet in deed, in the attitude of self-surrender (*islām*); to love like the Prophet in faith (*īmān*); to be aware of God's presence in all things including him- or herself; and to act appropriately (*iḥsān*—to act well or do what is beautiful, *dhikr*—the recollection of God).[17] In doing so, one becomes a "friend of God." Being one of the "friends of God" (*awliyā'-i allāh*) or saints, according to early Sufi masters, was the main principle of Sufism, and was characterized by an unflagging responsibility for the worship, devotion, and obedience to God and by God's responsibility and protection for the friend.[18] Because of the preeminence of the Prophet Muhammad, however, the mutual love relationship that distinguished saint or friend of God was understood generally by the Sufis as subordinated to the role of the Prophet, the latter being understood as public, the former as private. Such a hierarchy and distinction was one way of trying to relieve a very real tension (doctrinal and experiential) between the authority of the Prophet and God's revelation through him, and the ongoing, open-ended divine inspiration that typified the friends of God or Sufi saints.

For most of the Jewish mystics, the deeper meanings of the Torah are expressive of God's passionate love for humanity. The *Shir ha-Shirim,* the "Song of Songs," exemplifies this love, becoming not an inter-human ode, but a fervent, adoring love poem between God and human beings as lover and beloved. This intimate love relation between God and humanity is the mystical theme of the Quran for the Sufis. To evoke their intimate relation with God, many of the Arabic and Persian Sufi writings are filled with such images adopted from the courtly literary tradition that are Islamic and pre-Islamic in origin.[19]

As Armstrong observes, poets (and poetry) had played the crucial role in the political and social life of Arabia in the sense of fulfilling the function of dissemination, interpretation, and influence that our modern-day press does today.[20] In regard to Holy Scripture, the effect and import of poetry was even more profound.[21] Sufi poetry was not an autobiographical or *self*-expressive vehicle (as poetry tends to be today). The subject matter of the poetry was not the individual, but the *evocation* of the presence and power of God as Lover and Beloved in manifold ways, the evocative description of the generosity of the soul, the loving devotion of the individual in the presence of God, and the personal witnessing of the primordial covenant between God and humanity. This is not to say that there was not a scholastic language utilized in earlier trends in Sufism, but by the Classical period, many Islamic mystics expressed themselves in the form of poetic imagery.[22] One could also understand the use of poetic imagery as a favored medium of expression of the mystics because, simply put, it is beautiful and done well (*iḥsān*). Thus, it is not by default that the Islamic mystic resorts to poetic imagery; rather, it is the *way* the infinity of religious experience can be expressed most beautifully, given the finitude of language.[23]

It is true that this poetic form or the expressions that are couched in rich symbolic imagery might strike us as unfamiliar and even unfathomable. But despite its difficulty for interpretation, it nevertheless provides us with a form of first-person description of the lived-through presence of God on the part of the mystic. This observation is particularly relevant for the writings by Rūzbihān Baqlī that I consult.

Michael Sells outlines four basic phases of Islamic spirituality: (1) the pre-Sufi stage, which includes the Quran, Muhammad's mystical journey ("The Night Journey" [*Al Isrāʾ*, 17:1]; Arabic, Persian, Ottoman, Urdu poetic traditions; and early ascetic piety beyond what was prescribed by the *sharīʿa* or revealed law; (2) the early period of Sufism and Sufi masters, extending from Ḥasan of Baṣra (d. 110/728), Rabiʿa (d. 247/869),[24] Bisṭāmī (d. 260/874), Junayd (d. 297/910), Ḥallāj (d. 300/922),[25] to Niffarī (d. 354/965); (3) the formative phase of Sufi literature in which Sufism is a self-conscious style of spirituality integrated into all aspects of social and private life, spanning Sarrāj (d. 378/988) and Qushayrī (d. 465/1074); and (4) the works of seventeenth/thirteenth-century Islamic mystics, including ʿAṭṭār (d. 627/1230), Ibn ʿArabī (d. 638/1240), and Rūmī (d. 672/1273).[26]

For my purposes, more relevant to this sketch, however, was the broad bifurcation into two distinctive trends in Islamic mysticism, one that occurs within the early period: the Junaydī, after Abūʾl-Qāsim al-Junayd (d. 297/910), and the Bisṭāmī, after Abū Yazīd al-Bisṭāmī (d. 260/874). They are most commonly contrasted as the ways of "sobriety" (*ṣaḥw*) and "intoxication" (*sukr*, i.e., spiritual intoxication, rapture, ecstasy). While the mystical path of the former is generally characterized by the strict adherence to the *sharī'a* or revealed law, for the latter the perfect adherence to the Prophet can be satisfied neither by perfect adherence to the *sharī'a*, nor merely by faith alone.[27] Since one could always follow the law without interior faith, and since one could always have faith (abstractly at least) without being an exemplar of loving, service to others, humility, righteousness and charity, compassion, and so forth, it is necessary to cultivate an "interior" path.[28] The tension between these two ways was so pronounced by the fourth/tenth century, that the famous mystic Sarrāj attempted a détente between the followers of the intoxicated and sober paths.[29] Rūzbihān Baqlī's own spiritual experiences place him directly in the line of spiritually "intoxicated" Sufis, the one shared by the Sufi martyrs Ḥallāj and Bisṭāmī, for example.

The exact spiritual lineage of Rūzbihān Baqlī (522/1128–606/1209) is uncertain. Ernst reports, relying on Baqlī's own account, that he was born into a Daylamite family and was surrounded by people who had no real sense of religion.[30] Recalling having profound spiritual experiences at three, seven, and fifteen years of age, he left his vegetable store and all possessions, and wandered in the desert (anywhere from a year and a half to six and a half years). He then joined the Sufis and was most likely associated with the Banu Salbih family, where he would have had access to a library holding the writings of Ḥallāj. Later he retreated to Pasa, the town of his birth, and became a disciple of Shaykh Jamāl al-Dīn. He is believed to have studied with leading scholars of Shiraz (such as Fakhr al-Dīn ibn Maryam and Arshad al-Dīn Nayrīzī), and to have preached avidly in Shiraz until his death.[31]

As I have noted above with respect to both St. Teresa of Avila and Rabbi Dov Baer, my own concern is not with autobiography per se, but with descriptions of experiences as lived in order to discern the structures of mystical experience as modes of verticality. Even though there is a dearth of autobiographical literature in Islamic mysticism, there is a first-person genre of writing called supplication (*du'ā*), the calling upon God that expresses the deep personal relationship with God.[32] This, however, does not exactly provide detailed descriptions of the personal experience of God in the sense that I am utilizing here.

I feature Rūzbihān Baqlī both because of the first-person form of his descriptions and, most importantly, because of the originality and frankness of his descriptions. As we will see, although loyal to his tradition, he does not let convention dictate the overwhelming faithfulness to his intimate experiences of unveilings. Unveiling (*kashf*) is essentially experiencing the presence of God directly and personally. Even though the Islamic mystic, like Baqlī, will take Holy Scripture or the Quranic Revelation as his or her guide, and let the *sunna* of the Prophet provide the model of conduct, the path of unveiling is nonetheless distinctive both from the path of reason and from the blind acceptance of the messages related by the prophets and messengers. It is precisely with the writings of Rūzbihān Baqlī, and in particular one of his most important works, a mystical diary of sorts entitled *The Unveiling of Secrets,* that gives us a privileged phenomenological account of vertical experiences in the religious sense.

Modes of Unveiling

The modes of presence that exceed presentation can only be regarded as a kind of absence to the extent that presentation is our standard of givenness, namely, as "other than" presentation. But because other kinds of experiencing are given, they can be discerned and described; that is, they can be treated philosophically in the spirit of phenomenology no matter how curious they may seem from the standpoint of presentation. These kinds of evidence do not presume an "absence"; rather, they testify to different kinds of presence, modes of vertical givenness. We have examined these other kinds of givenness in St. Teresa of Avila as "prayer" and in Rabbi Dov Baer under the rubric of "ecstasy." For Rūzbihān Baqlī, the Islamic mystic, one of the predominant expressions that evokes this kind of vertical presence is "unveiling."

Unveiling (*kashf*) is a significant expression in Islamic mysticism. In Muslim societies, the veil demarcates a domain of intimacy, seclusion, privacy; and removing the veil signifies a privileged entry into that domain. For Baqlī, the imagery of the veil pertains not only to social relations, but most profoundly to inter-Personal relations. Where the veil signifies the transcendence of Allah, unveiling expresses the self-revealing or epiphany of God and the entry of the human person into the intimate sphere of divine presence.[33] The experience of the veil and the description of uncovering prompted Baqlī to write a treatise, *Commentary on Veils and Coverings,* or *The Book of the Clouding of the Heart,* which Corbin refers to as a kind of "phenomenology of Spirit" that is not concerned with the sense of history, but rather with the sense of prophetology.[34]

While Baqlī's numerous works were written in both Persian and Arabic, and although he was an extremely prominent figure in his own time and in generations to follow, very few of his own works have been published, let alone translated into Western languages. Henri Corbin has translated and published portions of Rūzbihān's work from several sources in French,[35] and Carl Ernst has translated and published a significant document in English. This latter work bears the English title *The Unveiling of Secrets* [*Kashf al-asrār*] and is a diary of mystical experience occasioned by a friend seeking guidance into the ways of "mystical knowledge and oneness" (§4). "Now I will write with God's aid," records Baqlī, "of the affairs of unveiling, the mysteries of witnessing, the marvels of the kingdom and the angelic realm, the gracious colloquies, and that which appears in ecstasies, God willing" (§56). On his own account, he began writing this "diary" in 577/1181 at the age of fifty-five and completed it in 585/1189 (§7).[36]

Contrary to how we might think of a diary today, that is, as a forum for recording our own reflections for private use or documentation, this diary was written out of love for God and for the spiritual enrichment of other human persons. In fact, it was written, not of his own accord, but at the behest of a friend: "I would like to describe them [the stations and states] to people so that they would love him [Allah] passionately, and be annihilated in the sublimities of his greatness. This is from my love for him, my mercy for his servants, and my sorrow for them; how can they be cut off from him, with nothing?" (§186).

Complying with his friend's request, Baqlī faced a difficulty cited by almost all of the mystics in conveying their experiences to others, to wit, he was asked to present mystical stages and experiences that remain inaccessible to people attuned primarily to ordinary or mundane experience (§5). This difficulty is coupled with another set of difficulties that are not as contingent, that is, they are not due simply to the fact that others may not share the same level of experience. These difficulties are twofold and concern Rūzbihān's attempt to evoke experiences that transcend the very process of description.

First, Baqlī must resort to metaphor because in his estimation experiences of divine presence are beyond *his powers* of description; he blames his inability to describe sufficiently his experiences that surpass "worldly creation" on his own weakness and incapacity and on his lack of comprehension concerning the "qualities of eternity" (§87, cf. §§104, 107, passim). Second, Baqlī writes on other occasions as if these experiences are in and of themselves beyond description independently of his own compromised abilities. "If every atom from the throne to the earth were a tongue for me, I would be unable to describe the Most High, from his perfect beauty and loveliness" (§107). Such an excess, in other words, is due to the fact that these experiences are *of* God, who is ineffable, and *from* God, who transcends any conceptualization, imagery, or attributes: hence, God by nature transcends every expression (§134; cf. §§59, 101, 161, 162, passim).

As we saw in chapter 1, the fact that we cannot give a description adequate to the experience does not necessarily hamper a phenomenological investigation of this sort. Even perceptual experience only gives us "sides" of the object, though it is there fully and inexhaustibly, and hence available for description. In the realm of vertical experiencing, what is required is the power *to evoke* the lived *experience* in such a way that it opens us to a possible experiencing and "seeing" in a "like" *manner.* Rather than these de facto and de jure considerations reducing Rūzbihān to silence, however, he does speak and write, and feels compelled to speak and write—like the other mystics—but he must do so while not taking himself or his metaphors too seriously and by running risks of misunderstanding.

These risks and dangers of misunderstanding include those of anthropomorphism (*tashbih*), the attempt to associate God to human likeness or to any created being; abstraction (*ta'til*), God being removed from creation; and incarnationism, abolishing the majesty of God in the manifestation of God. True enough, Baqlī feels himself particularly susceptible to such accusations at times because God gives himself in Baqlī's visions under human form—even though there are Quranic sources for such anthropomorphic expressions. For example, God gives himself in his visions as in the form of Adam (§116), with hands (§§59, 61), with a face (§124, passim), sitting on a throne, even as playing the lute at the door of the lodge (§114). Still, warns Baqlī, anyone who has not experienced these kinds of unveilings may arrive at the absurd conclusion that his descriptions are actually giving God the form of man (§148). "God forbid that he has a likeness!" writes Rūzbihān, and, quoting Quran 42:11, "'There is no likeness unto him'" (§87 cf. §§112, 191). "God transcends what runs in the thoughts of those who reduce him to abstraction and the fancies of those who understand God in human terms" (§186).[37]

By God being manifest, Baqlī means "the dawning of the light of God's care for the hearts of those who care for him."[38] For the Sufi, this does not mean that God is reducible to creation or is exhausted in creation; such an understanding is what the Sufi wants to avoid in what they understand as the doctrine of incarnationism. If God were manifest in human materiality and not merely human form, the revelation of divine beauty in the beauty of human form, one would run risk of reducing God to the human being. In loving, one does not become identical with the beloved.[39] Thus writes Rūzbihān: "When God, by love and inclination, makes of His faithful one the Desiring and the Desired, the Lover and the Loved, this serf of love assumes toward God the role of Witness-of-contemplation. It is God who, from an eternal contemplation, contemplates Himself in him and clothes him with his own Attributes, without there being any hint of incarnation, since He remains at a distance from everything that is creaturely. Or rather, it is something that escapes the understanding and intelligence."[40]

What we witness here is an understandable hypersensitivity to reifying God and to associating anything or anyone with God (*shirk*)—or anything that comes close to this. The fear expressed here is that if God is "incarnated" in humans, then God is reducible to human presence; one is no longer a prophet or a messenger, but "God." Accordingly, the tendency is to keep God at a remove.

The three dangers mentioned above are in sum reducible to one, namely, *shirk*, or idolatry, to which Muslim spirituality is especially responsive. God does give himself to Rūzbihān in the "theophany of beauty," which is understood as an act of eternal love, the revelation of divine beauty in the beauty of the human form.[41] But because he feels himself particularly susceptible to such criticisms, Rūzbihān is overcome by a need for reticence when describing the supernatural visions of God as they are experienced by him. He complains: "Understand, were it not for fear of the ignoramuses who accuse us of making likenesses of the cause, I would have indicated something of what I have seen of the Truth (glory be to him)" (§129).[42]

Such a problem of the mystic being misunderstood is especially evident in the phenomenon of "ecstatic expressions" (*shaṭḥiyyāt*) or divinely inspired speech within the context of Islamic mysticism in particular, and mystical experience generally understood. This is a topic that is worthy of its own singular treatment, and something I can only mention in passing here.[43]

Ecstatic expressions are not uncommon within Islamic mysticism; in fact, the phenomenon was prevalent and troubling enough for Baqlī to have devoted a commentary to this matter.[44] Perhaps the most frequently cited and most well-known examples of ecstatic sayings within Islamic mysticism come to us from Abū Yazīd al-Bisṭāmī, "Glory be to Me!" and Ḥallāj, "I am the Truth." Examples can certainly be found in other mystics and in other traditions. The basic problem is that taken out of context, removed from the lived, experiential dimension of the mystic from which the expressions emerge, and taken in a mundane sense, the ecstatic sayings on the surface appear not only to go beyond propriety, but to be blasphemous, idolatrous, inconsistent with scripture, or in violation of revealed law.

But *from within* the experience of God (e.g., within "union"), uttered from the dynamic, personal witnessing of God in which God is experienced as the only true "Self" and in which "I" am annihilated within God, it would not necessarily be inconsistent for the mystic to utter something like "I am God." They are not merely "deluded," "idolatrous," or "immature." Furthermore, if from the immanent experience of God the mystic is removed from the veil of the dualism of everyday life in which God is regarded as an exterior object or the pole of attributes, it is not necessarily nihilistic to assert something like "There is no God" or "God is dead." But again, such statements would have to be interpreted by those "of understanding" (Quran 3:7); or if we take dualism as our standard of understanding or "knowing," then such statements would have to be interpreted by the "unknowing."[45]

Stations and States

Just as in the Christian mysticism of St. Teresa there is common distinction between prayer that is acquired and prayer that is given as supernatural or infused, and just as in the case of Rabbi Dov Baer there is a distinction to be made in modes of ecstasy between what we gainsay by our own efforts and what is given by grace, independently of our efforts, so too in Islamic mysticism a common distinction is traditionally made between a station (*maqām*) and a state (*hal*).

Traditionally, a *station* refers to that which is attained by an individual's own striving, acquired, for example, by self-discipline and spiritual exercises. According to the mystic al-Qushayrī, one cannot move from one station to another unless he or she has fulfilled the provisions of the first. For example, whoever has not attained contentedness is not prepared for the station of trust in God; whoever has not acquired the latter is not ready for the station of surrender. In distinction to a station, a *state* is something that comes by the grace of God, is independent of a person's intention or effort, and rather than being acquired, is bestowed and freely given by God.[46]

It is generally understood that the Islamic mystics operate with such a distinction between stations and states. According to Schimmel there is a basic uniformity in the main steps, which entail stages of repentance, trust in God, poverty, varying degrees of love, and gnosis.[47] Yet even a cursory glance at such well-known Islamic mystics as al-Qushayrī, as-Sarrāj, al-Hujwīrī, or ʿAṭṭār, not to mention the vast array of other Sufis, shows clearly that there is anything but uniformity among Islamic mystics as to which experiences qualify as stations and which as states, which stage follows upon the other temporally, in which hierarchical order they are given structurally, the depth or duration of each stage, and so forth.[48] Indeed, I think we should be suspicious if there were *this kind* of uniformity among the Sufis (or among any of the mystics), for the stations and states are expressions of the presence of God; they are ultimately dependent on the spontaneous character of "unveiling," on the uniqueness of the person, and on his or her relation with God. Since the stations and states emerge through that spontaneously creative encounter with God on a radically personal or inter-Personal level in which there is no guarantee for a station or state and no preset formula for its bestowal, one would indeed expect the vertical modes of experience to be unique and peculiar to that individual.

If we are looking for a systematic ordering or for a conformity to a tradition with respect to stations and states, this is not something we will find with Rūzbihān Baqlī. On the surface, this may appear to be a disadvantage, because it is less easy to find familiar markers along a spiritual path, and in terms of exegesis, we cannot just subsume his language under ways of speaking to which we might otherwise be accustomed. But what we lack in conformity, we make up for in the richness and uniqueness of "phenomenological" description. In other words, one of the real benefits we gain from tracking Baqlī is that his descriptions evoke precisely the spontaneity of experience, without trying to conform to a preset standard.[49]

To take a striking and important example (and in distinction to what we might read as a conventional approach), Rūzbihān does not adhere to the "traditional" terminological distinction between a station and a state. This is not to say that he does not work within these conceptual categories or with the meanings that we try to express through these terms. He does. In one revealing section he evokes precisely this difference without the use of these terms. For example, he recalls an earlier time of his own discipleship when, for over a period of twenty years, "the requirements of striving" that had overwhelmed him eventually fell from his heart as though he "no longer approved of them in the court of knowledge." For now, according to Rūzbihān, knowledge was not associated with his own efforts: spiritual exercises, imaginings, discipline (*riyaḍā*), striving (*mūjahidā*), recollecting (*dhikr*); rather, it was accompanied by "grace and other things besides discipline and striving."[50]

If there is to be a witnessing of God through the veils, such an unveiling can only be given by God such that these favors are bestowed "through what he [God] wishes, to whom he wishes, as he wishes." In another locution, God tells Baqlī: "There is no way to me except through me, and by the unveiling of my beauty"; and citing Quran 57:29 as support of this experience, "'Grace is in the hands of God, he gives to whom he wills'" (§164, cf. §148).

What we can gather from these and other telling passages is that, like most of the mystics, Baqlī does operate with this common distinction between *that which is attained by strivings* and *that which is given by grace*—even though the experiences he reports tend to be of the latter nature and no longer as a result of strivings. However (and with the exception of about a dozen instances), rather than using the conventional term *hal* ("state"), as one would expect, to describe the grace-filled unveilings, the overwhelming term he uses is *maqām* ("station").

This tells us that Rūzbihān is less concerned with being compliant to a tradition than with appropriating the usage of the exemplar of mystical experience, the Prophet himself. On several occasions Rūzbihān invokes that spiritual "position" assigned to Muhammad by God, a position that is called, following the Quran, the "praiseworthy station" or the "Station of Praise and Glory" (*maqām mahmūd*) (17:79). In one vision, Rūzbihān asks after both the meaning of the praiseworthy station and the continuous light from the Divine Presence upon an individual's face. According to the locution to Rūzbihān from God, this "place" was the praiseworthy station, and the individual's face was Muhammad's, reflecting the "light of manifestation." "'If you had been able to enter, you would have seen God (glory be to him who is transcendent) without a veil.' And it was said to me, 'This *station* is exclusively Muhammad's, and no one else has access to this station'" (§31, my emphasis; cf. also §§152, 179).

Accordingly, in distinction to the more traditional usage of the term, notice here that station (*maqām*) refers not to one's effort (the convention), but to a grace-filled epiphany and presence of God, or what is in other Sufis' terminology denoted by "state." This is precisely the way Rūzbihān uses this term already before the beginning of his diary proper. He writes: "Praise be to God who ennobles by these *stations* his saints and his prophets *without cause or reason, not because of their striving or discipline*" (§56; my emphasis). It is *this* language that Rūzbihān tends to employ.

To make matters even more complicated, rather than simply reversing the meaning of the terms (so that now "state" would refer to that which is attained through my strivings), in many instances Rūzbihān uses the term "state" (*hal*) interchangeably with "station." For example, he will speak both of a station and a state of the "nearness of nearness" (cf. §47 and §126), and sometimes union is spoken of both as a station and as a state (cf. §126 and §158). Moreover, Baqlī also uses the same term (say, astonishment) for what can occur in an experience that is induced by striving and for what is given through an unveiling.

More importantly and more interestingly, Baqlī does not follow the ordering of the most common stages (e.g., those I named above according to Schimmel). It is not that Schimmel is incorrect, of course, but that Baqlī does not fit this characterization. What we witness instead is an energy that is much more directed to describing as faithfully as possible experiences that seem to transcend ordinary experience and for which there are no ready-made markers. Of necessity, they must be creative evocations. The names of his "stations" therefore reflect the intensely personal, spontaneous nature of the experience, so he names a station according to what takes place in it. For instance, while we might expect something like the "station of annihilation" (§§57, 78, passim), the "station of oneness" (§136), or even the "station of intimacy" (§§32, 138, passim), at first blush it strikes one as peculiar to read the colorful "station where breezes of power scatter" (§185), or the "stations of the witnesses of majesty" (§186), or even the "station of laughter" (§65). In recording such experiences, we are aware of movements obtaining between several stations, within an episodic station, and from higher to lower and from lower to higher experiences.[51]

In brief, by attempting to express the subtlety of variegated experiences, he at the same time tends to gerrymander the traditional lines drawn between the experiential jurisdiction of one stage and another. Since most of these stations are unique in relation to each other, they demand other kinds of expression to evoke their peculiar flavor.

Hide and Seek

Consistent with experiencing the presence of God in terms of "unveiling," the relation between God and Rūzbihān is often couched in terms that are reminiscent of the child's game of "hide and seek." Indeed, Rūzbihān will frequently go so far as to ask God for a particular dimension of unveiling, sometimes receiving the unveiling, sometimes not: "I sought God most high at dawn, but I did not find him" (§116). Or again: "I saw intimations of the cloak of divinity, and I said, 'My God, my friend, and my lord, how long will you make me see the chosen vision within the limits of the cloak of divinity? Show me pure eternity and divine presence!' And he said, 'Moses and Jesus perish in this station'" (§45). We even get the sense of self-admonishments from him for entering a childish "station of censuring and complaining" when he does not get what he desired (§58).

On the one hand, the reported entreaties convey that there is an intimate, friendly proximity between Baqlī and God, that he is so close to God that he can ask "favors" of him, though they are not in and of themselves the goals of the experience. The entreaties have more the sense of wanting to be more intimate with or spending more time with a loved one, pleading with God not to let him associate other things with God.[52]

On the other hand, such an appeal shows God as comforter, and it betrays an underlying confidence on Rūzbihān's part that God will grant a station or state to the faithful, that is, one attempting to live from "perfection" and a sincere heart. Despite the fact that Baqlī is the one doing the asking, it is not Baqlī who manages the spiritual stations, but God, and only at God's will. Accordingly, Baqlī's entreaties are not anything like a "cause" or a provocation. As Baqlī confirms over and again: "I saw nothing with these forms except what God wished" (§133).

The game of hide and seek that we see played on the field of Rūzbihān's heart and conscience (examples of which are replete in this journal) shows something still more. We ask after the presence of God because we are often not attentive to the presence of God as he gives himself *in the first place:* "So I implored him; I saw him in the outer world of the hidden, and I did not recognize the reality of union with him." We look, we search, we implore, but we are not attentive to that presence: "And I said, being in a mood of expansiveness, "Where were you when you hid during the music?' And he who is transcendent said, 'I was with you, as I am now, as you see me!' . . . And I said, 'My God, why did I not see you there?' He said, 'I was behind you, and above you, watching you, and on your right and left, as you see me now.' . . . And I saw the ocean of holiness, and he manifested himself in the whole of it with the sign of satisfaction. It was as if he were laughing in my face with these lights. I learned that this was the station of laughter, and my conscience and my state at that moment were happy" (§65).

In the beginning we seem to be pro-active, according to Baqlī, but in the end, even our efforts are really not our own efforts, but God working through us for his glory. For as it is stressed in the Quran, God is closer to us than we are to ourselves (50:16). Thus, it is not simply the case that we are seeking God in our efforts but that it is God who is and has been seeking us, and what is realized is that our seeking God is ultimately God seeking us for himself. In another interlocution from God, Rūzbihān relates: "You are seeking me and I am seeking you; if you look, you will find me in yourself, without taking the journeys of the hidden" (§196). Or again: "I reached the fields of pre-eternity, and the Truth (glory be to him) welcomed me and said, 'I have journeyed for your sake from the heart, from the valleys of identity; in each of its valleys existence is smaller than a mustard seed. My only goal is to visit you; sometimes I have helped you while you are sleeping, from the start of the evening to the time of awak-ing.' Then he manifested himself with a thousand attributes in a thousand stations, each with the quality of annunciation and satisfaction. Whenever I saw him in an attribute, he said to me, 'I love you. No sorrow will affect you, because [one only feels] it after a loss. I remain yours, so do not sor-row, nor be distressed because of thoughts and calamities'" (§198).

Having seen the tenor of the interchange between Rūzbihān Baqlī and God, I want to turn now to the issue of how the experiences (the stations and states) are ordered so as to discern the different modes of presence of God in his experience.

Ordering of Experience

At the age of fifty-five, the time he wrote his diary, Rūzbihān Baqlī reports one of his first callings to the mystical path. He writes that he was fifteen years old when it was as though he were being addressed from the hidden world. After going into the desert seeking water for ablutions, he was agitated by a beautiful voice saying "something concerning the divine oneness," and he remained there until the night. He records being afraid from a ravishing and a bewilderment that befell him, and then not returning to his grocery shop until dawn "in ecstasy, distress, sighs, and tears." We read: "On my tongue without volition came the words 'Your forgiveness! Your forgiveness!' . . . My tongue was stilled, and it was as though I was sitting for days together." After ecstasy overwhelmed him, he threw into the road the money box and whatever was in the shop for time of scarcity; he tore his clothes and headed to the desert. He then recalls remaining in that way for a year and a half, ravished and astonished, weeping and ecstatic. "Great ecstasies and hidden visitations happened every day. . . . Then I settled down from that distress" (§§10–11).

Having recovered from the "veiling" of his early life, he longed for the service of the Sufis, shaved his head, entered among the Sufis, "and worked in their service and undertook strivings and exercises." It is patent from his account that these ravishings, bewilderments, ecstasies, astonishments, tears, still had the tenor of experiences that correspond to his own strivings and exercises. He confirms: "But nothing in the way of hidden unveilings happened to me until one day I was on the roof of the lodge, meditating on the hidden world." It was at this time, as yet without a master, that the Prophet, Abū Bakr, 'Umar, 'Uthman, and 'Ali all passed in front of him—an event he discerns as his first unveiling (§§12–13).

From the record of these early experiences and what has been said previously, it is already clear that Baqlī operates with the distinction between those spiritual experiences that can be attributed to our own efforts and those that are given without prior cause or motivation. Spiritual practices, recollection, strivings, and even asceticism are all necessary in the beginning, as long as they are carried out from loving. This will dispose oneself to possible experiences that transcend what we ourselves "can" do.

In this respect, his understanding is similar to what we have encountered in St. Teresa of Avila and Rabbi Dov Baer. Just how he understands the ordering of those states or stations, however, is another question. On this, Baqlī is not clear, though admittedly, it was not his purpose to clarify that ordering of experience explicitly. It was enough to record them for his friend, and in the process of doing this, to cite the distinctiveness of those that were more pronounced or significant for his internal growth and closeness to God.

Yet even if Baqlī is not entirely consistent in his characterizations or terminology, there is enough uniformity to warrant interpretation. By carefully considering the passages in which he speaks of these stations, it is possible to discern, at least in broad strokes, not just their internal character but their relation to one another.

Since they are the main focus in this journal, I am concerned here primarily with the stations/states that occur by virtue of grace. Proceeding from "lower" to "higher," we can begin with what Baqlī terms being "clothed with divinity" (iltibās)—a term that he borrows from the Sufi tradition. "Being clothed with divinity" is an experience that actually covers several stations. In effect, it is the presence of God as apparent in visible form, symbolically mediated experience; it concerns the human self being clothed by the selfhood of God (cf. §§153, 175, passim).[53]

Moving in terms of the depth of experience, we can situate what Rūzbihān terms the *station of intimacy*. The station of intimacy is often described along with the station of love and the station of longing and passion. Here he will speak of "visitations" (wāridat) from God, which are distinct from mere apparitions, since the former appear and disappear, whereas the latter "enters the heart and settles in the heart, encountering the conscience. . . . The basis of visitation is the unveiling of the goal of the Gnostic, which enters spontaneously, increasing his longing."[54] As Rūzbihān writes in his diary: "Oceans of ecstasy, spiritual states, gladdening visitations weighed with longing, love, and passion. . . . I was in the station of intimacy, happiness, and the spirit was in a place such that I melted (unveiled and hid)" (§143).

The station of intimacy is further described as a privileged proximity to God, but one nevertheless that still admits of a spiritual distance between himself and God. "Then he hid, and then his face appeared from the window of the angelic realm, and he plundered my heart and spirit.

Then his essence and attributes appeared, and he drew me until there was only *a cubit between us*. I looked at his majesty and beauty, and I was intimate with him, and passionate, and I remained in that state for hours" (§167; my emphasis).

Finally, as admitting of distance between himself and God, "intimacy" is given as prior to union. His heart, he tells us, is between veiling and manifestation (*tajallī*) or "the dawning of the light of God's care for the hearts of those who care for him," between ecstasy (*wajd*)[55] or "the heart's comprehension of the sweetness of encountering the light of pre-eternity, the purity of witnessing, and the delight of speech," and nothingness; his intellect is awaiting lordly commands, his conscience witnessing might, his tongue describing eternity, his eyes burning with tears.[56] All this remains *until* "the Truth (glory be to him) witnessed me in the form of sweet union, and I witnessed the Truth with unveiled majesty and beauty" (§132).[57]

In distinction to the station of intimacy (and those stations associated with it), the *station of nearness* is characterized as an experience of God now with complete proximity, revealing a closer relation to God. Such an experience is marked by a forceful overwhelming of Rūzbihān by God. God is portrayed, for example, as seizing Rūzbihān with his hand, or again, his heart is described as living steel, and God attracts it to itself as if a "magnet of oneness" to the station of nearness (§170). God promises to show him his beauty and majesty and to give this to him forever, just as he wishes, without a veil; this experience is accompanied by not only visual but also auditory beauty (§37, cf. §104).

He writes: "The Truth (who is transcendent) honored me, *no distance* remained between us. I saw from the face of God most high a beauty and a majesty and glory, from seeing which the inhabitants of heaven and earth would have all died from pleasure. Then I saw the regions of heaven and earth filled with him. And I was with him, until he made me present in the station of nearness of nearness, above everything, and he manifested upon me seventy thousand majesties, beauties, and perfections" (§47; my emphasis). In the station of nearness, God manifests himself to Rūzbihān in a special way with no one between him and God. He cries out, weeping, drowning in what he calls the oceans of nearness. "Then he approached me until no distance remained between us, and I was sitting by him" (§104).

Above the station of intimacy and beyond complete proximity that characterizes the station of nearness, is the *station of union*. Since the former stations are also given by God without cause or being linked explicitly to our efforts, it is likewise the Holy who raises Rūzbihān to the station of union. Notice, for example, that what Rūzbihān calls "sweet union" is dependent on God raising him to himself, "witnessing him" in it, which corresponds to Rūzbihān's witnessing the Truth in unveiled majesty (§132). It is important to note here that while Christian mystics generally characterize union or some dimension of union as the ultimate mystical stage, meaning a kind of divine oneness with God, this is not the case with Baqlī and some other Sufis. Indeed, Baqlī does also speak of a *station of oneness,* but we should not conflate the two experiences, union and oneness, or presuppose out of hand that they are the ultimate stages.

The station of union emphasizes the inter-Personal dimension of experience that transcends both distance from God and proximity to God (intimacy and nearness). The station of oneness, however, has a slightly different nuance; it emphasizes our taking God absolutely as absolute, beyond imagination, strivings, likenesses, or temporal and spatial dimensionality. Here, it is all external, relative spatio-temporal things that are "annihilated" such that it is God, as essence, who stands alone: the focus of our witnessing is nothing else but the holiness of the Holy (§135). In Baqlī's diary, such an experience of oneness takes place at a deeper level of intensity than the station of union. We read, for example: "I remained in his majesty and beauty, and that is the state of the nearness of nearness, and the union of union. That state remained *until* he annihilated *everything but himself* from *my* thought and *my* conscience. I remained there, in the essence of the essence, and the reality of reality" (§126, my emphasis).

This sense of oneness is again confirmed in other passages. For example, in a station that he cites as having been nearer than any he had been granted by God heretofore, Rūzbihān again recalls what almost has the tenor of a reproach or instruction by God: "Have you seen anything of existence, have you seen space, have you seen time, have you seen form, have you seen anything of temporal causes or existing beings? It is I, you see me in the form of majesty, power, and divine presence. This is the world of oneness, and this is the station of oneness" (§152). Things no longer have any significance for the mystic; everything else is extinguished; only God stands alone.

The station of oneness, however, is not the deepest of stations. Characterizing an even deeper level of experience and gift from God is the *station of annihilation* [*fanā*].[58] Annihilation is deeper than union because in union there is still the experience of (the self) being united with God. Annihilation is also deeper than the station of oneness because, while there is the experience of all spatio-temporal creation as if it were nothing (nothing, that is, compared to greatness of God as essence), the status of the self is as yet not described in this experience except as precisely witnessing the oneness of God. In annihilation, however, it is the self that is annihilated in God and that is of no essential significance. According to Baqlī, in the station of annihilation one does not experience with the intellect; the consciousness of the self vanishes. Or to it put differently, one does not see with his or her own eyes (§78, cf. §66). All creation and all creatureliness, including my consciousness of self, is annihilated in the brilliance of God. "Anything but God most high is annihilated in less than an eye blink. The Truth remains unveiled in the beauty of oneness and the power of endlessness. He said, 'Everything is perishing but his face' [Quran 28:88]. That is the station of singleness and annihilation. I remained astonished and was annihilated, and I do not know where I was" (§109).

In a strict sense, when one experiences annihilation, he or she cannot properly speak of a station of annihilation because "I" am not, but only "am" (in) God; perhaps this is the sense of Rūzbihān's speaking of a station in which no station remains (§148).

Finally, Baqlī relates another experience that transcends even that of annihilation, namely, *subsistence* or "abiding" (*baqā*). Although Abū Bakr al-Kharraz (d. 899) is credited with having been the first to discuss *fanā* and *baqā* within the mystical tradition,[59] the station of subsistence, like that of annihilation, has its source in the Quran (e.g., 55:26–27), and according to how each Sufi experiences these stations, he or she will give it a different nuance. Generally speaking, however, subsistence is understood as life in God, where, after annihilation, multiplicity becomes manifest once more in a modified form, as determinations of one Truth, one Reality.[60] In 'Aṭṭār, for example, the valley of union (*tawḥīd*) is followed by the valley of blessed perplexity (*ḥayrat*), which is followed by the valley of poverty and nothingness (*faqr o fanā*), which in turn is succeeded by subsistence (*baqā*).[61] He writes,

> After that, by grace restored those mortal birds
> to themselves, but with no further mortality.
> When all were restored to themselves without selves,

they came upon subsistence [*baqā*] after annihilation [*fanā*].
Recent or ancient, there can never be
any talk of that annihilation [*fanā*], nor that subsistence [*baqā*].
Just as that day is far far from our sights,
its description is far from being explained or described.
Thus our masters have only attempted to explain
this state of subsistence after annihilation through allegories.
(4271–4275)[62]

For Baqlī, *baqā* is the subsistence of the spirit in witnessing God without disturbance, or again, the subsistence of what he calls "conscience in unity"; accordingly, it is a difference, or personal individuation *sustained in* God; this is to say that the "createdness" of the creature abides (creation does not dissipate), yet it abides not as merely human or "animal," but as divinized.[63] As Baqlī puts it in a commentary on "unknowing," after the seeker becomes annihilated in his seeking, "subsistence brings him into the Essence (*'ayn*) so that subsistence may be subsistent."[64] Thus, rather than a self liquidated in God, *baqā* is a free giving of the "Self" back to the Self, now as a Holy "Self," as a living from God and by God. This is why the mystical journey for Baqlī (as for others), does not culminate in a dissolution of the individual personality or in a crude pantheism, for *baqā* indicates a sustenance of what we would call the person as "individuated" in God (on "Individuation," see chapter 7).[65] According to this reading, union would be understood as a distinctive station that is followed by the station of oneness, which is deepened by the experience of annihilation of Self and then culminates in the subsistence of the "Self" in and from God, as a kind of difference in unity.[66]

This, however, is not the only reading of these stations where Baqlī is concerned. A different one is provided by Corbin, though in its own way it confirms the order of these last three stations that I have presented. Rather than placing the station of union (*tawḥīd*) as prior to the stations of oneness, annihilation, and subsistence, Corbin understands the latter three stations as *different degrees of tawḥīd*, or union. According to him, the station of oneness corresponds to what Corbin calls a first *tawḥīd*, the movement from the "visible world" to God (*az 'alam-e molk be-ḥaqq*); annihilation corresponds to what he designates as a movement of *tawḥīd* from the personal self to God (*az khwod be-ḥaqq*); subsistence, finally, corresponds to the annihilation of this annihilation. For Corbin, this movement originates from God to God, but is the "resurrection and reappearance" from what had been merged through annihilation in indifferentiation in the identity of the Divine.[67]

At least where Baqlī's diary is concerned, however, I do not see the justification for reducing these latter three stations to mere moments of "union" whereby union itself would not be transcended by the experience of oneness, annihilation, or subsistence. There is nothing in a mystic's experience, generally, or in Baqlī's experience, specifically, that maintains that union must be the highest experience. Moreover, and perhaps more problematic, Corbin wants to express these latter stages in terms that are reminiscent of moments of a Hegelian dialectic (a positive oneness or union, a negation: annihilation of self, and "sublation" as the negation of the negation: subsistence). But this dialectical reading can lead to a profound misunderstanding if these stages are expressive of vertical modes of experience. Vertical experience has, not a dialectical, but an "absolute" nature. This is to say that both annihilation of self and subsistence are *positive* experiences, *positive* modes of presence given by/of God. One cannot derive the unique personal experience of *baqā* from the negation of *fanā*. Finally, even though one experience may be "higher" or more profound than another or may have factually been given before or after another, they are not essentially determined as temporally ordered. Rather, they indicated dimensions of "reality."

In the final analysis, although Corbin confirms the ordering of the last three stages, we understand the experience of union as a distinctive experience in Baqlī, one that is followed in terms of depth, and not necessarily chronologically in his case, by the experience of God as essence or oneness, further by annihilation of self, and ultimately by free givenness of personal individuation *in and by* God as subsistence.

Couched in vivid language, locutions, and visions consistent with Islamic mysticism, Rūzbihān Baqlī coveys what we call vertical experiences in rich and textured modes of "unveilings." Although it is guided by certain signposts within his tradition, the order of this religious experiencing does not follow a predetermined structure but is presented by Baqlī as lived-through. Straddling experiences like being "clothed with divinity" through union and annihilation and subsistence, such experiences are marked by a personal, qualitative uniqueness of his experience of the Holy.

Not only Baqlī's descriptions but indeed all of these experiences from the Abrahamic mystics are sure to strike us as unordinary, not just because they might be unfamiliar to us, stemming as they do from religious traditions different from our own, if from any religious tradition at all. Rather, these descriptions appear alien and disorienting because of the very nature of the experiences themselves, expressed here in terms of prayer, ecstasy, and unveiling.

We might ask, though, is it really meaningful to speak of evidence in the religious sphere, and specifically with respect to experiences covered under the rubrics of prayer, ecstasy, and unveiling? Is it sensible philosophically to grant to such religious experiences the very status of "evidence"? How would it even be possible for us to adjudicate the experiences as "authentic"? Are there not possibilities of fantasy, hyperbole, error, illusion, delusion, or expressions of unfilled wishes that intervene and hamper such a portrayal and intrude on the integrity of so-called vertical experiences? Do they even have any integrity, and if so, are not the experiences just simply too idiosyncratic? Even if we are at all willing to concede the possibility of evidence here, how can the mystics themselves, those who lay claim to the genuineness of such experiences, contribute any clarity to this predicament?

In the next chapter I address the phenomenological issue of evidence with respect to these kinds of vertical experiences (chapter 5), working out in the subsequent chapters the philosophical implications they have for the tenor of the vertical givenness called epiphany (chapter 6), the significance this has for the philosophical problem of individuation (chapter 7), and finally, the impact this has on our understanding of idolatry and the challenges it issues to verticality (chapter 8).

Matters of Evidence
in Religious Experience

My orientation from the outset has been that the matters described by the mystics of the Abrahamic tradition in terms of prayer, ecstasy, and unveiling are lived through human experience. As such they can be approached philosophically—specifically, in the style of phenomenology —no matter how difficult these kinds of experience are to deal with, no matter to what extent they seem to exceed the bounds of what we take for granted as experience, no matter how they rub against our own philosophical prejudices. To do this, however, this vertical dimension of experience *has to be taken on its own terms* and not subordinated to how objects are given to us in perception, or evaluated according to philosophical narrow-mindedness, or accepted or rejected according to presuppositions of religious belief. A religious experience can only be confirmed or treated as deceptive within the context of religious experience itself (a moral experience within the moral, etc.), in its own "language," as it were. This is certainly the case with the mystics I examine here. On the one hand, this means that we cannot appeal to standards outside of the lived religious sphere to measure the authenticity of a religious experience. On the other hand, as lived, as experienced, it thereby opens itself for us to phenomenological description and investigation according to its philosophical significance.

For a particular type of experience that falls generally under the rubric of "the religious," I have turned to the mystics rather than, say, to theological investigations into the religious. The mystics are personal witnesses to a radical kind of experiencing, what I have termed "vertical" experiencing. I have called the type of vertical experience peculiar to this religious domain "epiphany." By examining three mystics (St. Teresa of Avila, Rabbi Dov Baer, and Rūzbihān Baqlī), who for my purposes are exemplary of these Abrahamic traditions, I have attempted to depict *how* the Holy is given in these radically personal forms. It is these constitutive features that make up what we understand by "religious" and qualify the religious sphere as such. Having been attentive to these unique personal forms of experience, I am now in a position to describe the mode and the structure of epiphanic givenness and its kind of evidence. In subsequent chapters I examine the implications of epiphany in relation to withdrawal and the fundamentally related issues of "individuation," and then expound upon the nature of idolatry.

Religious experiencing constitutes its own sphere of evidence; it has its own modes of givenness that are distinct from presentation but no less genuine. This sphere of experience has its "truth" that cannot be governed by or adjudicated from outside of *this, its own,* domain of experience. Furthermore, it has its own problems and types of deception, modalization, negation, corroboration, and so forth. So for example, as we will see, self-doubt and pride are qualitatively distinct from, say, the kind of doubt we find in perception; the corroboration of a religious experience in historical efficacy has its own integrity and is not a simple modification of an epistemic object as it unfolds concordantly in time. To be sure, if experience is confined to what we call presentation, then anything taking place beyond that sphere could be deemed as merely arbitrary; it is simply "madness," personal quirkiness, something not to be trusted. But for the mystics, these experiences are anything but arbitrary. They have an internal coherence all their own, and there is a lived rigor intrinsic to them.

In this chapter I take up the matter of evidence as it is an issue for these mystics. I do this to discern what qualifies "givenness" in the sphere of religious experience, how it is distinctive, and how deception, illusion, and the like play their role in such a dimension of experience. These are the kinds of issues I address when following the ways in which these three mystics, in their own ways, grapple with and characterize the problem of evidence.

Crucible of Prayer

Mystical experiences have their own evidential character. In the following treatment of vertical experience, as suggested by the writings of St. Teresa of Avila, I discuss three elements of this evidence peculiar to epiphanic givenness: (1) the evidential force of epiphanic givenness, (2) the question of deception and self-deception (i.e., modalizations of evidence), and (3) confirmation and corroboration of evidence.

1. The evidence peculiar to epiphanic givenness is internal to the experiencing itself. According to St. Teresa, in the experience of a certain

kind of prayer, the prayer carries its own force of evidence such that we experience immediately that it is something issuing from God and not from ourselves. It is also from within this experience that one kind of prayer gets differentiated from another and is experienced as *that kind* of prayer in its own right. We have seen that this is something St. Teresa states in many different ways over and over in her descriptions and testimonies of each degree of prayer. But what, more specifically, gives the experience its evidential character?

The problem of evidence for St. Teresa is multifaceted because it involves not just the initial givenness of the Holy as a mode of prayer, but matters of corroboration and confirmation. One quality of experience is clarity (e.g., *Obras,* 534; *Collected Works,* Vol. 2, VI:3.12). For example, when the intellect or imagination fabricates words (in distinction to genuine locutions coming from God, and compared now to those from God), the words are given as though muffled, fancied; when they are from God, they are given with a distinct and *unmistakable clarity*. In addition, she appeals to the *power and authority of the experience itself* that grants certitude. Bearing a great majesty and great authority, "as though speaking with a holy person, even though one does not call to mind who it is that speaks them," they make one tremble, and they concern matters that are very far from one's mind (*Obras,* 135ff.; *Collected Works,* Vol. 1, 25.6ff.). In the case of prayer from God, they are listened to, and one does not have a choice but to hear deeply. (In fact, the term "to obey" originates from the Latin *obedare,* which means to listen deeply, or to pay heed to.) Furthermore, one does not lose a syllable of what is said, she contends, and there is no way of diverting one's attention from the locutions, even if one so desired.

Related to this, she cites the *depth* of experience. In one comparison, she writes that it is like the difference between feeling something on the surface of the body and feeling it in the marrow of one's bones (e.g., *Obras,* 510; *Collected Works,* Vol. 2, V:1.6; *Obras,* 561; *Collected Works,* Vol. 2, VI:10.2). Another important feature is what we could call the *coming-from-elsewhere* of the experience (e.g., *Obras,* 530–31; *Collected Works,* Vol. 2, VI:2.5–8; *Obras,* 569; *Collected Works,* Vol. 2, VII:1.9). The experiences are given in a way that they could not have originated from me; they are beyond the pale of what I could have thought or invented, what I could produce in myself. Even if I try to resist them, they are beyond my capability or will to do so. On some occasions she reports that when she did not want to be taught, she was *made* to understand. Furthermore, the words and visions coming from God affect one so strongly that they are not soon forgotten, even for a person with a poor memory. In short, they are beyond what I myself could contribute or diminish.

A further noteworthy characteristic of this kind of evidence is its *immediacy*. The immediacy of the experience suggests that rather than unfolding over time like a perceptual object with its undisclosed horizons, the experience is marked by a *"suddenness."* "We are taught without losing any time," she writes (*Obras,* 532–33; *Collected Works,* Vol. 2, VI:3.4–7; *Obras,* 554; *Collected Works,* VI:8.6), and this suddenness is clearly discernable from something that is composed, which implies a gradual building up or a temporal expanse (*Obras,* 534; *Collected Works,* Vol. 2, VI:3.12–14). Or again, God accomplishes in a moment what we could not achieve in decades (*Obras,* 96; *Collected Works,* Vol. 1, 17.2).

Similarly, one is "struck," surprised in a way that the experience is not only not anticipated but non-anticipatable (cf. *Obras,* 553; *Collected Works,* Vol. 2, VI:8.3). The elements of *surprise* and *novelty,* however, are not given as aberrations or anomalies in an otherwise concordant flow of events as would be the case for perceptual objects (e.g., while listening to a concert, one could be thrown off guard by a loud explosion or by the building intensity of a crescendo alarm); rather, suddenness is peculiar to the nature of the epiphanic experience itself.

Finally, and related to the former characteristics, peculiar to epiphany is the quality of the completeness or the *fullness* of the experience. I noted above in the chapter on St. Teresa that each stage of experience—be it on the model of watering a garden or of the interior castle—is experienced as fully given. It is not experienced partially or as awaiting now the next level. It is a kind of absolute presence of the Holy, given one time as consolation, another as delight, and so on. But each experience is unique to itself, absolute, non-negotiable, complete—even though such an experience might be surpassed by another gift. It is only by a subsequent experience viewed retrospectively that one can discern that one experience was not as profound as another. But again, they are different in kind, not incremental developments of the same kind.

This is significant for many reasons: First, there is not one kind of vertical experience pertaining to the religious sphere, but many modes of vertical experience that fall under the rubric of "the religious." Second, "mystical union" is not the only kind of vertical experience; rather, vertical experience in the religious sphere is differentiated such that there is a kind of hierarchy of experience, as it were, but not where the "lower" experiences are less authentic. Third, these variations are differentiated, not quantitatively but qualitatively, according to the manner in which they are given. Fourth, related to the former, just because one experience is not as profound as another, this does not diminish its integrity as an authentic experience of/from the Holy. It is still given as a gift, still "infused" or "divine" in its own way and on its own terms.

So when we examine the quality of givenness as described, in particular, by St. Teresa, we can say epiphany has an internal clarity, power and authority, depth, as coming-from-elsewhere; it is immediate, sudden, non-anticipatable, each experience being complete, full, given in an absolute manner. For St. Teresa, these are qualities of the experience that could only be given in the religious experience itself, even though she attempts to evoke them through her descriptions and imagery after the fact.

2. Questions nevertheless arise for St. Teresa on an intimate, personal level with the character of urgency and seriousness regarding the issue of evidence because she has experienced times when she was deceived. Although an experience might be given to her as issuing from God, such a "gift" might still remain problematic on certain levels. She is aware, for example, that convulsions and fainting spells may be mistaken for rapture but in reality have nothing to do with this kind of prayer; others may "fancy that they are being carried away in rapture"—which she calls this "being carried away in foolishness because it amounts to nothing more than wasting time and wearing down one's health" (*Obras*, 506; *Collected Works*, Vol. 2, IV:3.11; *Obras*, 538; *Collected Works*, Vol. 2, VI:4.9). One could similarly mistake melancholy or losing one's mind for an experience of God. Her concern, of course, was not merely epistemic in nature, since the real issue for her was how what we are calling "modalizations" of evidence influenced the ways in which she was and others are able to serve God. If one's "*ordo amoris*"—to use Scheler's term—is not finely tuned, if one mistakes loving for hatred or lives in a disorder of the heart, her fear is that one will ultimately do more harm than good, both to others and to oneself (cf. *Obras*, 491; *Collected Works*, Vol. 2, III:2.2–5).

There are essentially two kinds of modalization that she describes: self-deception and deception from another. In the first case, self-deception or self-delusion may be brought on because one may be so eager to experience the gifts and presence of God that she deludes herself by composing, unbeknownst to herself, things she wants to be told or things she wants to see, thinking they are from God (*Obras,* 534; *Collected Works,* Vol. 2, VI:3.14). St. Teresa's descriptions, in part, were to serve this purpose of thwarting self-deception: "My intention is only to explain the different favors there are on this road, insofar as I understand them. Thus you will know, Sisters, their nature and their effects, lest we fancy that every-thing imagined is a vision" (*Obras,* 560; *Collected Works,* Vol. 2, VI:10.1). There are some individuals, she writes, who "see" everything they think about; locutions, she continues, can be especially illusory when they occur in persons who are melancholic. In this case, it is imperative to take the activity of praying away from the person and to insist emphati-cally that she or he pay no attention to the locution (*Obras,* 531; *Collected Works,* Vol. 2, VI:3.1, 3). At other times one can construct a vision that is derived from "an intense reflection in which some likeness is fashioned." Moreover, delusion may also be brought on by a "weak constitution" due to a great amount of penance and keeping vigil.

Finally, and related to the first point, self-deception can arise from pride. In addition to the production of desired experiences that we might imagine are from God, pride can also issue in self-doubt. Pride is not just a matter of thinking "I'm great," but of taking the self as the focus of the experience, as if it were all about "me"—good or bad. I will come back to the issue of pride in chapter 8. For now, let me simply note that for St. Teresa, pride can make even those who are advanced in prayer go about being disturbed by some minor trial: "Everything in their minds leads them to think they are suffering these things for God, and so, they don't come to realize that their disturbance is an imperfection" (*Obras,* 490–91; *Collected Works,* Vol. 2, III:2.1–3).

The other source of deception is from the "outside," as it were. There are two possible outside sources intimated in St. Teresa's writings: another human being and the devil. In the first case, one can have a poor confessor who does not have experience at a profound enough level. Although the poor confessor or mentor may not wish to do ill, he can nevertheless con-fuse and frighten an individual because he is unsure of himself and fears what is beyond his experience; he finds something to doubt in every-thing and accuses every experience of being a product of melancholy or the devil. In turn—a consequence of this taken from her own life—the individual can suffer from self-doubt and not understand an experience when it is authentic (*Obras*, 41–43; *Collected Works*, Vol. 1, 4. 3–7; *Obras*, 526; *Collected Works*, VI:1.8, *Obras*, 554–55, VI:8.8).

Deceptions can also arise from the devil, according to St. Teresa. For example, the devil can create fears and cause confusion by making use of good virtues; he can create great desires so that one desires the impossible instead of being content with serving God by doing things that are possible; he can cause one to be distressed over the sins and failings of others, to mistake humility for pride so as to abandon prayer; he can transform himself into an "angel of light" so that one makes poor use of good virtues; he can simulate favors from God to leave one with smug self-satisfaction so as to alter a religious path; he can create serious illusions and deceptions so that one thinks she is making progress when she is not. In short, rather than the experiences leading to expansiveness of spirit, when they are from the devil, they are restrictive in relation to the values one prefers in relation to God and to others. For persons who have not advanced very far, devotional feelings and the like may denote a good beginning, but these persons can easily be deceived because the devotional feelings are themselves not sufficient for discerning whether the effects are from a good or a bad spirit (*Obras*, 136–37; *Collected Works*, Vol. 1, 25.9–13).

3. It is with the possibility of deceptions and self-deceptions that the issue of confirming and corroborating evidence of epiphanic givenness becomes an important issue. St. Teresa gives various experiential clues that one can look for and "tests" that one can implement to corroborate a givenness as an authentic epiphanic experience.

In the perceptual sphere, corroborating evidence could occur through the concordance or *Einstimmigkeit* of the object or through the repetition of it in remembering. In the case of epiphanic givenness, however, corroborating evidence can occur through what we might call the *historical efficacy* of prayer. St. Teresa is explicit about this: "But it is in the effects and deeds following afterward that one discerns the true value of prayer; there is no better crucible for testing prayer."[1] These effects of prayer, of course, do not belong to just any domain of experience. Their valence belongs to prayer in this large sense and can be detected only in their religious significance. I will address this issue later in this chapter where the problem is even more poignant for us, particularly in the case of Rūzbihān Baqlī. The point now is that the crucible of historical efficacy suggests that inter-Personal evidence is protracted and literally not "self"-contained. It is expansive, retroactive, future-oriented, and interpersonal. What are some of the effects of prayer to which St. Teresa refers?

It is not possible to mention all the effects, but here are some of the more prominent ones. If the prayer is from God, it leaves a great quiet or peace or calm; otherwise, one is left disturbed or distracted (*Obras,* 555; *Collected Works,* Vol. 2, VI:9.9–10; *Obras,* 90–91; *Collected Works,* Vol. 1, 15.10–12). It may happen, for example, that one begs God to be told something and takes the locution that tells the individual what he or she wants to hear as authentic. But in this case, there is neither peace nor interior delight. Or one may experience being outside of oneself, like in a sleep, but it only yields effects that are precisely like those of sleep (*Obras,* 534; *Collected Works,* VI:3.11–14).

When the favors originate from the devil, according to St. Teresa, not only do they fail to have good effects, but they leave bad ones; no mildness remains in the person, and one is left as though frightened and very grieved (*Obras,* 136–37; *Collected Works,* Vol. 1, 25.11). What at first seemed to be a prayer of quiet leaves an experience of disquiet, self-interest, self-satisfaction; and one is left displeased and agitated without any good effect; the supposed humility left behind is disturbed and without gentleness; there is an interior languishing, and the body is worn down because it was produced by our own strivings. But again, such discernments are only possible for a person of great experience and who is able to compare the "negative" experience against the "positive" one.

Moreover, she writes, one will know if the prayer is not from the devil if there remains a sign that the Lord was present in his prayer; even if the individual "falls," he rises again quickly. For there is a strong desire in prayer that is from God not to abandon it no matter what trial one may undergo. There is also no need, she continues, to go about dredging up things in order to become "humble," since God gives the prayer *in a different manner,* for example, in an embarrassment or a humility that "undoes one" (*Obras,* 92; *Collected Works,* Vol. 1, 15.14). If the prayer is from God, the virtues grow and one improves in service to God seen as love of neighbor; one experiences interior joy and is stirred to praise God. In this sense, the effects of mystical prayer are world-transformative. Furthermore, three distinct qualities are said to be left in the individual: knowing the grandeur of God, self-knowledge, and little esteem of mundane things (*Obras,* 543; *Collected Works,* Vol. 2, VI:6.10). This self-knowledge means directly a humility in the presence of God where such a humility puts a stop to all other thoughts (*Obras,* 535; *Collected Works,* Vol. 2, VI:3.17). If the prayer is not from God, one is filled with pride or self-complacency. In addition, the prayer, vision, or locution is said to issue from God when it remains for a long time and is vivacious; whereas, if it is from the self or from the devil, its duration is short-lived, and in comparison, it is as if dead (*Obras,* 557–58; *Collected Works,* Vol. 2, VI:9.7–10).

If we produce the words, the words do not produce any effect. But when they are from God, the "words are work" such that even when completely agitated and distracted, one is changed completely, and the thought of God or the enjoyment of God is not disconnected from service to God and the growth of virtues. Thus we can say that what St. Teresa means by "effects" here is that the very relation with God is not just a change in the so-called object of experience, but a modification of the very relationship and hence of the experience itself. *One becomes different through the experience,* in this case, *in the manner of holiness.* "I" am brought into divine focus, and through my deeds, the world is brought into divine focus. The lack of historical efficacy, however, should induce suspicion. This is why, when speaking of the prayer of rapture, St. Teresa writes, "If the beneficial effects are not present, I would greatly doubt that the raptures come from God; on the contrary, I would fear lest they be caused by the rabies, as St. Vincent observed" (*Obras,* 114; *Collected Works,* Vol. 1, 20.23; cf. *Obras,* 540; *Collected Works,* Vol. 2, VI:4.17).

Another way of confirming or corroborating prayer that is implied in St. Teresa's writings is to consider whether the prayers could have been garnered by oneself or in any human way (*Obras,* 529–30; *Collected Works,* Vol. 2, VI:2.4, 7; *Obras,* 569; *Collected Works,* Vol. 2, VII:1.9). One could try, for example, to counterfeit the clarity or the effects, composing these words in the same way (*Obras,* 534–35, Vol. 2, VI:3.12–16). There should, however, be a great difference between those prayers given without any effort on our part, and those that we generate or compose (*Obras,* 545–46; *Collected Works,* Vol. 2, VI:6:7–9). If one were to meditate for many years, she contends, one could not have these tears, these delightful pains, these emotions of peace, calm, and joy, since there is an experiential, qualitative difference. One could also try to resist the gifts and favors or to distract oneself from the prayers, as St. Teresa herself did. If they are from God, there will be no way to avoid them (cf. *Obras,* 694–95; *Collected Works,*

Vol. 3, "Foundations," 6.5–6; *Obras,* 132; *Collected Works,* Vol. 1, 24.2). Finally, a locution or experience has its origin in God, she writes, if it is in conformity with Sacred Scripture (*Obras,* 177, 137; *Collected Works,* Vol. 1, 32.17, 25.13)—which, it is noteworthy to add, is St. John of the Cross's avowed mode of assessment, at least in the most important or difficult matters.[2]

It is important to mention that these so-called "tests" cannot be understood as external measures to be applied from the outside or as "proofs" of the veracity of a givenness; rather, they are clues that only make sense for those undergoing such experiences, or more broadly, within the religious domain of experience itself—again, a point I take up later in this chapter. Only within the experience itself can we sense the integrity of the effects, for example, if what one took as a gift from God did not actually lead to virtuous actions, but instead induced pride or deception.

Identifying the difference between experiences is something quite difficult for beginners, St. Teresa contends. The more experience one has in these matters, the deeper the experiences go, the better able one will be to identify the differences between these experiences, to move with security, and not to fear counterfeit prayers (*Obras,* 530; *Collected Works,* Vol. 2, VI:2.6–7; *Obras,* 576; *Collected Works,* Vol. 2, VII:3.10). For if one has not had a great deal of experience, she observes, one will not be able to discern an authentic prayer from a disingenuous one—and in fact, one must have so much experience that one needs "to come close to the very summit of prayer in order to have such discernment" (*Obras,* 86, Vol. 1, 14.8). Nonetheless, even if advanced in prayer, one should still not go about with an overconfidence that could easily instill pride. A madman too, St. Teresa recognizes, cannot divert his attention or think of anything else or be reached by reason, but this does not mean that the prayer is from God (*Obras,* 695; *Collected Works,* Vol. 3, "Foundations," 6.7). Thus, such a test cannot be sufficient; the verification cannot merely be a self-test, as it were.

In addition to the inter-Personal dimension of such experience, another interpersonal dimension is still necessary in all phases and for all persons: what she refers to as an experienced, very spiritual person, or a "confessor."[3] She will even go so far as to say that although one may be quite certain, for example, that a locution is from God, if it concerns something serious about oneself or concerns another, nothing should be done without the consultation of a learned and prudent confessor and servant of God (*Obras,* 534; *Collected Works,* Vol. 2, VI:3.11). The issue of a confessor is not at all unproblematic. While an experienced confessor can facilitate the life of prayer and can help one recognize the difference between authentic and inauthentic prayer, an inexperienced confessor can cause much harm, as happened in her own case (see, e.g., *Obras,* 80–82; *Collected Works,* Vol. 1, 13.11–19).

A vision, a locution, or a prayer cannot, of course, be witnessed by the confessor. It may not even be able to be explained by the one who experiences it. For this reason, the confessor may rightly act with hesitation. But, she continues, if the confessor has experience and has undergone similar experiences, he will need little time to discern their origin. In any case, one should always give an account of prayer (*Obras,* 558; *Collected Works,* Vol. 2, VI:9.11–12).

The ultimate court of appeal for the authenticity and integrity of prayer is grounded in the very "supernatural," or "infused" experience itself. This comes out at those occasions when St. Teresa is forced to confront the opinions of other religious persons, confessors, and sometimes even scripture with her understandings gained by infused experiences, especially as they concern the "sacred humanity" of Jesus.[4]

My point in mentioning this is not to suggest that St. Teresa of Avila directly challenged religious tradition—though it must be kept in mind that at the time of her writing, she was held under suspicion by the Inquisition and her "Book of Her Life" was impounded by the church fathers. Rather, I am observing that what gives the experience of epiphanic givenness its evidential force is ultimately internal to the very experience itself, the inter-Personal movement itself, which is infused in interpersonal history.

I have noted that St. Teresa has a compelling interest in determining the tenor of prayer. Having said all this, she admits that we, in our limited ways, may never be in a position to do this completely. So rather than get entangled in evaluations of deception, possibly wasting one's time, and perhaps insidiously removing oneself from prayer (understood in its larger sense), she offers throughout her writings the following instruction:

First, one should love God without self-interest and with humility. Since virtue is a matter not of enjoying God's presence but of doing service to God in working, suffering, and loving, one should avoid desiring consolations, delights, and favors of all kinds.[5] St. John of the Cross also gives this advice, writing that sanctity and loving does not consist in feeling great things but in having great detachment and in suffering for the Beloved.[6] Even if a vision is not from God, writes St. Teresa, it will do one no harm if he or she acts out of humble service (*Obras*, 558–59; *Collected Works*, Vol. 2, VI:9.12).

Second, one should live obediently. This feature comes especially to the fore in the work of her "Foundations." The point of obedience lies not in relinquishing responsibility but in refusing to act from self-interest or from mundane motivations. Put positively, it consists ultimately in acting from God in the world, conforming one's will to the will of God.[7]

Trials in Divine Ecstasy

In chapter 3 I described ten levels of ecstasy discerned by the Mitteler Rebbe through which God can be said to be experienced. The first five Dov Baer described as "natural" forms of ecstasy requiring some effort on our part. The latter five were depicted as divine forms of ecstasy beyond our efforts and received as a special kind of gift.

When, in the course of his *Tract on Ecstasy,* Dov Baer deals with the problem of evidence, he appeals to qualities internal to the ecstatic experience. For example, the wealth of the ecstasy is gauged according to its interior, direct presence of God in distinction to an ambient exteriority; the more genuine the ecstasy, the more deeply it is felt. Authentic ecstasy is accompanied by a transvaluation of the divine and worldly, with a positive orientation toward God. Longing for God is yoked with a detesting of sin (*Tract*, 71); the more genuine the ecstasy, the more it is accompanied by expansiveness, warmth, great inner vitality, as being without cause, or given without limit (*Tract*, 77–78). Ultimately, the ecstasy is experienced as issuing from one will (i.e., not separate wills; my will and God's will are experienced as one [*Tract*, 83–84]).

This said, it must also be noted that Dov Baer's main focus in this *Tract* with respect to evidence concerns more the dangers of self-deception and delusions that can occlude the ecstatic/prophetic experience of God than the direct testimony to genuine experiences. Like St. Teresa of Avila, the Rabbi identifies these problems, not for the sake of cataloguing these or those difficulties, but because they effect the very becoming of persons and their style of loving and hating. He describes the various stages of ecstasies and the problems to which we could succumb in a typology of sorts so that those who truly seek God and desire nearness to God can take "good care to fix their souls and hearts firmly in the Lord" and not fall into self-delusion (*Tract,* 141). The danger, as Dov Baer puts it on several occasions, is that through repeated self-deceptions and delusions, our talent for "hearing" might cease; by becoming absorbed with things, we might ourselves sink into the category of inanimate things and regard other persons in the same way; through this inversion of values, our hearts may become dulled and no longer alert to God.[8] Rabbi Dov Baer targets these inhibitions of the presence of God in phenomena like delusion and self-deception rooted principally in pride. But whereas St. Teresa also adds to this the power of the devil, Dov Baer cites the divisive force of the *sitra achra.*[9]

Dov Baer identifies dangers along the spiritual path, formulated at times in the manner of rebukes—understandable, given the dialogical nature of his treatise—as they pertain to levels of experiencing. "This matter is very subtle," writes Dov Baer, "with many nuances in the stages of subtlety" (*Tract,* 71). While one could find many of the dangers to be mentioned at other levels of experiencing too, and even though these levels will share similar traits, there is a particular danger belonging to specific types of divine ecstasy, spiritual growth, or experienced presence of God.

In identifying delusions and self-deceptions, the Rabbi first of all treats sham ecstasies, that is, kinds of behavior that appear from the outside to be authentic ecstasy but are really corrupted. In the case of the so-called natural ecstasy of the "external cry," we find instances of excessive self-awareness resembling those who are typically proud and haughty in worldly matters. Neither an intention toward nor a desire for the Divine, this kind of experience is cultivated by those whose only interest is in the pure rush of ecstasy or the achievement of some measure of vitality. Dov Baer calls these people "addicts" to pleasure; they assert themselves before God in the hope that they might be "something" special, thinking, in the words of Isaiah: "I am, and there is none else." Such is the cry of "self-worship" (*der hören sich mehr mit*) and not at all "God-worship." The point of achieving ecstasy here is only for the individual's own pleasure and not the service of or cleaving to God, being "in no way for the Lord" (*Tract,* 67–70, 78–79).

If the former instance of sham ecstasy can be called a physical materialism, then the next form can be called a spiritual materialism. In this instance there is in fact an intention toward virtue, but its motivation lies in doing good deeds for one's own benefit or to acquire fame. Being perfectly righteous in their own eyes, those who live in this way want the Lord to be glorified for their own names' sake (*Tract,* 119ff.). Thus, although one may be attached to cleaving, this attachment ultimately gets in the way of cleaving to God.

According to Dov Baer, the presence of God in divine comprehension or *daat* is not due simply to the profundity of the intellectual inquiry or merely to the subject matter. If this were the case, it could not allow for the occasions in which very brilliant people remain "empty" or very complex subject matters leave one "dry." Furthermore, divine ecstasy has to be distinguished from the kind of "rush" one may get by finally understanding some very difficult problem, since the measure of the person in the presence of God is not intellectual adeptness. True cleaving is in no way comparable to intellectual comprehension, which is peculiar to the natural soul (*Tract,* cf. 68, 95, 97). One is "moved out of Egypt" into the prophetic voice, one "hears" or "tastes" in a divine manner, "only as a result of the Source" (*Tract,* 96).

Having mentioned these two main forms of sham ecstasy, let me describe, in ascending order, the confusions, pitfalls, and difficulties relevant to the five stages of *divine* ecstasy addressed by Dov Baer.

On the level of *nefesh,* the chief confusion for those who seek and desire the nearness of God is self-delusion. Self-delusion is not due to ignorance, explains the Rabbi, but rather to a "weakness of effort" and to a "general faint-heartedness in will and concern for all the words of the living God." Now it may seem contradictory to assert that a problem of self-delusion arising on the level of *divine* ecstasy is due to a lack of *effort,* since the modes of divine ecstasy are beyond our effort. Dov Baer's point, however, would seem to be threefold. First, our effort is necessary, even if divine presence is not provoked by our effort. Second, we delude ourselves in thinking that non-effort is the opposite of effort, for on this level non-doing is really just another mode of doing. If divine ecstasy comes about, it is not due to our effort or non-effort, since as a gift, it is beyond both our effort and non-effort. It would be a great sign of pride to think that we could usher in divine ecstasy by our non-doing as well as by our doing.

Third, faint-heartedness in will or effort does not arise on the basis of a general malaise, but on the basis of something else that now occupies the place of God. For example, because such persons may be completely absorbed in their business affairs with their whole being, they cannot bear the yoke of deep concentration, tending to remain "cold" and jaded, such that the Holy cannot become a *personal* concern (*Tract,* 142). Laxity shows up in not taking responsibility for the hindrances of and attraction to material things. "Even though his soul weeps in secret and he is truly aggrieved, pride and the ties of self-love cover everything, to the extent that he sees no fault at all in himself and in his own eyes the way of every man is pure" (*Tract,* 141). This attitude amounts to a relativity of values: "I'm OK, you're OK." Desiring God may sound good to us, but we have no deep intention toward God—a mode of comportment the Mitteler Rebbe calls trying to buy wisdom where the heart is absent.

This recognition of self-delusion is less a matter of "testing" the authenticity of the experience than it is of describing a particular danger peculiar to this level of divine presence. What we can say here is that if the ecstasy is genuine, it will be detached from "effort," where spiritual laxity cannot be equated with such a detachment. It is the former that leaves a spirit frigid.

The effects of ecstasy pertaining to the level of *ruach* arrive with some different difficulties but are linked to the problem of pride as a lack of humility. This modality of divine experience is accompanied by a talent for "hearing" and a desire for God to be revealed in the doing of good deeds. Yet it is not without its own difficulties. Being moved to ecstasy in the contemplation of divine matters, one can harbor the thought that it is *oneself* who has seen the light; it is *oneself* who is warm with the touch of God. The result is a kind of "egotistical lust": the individual removes the Holy from himself by becoming holy in his own sight, so much so that eventually he becomes greatly deluded and confused in values (*Tract,* 146). Because in some corners of his being this individual thinks it is he who is in control; he imagines that once he has been moved to ecstasy, he can simply return to "business as usual."

Seeing nothing deleterious and being elevated in his own eyes, he strives for immediate divine wisdom without humility, becomes spiritually lenient, and insidiously falls into worldly interests. "This is the main cause of their downfall, little by little, without their recognizing it in themselves at all" (*Tract,* 150–51; cf. 147). The effects of ecstasy then become hidden, just as if the ecstasy had never taken place.

Finally, such an experience of self-delusion diverts one from integrating the Torah into concrete practice. While one may be thoroughly familiar with the Torah and eloquent in response, this self-delusion makes one, observes Dov Baer, merely academic, merely scholarly. Now the so-called spiritual practice and divine ecstasy become mundane.[10] "For they have not engaged in the divine service of fixing the matter firmly in the soul with a strong and powerful attachment, actually to live by it" (*Tract,* 151). Lacking what he calls "*lebendigkeit,*" or vivacity, which only follows from the "labor in divine service and great effort in prayer," scholarship amounts to "*totigkeit*" or death (*Tract,* 151). This induces dejection, laziness, and heaviness of heart, which is to say, lack of enthusiasm, kindness, and interior vitality; whereas enthusiasm, kindness, interior vitality, and so forth, are all hallmarks of the Chabad mystic and the loving response to God.[11]

One way out of this death, according to the Rabbi, is true repentance (*teshuvah*), which is literally the turning around (toward God) and is linked to *tzedakah* (charity and righteousness). True repentance ushers in a "contrite and crushed heart" (Ps. 51:19) (*zu brochenkeit; lev nishvar*), or a profound humility that is not contrary to joy, for it is not a self-indulgent anguish. Rather, as a genuine anguish over one's remoteness from God and detachment of the self, the "broken heart" is conducive to such joy.[12]

A contrite and crushed heart, however, is converted into divine joy and delight, not by anything I can achieve as if I would cause it through repentance of my own accord, but *only because of the Divine* who revives the spirit of the contrite.[13]

Within the sphere of ecstasy associated with *neshamah,* one penetrates deeply into a subject matter and thereby "hears" God deeply. Since this ecstasy is not fully integrated into the "heart," one can become impressed with one's own talent for hearing—an "evil malady that destroys everything," laments Dov Baer (*Tract,* 152)—and that arbitrarily restricts this very depth of hearing: "The mistake should not be made of forbidding or invalidating this ecstasy, God forfend, but he should see to it that it does not cause a reduction in depth and length etc." (*Tract,* 153).

Dov Baer also warns of the problem of faint-heartedness, lived as an absence of deed, whereby one lives in a separation of loving and mindfulness instead of the love of God being expressed immediately in practice. In Dov Baer's words, one is not—as one should be—"well-cooked" (*ibber gekocht*). Rather than a great longing and true love from the midst of the heart, there is once again too little *zu brockenkeit,* too little humility, so the ecstasy is not drawn into the heart (*Tract,* 157–59).

The level of experience peculiar to *chayyah,* which entails an inner concentration of mind and essential ecstasy of the divine soul, is fraught with its own dangers. For example, because one has attained a profound experience of God, one might become over-zealous in trying to influence others, harboring the illusion that one's aim is altruistic, when it might really be an appetite for control or being inattentive to the uniqueness of the other person. On a different score, one might be lulled into enjoying the experience merely, and not serving the Divine in the experience. Thinking that he has attained self-annulment, such a person might develop a severe "self-vaunting" pride (*Tract,* 161). That one is secretly prideful is apparent when the individual becomes greatly disturbed by being reproached or censured. An even greater danger exists for one who realizes that he or she has not attained self-annulment—not so much in desiring to attain such annulment, but in regarding the latter as if it were the only thing lacking in him! This becomes a more insidious form of pride. At this level, warns Dov Baer, the significance of such a "fall" from God is even more acute.

Still, there are experiences that do not impede ecstasy through self-delusions and deceptions, since they are not directed toward reaching any stage at all. Desiring only the nearness to God, a nearness that is called "divine delight in true intention," one wishes only to serve (*Tract,* 163).

The Rabbi describes various kinds of confirmation where the authenticity of this degree of ecstasy is concerned. One is the effect of true humility, for the individual realizes his unworthiness; he attains "*nishkeit,*" or nothingness, with no "self"-awareness. Accordingly, he is not moved by any insult, since he recognizes that he possesses nothing in his own right. There are, however, many different distinctions in the depths of humility to be made, and even here the danger remains that one may delude himself by imagining that he has attained true humility.

Another effect or testimony to the divine ecstasy of *chayyah* is the attraction to the nearness of God during the whole day and particularly in action (*Tract,* 164–65). Loathing the worldly vanity of existence with empty mind and heart, the individual will be greatly troubled at the waste of time caused by gossip. Furthermore, he will partake little in mundane delights like fame, fashion, cuisine, and so on, for the world is not the main purpose of life, but rather the nearness of God in the light of the Torah, both inwardly and outwardly. Thus, for example, even when this person does engage in business affairs, he will not "hasten to be rich," that is, he will not seek profit, and will instead do only what is necessary to live. Not investing one's whole concentration, will, and soul in business affairs, or things like wealth, physical health, and happiness, only God alone is valued as absolute. For the whole depth of one's heart will not be engaged in these dealings with self-sacrifice: "for 'yes' and 'no' are the same to him . . . and [he] will cast his burden upon the Lord" (*Tract*, 165–66).

Yechidah, as mentioned above, is characterized by the simple, essential will and delight, which is higher than reason. While this kind of ecstasy is very rare, it is always possible for this ecstasy to be given, even if for only a moment. Its ephemeral nature derives from the nature of human beings as finite. In these kinds of experiences, the orientation toward God is so intense that there is no self-awareness, but pure spontaneity. In the very experiencing itself, it all but excludes the opportunity for self-delusion. The danger of delusion, therefore, is not integral to this kind of experiencing, writes Dov Baer—though certain types of mental pathology and manias might pose as counterfeits.

In sum and to be brief, the genuine experiences of the Holy are characterized in Dov Baer's descriptions by the related experiences of spontaneity, lack of self-awareness, self-annulment, the experience of grace, the service of God as service to one's neighbor, experiencing God alone as absolute and not things, an inner vitality of heart and mind in enthusiasm, and humility. By contrast, throughout all of these forms of ecstasy, Rabbi Dov Baer targets self-deception, which has at its root the delusion of pride, the focus on the self, the lack of humility, and a laziness of spirit.

Confirmations of Unveilings

In the chapter on Baqlī, above, I described those unveilings that are expressive of internally differentiated stations and states of the experienced presence of God. There are several observations we can make about the quality of these modes of presence recorded by Baqlī. Let me make them explicit here (I will not dwell on them all, since they are by now familiar to us through similar descriptions given by St. Teresa and Dov Baer).

First, rather than the stations coming on piecemeal, they are marked by a suddenness, a force, and a spontaneity. Thus, the qualitative gradations are not given gradually like perceptual objects are given; even when we notice a "progression" in terms of a deepening, each onset of the presence is without cause, creative, "full," in and of itself. Rūzbihān's expressions often evoke the suddenness and the spontaneous initiation on the part of God. For example, he writes that the heart "shot into the station of astonishment at lordship" (§190), or again, that "states descended like thunderbolts upon me, from the effect of the sublimities of his face" (§102).

Second, where it is an issue of stations, the latter are initiated freely by God and are experienced as ultimately beyond our control. Even if these stations are "requested" by the mystic (as in the case of Baqlī), we finite persons are not in a position to anticipate them, since it is not in their nature to be provoked by us.

Third, and relating to the former point, with respect to our own strivings and imaginings that might be characterized as "active," the stations or states are distinctively "passive"—if we mean by this that it is God who initiates the experience "in us" and that it can take place over and against what we might anticipate. Note that it is always God who makes something happen: "Then *he seized me* and *made me* enter the world of power and divine presence and eternity"; "He *approached me* and *made me* dance" (§119); "I *fell* in the stations of the witness of majesty" (§186); "Between the evening prayers I saw myself *fall into* the presence" (§101; my emphasis). Notice, furthermore, that Baqlī is "put in" oceans of ecstasy: God intoxicates him with the wine of his union; God ravishes him with perfumes of his intimacy; God increases his longing with cups of his expansiveness (§156); God *witnessed him* in sweet union (§132); and so forth.

Fourth, in and through these levels of unveilings, Baqlī describes how he is given to himself by God and how God is given to him. In reality, these are one and the same thing, just expressed according to the nodal points of the experience. So, for example, to experience oneself as God's essence is another way of saying, in Baqlī's language, that one has experienced God as manifesting himself from the throne, in the station of passionate love, in the station of intimacy. Certainly, such a remark has to be taken with the particularity of Rūzbihān's experiences and not as a template for all experiences. Still, it illustrates a way that he is given to himself according to how God gives himself; or, we could say, how God reveals himself is a unique kind of presence, that is, the "station" or "state" of experience.

These are some of the ways that Baqlī reports being given to himself: as a friend of God [*walī*], chosen for nearness (§§14, 156, 188); in the station of annihilation, he is given to himself as a "weak slave" (§40); approaching divine presence, he experiences himself as a "bewildered beggar" (§55). He is further given as a companion (§59), and in what he calls the "station of abasement," he is given as the "least of [God's] creatures," as God's "servant and the son of [God's] servant" (§77, §148), or similarly, as God's falcon (§63).[14]

In a related set of observations, we can ask in turn how God is given to Baqlī in the experiences he records; that these descriptions change speaks to the ever moving and evolving presence of God in the relationship. God is given, for example, with personal intimacy: "I am yours" (§77). God is given in awe, magnificence, greatness, majesty, beauty (§72, passim); through the presence of power; as a friend, as lord, in generosity (§55), loveliness (§77), oneness, (§66), fragrances of sanctity and intimacy, suffering mercy (§112); with the cloak of divinity (passim); as laughter (§144). He is given as in no place or no dimension (§175), as a sailor on the oceans (§193), and perhaps most strikingly, precisely as face to face (§207).[15]

In chapter 4 I indicated what Rūzbihān Baqlī means by stations and states, and I have presented an ordering of these experiences. Having just drawn out some implications of this kind of presence, what remains problematic is the issue of evidence involved in this kind of experiencing. To be sure, we say that these kinds of experiencing are from God, and we have spoken this way regarding St. Teresa and Dov Baer. But what in them makes them show themselves as "authentic," as "real" for Baqlī? True, as in the previous cases, they depart from the way perceptual objects are given. But this is all the more reason to pose the question concerning their evidentiary status, especially given the unusual imagery. In fact, judging from the space he gave to these considerations, it was implicitly, if not explicitly, an issue for Rūzbihān.

Let me begin the case for Baqlī by stating a point that should now be familiar but might nonetheless be elusive: such "vertical" experiences are confirmed as authentic according to the stature of the experience itself. What I mean by this is the following: Baqlī does not appeal to perceptual experience, for example, to confirm a different order of experience, say, spiritual experience. He neither appeals to a "proof" through rational demonstration, nor does he appeal to his own assessment of his so-called progress. Rather, there are "intersubjective" confirmations of his experiences, and these are given by the saints, by the prophets and angels, and by Muhammad himself.

Of course, such a corroboration might appear to be circular and to be presupposing what it should confirm. That is, if we are looking for some kind of proof that the experiences are authentic from the "outside" of those experiences—experiences that are "objective" and can be adjudicated by others as true or false—then such confirmations would appear to be just as much in question. Why do angels, saints, the prophets, confirm these experiences when we might say in turn, "That is all well and good, but what tells us that *these* confirmatory experiences are themselves authentic?" Do we not need another set of evidentiary confirmations to verify these intersubjective confirmatory ones? Do we not need something more "tangible," something that is precisely not of this religious order in order to verify this other order of experience? Otherwise, are we not just back where we started?

The fact that Rūzbihān cites *these* intersubjective sources and not others indicates to us immediately that the verification of the said experiences is *internal to its own kind of experiencing and occurs on this level of experiencing*. There is and can be no external adjudication or justification from outside the religious experiencing, since they can be authenticated only in the manner of this kind of experiencing. Perceptual evidence, for example, cannot authenticate spiritual experiencing; the experience of loving another or being loved by another can only be "confirmed," as it were, *within* that same kind of emotional experiencing, and not, for example, by rational reflection on the loving or any experiencing that is different *in kind*. Rather, it must be internal to or consistent with its own domain of experiencing. Just as perceptual experience can only be disappointed or confirmed within a kind of "perceptual faith," such that what is given perceptually can supplant a previous perceptual givenness and accepted as such, so too can vertical experiencing only be disappointed or confirmed within the context of a religious experiencing.

Confirmation of experiences for Baqlī came in many forms: conformity to scripture, corroboration by a master or teacher, the joy expressed by all things (cf. §§ 44, 49, 114, 116). But by far the most predominant manner of confirmation arose in the form of intersubjective confirmations by saints, prophets, and the Prophet, either by Rūzbihān observing the latter, or by their having direct interactions with him. Often coming from the orientation of holiness (expressed as from the direction of Medina), they console him, bless him, long for him, welcome him; he is given among the chosen ones; and God even intervenes at times on his behalf so that others will respect him.[16] We read, for example, "The doors of the angelic realm were opened to me, and I saw in the deserts of the hidden the great imams in a circle on a carpet of light. I saw al-Shafi'i, Abu Hanifa, Malik, and Ahmad ibn Hanbal, wearing white clothes and white turbans, rejoicing and congratulating one another at [seeing] my face. Then I saw above them the prophets, and I saw our Prophet Muhammad among his companions, above all other creatures. He left them and overtook me, rejoicing and smiling, and he was kind to me" (§199).

Or again: "Then I saw the chosen ones at the door of the presence. There in the field of pre-eternity was our Prophet Muhammad, coming from the right hand of the presence. . . . Likewise I saw Adam wearing clothes of pearl. The Prophet embraced me and kissed my face, and so did Adam. Adam was extremely kind to me, like a father with a son. Then I saw Abraham, Moses, Jesus, and the elect prophets. I went to the nearness of the presence and saw Gabriel in the form of the Turks . . . He [the Truth] manifested himself to me repeatedly, each time in a different form."[17]

The approbation and acceptances were not only direct, at times, but intimate as well: "Then I saw the Prophet coming toward me from Median. . . . He opened his mouth and took my tongue and mouthed my tongue gently. Then I saw Adam, Noah, Abraham, Moses, Jesus, and all the prophets and messengers coming toward me, and they mouthed my tongue. Then I saw Gabriel and Michael, Israfil, Azra'il and all the angels, and they mouthed my tongue. So [did] all the saints and sincere ones" (§146). Such a vision expresses not just a passing acknowledgment of Rūzbihān by the prophets, but a personal intimacy shared by lovers.

Concerned also with illusion and self-deception with regard to such experiences, Rūzbihān is forced to confront how he knows, for example, that the visions and locutions of the angelic realm come ultimately from God and not, for instance, from Satan or from himself. How is one able to tell the difference? "The accursed Satan knew of my condition, and he dived into the ocean of his deception. He presented me with satanic imaginings and psychic likenesses. I recognized them all, *but how did my thought insinuate that what I saw of the world of the angelic realm and the attributes of the transcendent Truth came from his miserable semblances and likeness?* My conscience feared and my heart was averse to that thought, and I was distressed when words fell between him and Moses: 'The one who speaks to you is not God most high.' And Moses ceased speaking until God purified him of his evil by revealing miracles. Beyond that, *God made me look differently on the thoughts that occurred to me,* saying, 'How can there be sighs, sobs, tears, the preparation of consciences with the occurring of lights, and the increase of longing for witnessing eternity on account of the likeness of Satan? Do not be concerned. I am I, the one who chooses to manifest himself to the pure in the form that pleases their hearts. There is no genuine ecstasy except from the manifestation of my witnessing, in whatever state it may be. I am the one who manifests himself'" (§183; my emphasis).

In this text we see, first, that Rūzbihān was able to detect the images of the angelic realm as deceptive and as originating from Satan, but he did not know how he was able to grasp the difference. In addition, we see, most significantly, that it is God himself who ultimately assuages Rūzbihān's distress and asserts that the veracity of the experience lies within the experience itself, because only God could give it in this way. All of this appeals to an *experiential difference* in the kind of givenness it is and presupposes that one has the kind of experience and attentiveness necessary to recognize such an experiential difference. For example, Rūzbihān speaks of a taste remaining in his heart, a witnessing with the eye of the spirit, an authority in the locution itself that distinguishes it from other ones, or a tenor in the difference between "mundane" conversations and conversations that are of a spiritual nature (see §§161, 74). Of course, one cannot simply assume a prior experience to discern a present one, since then one could not account for how a present experience could be discerned as authentic within that present experience. This is why Baqlī implicitly appeals to a *qualitative* potency in the experience itself. For example, words simply are experienced as not coming from me but as coming upon me with a force and magnitude: "I heard the word of the Truth (glory be to him) speaking from beyond these veils. It was as though I heard great peals of thunder, and great thunderbolts in this likeness. Creation and time were melting with awe of his word" (§163). It is in this respect that the detection or the discernment is, and can only be, internal to the experiencing itself.

If there are deceptions or self-deceptions, they have their root, on Baqlī's account, in our own weakness, in our fleeing from God, in turning to what is not essential, and in taking our (ego-filled) desires as essential (§188). These features, no matter how diverse they may seem, have their source in pride. And it is pride, according to Baqlī, that makes us more susceptible to distractions and satanic temptations. Rūzbihān recognizes this in himself: "I was sitting one night, and I spoke of my importance and my rank, so that I became stronger in the world of imaginings and familiar with satanic likenesses. My conscience reached the margins of the world of wrathful actions; it did not turn toward the presence, and it did not look upon the places where manifestation falls. It lowered its eyes from the witnessing of the hidden lights, and hours passed in that" (§189). According to Baqli, "I" become hidden from God because "I" am over-invested in myself; I become removed from the Essence because I am captivated by my own power and the things of my own creation. In this way, I become more adept at dealings with my own self in the sense of turning away from God, and as a consequence, more sensitive to evil. I am occupied with the material world, with my own powers, with "creation." "I" get carried away with myself, taking myself too seriously.

Even though it is our pride that opens us to such deceptions and self-doubt, it is ultimately not in our power to overcome pride; it is precisely "our power," the power of the "self," as it were, that has to be called into question—a point made by the other mystics as well. So even though God warns: "You will not be a true believer in one God until you forget yourself and all else besides me from the throne to the earth" (§77), it is God who bequeaths the refreshment of spirit and the forgetfulness of everything that is not God (§ 184); it is by the grace of God that pride is lifted, and it is God who quells self-doubt (§§187, 189): "I was hidden from him for a time. He removed the veil of pride from in between, though there was no in between (§138)."[18] Phenomenologically speaking, it is only possible to detect an act *as* selfish, *as* prideful, if the "self" is not living fully in the selfishness. One is not living fully in selfishness when one is oriented toward another, so that pride is revealed as such only in the presence of another, in this case, God.

• • •

St. Teresa of Avila, Dov Baer, and Rūzbihān Baqlī, each in their own style, describe ways in which the Holy is given. The givenness of the Holy constitutes the religious dimension of experiencing in its most profound sense. The evidence of these experiences as a whole is corroborated in the astounding character of their lives, which are lived in humble service in and from the direction of holiness. Evidence in the religious sphere has its own contours, and is not gained by simply grafting evidence from the sphere of presentation onto vertical experience.

We have learned from their descriptions that the Holy is given in an absolute presence. No matter what level of experience, each givenness—understood as prayer, ecstasy, or unveiling—is experienced as over-abundant. The Holy is not partially given in the experience, not present and absent like the presentation of the front side and back side of an object, but given "fully." Indeed, if we wish to equate fullness with objects of presentation, then we would have to say that epiphanic givenness is "over-full," superabundant, and, as in the refrain of the mystics, "without measure." To say that this presence is experienced absolutely and fully, however, does not mean that the Holy is exhausted in this experience; but if the experience is surpassed by an ever-deepening presence, or if it is renewed, it takes place uniquely. Moreover, these kinds of presence of the Holy are qualified as sudden, coming on of their own accord, spontaneous, creative, immediate, without any sense of our being able to anticipate or control them. It is God who is "active" in relation to which our participation in the experience is "passive." We do not cause or provoke epiphanic givenness; it is experienced as grace. Our "activity," as it were, is receiving. But the Holy is "received" in such a way that this reception *alters the structure of experience itself,* and this makes a qualitative difference in how we live with others and in the world.

Religious experience is not immune to what we might call "modalizations" of that experience. In this case, one might undergo experiences of self-deception or self-delusion, temptations, self-doubt or pride, distractions and concessions that creep in little by little. Examples of corroborating evidence or the experienced presence of the Holy include a confessor or spiritual master (the role of which we find in all three mystical traditions), the historical efficacy of the experience, scripture, service of God, love of neighbor, humility, and so forth.

The recognition of the different quality of givenness in religious experience has, as suggested, important implications for the matter of religious evidence. When we think of evidence in the modern worldview, we appeal to its ability to be repeated, not just by me but by others. As such, evidence as a mode of ideality becomes an aspect of justification, something that I can explain and that I or others can redo. In religious experience, self-evidence does not exhibit this structure of ideality and corroboration. In the first place, it is nothing "I" accomplish or there for *me* or another subject to redo. Even though it is given, it is not there anytime we want it. In the second place, since the experiences are spontaneous, creative, unique, owing to "person" and the personal nature of loving (see chapter 6), there is nothing "to redo" or that could be repeated like an ideal object. This does not mean that this evidence lacks a structure all its own or that we cannot see commonalities across cultures within the Abrahamic tradition, or again, that we cannot pursue a similar path. But if there is any kind of interpersonal "ideality," it would be found in the structure of exemplarity, that is, in living *as* another, past, present, or future, and not *like* another.[19] Consequently, the corroboration of religious evidence in the mode of self-evidence occurs within the style of religious experiencing itself and cannot be expected to conform to a style of confirmation alien to it, like when the geometer appeals to the ideality of self-evidence in repetition. True, these mystics do speak about their experiences. They do this, however, not in an effort to justify self-evidence or to provoke them in others, but to evoke them so that others might be guided along a spiritual path. The corroboration of their experiences lies in the transformative power of the experience such that "I" become a different person through the experience, and this evidence becomes self-evidence in the lives the mystics live in service to God as love of neighbor.

If religious experience is so "singular," one may wonder whether the so-called idiosyncrasy of the mystics is really not just a sign of their pathology, or whether psychoses are not really just what religiously inclined folks want to call "mystical experiences." The writings of the famed Dr. Schreber, analyzed and popularized by Freud, highlight some of the difficulties in discerning differences in such experiences.[20] For example, Dr. Schreber writes lucidly from his first-person perspective about being in direct communication with God, of having a mission to redeem the world and to restore it to its lost state of bliss, of being the recipient of divine miracles ("rays of God"), of becoming God's wife, of assuming passivity in relation to God, of bodily functions being evoked miraculously by God, of regarding "God Almighty" as his ally, of suffering and privation for God. He also notes that his experiences exceed human understanding; the "divine revelations" cannot be expressed adequately within the confines of human language, and for this reason he must resort to "images and similes."[21] Are these not religious experiences and attempts at expression like any other we have encountered?

There were of course "nuances" to these experiences. For example, Dr. Schreber describes, in an attitude of both rebelliousness and reverence, God's not needing to be acquainted with living human beings, since he only needed to have intercourse with corpses; he maintains that God is only "nerve"; he writes of his emasculation by God as a precondition for a new race of humans being created, of his "voluptuousness" as a taste of bliss, of his right to scoff at God, a right that belongs to him alone and not to others, and of his identification with Jesus Christ.

We must note several things here. First, the attempt to evaluate these descriptions, to the extent possible, is the attempt often referred to, within a religious context, as the discernment of spirits. Is not Freud himself attempting this, if only in an ambivalent way or against his intentions? On the one hand, Freud immediately situates Schreber's writings within the framework of psychopathology—due in some part, perhaps, to Schreber's own self-diagnosis. His ideas are said to be of a pathological origin; he is assumed to be a paranoiac and delusional.[22] On the other hand, when Freud writes that Dr. Schreber's attitude toward God is "so singular and so full of internal contradictions that it requires more than a little faith to persist in the belief that there is nevertheless 'method' in his 'madness,'" or even when Freud reduces these experiences to the order of "religious paranoia," is he not implicitly delimiting a sphere of religious experience, *via negative,* by detecting Schreber's experiences as not *true* religious experiences?[23] Are there not signs of humility on Freud's part when, faced with more than he can handle, he understands his efforts as "*Attempts* at Interpretation"?[24]

Second, within the context of religious experience, the relation between the mystic and "religious paranoia" may not always be clear for us. If the mystics, as I mentioned above, are "hyper-normal," then what it means to be normal, as it is unfolding within human experience, is still in the process of *becoming normal,* in the process establishing norms within experience. The religious life is in this sense optimal-izing, normal-izing, in the dynamic sense.[25] There is not a final sense of normality already worked out in advance, outside of human experience, that we could then apply to that experience. The genuineness of the experience cannot be measured against the past. If there is a difference between the "normal" in the sense of optimal-izing, and the pathological, it lies in the integrity of the religious experience itself and not in its conformity to a stock set of external standards. This is a "difficulty" for many levels of experience, but it becomes especially acute on the religious level. Furthermore, we cannot rule out the possibility that one could have religious insights, mystical experiences, and then lose them, misunderstand them, or misinterpret their significance, not just intellectually but at the core of one's being. It is entirely possible that psychoses might be taken as mystical experiences, mystical experiences as psychoses, or genetically speaking, that mental pathologies had originated as mystical experiences.[26] Tarkovsky's *Nostalghia* gives us an excellent example of the precarious nature and depth of such mystical experiences in the figure of Dominico.

Third, religious experience as I have been explicating it is fundamentally open, "generative" (optimalizing), and not closed. There are differences of experience because of the uniqueness of person and the inter-Personal nexus. Religious experience is not susceptible to a definitive clarity. It is not only psychoanalysis or psychotherapy that sometimes wants this clarity at the risk of betraying the experiences (in the name of doing justice to them); "religious" fundamentalists also desire this kind of definitiveness, such that when the "truth" is pronounced, everyone will be driven to accept it. It is within this attitude of closedness, fixity, of arbitrarily limiting the Holy by our designs, implicitly associating the Holy with thingness, that both secularism and fundamentalism become modes of idolatry, as we will see in chapter 8. Finality makes a poor bedfellow of "the Infinite."[27] Such a limitation in the name of definitiveness (either from the side of psychopathogy or of fundamentalism) is a sign of arrogance at best. It betrays a basic "ontological vulnerability" within the Holy to harbor the pretension that we could sort out the Mystery in any ultimate sense through, say, psychoanalysis or religious doctrine. It is an expression of pride.

Does this mean, then, that we must abandon any and all critical perspective of "discernment"? Although one cannot discern, say, psychoses from mystical experiences with absolute clarity and definitiveness (since the experiences arise within generativity and have to be taken up *within* it), we can note some clues for discernment, clues suggested by these mystics' experiences, but nevertheless clues that do not provide a final key for dispelling the mystery in which we find ourselves. After all, the preference for loving over hating is not arbitrary, since hating, a negative phenomenon, is founded in loving. For example, to repeat some of the features disclosed by the mystics and on the basis of the authority of their experiences (the mystics—who, I admit, I identify on the whole *as* having mystical experiences or who live a religious life—an unavoidable hermeneutical problematic), we could ask: Are the experiences expansive or narrowing? Do the experiences lead one to embrace all levels of reality or to shrink back from existence? Are the "effects" of prayer that one live in the service of God, love of neighbor, welcoming the stranger; or do they yield the shunning of others? Is there a devotion to God more than the devotion to the idea of God? Is one left cold, frustrated, indifferent, or with a sense of calm and "interior peace"? Do the experiences open one to deeper values or do they limit what can appear as value? Is the attitude toward "nature" a devaluation of it through *ressentiment,* or a revaluation of it in relation to spirit? Does a later experience or insight disclose something about a former one? Is one left humble or prideful? Is one left fixated on the "communications," "visions," "locutions"? Is there service or devotion despite the "gifts"? Do the experiences tend toward the abandonment of self or toward the attachment to self and to things?[28]

I have briefly touched on the ways these mystics attempt to corroborate their experiences, how they attempt "to discern spirits," and how they the treat the problem of deception, self-delusion, and the like. Here I want to take up a particularly vexing problem concerning what the mystics identify as the role of "our efforts" in religious experiencing.

The difficulty can be expressed as follows: The presence of God is experienced in terms of an epiphanic givenness or grace, hence, not provoked as is the case of the presentation of objects; yet this first degree of *religious* experience is somehow associated with our own efforts. This very formulation of the difficulty occurs for us because we live in the modern Western prejudice that the "self" is the point of departure for these or other experiences. The assumption is that the individual self is self-grounding, and furthermore that we are somehow outside of the presence of God at the beginning and then possibly enter into this presence. We assume ourselves to be secular and then have to add on a religious dimension. This, however, is a reversal and an abstraction. The experiences of the mystics that we examined here were testimony to the opposite. Comparing God to a palace (not to be confused with the imagery of the interior castle), St. Teresa, for instance, considers the possibility of ever being outside of this presence, even if we strive to be. She reflects: "Could the sinner, perhaps, so as to engage in his evil deeds leave this palace? No, certainly not; rather, within the palace itself, that is within God Himself, the abominations, indecent actions, and evil deeds committed by us sinners take place" (*Obras,* 561; *Collected Works,* Vol. 2, VI:10.3).

Are we then to abandon the achievements of the Modern period and the insight into the Self and the value of the individual? Are we then to commit ourselves to a social imaginary that is, in Claude Lefort's terms, pre-ideological?[29] Let us recall that the social imaginary becomes precisely "ideology" when we attempt to account for the divisions between the political and the social, power and civil life, *in terms of the social sphere itself,* and not by appealing to a transcendent dimension of power to justify the division. Machiavelli was perhaps the first to take this bold stride.[30] Ideology, be it in the form of bourgeois, totalitarian, or invisible ideology, is an appeal to the (human) self as self-grounding, and thus to a new kind of humanistic immanence—and in this return to immanence is able to give an account of transcendence and account for transcendence.

It is no longer a question for us of returning to a pre-ideological social imaginary; nor do I think it is desirable. This has to do with the distinctively moral implications of ideology that we cannot ignore.[31] Nevertheless, the mystics' evidence *points us* in a different way, to yet a different social imaginary that is not pre-critical. Thus, it is not a matter of a regression, but of a retrieval, orienting us vertically to what I call below the "Myself," to a verticality that animates but is concealed in the Modern period, that is buried over in favor of the insight into the Self as self-grounding.

Certainly, the precise nature of this relation has to be worked out (see chapters 6–7). My point is that the Modern prejudice is one that starts with the individual self and possibly adjuncts God; the mystics' experiences, however, reveal the "starting point" as the Holy. Such experiences are never simply "personal," but are always already inter-Personal such that we are not self-grounding. Such an understanding has important implications that I will have to treat later (e.g., we cannot commit horrific deeds here "on earth" while God remains all peace in "another world," the impossibility of God's withdrawal, etc.). Here I want to emphasize three things:

First, the initial degrees of prayer/ecstasy/unveiling are discriminations of presence already within the ongoing movement of the Holy; the "initial" degree of presence takes place within the inter-Personal framework from the very start.[32] Although one is already "in" this presence of God and never outside of this inter-Personal nexus, there are still great differences in the *ways in which* one is in this relation or the *ways in which* God's presence is given.[33] Not every experience of presence is union; but they are nevertheless vertical experiences. Accordingly, St. Teresa articulates the "first" degree of prayer already from the perspective of the "infusion" of God in the everyday. Described from the ultimate degrees, this vantage point allows her to see how the first prayer is already inter-Personal. Since we are not self-grounding, the religious dimension of experience cannot in principle exceed human experiencing but is a mode of human experiencing itself.

Second, the self-grounding character of the subject, or what we can simply call *secularism,* for our purposes at this juncture, is not primary, but when taken as the starting point, is already an abstraction from this ongoing generative movement that is the inter-Personal nexus, or the religious dimension of experience. Such a putative starting point represents an attempt to remove oneself from the relation of being given to oneself. Because the inter-Personal movement is what is primary, secularism, for example, is a turning away from the "ontologically" prior (or "religious") event of inter-Personality, or in the terms I use here, it is a mode of idolatry. Idolatry can be interpreted as nothing less than creatively resisting the inter-Personal nexus: there is no neutral position because the generative movement is already a "positive" movement. Moving together with the orientation of this positive movement can be characterized as loving (see chapter 6). Because there is no neutral setting, any contrary movement defies or resists; it moves in the direction of hatred. Accordingly, such a defiance or resistance is anything but "liberating." It is not a matter of whether or not one thinks he or she is secular, fundamentalist, agnostic, or religious, for that matter; what is decisive is the direction of those acts, or the orientation of that life, or the ethos of the culture that bears the quality of holiness or evil.

Third, the Holy already announces itself in and through the movement of verticality, and for this reason, one is always already "engaged" in a vertical givenness. One cannot usher or provoke the Holy into givenness; one cannot proceed dialectically toward the Holy as if through a negotiation of meaning evolving between two poles; one cannot proceed in increments toward a vertical experience; one cannot just increase or intensify a presentational mode of givenness to "get to" a vertical givenness. Rather, one is already "swept into" the relation and movement, and this is why there are no securities or guarantees outside of those vertical movements themselves. We are already qualified with respect to the movement, and there is no refuge outside of this movement itself where we could putatively remain neutral.

To return more explicitly to the issue of "our effort," then, far from doing nothing, our efforts are necessary—as we saw above in the case of Dov Baer's exposition—for laxity in effort is also a self-deception. As

St. Teresa counsels, one must seek God's presence and not just wait. We must exercise the intellect, even be vigilant in our spiritual exercises and activities, for otherwise we will be left just cold simpletons (*Obras,* 550; *Collected Works,* Vol. 2, VI:7.9); and even when we are recipients of God's favors, we must persevere in receiving (*Obras,* 505; *Collected Works,* Vol. 2, IV:3.9). It is God who suspends the intellect in his manner. But this does not mean that *we* can produce God's presence, or, as she writes, "induce" (*procurer*) prayer (*Obras,* 504; *Collected Works,* Vol. 2, IV:3.4). The danger here would be in thinking that we are the ones accomplishing something outside of the presence of God, or that our actions participate in the same logic of provocation that objects of presentation do, in other words, that our actions provoke God to be present in a way similar to the way we solicit perceptual things to appear by being attentive to them. Instead, the things we can do that are within our power entail clearing the way or enabling ourselves to be disposed to the presence of God. For Dov Baer, when someone "hears" or "tastes" in a divine manner, the divine soul is moved to divine ecstasy. Certainly, this is connected to one's intimate relation with the Divine, which is a necessary condition; but it occurs "only as a result of the Source."[34] Ultimately, disposing oneself to God is not something that the individual does; even this is given, which in turn predisposes the individual to such a vertical presence.

· · ·

These concerns with the manner in which the Holy is given, what I have called here a matter of evidence, are significant in the following ways. First, "something" takes place, occurs, and does so in a way that is different from the ways in which objects present themselves. We are not the ones constituting the religious experience, we are not the initiating force, nor are we even in a "constitutive duet" (Husserl, Merleau-Ponty) in the intentional correlation as is the case with matters of presentation. Thus, it is not a question of whether or not the secular person, layperson, or the fundamentalist could initiate such a givenness, because this formulation is already at a removal from the source. But there is a question of initiation (cf. chapter 7). Vertical experiencing is a distinctive kind of experiencing that is "absolute," immediate, spontaneous, beyond our calculation or control, creative, each time "full," not partial, not mixed with absence, not given as lacking. It is "vertical" givenness.

Second, this givenness is not theoretical or speculative but is *experienced* in the lives of these unique persons we call the mystics (though not exclusively in them) and concretized by the very nature of their lives. This givenness peculiar to a religious experiencing—that qualifies a religious experiencing—is a unique and irreducible mode of experience—for lack of a better term, what I have called epiphany. The mystics' concern with the manner of givenness of epiphany, no matter how they themselves evaluate it—through intersubjective confirmation, conformity with Scripture, historical efficacy, authority of the experience itself—shows us that it is a concrete, lived, experiential testimony to a different kind of givenness that does not conform to presentation. It belongs to its own sphere of experiencing and has its own integrity.

In the following chapters, I take up this distinctive givenness in the attempt to work out some of its implications, for example: What is the concrete form of epiphany in human experience, and what characterizes its unique kind of movement? What does epiphany mean for the individual person, specifically in terms of "individuation"? How is idolatry given in relation to epiphany, and how does it arise as a problem?

CHAPTER 6

Epiphany and Withdrawal

*The goodness of the Good—the Good which never sleeps or nods—
inclines the movement it calls forth, to turn it from the Good and
orient it toward the other, and only thus toward the Good.*

—EMMANUEL LEVINAS[1]

Having articulated the matter of evidence regarding the vertical
givenness peculiar to religious experience or "epiphany," it remains for
us to give epiphany more specific, concrete, experiential contours and to
specify the tenor of this kind of givenness with an eye to a particular set
of philosophical problems. On the basis of their experiences, the mystics
assert (in terminology peculiar to each of them) that the presence of the
Holy is absolute, that we participate from the very start in vertical givenness, in a givenness that is realized in varying degrees and stages according to how the Holy gives itself.

But a set of difficulties emerges. If we are given to ourselves from the
start in an inter-Personal movement (if we are not self-grounding), if God's
presence is overabundant, without measure, as the mystics describe, then
how do we account for lapses in this presence? How do we account for the
mitigation of vertical presence, the experience of not being "in touch,"
of being distant from the Holy, or even of being abandoned? If God's
presence is persistent, if it "never sleeps or nods," how is it that our lives
become so disjointed, so complicated, so out of hand? How is it that I can
become conflicted with God or even conflicted with myself?

For the mystics, an experienced absence of God can be given in many
ways. It can be experienced as a "dryness" with nothing to sustain one
(St. Teresa); as the "dark night" of the senses and of the spirit in which
God removes all light (St. John of the Cross); as "affliction" that is distinct
from mere suffering and that only God can bring about, often in the form
of social degradation (Simone Weil); as individual and collective "exile"
from God's presence, the *shechinah* (Dov Baer); as "veiledness" (Rūzbihān
Baqlī). We might articulate it otherwise: we seek God, but God does not
respond; we experience captivity and seek freedom but are subjected to

slavery; we want sanctity but experience the removal of God in genocides and holocausts; we want our lives to make sense, but, in the eyes of
Dostoevsky's Ivan Ivanovich, we witness the brutal, meaningless death of
innocents. In contemporary life, we have responded to these experienced
absences in many ways, the most prevalent of which are nihilism and
relativism.

In order to approach this issue, it is necessary to identify the sense
of the givenness about which we speak, to ascertain its quality and to
inquire into what characterizes it most profoundly. What is the meaning
of epiphany? What is the significance of this experienced absence? How
does it determine our responses?[2]

There are many contemporary ways of understanding these issues,
and they range from Camus's understanding of human existence as absurdity (upon which I touch in chapter 8), to a postmodern "death of God,"
to a Bergmanian God-as-puppeteer, to a fundamentalist conviction that
everything happens for a reason. However, for my purposes (namely, to
discern and to highlight the nature of epiphany), I want to restrict my
analysis to two primary ways that we could contend, philosophically,
with these issues. The one, we could understand as a rupture due to the
Holy itself on the model of a "withdrawal." The other, which is rarely
formulated as such, I take from the experiences of the mystics. Such
an absence has meaning in the face of vertical givenness understood as
epiphany and realized concretely and personally as loving.

Although we could find several articulations of the first view, no figure is more commanding, more rigorous, and more incisive than Martin
Heidegger. In my view, Heidegger sketches most profoundly the view that
I contrast with that of the mystics. It is for this reason that I take him as
representative of this approach and impose on the reader the following all-
too-brief exposition of this significant philosopher's thought. My intention is not a critique of Heidegger per se, but of the presuppositions of
such thinking and the implications it has for thinking and living from the
vertical dimension. To account for the sense of the issues and not the particular figure of Heidegger, I focus not on what Heidegger explicitly asserts
about God, the Holy, or theology, but on the movement of "Being" and its
implications with respect to what I understand as vertical givenness.[3]

For Heidegger, the human being is disclosed as Dasein, as a being
in relation to Being, where the existential and ontological problem of
"absence" or "removal"—if it can be stated in this way—is formulated

as a "withdrawal" of the source itself and as a "forgetfulness" on the part of Dasein that is inexorably linked to this withdrawal such that it demands a new kind of thinking. Heidegger has exerted such an influence on contemporary thought, explicitly and implicitly, that many thinkers following in his wake assume the structure of withdrawal/forgetfulness in their own work, even "religious" thinkers like Michel Henry.[4] This makes it all the more imperative for us to examine some of the features and presuppositions of this structure, withdrawal/forgetfulness.

Withdrawal of Being and the Problem of Forgetfulness

It is well known that Heidegger broaches the question of Being in *Sein und Zeit* through that being that poses the question concerning the meaning of Being, namely, Dasein.[5] Dasein is a mode of Being (*Sein*), a way of existing as "there" (*Da*), where this "there" is the place of disclosure and openness. The human being is a being who exists as Dasein, and in this sense, even though the human being *is* Dasein and perhaps the only species we know to have the being of the "there," Dasein is not strictly speaking reducible to the human being.

Dasein is not the only mode of Being, of course. Other modes of Being that Heidegger treats in *Sein und Zeit* include the being of the ready-to-hand (*Zuhandensein*) and the being of the present-at-hand (*Vorhandensein*), though there are others too (like the being of nature, of mathematics, etc.) that simply do not become a topic for this work, *Sein und Zeit*. In the former case, a being presents itself in meaningful relations and acquires its significance precisely from its context. In the latter case, a being comes forth when its function or its nexus of referential implications breaks down. This could be the occasion for critical reflection on the significance of the tool, but it can also issue simply in the presentation of a new "object," devoid of any context. Be that as it may, Dasein is distinctive from these and other modes of Being insofar as it is the being for whom its own Being is an issue.

The problem for Dasein is that it loses itself in what we might call an ontological anonymity, what Heidegger terms "*das Man.*" *Das Man,* usually mistranslated in English as "the they," does not essentially depict an anonymity, as if lost in a crowd, but rather a kind of third-person anonymity of Being, a conflation of itself with other modes of Being such that Dasein does not see the distinctiveness of who it *is*. It loses its distinctiveness when it understands itself through things, or when it gains its self-identity by interpreting itself in the context of *their* relations. Accordingly, even if there were only one factual being with the Being of the Da, Dasein could still exist in the way of *das Man* (this could clearly not be the case if *das Man* were reduced to a social relation). The ontological anonymity of *das Man* means, then, that Dasein conflates its own mode of Being (Da) with the mode of Being of objects and/or tools.

This conflation is evident in a twofold manner. Since Dasein is a modal determination, Dasein can take any being who exists in the mode of the Da as an object or a tool: I can take myself as an object or a tool and completely obfuscate the Da (my "thereness" of Being), or I can take another who exists in the mode of the Da as merely present-at-hand or as ready-to-hand, thus occluding his or her Being; I can employ others for service and reduce them to use-value; I can treat another as an object fulfilling my needs; I can, for example, operate on another in surgery without any regard for his or her ability-to-be as "there." What is lost in this ontological anonymity is not merely the distinctiveness of its ability-to-be *there* as a mode of Being, but the distinctiveness of the there as a mode of *Being*.

One way that Dasein can be called out of this ontological anonymity, at least according to *Sein und Zeit,* is through a peculiar fundamental mood or attunement that Heidegger calls "anxiety." Anxiety individualizes Dasein. But this individualizing does not concern Dasein, for instance, as a process of isolating one human being from others. This would only be the case if Heidegger's distinctions were sociological and not modal. Individualizing is a process of disclosing to Dasein its unique individuation as Da; it discloses Dasein as *unique*—as Heidegger writes—*einzig,* as uniquely Da, whereby it identifies itself through a first-person responsible reclamation of the Da. Individualization does not disclose Dasein, for example, as alone or *allein*.[6] Dasein is individualized "down to itself," namely, down to *itself as the openness of Being*. Precisely as this openness, Dasein is not an object or piece of equipment but a "place," a clearing of Being and, in this sense, no-thing. We can of course retaliate in the face of this nothingness and flee in fear toward objects, but fear is still founded in the experience of who we are as uniquely "there," precisely as an ability-*to-be* (**Seinkönnen**). Ultimately, what is disclosed to Dasein is not just that it is the *there* of Being, but the there of *Being*.

To be individualized *as* there through anxiety as an ability-*to-be* is to come face to face with our unique mode of Being as finite. This finitude is disclosed in Dasein's being toward death. Being toward death is not the intention to die but the radical experience of our existence as *possibilized,* or liberated from the movement of mere life. For Heidegger, this possibilizing liberation, experienced as the ability-to-be with the existential accent on the dimension of the future, is given as thrown, thus pointing to the essentially passive nature of Dasein's original emergence in relation to Being.

This passivity in the emergence of Dasein as such, however, does not mean for Heidegger that Being is a unilateral Ground of beings. The nature of their relation is instead characterized as a *belonging*-together (*Zusammen**gehören***). To avoid reifying the relation as just another object, Heidegger's highlights the "belonging" in the belonging-together so as to determine the "together" in and through belonging, rather than qualifying belonging by togetherness. This emphasis on the belonging implies a dynamic tension, an abiding difference of Being and beings, a perdurance that places beings before Being but holds them apart.[7] A belonging exists with the human being who listens to (*hört auf*) Being because it is appropriated (*ist übereignet*) to Being. For its part, Being concerns the human being as Dasein through the claim that Being makes on the human being.[8] In this sense, Being and human being are appropriated to each other, they *belong* to each other.

The following questions now come to light. First, if Being and human beings *belong*-together originally, how are we to understand the source of Dasein's ontological anonymity (whereby it neglects the Being of the There and the There of its Being), or again, the fact that thinking is "enframed" such that it tends to lose itself in a kind of thinking that is not sensitive to the There or Being, for example, in calculative, representational thinking? In *Sein und Zeit* Heidegger characterizes this problem as a "forgetfulness," as a *Seinsvergessenheit*—a forgetfulness of Being that is later qualified as the forgetfulness of the very difference between Being and beings.[9] Second, what is the source of this forgetfulness? Can it be overcome? Is it an essentially creative forgetfulness, spontaneously emerging from Dasein? Does forgetfulness somehow lie in Dasein's own Being? Or is Dasein given over to itself as forgetful? If this forgetfulness can be mitigated, what is entailed in its overcoming? Who is exemplary in this regard?

To respond to these questions, it is necessary to consult some of Heidegger's later texts in which he approaches the meaning of Being, not through Dasein but through the attempts to think Being without regard to beings. To think Being without beings has to be more than a change in attitudes for Heidegger—a change that would be reminiscent of Husserl's shift from the natural to the phenomenological attitude—for all attitudes, according to Heidegger, remain within the domain of representational thinking.[10] Instead, to think Being without beings is to execute a *step back* from representational thinking (and thus a spring into an abyss [*Abgrund*]) so as to bring into view the history of Being and the ways in which it is forgotten—a history that Heidegger terms "metaphysics."[11] The step back is the attempt to think Being without regard to metaphysics and its conception of Being as a being or as a unilateral Ground (*Grund*) of beings, or again as self-causing agent.

Heidegger attempts to solicit this step back in order to evoke the very opening of Being so as to rest in that letting-presence that cannot be identifiable as this or that and hence *cannot be personal* in any way. As resting in the sheer giving that is prior to the determinacy of something becoming present as a field of articulated objects, Heidegger is faced with the profoundly difficult task of evoking (if not saying or describing) an "enigmatic region where there is nothing for which to be responsible,"[12] the "back side" of the horizon that faces us, which is "openness" as such.

Our problem, in the words of *Zur Sache des Denkens*, is that in the beginning of Western thinking only Being is thought, but not what abides as concealed in its unconcealment as the meaning of Being. What abides as concealed is the It gives (*Es gibt*) that gives the gifts of Being, time, thinking, and so forth. The "It gives" has been missed by thought, not because of a deficiency in our thinking but because the It gives "withdraws in favor of the gift that It gives" and necessarily eludes representational thought.[13] If representational thought attempts to grasp the It gives, "It" is reduced to an It *that* gives, and hence is transmogrified into an agent behind detachable deeds of giving. So as not to be misleading, Heidegger further qualifies the It as "Ereignis." *Ereignis* is the unique event of "Taking Place," of "appropriation" through which Being and human being belong together and are delivered over to each other. Taking place *takes* place (*das Ereignis ereignet*); that place is the human being as Dasein, and it takes its place for itself. But in taking place, "It" *withdraws and expropriates*. Heidegger writes: "What we have mentioned just now—*keeping back, denial, withholding*

—shows something like a self-withdrawing, something we might call for short: *withdrawal* [*Entzug*]. But inasmuch as the *modes of giving* that are determined by withdrawal—sending and extending—lie in Ereignis, *withdrawal must belong to what is peculiar to Ereignis.*"[14]

Ereignis holds itself back and withdraws in the gift-giving movement toward us and is retained in the self-withdrawing "sending" that is our historical destiny of Being. "It" arrives, takes place, by keeping concealed in unconcealment.[15] What ensues as the sent unconcealment is the history of Being as metaphysics, but as keeping concealed, the "original sending of Being" becomes more and more obfuscated in the epochal transformations of this history.

Since withdrawal belongs to Ereignis, we are subject to what might be called an *original forgetfulness*. The original forgetfulness is the veiling (*Verhüllung*) of the difference between Being and beings understood as concealment, a veiling that "has in turn withdrawn itself from the beginning." Since forgetfulness belongs to the difference because the difference belongs to the forgetfulness—as Heidegger states—forgetfulness is not contingent upon or a consequence of mere human thinking, *but endemic to the withdrawal itself.*[16] Such a forgetfulness can be nothing other than a thrown, sent, destined forgetfulness rooted in the denial of the presencing of Being *on the part of Being,* in the withholding of the disclosure of Appropriation or Ereignis.[17]

The problem identified by Heidegger, then, is a *forgetfulness* that is embedded in the withdrawal of the origin of the difference between Being and beings and that gives Dasein to itself and appropriates Dasein for itself; the "It" gives is forgotten in a forgetfulness that even escapes itself.[18] Since this Taking Place (*Ereignis*) cannot be thought within the scope of metaphysics, the attempt on our part is to step back out of the forgetfulness of the difference as such and to recall thoughtfully this difference as the perdurance of unconcealing-overcoming and self-keeping arrival; it is to spring out of the forgetfulness of the difference as such into the destiny of the withdrawing concealment of perdurance.[19] This step back, announced in *Sein und Zeit* and mentioned again in *Zur Sache des Denkens,* is a gradual removal of obfuscations or occlusions that may gain for us a preliminary insight, a "sudden flash" in recalling-thinking (*Andenken*) into what gives itself as the destiny of Being.

Such a step back can be initiated in a willing to renounce the will, a releasement to let-in from somewhere else, where the trace of willing vanishes while releasing oneself.[20] In his attempt to avoid slipping into what he earlier called "the onto-*theo*-logical constitution of metaphysics," Heidegger is careful to add that this is clearly not a casting off of sinful selfishness and letting the self-will go in favor of the divine will.[21] Still, writes Heidegger, this god-less, a-theistic thinking that must abandon the god of philosophy, to which one can neither pray nor sacrifice nor fall to one's knees in awe, is perhaps closer and more open to the divine God than onto-theo-logic would care to admit.[22] I will leave it a question for now if and how Heidegger opens the door for another mode of givenness beyond Being—an issue for which Jean-Luc Marion, among others, has taken him to task on more than one occasion.[23] My point, again, is not to decide if and how Heidegger can account for religious experience, but to take Heidegger's rigorous formulation of the problem in terms of Being as withdrawal, and the corollary of forgetfulness, as representative of this position.

The matter now is to see who is exemplary for the process of *das andenkende Denken,* the process of a recalling, meditative thinking that steps back from representational thought. Within this schema, it is the poet. For through the poet, language/thinking is able to say the unconcealedness of being, found truth as concealing-unconcealment, and bring the openness of beings into the Open.[24] Working from the experience of thinking, the poet discloses a way of thinking the Taking Place of Being in the human being and of guarding the concealed in its self-concealment.[25] At the limit, it prepares us for a new fundamental mood peculiar to a new beginning—not for *thaumazein* of the first beginning, but for *Scheu.*[26]

To sum up, then, in situating the problematic place of human being, the human being *qua* Dasein is characterized as the place of openness where Being takes place and appropriates Dasein for itself. Being (in all its permutations) recuses itself from givenness in its gift-giving, and in this essential withdrawal initiates or throws Dasein as fundamentally forgetful "of" the concealing-unconcealment and thus of itself as the eventful place where Being Takes Place. It forgets the difference between Being and beings in a forgetfulness that escapes itself, such that Dasein reifies it in the onto-theo-logic constitution of metaphysics. The redeemer from this forgetfulness, who can say the denial-withholding in its unconcealment and who can be the harbinger of a new thinking, ushering in a new beginning, is the poet. The poet in his or her radical thinking is exemplary of overcoming the forgetfulness of the original forgetfulness.

For Heidegger, then, and the position expressed by him, forgetfulness, or an experienced absence of the sort described above, is ultimately rooted in an intrinsic and essential withdrawal of Being for which there is no responsibility, in part because at this level it is not personal. Endemic to this withdrawal is a thrown forgetfulness which is initiated by this very withdrawal and which motivates our forgetfulness of this original forgetting. Being gives "Dasein" to itself, for itself (for Being), in a belonging-together, whereby the poet in his or her radical thinking is exemplary of overcoming the forgetfulness peculiar to the history of Western metaphysics.

Vertical Presence as Epiphany and the Problem of Idolatry

Having explicated this Heideggerian perspective, I now contrast this view, which is articulated along the axis of Being as withdrawal and the problem of forgetfulness, with another that is informed by the mystics of the Abrahamic tradition that I have investigated above.

The mystics treated here do not speak in a philosophical voice. Rather than a detriment, this makes their descriptions all the more rich since they are not laden with so many philosophical prejudices, conceptual constraints, or methodological blinders. Still, it does require on our part an effort to tease out the philosophical implications from the description of their experiences. For ease of exposition, I rely primarily on the descriptions already presented in chapters 2–4 above.

The first distinctive feature worthy of note is that these mystics address their experiences primarily in terms of the *emotional sphere* of experience, something signaled by their unrelenting appeal to the order of the "heart": to emotions like peace, calm, consolation, and joy in St. Teresa; to enthusiasm, *devekut* (cleaving to God), *kavannah* (sincere concentration), ecstasies of the heart in Dov Baer; to the heart's comprehension, visions of the heart, and God as passionate love (*'ishq*) in Baqli. These experiences single out the emotional sphere as prominent, which has its own integrity, and even (with special qualifications) surmounts the order of reason.

Now, it may just sound simplistic or naïve to say that such experiences go beyond reason and knowledge. But what the mystics are testifying to here—as I have emphasized above—is a very special order of human experience that has its own manner of evidence, illusion, deception, fulfillment, powers of discernment, "clarity," murkiness, and so forth. It concerns, not functions and acts of perception and judgment, which have an integrity all their own, but functions of the emotional domain like sympathy, feeling, loving, hating. It is this that we do not want to ignore. It would simply be an act of unequaled arbitrariness to dismiss a domain of experience because it did not meet the criteria of reason or givenness as presentation, or to exclude it on that basis from philosophical investigations.[27]

Certainly, Heidegger did not himself ignore emotional experience. We need only consider fundamental "moods" (*Stimmungen*) like anxiety, awe, boredom, and the like to convince ourselves of that. Nor is he describing Being on the model of Reason; his turn to meditative thinking and the exemplary efforts of the poet, among his critiques of Western Metaphysics, surely belie that. This, however, is still distinctive from the predominately concrete emotional character of the mystical experiences. It is important to recognize this because it relates to the very tenor of the so-called giving under discussion. When we examine the mystics, we note that the quality of giving is *not neutral;* rather, it has a particular nuance, depending on whether God is experienced as Father or Spouse, Majesty or Friend, Judge or the Merciful, Truth or Kindness. But of all of these experiences, the most profound for the mystics is the qualification of such giving as *loving,* and hence, God as Lover and Beloved. This loving is "given without measure," "infused," "magnanimous," "without limit," "overwhelming," "overflowing," "overabundant," "vigilant," "absolute," "infinite," received as "divine grace," as "onslaught," and so forth.

Note well: I am not trying to deduce the quality of the "giving" or "givenness" from what Being or God is or is presupposed to be. Rather, the "being" (or "non-being") peculiar to this sphere of vertical experience is determined on the *basis of the mode of its givenness.* In other words, instead of beginning with a presupposition of *what* God or Being is, and then suggesting how it gives itself, we are attentive to the *how of its givenness* as a clue to the nature of this "absolute." So when I speak of loving in this instance, I am not asserting something like "God is love; therefore, giving is loving." Instead, by taking *the mystics' lived experiences as my leading clue* and their discernment of prayer, ecstasy, unveiling—these ways of presencing—primordially as loving, we then, and only then, determine the nature of the Holy as loving. It is in this sense that we can say that the Holy gives itself as loving, since loving most profoundly qualifies its giving. Accordingly, in distinction to a kind of neutral, anonymous, and impersonal giving in an "it gives"—with all due qualifications noted with respect to "it gives"—we have a concretely specified way of giving experienced as loving.

Loving, as it is used in common parlance, is at best ambiguous. It often carries romantic overtones; it is sometimes sappy, sometimes characterized as a general feel-good attitude, being a warm-fuzzy glow, a static sentimentality, an aimless gushing, or even a psychological state of mind, suggested by the expression being "in" love. It can also be understood as an internal feeling, something I undergo like when "falling in love." However, we cannot let it go at that. If we are going to take our clues from the mystics and speak meaningfully about loving as qualifying epiphany as a type of vertical givenness, we have to be more precise.

Loving, following Scheler (a phenomenologist who to my mind has given the most acute, rigorous, and incisive philosophico-phenomenological account of loving) is distinguished as an "act" and not as a "function" because it is a creative, "initiated" dynamic orientation or *movement* peculiar to the level of spirit, and not an anonymous, psychophysical operation that happens by itself and that can become an object in time. In the next chapter, I will treat in more detail the significance of the distinction between "act" and "function" as it pertains to the quality of spirit and the process of individuation. Let me stay here with the notion of loving and ask this: To what is loving oriented?

Initially, we can say that loving can be directed toward anything. I can love ideas, knowledge, beauty; I can love honor and nobility; I can love animals (e.g., my pet cat), trees (old-growth forests), even cars and utensils (my favorite fountain pen). But hidden in this question is another, namely, *how* is loving oriented?

In each case, loving is a dynamic orientation toward this "other" such that the latter's intrinsic value is not exhausted in the loving; rather, as allowing it to unfold of itself, it is open toward infinity such that this "other" toward which loving is directed realizes the highest possible quality, the deepest value peculiar to its own being. In this respect, loving is an opening to the richness or fullness of what gives itself. It does so precisely where this "height," this "depth" of what gives itself is not and cannot yet be anticipated.[28] The higher value, this depth in quality, can in no way be given in advance, because it is only revealed in and through the *movement of loving itself.* We love the other in the fullness of what the thing is or who the person is, which is simultaneously an opening of possibilities and an invitation "to become." Loving, which is already oriented to what is given, is simultaneously an invitation "to become" in the direction of the height or depth disclosed in the loving, and is only "creative" in this regard. It is a movement that "rests" fully in the beloved but is not exhausted here; it illuminates a way of becoming more deeply what or who the beloved is, according to its being. For this reason, loving is not an occasion for the promotion of higher values in the other, making the person "better" (which would be correctly sensed as patronizing or controlling); it does not "create" higher values in the other.[29] Even a loving response, a response to loving, is "creative"; it too is initiated and takes place of its own accord, "improvisationally," we might say. By contrast, feelings like happiness, grief, enjoyment, or instances of co-feeling, like sympathy, are merely reactions to what is felt and do not point beyond what is felt; they are not "creative."[30]

I will speak more to these points below. Here I want to observe how loving qualifies the being "who" loves. While Heidegger understood the human being who exists in the mode of the "There" as Dasein, we use the expression "person" for the human being who is revealed in and through loving.[31] Person is not any-thing and can never become an object, since person is this dynamic orientation of acts pertaining to the emotional sphere of existence; who he or she is, is or becomes precisely "in" the intrinsic coherence of its creatively oriented movement, the most profound revelation of which is loving.[32] It is in loving, the deepest of the emotional acts, that one sees most clearly the spontaneous, immediate, initiatory, improvisational, and directed character of acts. Revealed most profoundly through loving, the person lives in and through such acts.[33]

This dynamic orientation is *unique* because it is originary, improvisational; the person's originality, if you will, arises from its spontaneous originating, and as such, the dynamic orientation is irreducible to another, radically irreplaceable. It is in this sense of uniqueness that we speak of the person as "absolute." Recall that by the expression "absolute" we do not mean universal.[34] As unique, a person cannot be predicated of singularity or plurality (I will return to this in chapter 7).

Personal loving can be understood in two senses, as infinite and as finite. What distinguishes infinite Person from finite person is that the former's movement of loving is "irreversible"; that is, it lets be completely what can become in its fullness without reservation, which is to say, *infinitely*. The movement or *how* of its loving (i.e., infinite) qualifies the "being" that it is (infinite Person). The movement of infinite loving is what we mean by "holy," and it is in this sense that we can properly speak of "the Holy" or (infinite) Person. "The designation of God as a Person," writes Buber, "is indispensable for all those who, like me, do not mean by 'God' a principle."[35] By this expression, "the Holy" or "infinite Person," I do not mean, however, *a* Person in the sense that Infinite Person is either individual or collective, since individualness and collectivity pertain only to finite beings. God as Person, however, is, in our terminology, absolute. "As absolute Person, God enters into immediate relationship with us."[36] It is only the finite person (as absolute), as we will see, that can be individual or collective.

Although loving can be directed toward any thing, the highest form of loving relates to that which bears the intrinsic value of the Holy. Loving can be an invitation or lure to become who or what one is, whereby the intrinsic quality of the loved is not exhausted in the loving, since loving is essentially *open to infinity*. It is open in two senses. First, loving is oriented to the fullest possible becoming of the beloved, toward boundless fullness or depth. Second, it belongs to the nature of loving not to have any temporal restrictions constricting the love in advance. It makes no sense to say, for example, "I will love you for five years." Furthermore, one can even love another after this other person is dead, and in this sense, loving extends beyond finitude. When one loves, loving is open to eternity, even if finitude seems to disrupt it. One loves and binds the beloved "in the bond of life as an enduring source of blessing."

The Holy "cannot" remove itself from this "source" of loving, or rather, is identified as this dynamically originating source. As persons, human beings are capable of this kind of loving, that is, of becoming holy insofar as they coincide with this dynamic orientation. But human persons can also "reverse" or occlude this movement. Such is the spiritual sense of the human person's finitude and what qualifies persons as spiritually *finite*.

Givenness, qualified as loving, is essentially a free self-giving that is unconditional.[37] But part of what it means to be spiritually finite is that human persons can *withhold* loving; we can be miserly and selfish, dissimulate, hate, "walk to do good and run to do evil," and in general occlude the movement of loving. By not living up to what it means to be person in the fullest sense, we live—in terms of this work—idolatrously.

Infinite loving, however, loving as holy, is beyond the "possibility" of withdrawal. St. Teresa writes, for example, that our spiritual darkness is not due to an obfuscation on the part of the "Sun of Justice," but rather to our own withdrawal (*Obras*, 567–68, 578; *Collected Works*, Vol. 2, VII:1.3, 2.1). God understood as Person "cannot" abstain from epiphany.[38] This does not mean that the Holy makes itself present like an object; we are speaking here of vertical givenness. It is also important to keep in mind the difference within vertical givenness between what corresponds to "acquired" givenness and "infused" givenness, and to recall that the absence of the latter is not necessarily the absence of the former. That said, we can understand the movement of epiphany as absolute since it is neither confined to the past or present, nor to a certain period of time, but is unconditional, "omni-temporal," or overabundant. Only infinite loving is commensurate with this unconditionality. Accordingly, any clue or glimpse that the mystics or we may have of the Holy is initiated *from the side of the Holy*. We are given to ourselves as an unmotivated, non-rescindable "gift." Aside from the important implications that this being given to ourselves has for the issue of individuation and not being self-grounding (chapter 7), irreversible, infinite loving means that the Holy is always already being given. Finite persons are one of the originating sites of that givenness.[39] More particularly still, and with respect to the issue of "effort" mentioned above, we are not the initiating, constituting source for the presence of the Holy, that is, for religious experiencing in the sense we understand it here.

Epiphany for us, then, is the mode in which "Being," "Ereignis," and so forth, leaves the realm of *impersonal regioning,* and becomes radically *personal*. As Holy, epiphany understood as the movement of infinite loving is *beyond* impersonality and is, precisely, Personal. In this way, we have not an anonymous "it" gives, a Taking Place, or Being, but a giving that is qualified as personal loving. Personal loving as infinite is a vigilant loving—such that it never sleeps or nods, as Levinas might say—a loving that remains a persistent invitation to go the way of holiness, where holiness is understood as the quality of infinite loving. It is in the face of this vigilance that we have to understand the *meaning* of the experienced absence in whatever form it takes.

From the perspective developed here, the experienced absence always takes place within the inter-Personal nexus, this already being given to ourselves as the site of infinite loving. This can only make sense when we no longer live in the Modern prejudice that the Self is the primordial point of departure and assume it to be self-grounding. Not being self-grounding does not mean that something like absence is never experienced, even in extremely radical forms that many mystics, medieval and contemporary, refer to as "affliction." Affliction is not the same as suffering. For example, God is not necessarily absent for the martyr or for the impoverished, even though they do suffer. "Affliction makes God appear to be absent for a time, more absent than a dead man, more absent than light in the utter darkness of a cell. A kind of horror submerges the whole soul. During this absence there is nothing to love."[40]

It is true, as Heidegger says, that we are not responsible for withdrawal or for such an absence in the sense that we do not cause it. The withdrawal is not under our control. We would also have to admit that idolatry, in our terms, is not the "cause" of absence or of an experienced removal of God, since idolatry is a change in orientation against loving, a reversal and the constitution of evil (see chapter 8). But this does not mean that there is no responsibility on our part "for" the absence *in the sense of a responsibility in and through the absence.* The *meaning* of this absence, where there is nothing to love, as Weil herself writes, is to continue *to love through the emptiness,* which is the meaning of the response as well. There can be no such persistent invitation to holiness in an impersonal regioning and ostensibly neutral giving. Personal loving is vigilance despite experienced absence. The "reason" there is affliction (and not merely suffering) is the same "reason" there is grace. Or, one could say, there is neither cause nor reason for affliction, and likewise no cause or reason for grace.

The primordial inter-Personal nexus, which is the site of infinite loving, persists as a constant invitation to holiness, remaining operative such that ultimately we are responsible for living toward or in the direction of holiness, even through this abandon.[41] To take a contemporary example, Mother Teresa writes in letters that in 1946, on a trip to Darjeeling, she was called by Jesus to serve the poorest of the poor. The locutions, visions, and experiences of ecstatic union lasted for several months, until she actually began her mission. Almost immediately at that time, these mystical experiences—which are no less mystical because of their duration in comparison to other mystical experiences we have examined above—ceased and ushered the experience of being forsaken by God, "thrown away by God." She writes: "I call, I cling, I want, and there is no one to answer.

The darkness is so dark, and I am alone." She further expresses the "terrible pain of loss," of "God not wanting me," of "God not being God," of "God not really existing."[42] Mother Teresa endured this dark night of the soul and experience of abandonment for fifty years, until the end of her life, though she never abandoned her humble service to the "poorest of the poor" and never doubted these infused experiences. The loving of infinite Person was experienced as an invitation to love in the manner of holiness, an invitation to participate in the movement of divine loving, even through the affliction of the darkest night.

Although the meaning of this can only be explicated when we clarify the meaning of individuation, we can say here that there remains throughout a responsibility such that even the meaning of this experienced absence is still an orientation toward others, personal others and others other than human. But this does not necessarily mean withdrawal or anonymity. The experience of absence, the meaning of this absence, remains, even in affliction, an invitation toward holiness.[43] In St. Teresa's terms, its meaning is service, not enjoyment; in Rabbi Dov Baer's terms, its meaning is *avodah* (service), as a call to *tikkun olam,* the individual and collective reparation of the world, the gathering of the scattered sparks of Holiness by loving even through hatred. This is how the Holy escapes—*not presence—but anonymity* in the form of concrete, interpersonal presence. Rather than the poet being the exemplar of overcoming the consequence of withdrawal, it is for the mystics, the one who lives in the direction of holiness, the saint.

By "saint" I do not mean someone who is officially promulgated by church authorities, but the "friend of God" (*walīallāh*), the *tzaddik,* in whom the original orientation is toward the Holy in loving, toward persons and beings other than human. The saint is this loving orientation toward the Holy, disposing this person to a new revelation and to an "expansion" of the nature of the Godhead from the perspective of finite persons. There is no universal measure for the person of the saint, no norms with respect to his or her actions and efficacy. These are only established after the fact and on the basis of a "faith" in relation to them. Virtues, actions, works, deeds, are only expressions of the being and holiness of the person. Likewise, the things that he or she does are not proofs but witnesses to his or her uniqueness. The norms and laws that arise (i.e., as "religious" ones) do so on the basis of this creative personal movement; they found cultural life and are not confined or reducible to it. What one "obeys" is not the style of thinking but the style of spiritual living, the shape of the person, not rules or laws; or rather, one only "obeys" the latter insofar as they are ways of achieving free, loving devotion.

The shape of the person, his or her works and deeds, all coincide in the personality of the saintly person. For the "material" of the saintly exemplar is the *person* of the human being him- or herself, and one witnesses the works of the saintly person in the transformation of those he or she "touches" directly or indirectly. As such, the saint functions as an invitation for others to live along "with" him or her in the same orientation; this is how the saintly exemplar can evoke a loving community for all persons.[44] Notice, finally, that being a saint or "friend of God" is not something elitist in the sense of being exclusive, but a possibility open to every person.

Can we say anything more about this "absence"? Whence does it arise? Is it "our fault"? We might wish to interpret it, as some of the mystics have done, as God "pruning" the soul, purging the senses, preparing one for union; we might pursue it as God's intervention in history, as some of the prophets have done. We could understand ourselves as responsible even for the scattering of the sparks, even though "we" do not "cause" it. Here responsibility would be a response to a situation that is the presence of God in world history and where God has an intimate stake in the unfolding of life and the unfolding of spirit. Here there is responsibility only if there is a personal relation at issue. Ultimately, however, we have to say that this absence remains a mystery, though it is not the enigma for which there is no responsibility of which Heidegger speaks. We do not call it a "mystery" because it is impersonal, anonymous, or because we do not and cannot get a handle on it; rather, it is mystery because it is "Personal," which is to say, the core of creativity, generatively enacted in the inter-Personal nexus, that is, generatively enacted uniquely each time, depending on the uniqueness of persons. It is mystery because there is loving "without measure"; there is ineffability, not because of removal but because there is too much to be said.

If there were an impersonal enigmatic regioning for which there is nothing to be responsible, then it would make sense to appeal to a thrown forgetfulness, to a forgetting of this forgetfulness, and to our task as remote from the "It gives." But if, grounded in the experience of the mystics treated here, we determine the giving as infinite Personal loving or epiphany, the "problem" on our part cannot be conceived as forgetfulness; it is instead determined as idolatry, and the task posed to us personally involves moving in the direction of sanctity. Idolatry is a reversal of the orientation of loving and only occurs in the face of that vertical movement. Make no mistake about it: Heidegger is working at the core of the experience and its problems. But the task for us is not to rest in the letting-presence, which cannot be identifiable as this or that; rather, it is specified in terms of vertical movement. The giving of "It gives" is not vertical in this personal sense, and this is why the question of idolatry cannot be an issue for the human being from a Heideggerian perspective. As compelling as Heidegger's articulation is, it is ultimately misleading. For the mystics, there is no neutral giving; we are either moving in the direction of verticality or in the direction of idolatry. The meaning of idolatry cannot be fully explicated until we treat the issue of individuation. It is to the matter of individuation that I turn in the next chapter.

CHAPTER 7
On Individuation

Taking epiphany seriously as givenness in the mode of loving, we are lead to issues surrounding the problem of individuation. Individuation becomes problematic because givenness in the mode of loving concerns the place of that loving, the givenness of "creation," and, as it bears on this work, the givenness of persons. The problem of individuation, however, cannot be reduced to that of the factual individual or the mere "life" of the individual; rather, individuation concerns the being given to oneself where this givenness is taken up as personal becoming. As such, we confront the question of the subsistence of that personal uniqueness.

Given what we have already understood from the mystics, certain questions become pressing as they bear on the issues of individuation. We understand that vertical givenness entails a range of experiences much more articulated than union. But when the mystics do experience ecstatic union (the union of God and the individual), just *who* is undergoing the union? For example, Rabbi Dov Baer speaks of a radical loss of self-awareness; St. Teresa of Avila, at one stage, compares spiritual marriage to a bright light entering into a room through two different windows, or to rain falling from the sky into a river or fount "which cannot be divided or separated from the water of the river" (*Obras*, 571; *Collected Works*, Vol. 2, VII:2.4); Rūzbihān Baqlī writes of an essential union and annihilation of the self. But just who is undergoing such a literal consummation in spiritual marriage? Who is living through the loss of self-awareness in Rabbi Dov Baer, and how are we to understand this loss of self as an experienced ecstasy? Just who undergoes the experience of the annihilation of self and essential union in the case of Baqlī? In terms of the ecstatic mystics like Hallāj, who says "I am the Truth," or in Bisṭāmī, "Glory be to Me!"—just who is speaking? How can we speak meaningfully about such experiences? Is this somehow connected to the well-known adage that one must lose oneself to find oneself? Does the person who undergoes such experiences remain unique? Or do the mystics' experiences suggest that the individual is absorbed into "the One"? Is the famed experience of *unio mystica* at the same time a loss of personal uniqueness?

In this chapter I first examine the general problem of individuation in terms of the self and the Myself as the rudimentary sense of self. Because the notion of individuation is used today in so many different ways and in varying contexts, I distinguish between three senses of individuation—thisness, singularity, and uniqueness—specifying individuation in the proper sense as personal uniqueness. After explaining in what way the individual person is "absolute" and not relative in the inter-Personal nexus, I interpret this nexus in terms of solidarity.

Myself and Self

The mystics understand not just "favors," infused prayer, ecstatic experiences, or unveilings to be gifts from God, but their very selves as the experience of grace. We have understood by this that the individual is not self-grounding; the person finds him- or herself "in" an inter-Personal relation from the very start.

A phenomenological perspective in general is attuned to modes of givenness. With regard to the person, we do not immediately ask, in phenomenology: "*What* or *who* am I?" but "*How* am I given?" If we were to begin with the Modern prejudice of the self as the point of departure, we might jump to the conclusion that the self gives itself to itself, and consequently that the self is self-grounding. In terms of a phenomenology of time-consciousness, it would imply that there is *meaningfully* no before or after to my self, since I am its very constitutive source.[1] To the extent that I am self-temporalizing, I cannot simultaneously be constitutively before, after, or "outside" of myself. Birth and death do not and cannot become constitutive problems for me. I am the source of meaning, and I am the meaning source of my self; to that extent, I can be considered to be constitutively self-grounding. Here I could say, "*I am* eternally given to myself as *self-giving*" or "*I give* myself to myself, eternally." This is not to say that I, as a factual individual, was not born to parents and thus mortal, but that in terms of sense-constitution, I am the very source of time and of my self, and in this respect there can be no before or after prior to my self; I am given to myself as immortal, as self-grounding.

Now, the mystics' experiences testify to a givenness that goes beyond this kind of self-givenness. It is not that the self is not *a* constitutive source of some kind, but rather that the self as a constitutive source is nonetheless experienced precisely *as given to itself*, as receiving itself, and thus not as the ultimate constitutive source. What is primary here is not the "self" or the "I," but what I call the moment of the "Myself." I use the reflexive pronoun *Myself* here to convey the moment of receiving myself, of being given to myself. The experiences of absolute dependence and reliance on the Holy, the experiences of obedience (which I address later), and the like, are expressions of this being "given to *myself*." Rather than an independent ontological substance, this Myself is a relational movement rooted in the experience of being placed before God and only emerges as an experience in relation to the Holy or *as* this relation (a relation to be determined later as solidarity).

When we ask what it means to be given to Myself, or how it is that I am given to Myself, what can we glean from the mystics? Being given to Myself grants me the ability to take myself up as already given to myself: I am given to Myself with the *ability to be my self*. The problem arises when the ability to be my self, which is given as a gift, is detached from this being given to Myself. It is then that we can become concerned, occupied, preoccupied, even fascinated with the self such that it occludes this relation to the Holy. This is what we would call in other terms, "pride" (a topic of chapter 8 on idolatry).

I make this distinction between the "Myself" and the "self" as a provisional one. It is provisional in two senses. First, the Myself and the self are not separate "selves" but moments of a primordial experience; or rather, they suggest two ways of taking up this primordial givenness, one in the direction of the self as self-grounding, and the other as a "return" to Myself and as not self-grounding. Second, it is provisional because in the final analysis the issue of individuation will not be able to be settled simply on the level of the "self," but will have to be taken up on the level of person and *personal uniqueness*. I begin with the question of the self, however, because it gives us some insight into the highly problematic nature of the self in the mystics' experiences.

The problematic nature of the self gets expressed in the mystics' orientation toward the Holy because it is there that one sees efforts to "lose," "surrender," "forget," or "abandon" the self. Before determining what we mean by the self in this sense, let us examine the ways in which these three mystics portray losing oneself, since this gives us a clue to how they understand the self and how the self gets in the way of being given to Myself, and hence obfuscates my primordial relation with the Holy.

The process of losing the self is referred to as a "forgetfulness of self" (*un olvido de sí*) in St. Teresa of Avila (*Obras*, 574, 581; *Collected Works*, Vol. 2, VII:3.2, VII:4.11). One practices not only a detachment from all things but also a detachment from the self (*Obras,* 296; *Collected Works,* Vol. 2, "The Way of Perfection," 15.7) through techniques of meditation and vocal prayer, through practices of self-surrender in the positive orientation of service in which "I" am not at all at issue and in which there is no thought about favors or the glory of what one does (*Obras,* 70–71; *Collected Works,* Vol. 1, 11.1–4; *Obras,* 597; *Collected Works,* Vol. 1, "Spiritual Testimonies," 8, 10). In the words of St. John of the Cross, "going after God" entails "going out from oneself through self-forgetfulness, which is achieved by the love of God."[2] As St. Teresa writes, one only overlooks the self in and through abandoning oneself entirely to God, and where God stills the self (*Obras,* 96; *Collected Works,* Vol. 1, 17.2).

The question of agency is a peculiar one here, since there is a lived paradox, namely, *I* cannot *be* humble of my own accord (lose my self) since I cannot be oriented toward a negation of the self and still lose the self. Trying to forget the self directly is just another way of being occupied with the self, whether it be in the form of pride or self-doubt. Ultimately, it is God who stills "the freedom of the self," because it is he who occupies it in another way, such that this freedom reaches fruition as bound to the will of God. As I noted above, the mystics contend that while there is a struggle to suspend our mental activities in general, our efforts, our strivings, and the like cease to work only because God suspends them. Such a suspension is ultimately accomplished with God's aid because our efforts on their own can only strengthen our very efforts, our freedom of the self. It is only through the *awakening of loving* (i.e., being occupied in another way), which for St. Teresa has a Personal form (*Obras,* 503; *Collected Works,* Vol. 2, IV:3.4), that the self is no longer occupied with the self. By this awakening of loving, I am literally called back to Myself, and Myself as "Holiness." Let us recall that in her imagery of the Interior Castle, the self is portrayed as an inward spiraling movement, spiraling ever more deeply into its center. The seventh chamber is expressive of the core of the "self." At the moment that we discover the center of Myself, this "Myself" is revealed as Holiness. This is what we mean by saying that losing oneself is the discovery of oneself (or in our terms, losing my self is the discovery of Myself).

Rabbi Dov Baer expressed the problem of the self in the presence of God differently. For him it was the problem of "self-awareness." Self-awareness, in the way the Mitteler Rebbe uses the expression, indicates an explicit awareness of the "self" in the process of experiencing such that the self intrudes on the experience. Accordingly, the self in the self-awareness seems not really to be the self that is doing the experiencing, but the self that becomes an object of the experience: I take myself as a "great something," as a "somebody." The problem for him was that the awareness is not absorbed completely in "the good thing itself" or in the experience of God understood as ecstasy, but it turns back on itself, yielding a distance between myself and God. In fact, from one perspective, it is actually the intrusion of the self that distinguishes various levels of ecstasy. Since the self conceals the Divine presence, the task becomes one of paring away at the self to reveal its deeper meaning. What we are calling the Myself is the Divine in the manner of the concealment of the Divine by the self.

Natural self-awareness for the Rabbi becomes divine non-self-awareness from the side of the Divine. In Dov Baer's words, ultimately I *can*-not extend my "freedom of choice" (i.e., my "self") to choose not to be free or to choose not to be self-aware. Rather, a "diminution of self-awareness" is motivated by "an excess of light and inner vitality" and not by anything *I can* do; non-*self*-awareness, "spontaneity," and so forth *comes upon me* as an attenuation of self in *self*-awareness by the Source.[3] Still, Dov Baer is careful to clarify that one can still experience the ecstasy without the intervention of what he calls self-awareness: "Even though the ecstasy is sensed greatly in the heart, this state cannot be termed self-awareness." Yet he clarifies, "But for all that, it is an *experienced ecstasy*."[4] What is experienced is the presence of the Holy without the self's intrusion.

We also saw, in the case of Rūzbihān Baqlī, that one of the main stages of unveiling is the station of annihilation (*fanā*), the annihilation of the self. Let us recall that the detachment from things is a station preceding, in the order of intensity, the station of the annihilation of the self. In the former, things no longer have any significance for me; spatio-temporal creation wanes in comparison to the majesty of God, as if creation were nothing; only God stands alone, and everything else is annihilated. This was called the station of oneness and is the experience of union with God. But here, for Baqlī, "I" am still in some sense united with God, witnessing the oneness of God. *Fanā*, or annihilation of self is deeper than the station of oneness because the self is annihilated in God such that even the consciousness of self disappears in the brilliance of the presence of God: "I" do not see with my own eyes, speak with my own mouth. In a very real sense, Baqlī writes, "*I* do not know where *I* was" (§109; my emphasis). This is why it is difficult for Baqlī even to speak of a station of annihilation, as we saw, because "I" am not, but only exist in God.

To sum up these experiences, let me note two things. First, for these mystics (and others as well), the experience of the self is a fundamental problem with which all of them deal on an experiential level. I do not maintain that they deal with it in the same ways; rather, it is no coincidence that the self is an issue, indeed, an obstacle on the way of holiness. For the mystics, it is precisely in the presence of the Holy that the self gets called into question "with the help of God." My ability to be my self is realized as an ability to be Myself, which is to say, to be bound to and by God. The process of renouncing "my" will in order to conform to the will of God takes various shapes according to the character of the mystics and their unique religious traditions.

Second, in one way or another, they all speak of and through an experience of the loss of self. For example, St. Teresa writes of how the "soul feels when it is in divine union"; Dov Baer writes of a sensed ecstasy that in no way involves the "self"-awareness of the ecstasy; Rūzbihān Baqlī writes of the experience of the annihilation of the self. What sense does it make to speak of a non-self all the while *experiencing* the loss of self or *remembering* the experience of a loss or forgetfulness of self?

The question for us concerns the tenor of the "self" such that, on the one hand, "I" strive toward a self-forgetfulness, and on the other hand, still experience the very loss of self in union, in annihilation, in complete absorption in another. What can we mean when we speak of self-surrender and undergoing the loss of self?

It must first be acknowledged that these paradigmatic mystics operate with a rather general and often ambiguous understanding of the self. For example, they neither distinguish rigorously between, say, the "I," the "ego," the "soul," or the "self"; nor do they distinguish between reflective and pre-reflective senses of self as we are accustomed to doing today.[5] Nevertheless, there is a sense of self (or senses of self) that are in play, and they tend to be evoked in association with the various discussions.

What we are able to discern of the "self" in these mystics' writings often arises in the context of activities and abilities. It is not uncommon for the self to be a synonym for my individual bodily desires and appetites; my intentions; my particular interests; my powers; my faculties of the intellect, memory, imagination; my strivings; my spiritual exercises; and especially, "my will." But the self also arises in less "active" modes, for instance, when expressed in terms of "self-indulgence," "self-assertion," or "self-reliance," or when I am implicitly absorbed with my discomforts, when I am preoccupied with what I lack. The sense of self is also evoked when they write of "my honor," "my reputation," "my vanity," "my attachment" to things, and even "my prayers," "my ecstasies," unveilings made to me, prayers given to me. In these cases, the sense of self appears to get more and more remedial. But this also gives us a clue to the range of experiences that cover the "self" and what remains most elementary of the self for the mystics. Running through the various senses of self, and what bears on the self in its most elementary form, is the fact that all the experiences, be they active or passive, reflective or pre-reflective, *belong to me;* they are all *mine.* In one way or another, the experiences of self express what Dan Zahavi identifies as "mineness." To employ distinctions that are highlighted phenomenologically in Zahavi's latest work, *Subjectivity and Selfhood,* we have here in the mystics the self in the sense of an object of experience, in the sense of active egoic involvement, in the sense of passive experiencing, in the sense of agency, and in the sense of mineness.[6] So, what senses of self are at issue here in the forgetfulness of self?

We can say that all of these senses of self are in play in the mystics, and some of them are more or less directly implicated in the loss of self than others. For example, it is relatively unproblematic to speak of the loss of self where the sense of self is a special object, for this "self" could be surrendered while still living through the experience in its full integrity as mine.[7] "On the pre-reflective level, there is no explicit awareness of the experience being mine."[8] While we may not attend to this mineness in any explicit way, we can always reflect on this mineness and make this "background presence" an object; but the first-person experience of objects is not an object of this sort. These experiences, even the experience of the loss of self, are given to me in the first person, and this immediately reveals them to me as mine.[9]

Now we come to a much more problematic instance of the loss of self, namely, where it concerns the loss of mineness itself. Is it the case that the self as experiencing the mineness of the experience can be abandoned? Can *this* sense of self be surrendered? Do the mystics lose the first personal givenness of experiential life? So, for example, is there an experience of the mineness in spiritual marriage, in the ecstasy peculiar to the level of *yechidah* as the pure will of God, or in annihilation? When 'Attar writes of the thirty birds (*sī murgh*) who finally reach the King (*Sīmurgh*) and in seeing the King see themselves; when Meister Eckhart writes, "God's is-ness is my is-ness," are these mere ravings of madmen? Are they just over-joyous hyperboles?

There are three ways we can approach these questions. The first is to remain on the level of psychology and approach them in terms of psychopathology. I have already cited the attempt to do just that in the case of the Jewish mystic Joseph Caro. Many "experts" weighed in on the issue, citing hysterical manifestations, hallucinatory projections, inner cravings for supernatural knowledge and power, personality disassociation, and a qualitative suggestion of schizophrenic process.[10] We could find other contemporary examples of reducing such experiences to psychopathological manifestations in relation to other mystics as well.

Where we are examining, more specifically, expressions related to a loss of self, we might attempt to interpret them in terms of discordances within a putative normal range of experiences; they would then be understood as disturbances in the first-person perspective and the dimension of mineness. They would then be variants of what the phenomenological psychologist Eugène Minkowski calls the deficiency in ego consciousness. Take just one example that he cites: "I do not sense myself any more. I do not exist anymore. When someone speaks to me, I feel as if he were speaking to a dead person. I have to look at myself to be sure that it is I. I have the feeling of being an absent person." Or again, when asked if he had gone out the night before, the patient responds: "It was not really *I* who went out; it was as if some other guy had gone out and not me." And perhaps most poignantly, "I don't feel that it is right to use the expression 'I' and 'me'; they do not correspond to anything precise."[11]

On the surface, an account such as the one Minkowski gives bears a striking resemblance to the comments yielded by some of the mystics in the experience of union or in some of their so-called ecstatic sayings. To this extent it would be tempting to reduce the former and the latter to the same set of experiences and to treat them under the heading of psycho- or neuropathology.

Zahavi's work considers only psycho-physical and psycho-pathological phenomena as nonstandard modes of first-person experiences and does not consider the question of mystics and their first-person experiences or experiences that seem to challenge both the "normal" and "pathological" modes of self-awareness.[12] From the perspective developed here, however, any account of selfhood has to take into consideration the experiences cited by the mystics, no matter what one's conclusions might be on the matter of selfhood and the loss of self. To leave them out of account is to limit arbitrarily the field of phenomena for such an investigation.

The second way is to take the experiences as a distinctively novel field of phenomena. Such a distinctiveness would be grounded in the very quality of the experiences themselves. This is the more appropriate way of handling these issues *on this level*. Note that the mystics themselves are able to recognize the difference between everyday normal experiences and "abnormal" experiences (which they may term melancholy, self-deception, illusion, hallucination, etc.)—something that patients who suffer from schizophrenia are also able to do. The mystics, however, are not only sensitive to these distinctions, but they also distinguish between "normal" and "abnormal" everyday experiences on the one hand, and experiences that are "infused," or what we from our perspective call simply "mystical" on the other. Such differentiations are possible because there is an *experiential difference in their very givenness*. This is the basis for treating these kinds of experiences as distinctive. For the Abrahamic mystics dealt with here, the experienced loss of self is not the experience of its "illusory" or "fictive" character, nor does it have the tenor of a disturbing pre-psychotic self-disorder.[13]

I am not suggesting there are not pathological experiences, that everything is relative and just depends on the context, or that the normal and the abnormal are merely extremes on a sliding scale.[14] There are indeed pathological experiences insofar as they are determined as such in relation to optimal and concordant experiences that set the standards of experience *within* experience itself (i.e., not from externally imposed medical norms or therapeutic practices, or from eternal designs of nature or a divine being). My point is that these mystical experiences are not pathological or deviations from a standard, but are what we might call *hyper-normal* in the sense that they disclose a new optimal way of living and different revelations of selfhood that are grounded in new possibilities for humanity.[15] In fact, if we remain open to the field of experiences and to the distinctive kinds of evidence they bring with them, there is no reason to confine such mystical experiences to pathology—unless we arbitrarily impose on them the framework of psychopathology to which we have already ascribed. To do so would be, already and in advance, to define normal experiences *de jure* within this framework and mystical experiences outside of normality.

Given this, how are we to understand the dimension of self as mineness with respect to the loss of self? As suggested above, we can speak in an unproblematic sense of the loss of self where the self as an object is an issue, and even where we are concerned with active modes of self-reliance, self-ishness, attachment to self, and the like. Furthermore, we are not inferring, as Stace does, that the "Self" is a pure unity of the manifold of consciousness from which in mystical union the manifold itself has been eradicated.[16] The more problematic issue of the loss of self, and the more phenomenological one, occurs with respect to the sense of self as "mineness."

If Zahavi is correct in maintaining that nothing that lacks the consciousness of an experience in its first-personal mode of givenness, its "mineness," deserves to be called a self,[17] then in certain instances of mystical experience, we might very well be confronted with a loss of self, even in this "minimal" sense. To be sure, when we read accounts of the mystics who write even of an awareness of undifferentiated unity, we might be tempted to ascribe a sense of (self)-awareness to the experience. After all, is there not some remnant of self-awareness (or mineness) that makes any experience precisely an experience? But annihilation, spiritual marriage, and the like are not, properly speaking, "objects" of experience. When we are confronted with experiences like union and annihilation, or with ecstatic expressions of experiences like "I am the Truth (God)," I think we can no longer meaningfully speak of a self, even though these experiences may only be episodic. At that moment, the mystic is speaking, curiously enough, from the "perspective" of the Holy; the experience is not "mine," though there is an experience. Or again, the experience of "mineness" is so transformed as to make it meaningless to speak of a self in this instance. It is important to add that there is a loss of this minimal self without this loss of self being "pathological"—even if it does deviate from average or standard experiences. In sum, the loss of self in the mystics can include the "self" in the unproblematic senses all the way down in exceptional circumstances to the self as mineness.

Some may object that these kinds of questions presuppose a Western dualism and that to leave Western dualism (or "Western thought" altogether) is *ipso facto* to get rid of the problem of the self. However, I maintain that there is nothing essentially dualistic about the self and other, or in different terms, the home and alien, though it would be accurate to characterize them as both asymmetrical and co-foundational.[18] Certainly, my approach does not take into account the ways of Zen Buddhism or Eastern spiritual traditions. This, however, is not my task here. I am not asking if in all instances there can be a loss of self. Rather, working as I am within the context of the Abrahamic tradition, I am attempting to understand and to explicate the meaning of verticality and idolatry.

The loss of self in the sense of mineness, furthermore, is not experienced as voidness of own being in the way we might find the issue articulated in Zen Buddhism. In the latter, it would be grasped as a realization of the non-being of the self on the hither side of its being or non-being (*śūnyatā*). In the Abrahamic tradition, it is a matter of self-surrender, self-abandon with a positive orientation toward the Holy, or an experience that comes to me ultimately from the Holy. These are phenomenologically distinctive and irreducible experiences.[19] Even Foucault, who is more interested in "religion" as an instrument of power, recognizes such a fundamental experiential difference in spiritual orientation: Zen and Christianity are incommensurable, for while the former is geared to attenuating the individual, the latter, in its emphasis on loving between God and the individual, is trained on individuation.[20] Such a phenomenological and experiential position goes against the claim, made for example by Soelle or Stace and Smart, that there is no experience of the Holy that is ultimately distinctive from other mystical or spiritual traditions or that it is basically the same experience in widely different cultures, only "interpreted differently."[21] (The issue of intercultural differences is a topic for another work and cannot be dealt with here in a more systematic manner.)

I mentioned above that this approach was a second way of approaching the questions raised above concerning the loss of self and, more directly, the problem of individuation. Neither the first nor the second ways, however, are definitive. Ultimately, whether or not we conclude that the self is overcome in the minimal sense, this will not resolve the issue of individuation. Having determined the sense of human being through loving as person, it is on the level of person and with the issue of personal uniqueness that we have to address the question of individuation. The issue is not whether or not there is a loss of "self," but whether or not there is a loss of personal uniqueness and whether the inter-Personal structure is dissolved in union and the like, or whether and to what extent it persists.

One further qualification before proceeding: it should be clear by now from the preceding that what we mean by person is not reducible to a "narrative" concept of self. Zahavi, for example, speaks of the person as a narrative construction "because what is being addressed by this model is the nature of my personality or personal character" as a personality that evolves through time. Accordingly, for him, narrative personhood presupposes experiential selfhood (but not vice versa).[22]

One can agree that the narrative self is founded on the minimal self, but I have to disagree that the narrative self is reducible to the person. Person cannot be "constructed" through narrative but is given dynamically in acts peculiar to the emotional sphere, most profoundly through loving (and as we will see below, in the constitution of vocation and obedience as generative service). I agree that this individuation is fully developed in a "communal horizon" if what one means is that individuation involves the dimension of otherness.[23] But on the level of person, we have to give this statement a more nuanced qualification. It is not just that the self is "personalized *intersubjectively*."[24] Rather, it is that the intersubjective dimension is here qualified as an *interpersonal* one, which in terms of the religious dimension of experience is inter-Personal and morally inter-personal.

In the interest of grappling with these and related questions, it is essential that we become clear about the meaning of individuation in general and its distinctiveness in the inter-Personal sphere. Because this is such an important problem, it will be useful in what follows to work through the various possible notions of individuation in some detail, reserving, in the final analysis, "individuation" in the proper sense for personal uniqueness.

Individuation: Thisness, Singularity, Uniqueness

By individuation in general, I mean a dissociation or delimitation—internal or external—that makes this thing *this particular, individual* thing; what makes this organic being this *singular* being; what makes this person this *unique* person. Let me begin with the question of individuation as it pertains to inorganic being, then vital being, and finally spirit. I will then be in a position to address the so-called individuation of objects in contrast to the individuation in the proper sense as it pertains to persons.

Inorganic Forms, Objects, and Thisness

In and of themselves, inorganic forms do not dissociate themselves; they have no "inner being" and no "environment" (*Umwelt*).[25] We can find in inorganic reality forces and fields of forces, but these forces do not have a purposeful orientation; they are without internal direction or orientation, and they do not individuate themselves. While we have a pretty good idea of how tornados are formed in terms of climatic conditions required for their formation and while we know when and where they are more likely to strike, their appearances are essentially random and are open, in this respect, only to statistical meaning.[26] This is not to say that we cannot find regularity in inorganic reality and its forces. Tornados are almost universally cyclonic, that is, they spin counterclockwise in the Northern Hemisphere (though there have been documented cases of anti-cyclonic rotations); cloud-to-ground lightning occurs when a negative discharge is met by the return stroke of a positive electrical charge (though there is the phenomenon of "ball lightning" for which there is no adequate scientific understanding); obsidian rock cleaves regularly with a shell-like fracture; crystals (except for opal and glass) always have a regular atomic structure or "habit": one recognizes a trigonal system in calcite, an orthorhombic system in topaz, and so forth. Nevertheless, there is nothing in inorganic reality in and of itself that is self-differentiating, making it itself "singular" or "unique."

Instead, there are only "individual" or "particular" things on the level of inorganic reality, not because they are "self-individuating," but because human beings make these dissociations, practically and conceptually. How do such dissociations take place? How is the dissociations of objects (taken in a broad sense) different from early kinds of dissociation in the vital sphere and in personal individuation?

According to Edmund Husserl, all empirical objects are constituted in the immanent form of time. It is the form of time—present, past, future—that most basically gives objects individual existence.[27] While all objects will have some temporal position or duration, the problem of individual existence gets more complex when, for example, two objects appear simultaneously, like two red flashes in the sky, each one being "now." In this case, a second character, the spatial character of being-here, individualizes the object, but it essentially presupposes the temporal placement now (Hua 33, 292). The temporal and spatial placement of the object, here and now, constitutes an object, say, a pencil, as *this* individual object, distinct from every other object (Hua 33, 292, 301). In being this pencil, now, here, it becomes actual, existing, and not merely possible. Let's call such an aspect of thisness its individu*aliz*ation (as opposed to "individu-ation," which we reserve for persons).

Individualization bears directly on *empirical objects* because of their *Einmaligkeit*, their nonrecurring placement in time, and secondarily, on their spatial differentiation. This concerns what we call empirical objects. But what about another sort of object, what about essences or eidetic objects? With respect to *Einmaligkeit, essential objects* are not, *qua* eidetic objects, "individualized." They are, however, given to consciousness. The question for us concerns their distinctive mode of givenness. How is the essence given? To respond to this question, we need to examine the process of *particularization,* that is, *how* essences become particularized. Ultimately, although we can distinguish between the processes of individualization and particularization, given the concrete richness of the phenomenal field, the problem of the individualization of objects remains abstract without also bringing into play the particularization of the essence.

The particularization of an essence concerns the instantiation of the essence in a particular entity bearing the essence's scope (Hua 33, 300). If individualization is the direct result of the temporal placement of time-consciousness, and secondarily of spatial location, then the particulariza-tion of an essence is an indirect result of time-consciousness as a placement of the individual object in a temporal (and possibly spatial) position. It is one of the founding insights of phenomenology, already detailed in the "Sixth Logical Investigation," that an essence can only be given in a kind of *"Zusammenschauen"* or *"polythetic act"* (Hua 33, 310, 321). According to the *Logical Investigations,* an essence can only be given on the basis of a temporal or spatio-temporal empirical object of experience as it is given in "simple" perception. Essential insight, or the consciousness of essence (*Wesensbewußtsein*), is therefore founded in simple perception. Whereas an empirical object can be given as it is without putting into play still more basic acts and thus does not itself presuppose still other constituted objects (hence, it is simple and founding), an essential object presupposes the givenness of an empirical one in order for the essence to be given (hence, is founded). In this way, the essence is said to be a surplus over the empirical object, and essential insight (as a mode of categorial intuition), a surplus over simple perception.[28] Although it is a surplus in this way, an essence can only be given *in and through* a particular, while never being reducible to it.

Taken as a whole, essential insighting is said to be "polythetic" because two kinds of seeing are in play in order for the essence to be given: an empirical one, and, simultaneously in and through this, an eidetic one. Moreover, while an essence can be given in and through several particular individuals, only one particular instance is needed for the essence to be given as such. To assert that the essence is capable of being given in any temporal position or in any particular instance is another way of saying that any individual within a scope of possibilities can serve as a conveyer of the essence. Some, however, may be better conveyors than others; some may be "exemplary."[29]

But if immanent time is the form of givenness of *all* objects, the kind of surplus of eidetic objects over the temporality of empirical objects does not mean that essential objects have no relation to time; rather, it suggests that their temporality is not of an objective order (Hua 33, 321; 316–17). Accordingly, a universal is given with a temporal duration, but this duration plays an entirely different role from the duration in which an empirical object appears (Hua 33, 311). An essence has its *Allgegenwart,* its omnipresence in time, capable of being given in any temporal position (Hua 33, 311–12).

A concordance of temporal appearings does not constitute the essence's identity, just as different times do not extend its duration, since in one temporal instance the essence is given everywhere as identically the same (Hua 33, 310). So when the essence is grasped in repeated acts, we do not have different universals that are grasped and then associated; rather, the essence is given in a complete identification as identically the same in different temporal positions and as something that does not have longer or shorter duration.

Individual objects can only be the same—hence, particular instances —insofar as they endure continually through different temporal positions concordantly. If they suffer discordance, they could remain the same only by virtue of an overarching concordance. Otherwise, they would be "different" objects, uniform or similar to each other (Hua 33, 321–22). By contrast, an essence is given incidentally in such a time, since different times do not extend its duration, just as one particular time does not diminish its duration. For example, I may consume bread, and the bread can be said to endure as long as a certain amount of it has not been eaten. But the essence of bread is not thereby consumed in the eating of the bread. I cannot parcel out the essence "bread" in time to make it last longer.

Although the problem of individualization can be treated apart from particularization, where the concrete actual entity is concerned, individualization and particularization cannot be separated. We can see an intimate relationship between individualization and particularization in terms of a phenomenology of association or the materialized form of time-consciousness, for example, with respect to how an individualized entity can simultaneously be the particular entity homogeneous to another individualized entity that is also a particularizing of the same essence.[30] It is this that is at the heart of the problem of unity and difference where individualization and particularization are concerned.

When we consider a simple case of transcendent objects—for example, two red triangles—we note that prior to making any comparison, the triangles link up, forming a uniform pair with respect to redness and being triangles. Here color (red) distinguishes itself from figure (triangle) such that the two respective moments of red come into relief and exercise an affective force.[31] If we change the example so that we have two triangles, one darker, one lighter red, or more drastically, one red, and one blue, we would have uniformity with respect to the triangle, but similarity as a whole, since a dimension of contrast, or "fusion-at-a-distance" would intervene as constitutive of the appearance. (The same could be said *mutatis mutandis* with respect to immanent objects, say, two notes, both "C," but one staccato, one legato.)

How are the *individualized* entities also uniform or similar to each other, and thus *particular* instances of the same essence? In going from one present to the next, an individualized entity is held in retention, allowing the consciousness of a succession and thus a formal unity constituted by time-consciousness; but this *individualized* entity is also the bearer of a materially relevant character, say, red or triangle. Thus, this *individualized* entity is the *particular* conveyer of "red" and "triangle." Not being exhausted in the individualized/particular instance of the thing, an essential structure can function as the same for other nuances—not arbitrarily other nuances, however, for the particularizations are still bound by the essential structure.

While the particularization of the thing is a restriction of the essence, it simultaneously opens up a depth or richness that transcends it as a surplus. It is this "surplus" or "essential structure" that continues to be functional. Through the simple seeing of this individualized red triangle, the essences, red and triangle, are also self-given, allowing them then to become the "what" or the "common features" of the other individualized red triangle.[32] Here a synthesis of homogeneity can only take place because the essence is "self-giving" through the individualized-particularized entity such that it leadingly guides the perceptual train that unfolds in associative syntheses (of homogeneity, heterogeneity, etc.).

To get to an essence through one thing is to get to all things of that essence. In being intimate with one thing, I am always already intimate with all the others, even though I have never directly encountered the others. This operative dynamic of eidetic insight enables me to shift my gaze from this thing now and here to "the same" in the other thing as they are held in a formal unity through time-consciousness. Some possibilities will be more "alluring" than others and exercise a stronger or weaker affective force. Here the affective force will radiate out from the particular-individual in such a way that it accentuates objects (e.g., the red ones) that will fulfill the conditions for forming a configuration.

When we examine the phenomenon, not just in terms of formal time-consciousness but of the materialized form of time *qua* content, the process of individualizing objects cannot stand alone; it must be integrated into the problematic of particularization. The concrete actuality is *individual and particular.* This is what we mean by the *thisness* of the object.

To sum up, dissociation is only operative with the practical or conceptual intervention of human beings. Accordingly, where objects are concerned, the principle of dissociation is time and space disclosed through the processes of individualization and particularization. We can speak of an individual being as an "instance" where the individual object is subsumed under the *universal,* of its having a context in which it becomes meaningful, and this meaning being subject to our use of it or to our interpretations. We can speak of the object being *this* object, as nonrecurring and as different from other objects. But in and of itself, inorganic nature or "materiality" is not individuating. Dissociation is something that is imposed from without by human beings. Having examined the issue of dissociation as it pertains to inorganic being, let me now turn to this process as it concerns organic being.

Vital Being and Singularity

Organic beings are not merely "objects" for human beings who make external differentiations; they also have a being in and for themselves;

they are self-differentiating, self-limiting in both spatial and temporal respects. This level of being, to follow Husserl's and Scheler's analyses, coincides with what is called, in general, the "vital" level of existence or "psychic life."[33] The vital or the psycho-physical sphere spans plants, animals, and human beings, and as such they partake in their own way in the vital impetus (*Lebensdrang*). Scheler identifies four forms of psycho-physical life that I find particularly helpful as a way of organizing my exposition of singularity: vital feeling or drive, instinct, habit, and practical intelligence.

Vital feeling is present in plants as well as in animals and in human beings. Plants, for example, express the directedness of the vital in their growth, reproduction, and death; the vital feeling or drive of plants is also evident in their heliotropic or geotropic orientations, impelled, in an unspecified manner, toward the "up," the "side," the "down." Even though plants can be understood to have an interiority, their directedness is toward an "outside" in a general manner, directed toward possible resistances and realities encountered in the environing-world that are significant for the life of the organism. Although there is no reporting back of its varying states to its center, even plant life exhibits what Scheler calls "expressiveness." Expressiveness, this original phenomenon of life, is evident as the physiognomy of its inner states such as vigorousness or feebleness, exuberance or poverty.[34] Because there is evidence of spatial and temporal dissociative unity (*Geschlossenheit*) as manifested through drive peculiar to plant psycho-physical life, we can speak of a dissociation internal to this sphere of life, or more precisely, what we will call a "singularization," where plants are concerned, though the measure of this dissociative unity is somewhat more restrictive than in the case of animal life.[35]

Instinct, or instinctive behavior is the second form of psycho-physical life. By instinctive behavior, I mean that the organism comports itself with a sense-orientation as an immediate feeling-encounter with a specific environing world, or what I called in a different work, a "terrain."[36] Instinctive comportment is oriented in such a way that it is significant for the whole of the bearer of life or for the whole of other living organisms; it has a firm, unchanging rhythm and responds to typical reoccurring situations that are significant for the life of the species. Correlative to instinct is the emergence of relatively single (*Einzel*) sensations and ideas out of diffuse complexes, or of a single drive from an instinctive sense-complex of behavior that requires satisfaction. This goes hand in hand with the emergence of the single living being, freed from its bondage to the species. Making possible a larger variety of special situations that the single living being may encounter and to which it may respond, instinctive behavior as such nevertheless serves the species and not the individual; it is therefore not a response to specific factors in the environing-world that vary from individual to individual. Instead, instinctual comportment is always a reaction to a specific *structure*, an orientation toward possible portions of an environing-world that is typical for a species.[37]

Habit and the habitual mode of comportment—the third form of psycho-physical life—does, in distinction to instinctual behavior, tend to serve the individual and not the species. We see this evident in all living beings whose comportment can be modified on the basis of earlier experience in a meaningful way, that is, in human and other than human animal life, though it does not appear to be present in plant life. Habit is a function of what we might call, with Husserl, the associative laws of "passive synthesis," that is, the pre-reflective, primordial regularity of sense-genesis that functions in principle prior to the onset of active, egoic participation and active meaning orientation.[38] The laws of association, such as homogeneity, heterogeneity, similarity, uniformity, and contiguity, are not purely formal; they function in concrete contexts of *affectively significant* environing-worlds. Something that emerges for the living being as affectively charged can lure a "turning toward" it; it can link up with other similar features; it can provoke a reproduction of it in memory. In this way the living being can repeat it virtually and actually, imitate it, and so forth—a process that is the basis of trial and error. Such behavior can become sedimented and integrated into patterns of behavior, forming not only a habitual style of the single individual being but a "tradition" among social forms of animal life as in herds or packs.[39]

It is not my goal to discuss all the elements of this very rich process of habit and passive association. I am only pointing out that we can witness various dimensions of self-dissociation in psycho-physical life. Through the efficacy of habit, the single individual emerges more directly than in the case of instinct because here the individual can adapt itself to new situations that may not be typical of the species or may function in ways that do not always serve the reproduction of the species and in this way discloses a new dimension of possibilities for the enrichment of life.

Whereas instinct appears rigid for the "individual" with respect to the possibilities disclosed through habit and associative memory, the latter itself appears fixed with respect to practical intelligence. In practical intelligence, the fourth form of psycho-physical life, a living being is in a position of responding to a situation meaningfully without trial and error because it is capable of elementary forms of choice. An organism manifests intelligence, on Scheler's account, insofar as it is able to comport itself meaningfully toward a goal "suddenly," independently of the number of attempts (trial and error), and "cleverly" (attaining it) or "foolishly" (missing it). Only a being who manifests intelligence can be clever or foolish. Moreover, this intelligence, which is expressive of the vital impetus, is itself bound to life insofar as the behavior serves the agitation of drive or the satisfaction of a need. Finally, intelligence is practical because the sense of it is to attain the living-being's drive-oriented goal through a "doing" (Handlung). Intelligence is only raised above prudence, cunning, and cleverness when it serves goals peculiar to the sphere of spirit.[40]

In practical intelligence as a psycho-physical form of the life force, then, the single individual being emerges even more distinctively. Now, when the individual living being encounters a situation, it may not be just new or atypical for the species (as was the case in habitual behavior), but it can be new for the individual. Things that appear in the environing-world are not only affectively significant, they acquire the dynamic functional value of instrument; through such instrumental behavior there is genuine discovery that is relevant for the individual. An individual living being can intervene abruptly in the constellation of drives, can circumvent immediate gratifications to attain distant ones: through practical intelligence, it can live *pragmatically*.

Having identified these four forms of psycho-physical life, we can make the following three concluding observations before we go on to individuation in the sense of personal uniqueness.

First, inorganic reality only admits of dissociation through our practical and conceptual intervention. In this case, we can speak of the material world and objects being individual-particular, we can speak of *thisness*, but materiality itself is not a principle of individuation.

Second, depending on the manifestation of the psycho-physical form of life, there are different kinds of self-dissociation within the sphere of the vital. These manifest not "thisness" or "individual-particularity," but *singularity*. In each form of the life impetus or vital urge, we can see a different degree of singularity with respect to the life force, and this singularity will be more or less pronounced, depending on whether vital feeling, instinct, associative habit, or practical intelligence is prominent in that living organism.

Third, while these psycho-physical forms are distinctive and enable an interior dissociation to emerge to a weaker or stronger degree, they are still essentially expressions of the *organic* sphere of reality and ultimately serve the ends of life. Although we may find it useful to speak of an "outer" physical dimension of organic reality in relation to and expressive of an "inner" psychic one, fundamentally, it is still one single vital drive that constitutes organic reality and that directs itself as a proliferation of forms for its own aggrandizement.[41]

In sum, the problem of dissociation, understood as the emergence of singularity and expressed in psycho-physical spheres, from vital feeling to practical intelligence, is still contained within the dimension of vital life. It pertains to organic beings to a simpler or more complex degree as it ranges from plant life to human beings. A psycho-physical organism has an ontic "center" in the sense that it is "self-limiting" or "self-dissociating." On the level of drive, we find the inkling of interiority in expressiveness as an original phenomenon of life; on the level of instinct, we have the emergence of sense-orientation and a single drive from an instinctive sense-complex of behavior that liberates the single being from the species, making possible a larger variety of special situations that the single living being may encounter and to which it may respond. On the level of habitual behavior, we have the operation of the associative principle that expresses a further liberation from the species, the increase of centralization, and the ability to react to new, nontypical situations of the species. Finally, on the level of practical intelligence, we witness elementary forms of choice and a behavior that can respond in ways that are new and relevant for the individual itself.

However, as manifestations of the life force, these forms of singularization do not yet bear on individuation where the dimension of "spirit" is concerned; singularization does not yet get to the problem of the human being *as* person and hence to the problem of individuation as personal uniqueness.

Spirit and Person

Maurice Merleau-Ponty writes that the body's role is to ensure the metamorphosis of invisible into the visible, transforming ideas into things. Through the vital appropriative and disappropriative structures, what was

previously merely "interior" or only "theory" attains its incarnate significance; the body realizes existence as transcendence, which is a different
way of saying, as he does later, that flesh "is" an element of Being.[42]

Behind these rather prosaic, cryptic, and almost innocent-sounding
statements hides a presupposition about the dimension of spirit in relation
to vital being. If inorganic and organic being can be said to be "real," or
qualify reality, if the real is force, modified in different ways as vital urge,
then spirit in distinction to the real is "impotent," not "real."

Someone may object, however. "Why take all the trouble to expose
the religious dimension of experience in the mystics as something to be
taken seriously and to broaden the sphere of evidence to include, as it
should, religious dimensions of experiencing, when one now maintains
that spirit is impotent and not real?" Here we must be careful. For to follow a long phenomenological tradition beginning with Husserl, to say
that something is not real does not mean that it is not *actual*. The sphere of
spirit is actual, and it is efficacious, but not in the sense of "real" force or
power. As we will see, its efficacy lies, in part, in its ability to direct and
to guide. Since force can be force without internal direction or orientation (e.g., tornados, lightning), it is not dependent on spirit to be forceful;
whereas spirit, which is in and of itself not "real" or "force" in this sense,
is dependent upon the real in order to direct or guide, and in this way to
effect change in the world.

But let us be clear: spirit is a genuinely unique phenomenon that cannot be derived from or reduced to basic drive or the vital impetus. Let me
take up the role of spirit here to clarify the individuation of person. For
the purposes of this exposition, I treat five aspects that are unique to the
emergence of spirit. I consider them for the moment in their distinctiveness and then understand them in terms of the person as an integrated
whole.

1. Spirit is actual in two senses. First, spirit is actual in the sense that
it has an existential density that is distinct from what we have called
"reality"; although it does not give itself in the mode of "reality" and can
be said to be "irreal" in this sense, it does give itself in other ways, for
example, in emotional, rational, and volitional acts. Second, and related
to the latter point, spirit is actual in the sense that spirit has its being in
the creative execution of *acts,* not functions.[43] Acts, which are lived as
a dynamic orientation, reveal the presence of spirit and can never be an
object; acts are "initiatory," "spontaneous," "creative," in the sense of

improvisational. This is the reason I mentioned above that person, who lives in and through acts, can as such never become an object, or that it is an act of violence to attempt to objectify persons.[44] Of course, the being that is also the bearer of spirit is able to objectify its own physiological functions and psychological experiences, for example, through reflection; we can also speak meaningfully here of psychic states and the like. The main issue now is that while spirit as act-ual can never become an object, we can nevertheless be attentive to spirit in different ways otherwise than objectification. The mystics try to capture this by appealing in their own ways to "recollection," to *kavannah,* or sincere concentration, to focused meditation, and the like; Scheler appeals to "collecting" ourselves (*sich sammeln*) and "concentrating," Heidegger to "meditative thinking"—all of which are different from objectifying.

2. The bearer of spirit can inquire into the meaning of things and not just take them for granted; it can interpret reality *as* it is given, as such. There are many ways in which we could express this. Important to note here is that spirit is not practical or technical intelligence, which also belongs to the psycho-physical sphere of existence, but is revealed in what phenomenologists call "ideation." Scheler gives a striking example of the Buddha here. After leaving his sheltered existence in his father's palace, Siddhartha Gautama encountered a single person who was poverty-stricken, a single ailing person, and a single dead person. He immediately grasped the essential condition of the world as suffering. This grasping is phenomenologically distinct from practical intelligence that could only recognize pain and then ask after its cause, how it could be removed, and so forth. The latter, however, is quite different from encountering the "strange and surprising essential condition" that the world is riddled with pain, evil, and sorrow.[45] Ideation need not be understood as a one-time affair, however; being guided by original insights of this kind initiates a pathway to further growth and development of spirit as person.[46] This is a process I have characterized in another work as the operative dynamic of eidetic insight.[47]

3. Even if it is my pain that I experience, and even if my pain is given to me immediately, I can still detach myself from it. This leads us to another observation, not to the practice of intelligence but to the practice of *detachment* that is peculiar to the dimension of spirit. In one respect, to detach oneself from psycho-physical as well as inorganic being can have and has had disastrous consequences in the West because it has issued—just to

name one instance—in a domination of the human being over beings other than human. This feature, however, is *not intrinsic to spirit* or to the practice of detachment, but to a mode of idolatry specific to the ecological dimension of experience, where we do not live out the interpenetration of spirit and reality, and where the Earth is disregarded in its aesthetic function as ground. (This is a topic for another work on the Earth and forms of "idolatry" in relation to genuine ecological experience.)

I emphasize this feature of detachment here because it is a practice cultivated by the mystics. Indeed, one might even say that their attempt is *to actualize* spirit through the *de-realization* of the self. Specifically, loving can "de-realize" through its orientation toward the Holy, toward other persons, and toward beings other than human. This is undoubtedly what Simone Weil means when she writes that "we participate in the creation of the world by decreating ourselves."[48] De-creation, de-realization is "conversion" or the process of returning from the reversal of idolatry in the sense of being attached to the real at the expense of spirit. To de-realize my self is to actualize Myself; yet detachment, de-realization is not a negation of reality, since it is a *qualification of the real through loving* and hence the process of "redemption." This leads me to the next point.

4. The human being uniquely concretizes the spheres of the inorganic, the organic, and spirit. While we have been viewing spirit in its differentiation from the inorganic and organic to focus on its distinctiveness, we run the risk of losing more than we have accomplished if we do not also emphasize the interpenetration of these levels of being in the concrete unity of the human being. Indeed, in the Modern period, the predominant view of the human being was its rational character removed from the roles of affect, impulse, drives, and desires. Marx, Nietzsche, Freud, and more recently, Deleuze and Guattari, have shown in what ways we are not governed by reason but are influenced by impersonal anonymous forces, historical milieus, subliminal interests, drives, productive desires, instincts, fantasy life, the subconscious, and so forth, which manifest themselves in individual choices, addictions, social behavior, historical patterns, and the like. They are so intertwined with who we are that it is not entirely clear at times just "who" is the initiator of acts or to what extent they are even "freely executed."

But rather than this plunging us into a vitalism, it conversely highlights that in the human being as person, who is the locus of spirit and life, the *vital is not merely the vital;* in the human being, addictions and desires are as much "spiritual" as they are vital or psychic. Furthermore, it does not mitigate the phenomenological distinctiveness of the emergence of spirit (which is not reducible to reason) in relation to the vital; rather, it underscores the seriousness and difficulty of the undertakings by the mystics to suspend, for example, through ascesis (as one way among others) the operation of the vital in relation to which the world appears as resistance and at the same time as the precondition for all sensory experience.[49] In phenomenological terms, their lived epoché, their lived reduction, as it were, *liberates the vertical dimension inherent in the vital.*

My suggestion is not simply that we can never completely suspend the vital or untangle the knots of intercultural influences. As Luther points out, it is futile to view spirit and drive as antithetical. They have appeared, and they have done so in such a way that precludes contest; it is meaningless to assume that there can be a struggle between something in the realm of reality and force (basic drive) and no-thing in the realm of irreality (spirit).[50] Indeed, spirit and life are essentially related in the human being. Rather, any attempt "to suspend" or "to liberate" is in and of itself evidence of the originality of spirit in relation to the vital and is testimony to its irreducible character. More exactly, the efficacy of spirit lies not in generating or negating instinctual energy but in *directing and guiding* vital forces, and in this way *realizing* ideas and values.[51] Spirit (irreal) appeals or lures drive (real) by presenting ways of being toward the infinite fullness of its ownmost possibilities; that is, in being spiritualized, it draws the real from itself as limited toward itself as infinite.[52]

5. Peculiar to the level of spirit is not merely reason, ideation, detachment, but the emotional sphere of existence that is manifest as acts like loving, hating, and, insofar as they are initiated, sympathy and feeling.[53] As noted above, just because the emotional sphere is not rational does not mean that it belongs to the level of drives or instincts. While we can find generosity, help, reconciliation, and the like among psycho-physical life, on the level of spirit, we can *prefer,* for example, the pleasant to the useful, the joyful to the pleasant, as values in themselves. Moreover, loving and hating express something new in relation to the vital sphere. Whereas vital values end with the vital (or tools as such end in their usefulness), whereas in life we live to die, in loving and hating, we are in principle open to infinity and can persist beyond death (e.g., we can love someone even after he or she is dead), even if the love only *de facto* lasted a short while. Loving can actualize (spiritualize) vital drives and

forces, ultimately, in the direction of holiness.[54] In and through loving, the human being, as the interpenetration of spirit and vital orders, is concretized as person.

Where do we stand now on the issue of individuation? What makes me irreducible to another? What is the principle of individuation where persons are concerned? We have seen that it does not reside in inorganic materiality. There is no intrinsic dissociation of any kind on this level of being. Spatio-temporal thisness is imposed conceptually and practically from the outside; these conceptual and practical performances might treat the human being as a so-called "cultural object," different from other "cultural objects"; we might then understand *this* human being as a particular human being in relation to universal humanity. But aside from these approaches, which represent a profound misunderstanding of the person, spatio-temporal dissociations in the form of individual-particular thisness cannot speak to the issue of the individuation of persons.

Moreover, the principle of individuation is not vital being. There are intimations of such internal dissociations on the level of the vital that in varying degrees express a *singularity* of the individual living being. But even on the level of practical intelligence or pragmatic behavior, we do not find creatively initiated acts as distinctive from the movement of vital being. The singularity appears and vanishes with the movement of the vital since it is internal to the movement of life and death. Yes, my body separates me from another; as expressive of the life force, I become singular through it. Yes, I have my individual desires that are different from other individual desires. My perception of color is different from all others who see the "same" color. I am singularly different from the squirrel outside my window, but as a singular being, I am not ultimately irreducible to the squirrel.

This does not mean that we as vital beings are not all vitally connected. Merleau-Ponty was correct in citing and exploiting the essential *reversibility of the flesh,* the lived-body: all lived-bodies are of the same flesh (*la chair*); as such, they exist in a relationship of reversibility. As singular, each living being in its peculiar reflexive character is, as he writes, exemplary of this general reversibility. Flesh, as an element of Being, is Tangibility, Sensibility, Visibility, Audibility; and all tangibles, etc., not only share essentially in this movement but are expressive of this movement.[55] As such, however, the flesh is not and cannot be a principle of individuation. This is why, for example, Merleau-Ponty and Levinas write of two different levels when the one, Merleau-Ponty, understands the handshake as reversible, and the other, Levinas, understands the handshake as expressive of irreversibility and asymmetry. In the latter case, it pertains to the absolute uniqueness of the other person.

If there is an individuating principle such that it makes "me" irreducibly unique, it is not to be found on the level of inorganic or organic being; it is not evident through conceptually and practically applying differentiations from the outside. Rather, it occurs internally, on the level of spirit, and more precisely, concretized as person. I approach this individuation as a twofold movement of personal uniqueness.

Personal Uniqueness

Given-Givenness

If we understand givenness in a broad sense, we would have to say that all creation is a givenness to itself. Inorganic being, vital being, and personal being are all "given"; all beings, inorganic, organic, spiritual, are not self-grounding. So how is givenness distinctive in the case of persons, and how does it relate to the problem of individuation?

Not being self-grounding means more, where persons are concerned, than being born to parents or being born into a homeworld. I am not just given in relation to the Holy; I am not just thrown into relations with others.[56] I am given to Myself. Intrinsic to this givenness is a given, a given-givenness.

The relation to the Holy through which I am given to myself charges me with a kind of "ought." This "ought" that comes to me, comes to me "alone" such that it can neither be exchanged for another "ought" nor transferred to another person. It is given independently of my explicit knowledge of it and before I could choose it for myself. Yet it is given in such a way that I, as human being, can have a pre-reflective *eidetic* "value-insight" into my person.[57] I can grasp it *as* meaningful for myself and as peculiar to Myself, as a good-in-itself-for-me.

Is this not contradictory? How can there be a good-in-itself *for me alone*? Does not the very notion of the in-itself imply universality such that it applies equally to everyone? Here is one place where we find the "universal" and the "absolute" parting ways. The good-in-itself is necessary, binding, decisive, and in this sense, absolute. This good-in-itself, which qualifies Myself in inter-Personal loving in this primordial epiphany, is received whether we want it or not and "before" we could subject it to our volition. It cannot be explained, argued with, argued out, transferred, exchanged, or negotiated. It is unconditional and binding, yet it is absolutely binding *on me* and me *alone,* even if others have the "same" good-in-itself-for-me. *It is unique to me.* The absoluteness of this good-in-itself that comes to "me alone" in part pre-defines my personal uniqueness in the world and among others. Given as the givenness to myself, the good-in-itself-for-me might go unrecognized (for reasons I will mention below), but the extent to which it is made thematic in the spiritual act of personal discovery (which may require a lifetime) is the extent to which it is grasped as my "vocation," my "calling." Such a uniqueness of the personal vocation can be predicated neither of plurality nor of singularity, for it is a relation *each* person has precisely in his or her difference, whether there are many who have this "same" vocation or only one actual individual. The good-in-itself-for-me, grasped as my vocation, is one moment of personal individuation that individuates me as *unique.*

There is certainly a question of how this vocation is grasped. It may come in a moment of insight to which only we have access; it may be glimpsed by another who "knows us better than ourselves"; it may come into relief when we turn away from it, allowing us to detect it, *via negativa,* only by the traces it leaves or the silhouette it casts, like the norm that stands out only by deviating from it. Secretly at work in us, always directing and guiding us without forcing us, it may never be perceived in any explicit manner, and certainly not as a distinct content of consciousness.[58]

There is a Chasidic tale of a rabbi, a teacher of renowned goodness, who at the ripe age of 92 anguished in the last hours of his life. His students came to him asking, "'Master, why are you so troubled? What have you to fear?" The rabbi replied: "I am afraid of a question God may ask me: If he asks me, 'Jacob, why, in your long life, have you not accomplished the great tasks that Moses had accomplished?' I would have a reply: I would say: 'But Lord, you have not given me the gifts of courage and leadership that you had given Moses.' And so I would have an answer. And if God asks me, 'Jacob, why, in your long life, have you not done the deeds that

Maimonides had done?' I would have a reply, I would say: 'But, Lord, you have not given me the intellect you had given Maimonides.' And so I would have an answer. But if God asks me: 'Jacob, why, in your long life, have you not done what only you could have done?' For this, I would have no answer. It is this question that I dread."

Such a task, which is already given personally in this inter-Personal relation, can only be realized in and as the unique life who is this person. This is why Kafka's portrayal of the man standing before "the law" stuns us, just as it does the figure in the parable.[59] How can I be kept from a law—"the" law—which by its very essence is universal and valid everywhere and for everyone? I keep myself from it precisely when I take it as universally valid, subject to the norms of reason, when I try to confine this absolute relation to the strictures of the autonomy of reason. But it was meant only for me, the parable concludes.

The story shocks us because we are faced with a seeming paradox: *The law* (universal) that is meant only for *me,* and for me *alone* (individual). When we approach it this way, the parable is inaccessible because we cannot reconcile, rationally, the universal and the individual. Inter-Personally, however, the parable takes on its full meaning because the "law," the good-in-itself, is given only for me, personally, uniquely, absolutely. It is the good-in-itself-for-me, grasped as vocation, my given-givenness.

This is why, to borrow a phrase from Simone Weil: "Nobody but myself [Myself?] can appreciate these obligations."[60] This is further why only I can feel guilty about falling from my vocation: "guilty," because it is experienced in its absoluteness prior to my reflective deliberation about it and because I stand before another, the Holy; "I," and no other, because it is experienced as *for-me* and for me *alone,* uniquely. (Or rather, no one can experience guilt about my falling away from my vocation the way I do in my personal uniqueness. However, it is possible to have a collective guilt [for another to experience guilt] about another person's falling away from his or her vocation in the sense that we, as persons, are collectively responsible for the becoming of the individual person.)[61]

Obedience or Disobedience

We understand the givenness of the good-in-itself-for-me as generated from primordial loving. It is what we have called above "primordial epiphany," which is the inter-Personal nexus. Being given to Myself, personally, in primordial loving, "I" am given to Myself as this good-in-itself-for me. As loving, this givenness qua epiphany, intrinsically invites a loving response of some kind.

The givenness of this good-in-itself-for-me is one aspect of personal individuation. It is a givenness that is given. There is another. This good-in-itself-for-me that I cannot negotiate solicits a response—a response that is executed "freely," spontaneously, improvisationally, of its own accord. The highest form of response is what the mystics understand as "obedience." To be sure, the mystics speak of obedience in a variety of ways. Often the mention of obedience in the Jewish, Christian, and Islamic mystics occurs in the context of obedience to a superior, to a spiritual master, or to a confessor. But these figures are understood as helpers, as it were, so that the individual learns in service to surrender him- or herself, to uncover without attachment the good-in-itself-for-me as a way of aligning my will to the "will of God." As Weil observes, properly speaking, we never accept or refuse; rather, we obey or disobey.

It might sound terribly simplistic to say that we either obey or disobey. Does this not already presuppose that we "know" our own unique calling—provided that we even care to find it at all? If it is *for me,* how does it come to pass that I may *not* know this good-in-itself-for-me or struggle to find it? This is precisely the paradox of Kafka's parable. The good-in-itself-for-me, this vocation, is not at all given like an object and is not something I can grasp initially in a rationally cognitive manner. Since it bears on the core of the person, it is given with respect to the emotional sphere. So just because it is not something to know initially does not mean it is nothing, either. Given as it is with respect to the emotional sphere of existence, it bears on us with an affective, emotional significance. Is it no coincidence that we spend so much time with friends, counselors, therapists, clergy, in figuring out Who am I? What is my place in the world? What am I to do? If our existence were merely a rational one, perhaps this vocation would be transparent, and simply knowing what signifies me, what makes me who I am, would immediately satisfy me. But the good-in-itself-for-me is not just something out there to grasp; it *plagues* me. It seizes me "before" I could get a hold on it; and if I am unable to comprehend it completely, I am not able to escape it, either. What dignifies me with my very sense of being, what makes me me, does not necessarily make me happy; it constrains me, burdens me, can give me "issues," can make "me" conflicted with "Myself."

To be obedient is to allow myself to be thrown back on Myself, perhaps in confusion, in humility, recognizing a failure in "myself" to live out its/my significance. The mystics in particular become obedient by engaging in spiritual exercises, fasting, meditation, asceticism, and the like, in order to mollify the ossification of spirit, to remove distractions, enabling them to become more and more attuned to their own "dignity." For them, being obedient means harkening to their dignity as given by God, which is to say, serving God completely in humility.

It would not be far-fetched to say that for the most part we live in disobedience. We do not allow ourselves to be plagued by what dignifies us; we take shortcuts, by design or necessity, to hand-picked professions; we become attached to what we our selves want to do, without any consideration of the inter-Personal sense of this good-in-itself-for-me. Having passively become inattentive to, distracted from, or having actively displaced the good-in-itself-for-me for so long, it comes as a trial when we seek to discover it. This is the necessity of religion, ritual, cult, and, in most of the spiritual and religious orders, of a more specific sense of obedience to a master, teacher, sage, or confessor. I am not considering here how such an obedience might be exploited, as in the case of popular cults or in the hands of demagogues. Nor am I depreciating the role of critical insight into the value dimension of persons. Obedience on the level of experience that we are treating here presupposes a mutual loving that founds trust. We recognize an authentic form of self-love through which the person approaches this vocation and obedience (see chapter 8). It is when self-interest in any form intervenes, on either side (either the spiritual "master" or the novice), that the interpersonal sphere becomes distorted, and indeed can become violent; it violates. But having recognized this, we have to be clear: The problems we encounter do not lie in the nature of obedience peculiar to the structure of inter-Personal loving but are rooted in the distortion that I have termed idolatry.

Rather than pursue this line of thought here, let me stress that while we may ordinarily practice resisting the good-in-itself-for-me, that is, practice "disobedience," the mystics, at a particularly advanced degree of prayer/ecstasy/unveiling, embrace it unconditionally. They live for obedience, that is, service in humility, and this living in the direction of the call *qualifies that direction personally.* Such a "qualifying it personally" is of its nature ambiguous because it means at the same time (1) qualifying that loving which is epiphany (which we have understood from the mystics as co-participating in God's creation, restoring the *shechinah* and repairing the world, restoring God's glory or presence), and (2) qualifying Myself uniquely. While both of these senses are in play in any obedience or disobedience, we recognize that any obedience or disobedience is a creative origination of this good-in-itself-for-me; it qualifies this Myself personally and individuates me uniquely.

So not only does this good-in-itself-for-me individuate me uniquely, but obeying or disobeying the good-in-itself-for-me individuates me personally, uniquely. The good-in-itself-for-me is a kind of origin co-original with Myself, and obedience and disobedience to it originates this "origin" originally. When I meet someone, he or she is like no other, for better or worse. I may be able to typecast this person or make subsequent comparisons, but as person, he or she is not this, neither particular nor individual, but beyond every numerical qualification, singular or plural. The distinctive directedness of personal act-orientations reveals the absolute uniqueness of the person. The deeper the human being is revealed in loving—and these depths are possible only in loving—the more a human being is revealed as *person:* as irreplaceable, as irreducible, as individuated, as absolute, as unique.[62] This is why, in the context of the person, it is improper to equate "absolute" with "universal."[63]

It is with this density that we can speak to the unique and irreducible person as "Anne," "Samuel," "Rachel," "Joseph." This "density" of which I spoke, however, is not an object, nor can it become an object. One becomes "Rachel" in and through each act, such that the whole person is brought to bear in this living present; "Rachel" permeates each act fully but inexhaustively. The person, "Rachel," however, varies throughout each act-orientation without being like a thing changing in time, for the person is personalizing/temporalizing. Who "Rachel" is cannot be limited to past accomplishments as finished events, is never an object, but is "identified" and can only be identified personally by the orientation of personal acts that are unique. In this way, "Rachel" is the process of an unflagging becoming-otherwise, even if living through acts of the same orientation.[64] Only Rachel can reveal the Holy (and herself) in this unique, personal way. Only Samuel can reveal the Holy (and himself) in this unique, personal way.

Though this is not the explicit topic of this work, it is with this density that we can speak not only of the "individual" finite unique person, but of the "collective" finite unique person. That is, since the individuating principle is not inorganic or organic being but takes place on the level of spirit, we meaningfully experience persons in their full sense as both individual and collective. A "homeworld" or "alienworld" of any kind can be understood as a unique finite collective person and is given as such through the collective orientation of its acts. However, let me return to the person in the former sense.

In a *personal* manner, the origin is taken up in such a way that the origination continues to accomplish the individuation of the person. On the one hand, I am not before my origins, since I originate them in creative acts. On the other hand, I am before my origins because I am "within" the dimension of the Holy from the start; *I* take "it" up as it is given "before" me, or given when I already come on the scene. This is how I participate in more than myself. I am already before my origins as being given to myself by the Holy. In this sense, my own origin becomes a constitutive *problem*. I reflect on origins of the world. The world becomes a "problem"; *I* become a "problem." But I become a problem because I am already beyond myself, as given to Myself, and in originating acts, becoming personally, uniquely, who I am.

Person to Person

Let me return now to the explicit problem of individuation and to the questions posed at the beginning of this chapter. What happens in the experience of radical union expressed by the mystics in the descriptions of spiritual marriage, the divine ecstasy of *yechidah,* or annihilation of self? Is the integrity of the person as individuated called into question? We can take up these and related questions within a phenomenological context in two ways.

1. The first way would be to take birth and death as constitutive features of our being and to reflect on what this means for the problem of individuation. I noted at the outset of this chapter that within a phenomenology of time-consciousness it made sense to assert that the transcendental subject is immortal. Concerning the past, we could say with Husserl, I *was* eternal; concerning the future, I *will be* eternal. There is symmetry here with respect to past and future. But when we consider the deeper dimensions of givenness and being given to Myself, "mystery" becomes constitutively significant. Here we can say phenomenologically: I am given to Myself. But unlike the case within genesis, here

the *motivation* (to use a phenomenological term) for my emergence cannot be traced back; the motivation for my being, why I was given to myself, and so forth, is not clear and perhaps may never be clear; nevertheless, I am given to myself—this is apodictically certain; that is, it cannot be "crossed-out," it is *undurchstreichbar.*

If we have an apodicticity with respect to being given to Myself, do we have such an apodicticity in the other direction? For example, can we say apodictically that "I will not be taken from myself" or that "I will be taken from myself"? Is a not-being-taken-from-myself apodictically certain? Let us recall that we are not speaking simply of vital birth and death. To assert something about the future in this regard would amount to being able to experience this being-taken-from-myself, and we cannot too hastily claim that being-taken-from-myself is equivalent to empirical death. We cannot identify these two out of hand, first because we *do* have the apodictic evidence of being given to ourselves. If you like, this being-given is a phenomenological given. We are given to ourselves as the source of meaning in relation to the world, and so forth.

Since individuated finitude is not reducible to material nature but is intrinsically tied to being-given, empirical death cannot *ipso facto* be a phenomenological being-taken-from-myself. Because individuation is rooted in the personal act-orientation and origination, vital death does not automatically mean that I lose this individuated uniqueness. Accordingly, empirical death cannot mean that the person is stripped of its absolute character such that it would be merely *relative* as relative to infinite absolute Person. Of course, this is not to assert that I will not be taken from Myself, either. What we can say is that in our given absoluteness as unique persons, we are relative to infinite absolute person as the *absolute* source of our experienced absoluteness. We can say nothing apodictically with respect to the future on this issue. Phenomenologically, mortality cannot be decisive.

This being said, on the basis of this individuated structure, we do have grounds *to assume* that we will not be taken from ourselves, that being given as absolute ourselves and relative to the absolute infinite Person as the source, we will somehow endure. This opens up to the dimension of hope. It is essentially different from asserting, within the strictures of time-consciousness, that I will be eternally. Thus, whereas the dimension of the past as birth yielded the constitutive problem of mystery, the dimension of the future as death yields the constitutive problem of hope. But this remains an assumption, or at the limit of givenness, and is not itself a phenomenological given.

Finally, let me entertain the question concerning the place of birth and death as a constitutive problem. I noted above that there is a constitutive asymmetry of the past and future that corresponds neither to the symmetry with respect to individual time-consciousness or transcendental genesis, nor to the symmetry with respect to empirical birth and death. While we do have apodicticity where birth is concerned—I am given to myself, although I can find no motivation for it—there is no apodicticity concerning the future. Just as I cannot assert that I will be eternally, I cannot assert apodictically that I will be taken from Myself, that my individuation will dissipate with my death. This is not to say that death is not a transcendental or constitutive feature; it is. Rather, the evidence for it is not decisive or apodictic like it is for birth. Consequently (and to use Heidegger's expression), being toward death cannot be an apodictically constitutive phenomenological feature, even if we expand our scope from genetic self-temporalization to generative considerations. Only a phenomenological mortality could have, as an apodictically constitutive feature, being toward death. And although I do not want to equate "natality" here with Heidegger's "thrownness," at least the extent to which his understanding of thrownness entails a not being self-grounding, thrownness cannot be subordinated to being-toward-death, but just the reverse. There are no decisive experiential grounds for phenomenological mortality, and phenomenological mortality could give no decisive response to, let alone resituate, a phenomenological immortality.

Rather, what becomes the new guiding feature for phenomenology is natality, the phenomenological meaning-orientation of birth. Only phenomenological natality can respond to or convert a phenomenological immortality such that immortality is integrated into and situated by natality. It is worth remarking as a concluding note that the issue of birth and death would have to be evaluated quite differently if taken up from a Zen Buddhist perspective—a perspective that I am precisely not working here. In that case, it would have to be investigated from the perspective, not of Generativity, but of śūnyatā (emptiness) or zenki (undivided activity).[65]

2. Considering the vital death of the person as the limiting case of individuation eventually requires us to speculate on whether or not the

integrity of the person is maintained after death—and if not speculate, then at least make various assumptions. Let us, however, take a different approach.

The human person was described above as the integrative locus of the vital and spiritual dimensions. This is an important issue: since vital-life is *not* the principle of individuation, vital-death cannot in and of itself eliminate the uniqueness of the person either. The matter of individuation cannot be determined on the level of the vital. The issue for us, ultimately, is whether there is a removal of the "spiritual" density in the sense of personal integrity or uniqueness of the individual—*even within the vital life of the person*. In other words, where individuation is concerned, the question is not really whether or not we survive *vital* death. Independently of vital death, we could also lose our spiritual or personal core of who we are. Since the vital is not the individuating principle, the question, then, is whether the integrity of the person is sustained *even in vital life*.

This problem is raised experientially for the mystics. Rather than examine all of the three mystics here, let us take our cue on this matter from Rūzbihān Baqlī's descriptions of mystical experience, since the issue is brought to the fore in an especially sharp manner. In this way, it clarifies the experiences brought to the fore in these Abrahamic mystics.[66] We have seen that for Baqlī, higher than union or annihilation of the self is the experience of *baqā*, or subsistence. This is not insignificant. In fact, such an experience goes against most assumptions, philosophical treatises, and cross-cultural studies, which hold that union is the highest degree of mystical experience. It illuminates a dimension of experience in which there is distinction within unity, as it were, but where such a distinction comes "after" union and is not a penultimate stage to it. In chapter 4 I noted that *baqā* is the subsistence of the spirit, or again, a personal differentiation, a personal individuation *sustained in* God. In *baqā*, beyond *fanā*, or annihilation, creation is not dissipated; the "createdness" or "creatureliness" of the creature perdures; but at least where persons are concerned, creation abides not merely as human or as "animal" but as divinized.[67] To cite once more a statement from Baqlī's commentary on "unknowing," he writes that after the seeker becomes annihilated in his seeking, "subsistence brings him into the Essence ['*ayn*] so that subsistence may be subsistent."[68] Rather than merely being vanquished in God, *baqā* is the experience of receiving Myself, now as Holy, as a living from God and by God, not from or by the world. The person is experienced as "individuated" through God; that is, in loving, as loving, God freely "honors" the personal integrity of the finite person. This is what is experienced as the uncaused "giving back" of the person.

We need not interpret the annihilation of the self and subsistence as temporally ordered stages. Even though one experience may be more profound than another, "higher" than another, or factually may have been given after the other, they can indicate different depth revelations, or as we would say, epiphanies in the experience of God.

In addition to this experiential clue, given what we have elaborated upon above, we would have to say that even if the self in its most minimal sense of mineness is lost, the person as such is not dissolved in union and the like. The person as dynamically originating the origin lives in and through this dynamicity in an initiatory, "creative," improvisational manner, becoming who he or she is irreducibly. Not only are finite persons irreducible to one another, but finite persons and infinite Person are irreducible. Furthermore, it is peculiar to the nature of loving to let be or to become from the integrity of who (or what) the other is. Loving is oriented in its nature, not to overcoming the dynamic density of the other person, but precisely toward the absolute character or absolute value of person in his or her uniqueness. This is of course a mystery. But there is no phenomenological basis for asserting that the Holy as loving would violate this personal integrity of another. Admittedly, this is to place the Holy as all-loving, merciful, and compassionate above God as omnipotent and omniscient.

On this point I disagree with Michel Henry's contention, as I have done on another occasion,[69] that the relation between the Holy and the human, or the infinite and the finite, is that of the absolute to the *relative*. For Henry, we have on the one hand the self-affection of *absolute* Life in which this life is self-engendered, and on the other, the *relative* self-affection, in which I experience myself as given to myself.[70] Because Henry regards the former as absolute and the latter as relative, he can write that in the final analysis there is *only one* self-affection, namely, "that of absolute Life." As a consequence, our actions are not ultimately those that are integral to the finite person, since what we do is "*nothing more* and *nothing other than*" the self-accomplishment of absolute Life.[71] In other words, our doing, our actions, do not have an integrity all their own for Henry; they are not simply in humble service of absolute Life, but *merely* relative and *ultimately* reducible to absolute Life.

By contrast, from the position developed here, the person has an experiential density and is given as absolute, though finite. The good-in-itself-for-me that qualifies the person absolutely, this given-givenness originates me. What we do in relation to that "origin," furthermore, originates a personal orientation that is absolutely distinctive, qualifying our finite personhood. As not self-grounding, the person is relative to the Holy; the finite is relative to the infinite. But—and this is decisive—the relation of the finite to infinite is not a relation of the putative relative to the absolute—though this is an easy assumption to make. Like in the case of Henry, this would make the human person merely a function of divine thought or divine self-affection. If idolatry emerges, then idolatry would itself be a function of God, and the function of forgiveness, salvation, and so forth, would be pointless. Now this may go against the grain of certain theological convictions; it may even hark back to a form of the problematic addressed by Augustine and the Manicheans. Be that as it may, I am not appealing to theological convictions, but only drawing out some implications based on such a reduction.

Instead, from our phenomenological perspective we would express it this way: *Absolute finite* person is *relative* to *absolute infinite* Person. Although the finite person is relative to infinite Person, this being "relative to" does not thereby render the person relative. For example, if God knew in advance each concrete aspect of the person, if God predetermined the content of actions of an individual (which contradicts loving), then we might say that the individual would be merely "relative." If our actions were merely God's and made no contribution to the "reparation of the world," or to ushering in the "kingdom of God," or to the concrete density of being that the person gives to him- or herself through his or her life, then the individual could be merely "relative."[72] Rather, being "relative to" means instead that the finite person is given to itself as not self-grounding, and in its finitude is relative to infinity, but as absolute to absolute. Our actions in this sense are not God's contributions but our own contributions, bearing within them the sphere of morality, social responsibility, or, as Leo Baeck calls it, "religious ethics."[73] There is not necessarily a contradiction here, but what the mystics would call a matter of grace. The inter-*Personal* structure is a dynamic tension between absolute finite and absolute infinite. Thus, it is not a matter of theism, or monism, or pantheism,[74] but of "personalism" in its most radical sense.

Only in the sense that absolute finite person is relative to absolute infinite Person can we speak meaningfully both of service in humility and of opening the *moral sphere* of experience. If finite persons were ultimately reducible to infinite Person or to each other, there could be no field of responsibility; there would be no point to the *interpersonal* field of action. Moral action amounts to affirming, ultimately through community and loving, the absolute inviolability of the other person as person, a being-with others, without sacrificing the irreducibility of the other person. In Henry's version, loving can have no moral dimension.[75] The dynamic tension of which I spoke is maintained in and through person's absolute—which is to say, personal—difference, and "because of" this personal difference through loving. Loving is the regard of this absolute difference. This inter-Personal nexus is captured best, not by Heidegger's "belonging-together," but by what we understand as "solidarity," which is informed by absolute uniqueness.

Solidarity

There are two senses of solidarity that are intertwined, between infinite and finite persons, and among finite persons. Solidarity in the first sense is inseparable from the latter because it involves communal, cross-cultural, inter-personal participation in the presence of the Holy. They are further intertwined because, as I noted above, person is given both in individual and collective senses. This is one reason why Scheler writes of the impossibility of substituting one person or a group (collective person) for another as an inviolable, fundamental principle.[76] This has important implications for how we regard radically incommensurate worldviews, religious or spiritual traditions; that is, other persons, histories, and cultures that are fundamentally irreducible to our own—in particular, the irreducible relation expressed between, for example, the Abrahamic tradition (with its insight into the generative structure of Person and persons) and Zen Buddhism (with its insight into emptiness). I reserve a more thoroughgoing discussion of this matter for another work. What I can note here, however, is that historical culture, including religion, is not the foundation but the result of being guided by insights into what we might call ultimate reality. This implies further that religious/spiritual experiences and religious communities are foundational for cultural experiences and cultural communities. At this point I touch only briefly on the structure of inter-Personal solidarity. For reasons that hark back to chapter 1, I continue to describe this structure within the Abrahamic tradition.

By inter-Personal solidarity I understand, on the one hand, the phenomenon of self-givenness (as givenness to Myself) as being not self-grounding; and on the other, the actualization of infinite Person through the self-becoming of persons, most deeply in the direction of holiness.

We see in the mystics—before they were understood as or understood themselves as mystics—a fundamental, rudimentary personal commitment to the Holy. We can understand this as a "response to" or "origination of" primordially being given to Myself. The main point here is that this commitment, first, was not the effect of rational reflection on, or theoretical conclusions about, the deity, carried out as a mere belief in God or the result of feeling confident about the existence of God. They did not say, "First, You show me something I can grasp, then I will love You." Their religious orientations were not lived out of coercion or insecurity, but lived from freely initiated, improvisational loving. The latter did not just arise as a shot out of the dark, but as a "response" (sometimes peaceful, sometimes not so peaceful) to the open meaningfulness of all there is. The evidence peculiar to religious experience, as we saw in chapter 5, is only given within this sphere of experiencing; it is an evidence that is intrinsic to and corroborated in the loving itself, which is "revelatory" of holiness.

Second, and related to the former point, aside from the fact that the mystics are sometimes rather misleadingly called "contemplatives," their task as individuals was not simply to think about or to speculate on God, but *to live* in such a way as to conform to the movement of the Holy, that is, to realize the meaning of their freedom as bound to the movement of the Holy, to live in humble service, and in this sense "to obey" the movement of holiness. This is one aspect of what I mean by "solidarity."

But the term solidarity also suggests more than obedience, even in the sense we use it here, namely, that one is involved inextricably *with others* and is informed *by absolute uniqueness, not by sameness*. Solidarity, generally speaking, means a co-orientation whereby each unique person, living in his or her own way, lives in the same core orientation. Each person is irreplaceable and unrepresentable in this solidarity (since the contribution is unique according to one's way).

Solidarity, as it concerns infinite and finite persons, as mentioned above, entails conforming our orientation to the orientation of God or holiness concretely, as loving in the sense defined above. This also means, conversely, that the Holy is in solidarity with finite persons and world history. In this respect, God or holiness is not "hither" or "beyond" in a world of peace while human persons merely toil and struggle.[77]

Solidarity, while pointing in the former direction, also points in the direction of finite persons. The "with others" mentioned above signals not an orientation toward "humanity" as a concept or toward impersonal institutions, but a "person to person" nexus such that my personal destiny is essentially joined with other persons ("individual" and "collective"). The mystics experience this as humble service. Mother Teresa put it in this way: "We all have the duty to serve God where we are called to do so. I feel called to serve individuals, to love each human being. My calling is not to judge the institutions. I am not qualified to condemn anyone. I never think in terms of a crowd, but of individual persons. If I thought in terms of crowds, I would never begin my work. I believe in the personal touch of one to one."[78]

I mentioned above that solidarity is a task involved with others. From the perspective developed here, this solidarity is *personal,* that is, a solidarity of Person and persons, and among finite persons. The meaning of what we understand by *personal solidarity* where the mystics are concerned is understood as the task of "redemption." Redemption is not taken in the individualistic sense of the exclusive salvation of my soul—but as the liberation of all creation. This has been expressed as "gathering the scattered divine sparks," as helping to establish the kingdom of God on "earth," as acting for the glory (or presence) of God, as living in such a way as to hasten the messianic era. It is the process of appreciating (in the literal sense of the term) the vertical in all things, all beings, participating in their ultimate, illimitable actualization in the direction of holiness. Running water in a brook can be experienced merely as quantitatively pure drinking water, as H_2O, as spring runoff, as something ice-cold, as evoking a hiking partner, or as the presence of God. While we will in every instance encounter the mere physicality of the "water," what remains open is whether or not it will be lived vertically, ultimately toward infinity (i.e., "redeemed").[79] To limit the encounter *merely,* say, to H_2O, or to something ice-cold, without it simultaneously opening beyond itself (vertically), is a form of idolatry (see chapter 8, section 3 on "delimitation").

Redemption, then, is the process of "infinitizing" the finite, spiritualizing or actualizing the real, with the effect of liberating finitude. I noted above that for the Jewish mystics, the paradigmatic event of the exodus is not merely a historical event. The term for Egypt, מצרים, is transliterated and pronounced as *Mitzraim;* but this term, מצרים, is also the term for "limitations," transliterated and pronounced as *metzarim.* For the mystic, the exodus expresses the process of living vertically, toward boundlessness, toward the Holy, and in this way being liberated from both material and spiritual limiting and constraining conditions. What we have designated as the liberation from limiting conditions is, as Luther puts it, to be "saved" in the deepest possible sense of the term.[80] Thus, the liberation of finitude cannot most profoundly be the liberation from life and death, but is the liberation in the spiritual sense of finitude, namely, from the reversal of infinite loving (idolatry)—which in the myths of the Abrahamic tradition coincided with death, pain, and suffering. Or, we can say, redemption is the liberation from life and death to the extent that it is the liberation from idolatry.

We certainly risk the danger of misunderstanding when we speak of solidarity as conforming one's orientation to the orientation of holiness if we think that this entails converting or demanding others to live like we do. This, however, violates the principle of unrepresentable solidarity, which is grounded in the uniqueness of the person and his or her relation to infinite Person. Naturally, we live our way as decisive. Like all true teachers, writes Buber of the Buddha, he desires, not to teach one view among views, but "the" way.[81] Explicating this demands treating the notion of exemplarity and cross-cultural interaction. For now, let me say that because some homeworlds or cultures have, over time, developed insights and modes of access to "ultimate reality" that are simply not available to us or to others and may never be, and because these paths cannot exhaust the epistemic or moral world, the point of solidarity cannot be to convert or to dominate others. Indeed, the encounter with another "way" forces us to examine ourselves critically, not to reduce others to our way.[82]

The point as a Jew is to live in such a way that the Muslim becomes a better Muslim, as a Christian, that the Jew becomes a better Jew, and so forth.[83] From the Abrahamic perspective, in which there is only one God, even encountering the Zen Buddhist, for whom there is an insight into emptiness and not absolute Person, solidarity entails recognizing the absolute value of this person, even if he or she does not live "ultimate reality" in a personalist way. The point here is to live as a Jew, Christian, or Muslim in such a way that the other becomes a better Buddhist. At the very minimum, such an encounter throws us back on ourselves such that others, in their ways, enrich our unique ways as lovers of the Holy.

In the Abrahamic tradition, redemption is the personal meaning of solidarity as the redirection of verticality and the liberation from idolatry. Despite the fact that, or perhaps precisely because they are mystics, the task of redemption is lived with a sense of urgency, an urgency that also filled the prophets. There is an urgency because although we live at least implicitly from holiness, our actions are either carried out toward infinity or toward limitation with no benefit of a neutral position; we live either in the direction of verticality or in the direction of idolatry.

Having addressed verticality in the sense of religious evidence, givenness as epiphany, and the meaning of individuation, it is to the phenomenon of idolatry that I turn in the next and final chapter.

CHAPTER 8

Idolatry

Experience is not restricted to the presentation of perceptual or epistemic objects. Epiphanic givenness, which has been clarified personally as loving, is one such example of a much broader sphere of evidence, a sphere of evidential experience that I have termed, in general, "verticality." Idolatry, by contrast, is the expression I use to convey the reversal of vertical relations, the negation of verticality. This exposition of mystical experiencing has suggested that once this dimension is given in human experience, that is, religious experiencing as epiphany, there can be no neutral position. We are either oriented vertically, such that the meaning of our lives takes on a predominately vertical *qua* religious, Personal significance, or the meaning of our lives and actions is qualified by idolatry.

By articulating verticality throughout this work, I have implicitly elucidated idolatry. It was necessary to begin by clarifying the meaning of vertical givenness because idolatry can only be detected as a problem within the possibility of verticality. It is within this structure of verticality and idolatry that our experiences as persons in the most radical sense are to be understood. Without these dimensions, our history as we usually understand it cannot take into consideration the fullness of what it means to be persons; nor are we able to grasp or to address adequately both the interpersonal goodness and the interpersonal catastrophes we face in that history. The point of highlighting idolatry is not to theologize the difficulties we face today and unload them on something beyond our ken; it is not to deny imprudently the experiences and efficacy of impersonal forces described, for instance, by Marxism, structuralism, or psychoanalysis. Rather, it is to rediscover in them their profoundly *personal* dimension.

The task of this chapter is to draw idolatry into sharper focus. Idolatry as an experience, or at least as an important philosophical concept, has emerged within contemporary philosophical discussions.[1] This is due in no small part to Jean-Luc Marion's pioneering works that treat idolatry, for example, his *Idol and Distance, God without Being,* and to some extent, *Being Given.*[2] Bruce Benson has done this notion further philosophical service in his recent study, *Graven Ideologies,* by clarifying the insight into idolatry that has been functioning in contemporary Continental literature through several principal "idol detectors" such as Friedrich Nietzsche, Jean-Luc Marion, and Jacques Derrida.[3]

In this chapter I am not so much concerned with treating idolatry as a mode of theological and philosophical aporia. In fact, what might be understood as idolatry on the basis of theological and philosophical conviction or religious tradition can often be called into question experientially in the lives of various mystics. For example, ecstatic expressions like those witnessed in Baqlī or Hallāj, understood on their proper experiential foundation, are not necessarily and *a priori* "idolatrous."

More than worshiping false gods or bowing down before images, more than the visual metaphor of the gaze explicated in a theology of the icon, I take idolatry as a *lived movement*, a uniquely *personal* orientation that arises within the context of vertical givenness; and my clues for elucidating this movement arise from the experiential basis of epiphany as described by these mystics of the Abrahamic tradition. Idolatry here is determined in relation to the vertical givenness of epiphany and its distinctive religious sense. While idolatry can be specified in terms of human sacrifice, harking back to a novel moment and addressing contemporary acts of evil such as the Holocaust and genocides,[4] I do not understand this as the exclusive moment of idolatry where *the religious sphere of experience* is concerned. "Human sacrifice" would belong properly as a moment of the moral sense of idolatry as "evil"; explicating this remains the topic of another work on the moral sphere of experience, its modes of givenness, and the kinds of idolatry that are unique to it.

In its contrariety, idolatry illuminates what is taking place in vertical experience. In this way, understanding idolatry also points to challenges to idolatry. In this chapter, I identify three principle and interrelated moments of idolatry that bear on the religious sphere of experience: (1) the self and pride; (2) the attachment to "world," which is expressed in both secularism and fundamentalism; and (3) what I term "delimitation," or the mono-dimensional character of experiences that fail to point vertically.

Idolatry and the Self: Pride

Let me note from the very beginning that there is a self-love that is authentic and that is not reducible to pride. While idolatry allows us to live the good-in-itself-for-me without obeying it, or at least without letting it trouble us too much, self-love in the positive sense is the orientation toward the fullness of who we are, that is, toward the good-in-itself-for-me. This does not mean that in self-love I do what I think best for my self-interests or even act according to what I think I deserve. This good-in-itself-for-me, my vocation, is given, and as such it is a givenness in relation to the Holy. Authentic self-love is the openness to oneself in accordance with this vocation as one stands before the Holy. We see ourselves as if through the eyes of God, to employ Scheler's expression, and as placed in the total moral universe.[5] Self-love is the movement of realizing this vocation and turning away from any image of ourselves that we have constructed. In self-love, I divest Myself of my self in a readiness to serve. The Jewish mystics have a term for this experience, an experience that has biblical roots: hineni. When God calls to Moses, he responds: hineni, "Here I am." When God calls to Abraham, he responds: hineni, "Here I am." Whereas in the myth of Adam and Eve human beings hide from God, hineni expresses an immediate, absolute, unconditional readiness to serve. This is what we understand as genuine self-love and is compatible with the disposition of humility (about which I will say more below).

Self-love is oriented toward the emergence or realization of who I am called to be as placed before God with others. Since the personal "self" in question is experienced as being given to Myself, and the "loving" as being open to that good-in-itself-for-me, it is not an experience of being self-grounding.[6]

Pride, however, is to be understood in contrast to self-love in the sense described above. Let us further distinguish this pride from a kind of esteem or "pride" that we might take in others or in things, like when we say we are proud of our children or that we take pride in our heritage, or are proud about a job of painting the house. According to Scheler, one could take pride in things that have an intrinsic value, but in this case these things still have their value independently of that pride.[7] Of course, one could become vain or haughty with respect to these matters. But whereas vanity is only ridiculous, pride in the more profound sense is diabolical.[8] Bowing before the images we have of ourselves, pride is not love in any genuine sense, but rather, as St. John of the Cross so keenly put it, makes a festival of and for myself.[9] In the writings of the Islamic mystic Al-Muḥāsibi (d. 243/857), pride (kibr), as distinct from conceit, vanity, or self-delusion, is precisely a matter of placing oneself in the place of God (and not realizing Myself as placed before God as "human godservant").[10]

There is certainly a long religious tradition of citing pride as "diabolical." In the Judeo-Christian tradition, Lucifer, one of God's highest beings, displays an inordinate love of himself, putting himself above God and refusing to serve God. Here pride harbors an explicit religious moment in the sense that it relates directly to God. In the Islamic tradition, Lucifer (Iblis) has an inordinate love of God but will not bow to human beings. Here pride has an explicit moral dimension in the sense of refusing to serve human persons; Lucifer's pride lacks the dimension of ethics and justice, and in this way has an impact on the religious dimension. In the Jewish tradition such a lack of the moral dimension would be a lack of the religious as well, and vice versa, since one cannot serve God while not loving other persons.[11] In both cases, directly or indirectly, Lucifer winds up esteeming himself above God and refusing to serve. He values his own conception of himself above God's command and withdraws himself from the subjection to and presence of God. Similarly, Dante considers the last circle of hell, the pit of Cocytus, to be treachery to others, in particular, to "superiors," which elucidates why the first cornice one must pass through within purgatory deals with the prideful.[12]

These theological, mythological, and literary conceptions of pride and evil bear an existential and phenomenological truth. The whole issue of pride would not be at all a pernicious, delicate, and sometimes elusive experiential issue for the mystics or those leading a spiritual life if persons were not given with intrinsic worth, as absolute, unique—that is, if we were only *relative* in relation to the Holy as absolute. Pride is problematic, not because it recognizes intrinsic personal worth, but because it fixates on this personal absoluteness and uses it as an excuse to sever the relational character of that absoluteness. One takes the experience of absoluteness now as testimony to being self-grounding. Arrogance and presumption follow from this false sense of sovereignty.[13] On the one hand, self-love affirms this absolute character and uniqueness in the moral universe, but as placed before the Holy and others. Yet if self-love is taken in abstraction from this vocational element and service, we can no longer speak of loving in its fullest sense. In pride, there is no vocation other than the one I give to myself, with the danger that we become fascinated with ourselves (and only then as a consequence, vain). The problem, then, is that by being consumed with ourselves, by being carried away with ourselves or taking ourselves too seriously, we implicitly turn away from Holiness, becoming, as a consequence, more susceptible to evil. That is the real problem of pride.

One could always insist that in principle I might be able to give myself the "right" vocation independently of God, and that from the standpoint of independence, I am instead independent "before" God; in fact, one might object, this "being before God" is what should be called into question. Put in this way, it is impossible to argue one way or the other.

Nevertheless, I would like to insist on a phenomenological difference between humility and pride that cannot go unmentioned since they are intrinsically different kinds of movements. Phenomenologically, pride arises along with an experienced lack of self-confidence such that in pride one clings ever more tenaciously to the self. Pride and self-doubt are fraternal twins. Indeed, self-doubt, like self-loathing, or reflecting on one's own inferiority, is a sign of the self-same pride, since it only calls attention to the self. "To doubt oneself," writes Bernanos, "is not to be humble, I even think that sometimes it is the most hysterical form of pride, a pride almost delirious, a kind of jealous ferocity which makes an unhappy man turn and rend himself. That must be the real truth of hell."[14] In true humility, the self becomes so "annihilated" that one no longer even reflects on one's own unworthiness.

Accordingly, pride is not just humility without God, only called by a different name. In humility, the life, the work, or the act is *other* oriented; it points to God or to others in service. In pride, the point of the life, the work, and so on is the self; the movement of the work—if we can call it movement at all—ends in the self. However, just because one is "other oriented" does not mean that the movement is one of love. Both Nietzsche and Scheler have shown that "altruism"—the putative love of the "small," the "weak," the "oppressed" (as opposed to genuine love of others)—is a sign of moral *ressentiment* and is accordingly expressive of self-hate.[15] Here, turning toward others is a result of fleeing from oneself; sensing one's unworthiness, one is impelled to seek refuge in the "other" merely because it is other than myself.

If we take Tarkovsky's film *Andrei Rublev* as an example, we observe that the film concerns more than Andrei Rublev as an icon painter. Not only does it portray icons in the film, not only are some of the visual shots themselves styled after icons, but Andrei himself, through his affliction (or "passion") and awakening (the "bell" and his return to speaking and painting), becomes iconic and exemplifies this iconic movement that does not end in himself but points beyond himself, through him, to the Holy. Andrei is seen in sharp contrast to his counterpart, the insecure Kirill, whose concern as a painter ends only in himself, admitting to Andrei toward the end of the film that he had been governed only by pride and, in relation to Andrei, envy. Thus, we have the contrast of affliction and humility on the one hand, and suffering and pride on the other; we have the movement of the icon in the first case, and the "movement" of the idol in the second. Pride is articulated as the root of idolatry.

Pride not only impoverishes Myself, but it impoverishes the world since it fails to recognize the value of things unless they relate to me or serve me. In fact, I feel that I deserve everything, and if I deserve everything, nothing can be experienced as gift, which is another kind of impoverishment. For those who serve in humility, however, nothing is experienced as deserved, and everything is experienced as gift, even and especially this absoluteness of the Myself.[16] This is the realization arrived at by the mystics. St. Teresa writes, for example: "The first sign for seeing whether or not you have humility is that you do not think you deserve these favors and spiritual delights from the Lord or that you will receive them in your lifetime."[17] Similarly, for Dov Baer, in humility one attains divine delight without any intention of reaching any stage, without any self-congratulations, practicing only self-abandonment in service; in this way one "is not moved at all by any insult" and one experiences that he possesses "nothing in his own right, and this is the very opposite of pride. . . . In this, too, there are many different distinctions in the aspect of the depths of humility."[18] For the Chabad mystic, service (avodah) is only truly service when it is done with gladness and a joyful heart and when one does not go around depressed, anxious, and full of self-doubt or sorrow; for according to him, these are either expressions of a lack of faith in God's forgiveness or expressions of pride.[19]

It would seem that in order to circumvent the pitfalls of pride, all one has to do is to jettison the self—a concept we have met above in chapter 7 regarding self-forgetfulness. One must be careful with such an assertion. The mystics are forthright in saying that one must do what one can in "perfecting" oneself through self-surrender. But it would not do to denounce or to scorn the self as something hateful or to take it as a negative value in the attitude of ressentiment. In the first place, the self is a positive value; it can only be "abandoned" genuinely when recognized as *positive*. In this case, however, it is renounced, not out of, say, self-loathing, which Weil recognizes as a new "crime of idolatry"; but rather, it is renounced in its positivity, out of service to another, since the self can only be "renounced in favor of God."[20] She writes: "Attitude of supplication: I must necessarily turn to something other than myself since it is a question of being delivered from self . . . Any attempt to gain this deliverance by means of my own energy would be like the efforts of a cow which pulls at its hobble and so falls onto its knees."[21]

It is easy to speak cavalierly of losing the self in order to find the self. These expressions are commonplace. We have seen, though, that calling the self into question is not in the last analysis the result of one's own efforts. Even the suffering inflicted by others, the world, or oneself has mundane origins and is something I or another can in principle remedy. In Weil's experience, for example, *affliction* is not at all identical to *suffering* for this very reason: "Nothing in the world can rob us of the power to say 'I.' Nothing except extreme affliction. Nothing is worse than extreme affliction which destroys the 'I' from outside, because after that we can no longer destroy it ourselves."[22] Affliction, which is the experienced absence of God, only makes sense in terms of vertical experience, and curiously, as a gift: "Yet until a soul is placed by God in the passive purgation of that dark night . . . it cannot purify itself completely of these imperfections or others."[23] In humility, one is carried along in the movement of holiness, and one is opened to others and the world without haughtiness or vainglory.

Does this mean that only the "mystics" can be liberated from pride? Does this imply that without such "supernal" experiences we are doomed to live in idolatry, at least to some degree? How can this speak meaningfully to those of us who do not have such "mystical" or "infused" experiences? These are questions to which I return at the conclusion of this chapter. Suffice it for now to spell out the gist of these remarks.

Pride is explicated here fundamentally as a *religious* concept and within *religious* experience, which is not to say that this exhausts all modes and shades of pride, but it does focus on the most *personal*, most radical, and most fundamental sense. Pride is a kind of idolatry, in contrast to verticality. We are either living in the basic orientation of verticality or of idolatry. This is the religious meaning of these experiences; there is no neutral posture. At this level of human experience, the only undoing of pride is verticality, which may come in any number of ways of what the religious masters call gift or grace: in the prayer of quiet, in a child's smile, in a coastal mist, in an arietta, in a painting, in a conversation, or in affliction.

Idolatry and Taking the World (Literally): Secularism and Fundamentalism

Pride is a mode of idolatry that can be called an idolatry of the self. There is a related movement of idolatry that we can understand as idolatry of the world. One of the consequences of this, but not the only one, is "secularism." I understand by secularism the process of living in the world, *from the world*. Allow me to articulate this movement of idolatry first by explaining two different, yet interrelated senses of "world," and then by developing the implications of this for the movement of idolatry.

World as Object

The first sense of "world" I take from Edmund Husserl's earlier works, namely, the world as the being of all beings, as the totality of all entities.[24] In this respect, the world is fundamentally no different from an object; it is the *cogitatum* writ large.[25] When I am oriented toward objects, be they perceptual in the sense of spatial/temporal objects, or epistemic in the sense of ideal objects, they are given to me as correlative to my intentional acts. Their meanings are relative to these acts and to a contextual nexus of the act-sense correlation. The world as totality is no less an "object," no less relative, even if it is understood as the synthetic totality of all synthetically connected intersubjective accomplishments; "world" becomes no less an objective-sense than a particular object like "tree" or "car."[26]

Notice that the object's character as relative does not necessarily fluctuate by being material or intellectual, particular or universal, divisible or indivisible, ephemeral or omni-temporal. A loaf of bread may satisfy my hunger; I can share it with others, and it can perish by being eaten. The idea of bread cannot in principle be limited to me or to some of us, but in principle it can be shared by all; it is not subject to fad, style, and number of people who have partaken of it or who will partake of it. Here we would distinguish between the material object and the eidetic object, the particular and the universal, the instance and its concept. But the relativity of beings applies to both of these objects. Relativity is not a distinction between the particular and universal but is discerned by the quality of its givenness.

Idolatry arises in the religious sphere of experience when we take something relative as if it were absolute, giving absolute weight (here, the weight of the Holy), to the relative thing. In this way the thing (object, desire, pleasure, idea) occupies us with the tenor of absoluteness and takes on the unconditionality of the supremely valuable. This inversion may be conscious or quite unconscious; in either case, it can be borne out by the test of our practical conduct, since in it the relative being is accorded the highest weight, behind which everything else is valued.[27] Becoming bedazzled, obsessed, preoccupied, fixated with the thing or idea, we "deify" it and become enamored of it. "The finite good is torn from its harmonious context in the world of goods: it is loved and pursued with a total lack of compromise wholly out of proportion with its objective significance; the human being seems magically enchained to its idol, and behaves 'as if' it were God himself."[28] For example, we might become obsessed with the maximum acquisition of economic goods, with the patriotic idea of our country, with limitless knowledge, with sexual conquests, with winning at sports, with weight loss. But idolatry is not only evident in such "mundane" experiences. Mystics even warn of being attached to so-called religious objects: to clothing, a book, a monastic cell, a particular place of prayer, a particular design of rosary, a crucifix, ideas, even to one's own spiritual progress.[29] This would constitute a kind of spiritual materialism or spiritual pride and would be the contrary of the poverty of spirit. Being attached to things is more harmful, according to St. John of the Cross, than committing what is known in the Catholic tradition as venial sins: "It makes little difference whether a bird is tied by a thin thread or by a cord. Even if it is tied by thread, the bird will be held bound just as surely as if it were tied by cord."[30]

Addictions that dominate one's actions and serve as the focal point of one's life, be they consciously or unconsciously manifest in gambling, drinking, substance abuse, sex, and so forth, are not most profoundly genetic, physiological, or psychological, but spiritual disorders.[31] This is not to say that caffeine, nicotine, and alcohol are not physiologically addictive; they are. This is not to say that opium, "ecstasy," or crystal meth are not psychologically addictive; they are. Rather, addictions of these and other sorts are more than that; they are ultimately disorders of the heart. To appeal once more to Simone Weil: "In the same way the man who thinks he is in the power of pleasure is really in the power of the absolute which he has transferred to it. This absolute is to pleasure what the blows of the whip are to the master's voice; but the association is not the result of affliction here; it is the result of an original crime, the crime of idolatry."[32] Addictions carry with them a value directedness whereby a relative thing (such as pleasure) enjoys the status and privilege of being absolute. I am enthralled by it, I am captivated by it, I orient my life's behavior around it, I structure my family and their needs around it, I plan my life to accumulate wealth, I squander savings so I can gamble at the peril of my family's security, and so forth. The relative, finite thing orients me, but only because in its image I extol my own—in this way rejoining pride. This is the reversal I have termed idolatry.

Inversely, one could misplace an experienced "void" on the religious level of experience (which presupposes at some time an absolute experience) in terms of the need for objects. In fact, capitalism literally "banks" on this inversion. This is why advertisements must elevate the object to the status of an absolute to induce in the consumer the expectation of filling such an experience with finite, relative objects. And because the latter are relative and finite, they need to be replaced infinitely. The fact that relative objects cannot by their nature be absolute and cannot generate an absolute experience (say, a religious one) is not ascribed, in capitalism, to the object and its finite relative nature, but to the consumer. We are at fault. As a consequence, we must continually (infinitely) search for (consume) more objects to make up for the infinite lack on our part. At the extreme, God then becomes a projection of our needs, a theistic object, an idol, to placate our vulnerability.

I am not suggesting that we somehow elect to live in the reversals of idolatry. Evidently not. For we rarely detect them as such. I am not asserting that we, in good conscience, just privilege relative, finite things over persons and Person. Then the problem of challenging the reversals would only amount to an act of voluntarism. Instead, there are forces that militate against confronting the reversals by encouraging us, and at times demanding us, to elevate a thing to the status of an absolute. These forces are our inventions, original and creative; they are political and economic historical forces like racism and capitalism that train us to accept things as absolute and to reduce spiritual beings to use-value; they demand that we thrive on, and in many instances survive on, surplus value, that is, exploitation. There are instituted systems that operate under the veil of anonymity that over-attune us to things so that we slip all the more easily into taking persons as "its" and "its" as gods. It is in this sense that these forces can be rightly called "demonic," not because they stem from some outside source, but because of the meaning of what they accomplish, namely, the systematic obfuscation of vertical relations, the frustration of vertical movements, such that it becomes more and more difficult for us to find a way to confront idolatry as such, to say nothing of seeing our way out, to tackling the reversals. Recognizing the role of systemic forces hiding under the veil of anonymity does not, however, mitigate our responsibility in initiating idolatry, compromising vertical relations, and continuing to condone idolatry through micro-actions, thereby institutionalizing it. Such forces may indeed impede a "vocation" or even render it invisible; but this just makes the situation all the more tragic.

Let us return to the spiritual dimension of addiction and place it in the context of what Margaret Miles addressed in her work devoted to a new asceticism as directed toward the fullness of life. We live in an age of unacknowledged asceticisms, she argues, that deaden spirit and are destructive to the body; they do not make us more alive in the flesh and in spirit, they do not aid us in self-understanding, focusing energy, intensifying and expanding consciousness, or evolving in purity of heart— which is the real mission of asceticism.[33] Alcoholism, drug dependence, overeating, overwork, promiscuity, self-indulgence are modes of a misguided asceticism in our times.

Fasting, meditation, or even the sacrifices we make daily of living in crowded cities for the sake of our work or the delight in the company of others, Miles maintains, can become ascetic in the positive sense if they are lived in the direction of spiritual values. Today, however, most of our practices are oriented toward death and not ascetic in the true sense when they become disconnected from the source of life and being: "Historic authors variously named this loss of the sense of our connection to the source of all things 'sluggishness,' 'fatigue of body,' 'inertia,' 'torpor,' 'dullness of apprehension,' 'smallness of soul,' and 'indifference,' to name only a few."[34]

Scheler goes so far as to say that our specifically modern type of asceticism, which is completely alien to antiquity and to the Middle Ages, is founded in *ressentiment*. Whereas the ideal of asceticism was to attain the maximum of enjoyment with a minimum of agreeable and useful objects (what Miles calls the "fullness of life")—enhancing one's ability to gain pleasure from the most simple and accessible things (hence, voluntary poverty, obedience, chastity, contemplation)—*modern* asceticism developed an ideal whose ethical sense is precisely the opposite. Now, based in the *ressentiment* of a superior ability in the art of enjoyment, asceticism is the "ideal" of the minimum of enjoyment with a maximum amount of pleasant and useful things. It is the basis of capitalism and sheds light on the culture of "entertainment" as we know it today.[35]

When we become attached to goods, which have intrinsic value as finite and relative, hoping that they can "provide the infinite life and satisfaction for which human beings long," that is, when they are taken as absolute and infinite—or in our language, when they become idols—when we refuse to acknowledge that we require of them what they as relative, finite beings cannot supply, namely, absolute being and spiritual joy—what we have called idolatry—we become, in Miles's words, *addicts*.[36]

But, one may object, "What does it matter if I take something in this obsessive way when I don't believe in God in the first place? Where is the violation? Why is not one pattern of action simply different from another? How can you call this 'idolatry'? How is it that one can vilify this set of actions and glorify another?"

It is noteworthy that Camus, in his *Myth of Sisyphus*, is entirely consistent in this regard. For him, absurdity is the fundamental situation of human existence. Absurdity does not signify "nonsense," but rather, the human condition of living without any predetermined guarantees of either meaningfulness or meaninglessness. Because one can neither assert nor deny what is not experienced as truth in the "flesh-and-blood"—an empirical presence one cannot deny[37]—and because for him no absolute of any kind can be given in experience, one can make appeal neither to some eternal meaning nor to some eternal meaninglessness. One neither scorns reason nor laments the irrational. Living honestly in the absurd, one lives a life without appeal—appeal, that is, on the one hand to some divine being that orders the universe, gives it a reason, gives hope, and makes the separation of the world and human consciousness *heimlich*, or on the other hand, to some predetermined meaninglessness that would justify despair and possible suicide.

The experience of the absurd is the experience of no absolute whatsoever, such that it is impossible to make value judgments and impossible for any difference to make a difference. In place of the ethic of quality, which would presuppose the order of the saint, the absurd person lives an ethic of quantity.[38] Absurd creation is absurd indifference, is relative relativity. To live one thing over another as if it were intrinsically better; to value one kind of experience over another, even out of habit or carelessness; to let one idea, one passion, one experience dominate any other, unconsciously or implicitly—this would constitute a betrayal to the fundamental experience of the absurd that defines human existence. It would be to admit that there is an absolute in some form or other, *even under the banner of addiction*. To admit quality, value preference, a difference that makes a difference, is to admit the experiential sphere of the absolute. To live without addiction, with utter indifference, merely collecting experiences whose ultimate values are relative, is to live the absurd with perfect lucidity, to mask nothing, and to play at everything, and hence for Camus to realize the meaning of human existence—as absurd. "Jeopardy" and "Trivial Pursuit" are Sisyphus's dream epistemology: amassing and expounding upon an internally disconnected quantity of information with no qualitative difference or context to sort them out in any direction (*sens*), hierarchy, or qualitative significance. "One must imagine Sisyphus happy."

Failing to see these profound implications of the absurd would be for us to fall short of grasping the radical and incisive character of Camus's observations: either there is relative relativity, or there are spheres of absolute experience; either there is an ethic of quantity and radical indifference, or there is an ethic of quality and radical value preference.

Of course, the consistency and correctness of Camus's descriptions hang on one presupposition; this is the lynchpin of his analyses (and by implication, my own): for Camus, experience is only as robust as material and perhaps ideal objects, what I have called objects of presentation. One cannot assert or appeal to anything beyond the experience of so-called flesh-and-blood truths. This is why to acknowledge an absolute kind of experience, which would include the experiences related by the mystics and the saints, would either be counted as a product of longing for that familiar immediacy of Being, an unjustified nostalgia, or an inconsequential appeal to what we cannot know. Even in terms of addiction, letting something dominate our lives as if it were absolute would just be a failure on our part to live human existence as it is, namely, absurd.

But what if, as I have tried to show in this work, experience is not limited to objects of presentation, even if such an experience has a different logic from objects of presentation? What if experience is broader than this, so that it includes, in its own way, the evidence, say, of loving, kindness, hatred, and so forth? What if there is a unique order of absolute experience?

Either the absurd, or verticality and idolatry; there is no in-between. Camus's work makes this point as neatly as the writings of the mystics.

It is noteworthy, phenomenologically, that in our experiences, independently of belief in some deity, something can take hold of us in an absolute manner. The fact that something can be taken as absolute, even some relative thing, and is able to exert its force as absolute even though it is something relative by virtue of its givenness—even where God is not an issue—this is testimony to an experience of the sphere of the absolute in our lives. "It is not surprising," writes Weil, "that in temptation men so often have the feeling of something absolute, which infinitely surpasses them, which they cannot resist. The absolute is indeed there. But we are mistaken when we think that it dwells in pleasure."[39] Idolatry is a kind of service, but a service that Rabbi Dov Baer calls an *avodah zarah:* the service of other gods, the service of foreign, alien, strange things. From the standpoint of Divine service, it is a strange service, an estranged service.[40]

For me, given the broader sphere of experience I have described in this work, this means that when we become obsessed with things or ideas that hold sway and acquire an absolute weight in relation to which everything else is measured, when some fascination rules and orders what we do over all else, it has to be qualified as a misplaced directedness, a reversal of the relative and the absolute. What is relative gets the weight of the absolute because there is an experienced absolute, the Holy, and the Holy by implication becomes relative to that relative (now absolute) thing. In this process, we make ourselves and other human persons of relative value in relation to things, allowing us thereby to view injustice with callous equanimity; we become fascinated with mere details, disconnected facts, and fragmented images ("Trivial Pursuit," and the like), fetishizing knowledge as information acquisition. Is this not idolatry?

I have depicted idolatry in this section as a reversal of the absolute and the relative. Left like this, however, such a characterization is misleading. It is not as if, in the experience of relative things or the Holy, one simply changes "objects." "If I could only substitute God for drinking; if I could only metabolize my obsession for running into an obsession for God," we might imagine someone saying. Phenomenology has shown—in figures like Husserl, Scheler, Merleau-Ponty, even Hegel and Levinas—that what is primary is the relation itself, not the "subject" or "object," such that the transformation of the "object" of experience alters the structure of the experience itself.

On the one hand, it is possible to transfer an obsession with something that is physically or psychologically harmful—say, drinking, eating, or drugs—to a passion (or obsession) for something that is healthy, like running and competing for marathons, because these occur on the *same order of experience.* But it is something else to speak as if one could transfer an obsession with the former or the latter for an "obsession" with God—unless God were merely identified as just another thing, in which case it would not concern the sphere of the religious in the genuine sense. On the contrary, "I" am not the same "I" in the love of the Holy as I am in the "love" of or fascination with things. The movement of obsession with respect to running or drinking as "absolute" is not the same as the movement toward the Holy as absolute. It only perpetuates confusion when "God" is used as saccharin; it only buries the problem of idolatry even deeper.

The recognition that the change in "object" constitutes a modification in the quality of experience and hence a change in the "subject" is why Martin Buber contends that the "I–You" and the "I–It" are "word pairs" that one speaks with his or her whole being.[41] The "I" in comporting itself to the world or to a thing gives itself differently from the way the I is given in relation with the Holy, another person, or nature. That is, the "I" is inseparable from the word pair itself; it is only abstractly that we conceive of a subject that would be equally and indifferently the same from one involvement to the next. Indeed, according to Buber, the "I" is only fully revealed as person in the I–You relation.[42] Thus, strictly speaking, if I am obsessed by a thing and erect it so that everything is subjugated to it, then it is incorrect to say that I can turn my obsession now to God and escape idolatry. The movement toward the Holy qualifies this relation as *a different kind of movement,* and I am a different kind of person in the process. Buber writes: "He who is dominated by the idol that he wants to acquire, to have, and to hold, he who is possessed by his desire to possess, he has no other way to God than by returning [*Umkehr*]; this returning entails not simply a change of goal, but an alternation of the kind of movement."[43]

Such a turning back or returning is actually a reversing of the reversal. This is to say, the orientation of possessing things, idols, whereby they take on absolute worth is not primordial. It is a distortion or disordering in which relative things are lived as if absolute and the sphere of the absolute is held in no higher regard than relative things. The now so-called religious sphere can be taken as some*thing* incidental to our lives, something that can then be adjuncted when we feel like it, changed at our discretion, abandoned when we don't feel like it anymore. It is not that there are not proper involvements with things, but they deserve a relation appropriate to them, namely, as relative. The violence of idolatry emerges when we treat relative objects absolutely, inverting the absolute and the relative, constituting a de-spiritualization of our lives.

Just as the "I" is not neutral in its orientation but is qualified as such in verticality or idolatry, so too are these two movements not neutral in relation to each other. The more talented we become in living the reversal of idolatry, the less adept we become at living vertically and the more difficult it becomes to return from or to reverse the reversal. In accommodating ourselves to objects, we proliferate idols and the way of being with idols so that idolatry now seems natural to us.

World as Mundane

By understanding the world as object, I have described idolatry as a reversal of the relative and the absolute. There is another interrelated sense of world that speaks even more directly to the problem of secularism as idolatry, and that is the world in the sense of mundaneity.

The sense of mundaneity is twofold. First, the world is what we live every day in a straightforward attitude of acceptance. It corresponds to the concept of mundaneity when we take its very meaning for granted as always already present, that is, when we take the sense of world-meaning for granted. This everyday concept of the world corresponds to the phenomenological notion of the lifeworld.[44]

Second, in distinction to the commonsense worldview, the world as mundane corresponds to the objectivistic worldview. Here the world is determined as objective reality, subject to causal laws, or as nature inherently capable of quantification. Falling under the aegis of world as mundaneity are both the "subject" and the "object" insofar as they are both determined by objectivistic principles, insofar as both are "worldly" in this uprooted sense.

Notice that these two truncated ways of understanding the world correspond to the two ways in which Husserl portrays the so-called natural attitude. In the former case, the world is given in the natural attitude as the natural concept of the world; in the latter, it is experienced in the naturalistic attitude as the scientifically mathematizable world. Of course, by taking the source of the world for granted, one can easily slip from that natural everyday concept of the world, or lifeworld into an objective, quantitative view of reality. In this way, the latter is grounded in the former, while the naturalistic worldview is a possibility within the natural, but not the reverse.

But what both attitudes and senses of mundaneity have in common is that the source of the world is taken for granted. They amount to living in the world from the world, where the world is its own ultimate source of meaning. This is the root sense of secularism: living in the world from the world as its own source, as if the world were absolute.[45] As a consequence, human history can be counted as the self-contained domain of human actions and initiatives in its possible confrontation with nature, and nothing more. The denial, or so-called death of God, is only a result of this movement.

In contrast to living in the world from the world, we point vertically. Vertically speaking, secularism lives in the world while taking the source of the world for granted. Living in the world, from the source of the world, or living *in* the world *from* the Holy, is not a retreat from world-historical or interpersonal transformation, but the very process of sanctifying the world and the interpersonal nexus. In the Abrahamic tradition, this has been expressed as *tikkun olam,* the reparation or redemption of the world, realizing the presence of God or performing works for the glory of God, participating in salvation history.

To live in the world from the Holy can mean, as suggested above, to love one's neighbor as oneself; to live in humility and poverty; to clothe the naked, feed the hungry, and forgive one's enemies. In this way I do not treat the other person as a creature who is merely differentiated from me in space and time, as just another human ego, but as absolutely unique, with his or her own "good-in-itself-for-me," that is, in solidarity. I love my neighbor as "Myself" in this more profound sense.

Of course, one could always execute actions so that they look the same from the outside. Superficially, I could put on the appearance of fasting, but not fast in spirit. I could put money in the "poor box" and make a difference in this sense, but just want to feel good about myself or put down "community work" on a curriculum vitae. Or again, I may not countenance any explicit belief in God, but still act for the liberation of my sisters or brothers in my community. Or conversely, I may want to effect a change in the world out of love of others, grounded in an explicit religious experience, but try as I might, all my actions may be ineffectual and to this extent perhaps in vain.

Does the salvific role of one's actions depend upon actually effecting such an external change in the world? Is there a limit to when that change is effected? Now? Generations in the future? It is true that one can pretend to be loving toward another and really be preparing acts of violence; but can one love one's neighbor as "Myself" and still do acts of violence? Can one, for example, enslave others (being well-meaning or not) and further the kingdom of God?

The point of practicing mercy, for example, is not to conform to an exterior model and to imitate the show of mercy, as Henry has shown,[46] but to live in such a way that the acts, whatever they may be, *bear the essence of mercy,* with the hope that they will be efficacious in this way. To borrow a distinction that Scheler makes, the Christian does not live "like" Christ in the sense of copying the exterior operations (having long hair, being a carpenter's son, and the like), but lives "as" Christ such that whatever the acts may be (though they cannot be just anything), they bear inextricably the essence of or the internal sense of that life, though they are irreducible to that essence. Without our being able to know the ultimate meaning of living in the world from the dimension of the Holy, the most we can say is that there is nevertheless an *experiential, lived difference* between living merely "worldly," and living in the world, from the Holy; this is a difference we can sense interpersonally, historically, in the world.

In point of fact, one cannot effectively resist injustice or hatred on its own terms, challenging secular history with merely secular means (which would, furthermore, arbitrarily delimit a dimension of human experience). The experience of the mystics is prophetic in the deepest sense. In the face of perpetrating and condoning violence, tolerating hatred, being complacent at cruelty, and practicing deceit, one does good deeds, which is to say, brings the world into divine focus. Human history, and the situation in which we find ourselves in this history, can therefore only be understood most fully in connection to the Sacred. Religious experience is not an "option" at our disposal, an add-on to culture; nor can it be realized most deeply as a mere political technique. Nevertheless, to live in the

world, from the Holy, is to cultivate human spirit and thereby revolution-
ize history. World history is only *essentially* changed when transformed,
not in its own terms, but by living from the dimension of the source of
the world.

Secularism vs. Fundamentalism?

RELIGION AND CULTURE

To transform world history vertically does not mean to do this in
terms of "religion." There is an important distinction to be made between
living religiously, in the sense of living from the immediate and direct
experience of the dimension of the Holy, and religion merely as a social
and cultural phenomenon. In certain respects, thinkers like Foucault,
Bergson, and Durkheim are entirely correct. Religion can be a persuasive
institutional, political force, a "superb instrument of power for itself,"
carrying tremendous historical weight.[47] It can be regarded statically
as a human force that simply ties the individual to social life and com-
pensates for the imposition of human intelligence in the natural world,
offering security and serenity.[48] Religion can be taken as a social institution that responds to human needs, that issues in systems of practices
(ritual conduct, festivals, rites, etc.), and that derives from systems of
ideas that express the world.[49] There can be no doubt that religion is a
human expression, a cultural emergence, a social event. Religion is our
making. To this extent, religion can become idolatrous in a fashion no
less invidious than, say, militarism, that is, when we absolutize our own
fabrications, trust in our own creation, as the prophet Hosea observed.
I will take this up below when I consider fundamentalism as a mode of
idolatry. The question to consider now, however, is not whether religion
can be interpreted as having a human origin, but whether and to what
extent it has a *personal* one.

If we understand culture as intertwined with desires, interests,
sufferings, even climate, geographical factors, and the like, and not as
in opposition to "nature"[50]—without culture or *Geist* being a product
of psychic or physicalistic or "natural" factors—there is no reason to
oppose religion to culture, no matter how "primitive" or "advanced"
(in Durkheim's sense) the particular forms of religion might be. It is not
religion but *religious experience* that is the foundation of culture, and cul-
ture/religion is transformed, not within culture but from the foundation

or source of culture.[51] In other words, if religion and culture are somehow on the same level of experience, as I am inclined to express it, it is not merely a result of human action.

Despite certain inconsistencies in his presentation of the *élan vital*, Bergson is not a vitalist. As is well known, Bergson distinguishes between "static religion" and "dynamic religion."[52] Static religion is the product of the myth-making function that counteracts the emergence of intelligence in the human species and attaches the human being to the particularity of life and to the social whole. Dynamic religion, by contrast, emerges from the creative impetus itself and puts us in contact with the creative effort that life manifests (what Bergson understands as God). This is the point of mysticism for Bergson.[53] So static religion is founded in dynamic religion, and mystical experience, taken in its immediacy, is the religious foundation of morality, both "open" and "closed." Not the vital urge but the experience of the Divine—religious experience—is the foundation of religion. One might ask to what extent dynamic religion or mysticism can any longer be regarded as a vitalism, since even for Bergson, the generativity of the vital impulse reveals itself personally.

Here I am not considering what might be called, using traditional terminology, a "natural" religious experience; this I reserve for a subsequent work. I am considering it directly in a personal dimension. What distinguishes so-called natural religion from positive religion is not rational knowledge, metaphysics, and direct experience or "revealed" religion, but rather *different kinds of givenness*. In the personal sphere, for the givenness to and through persons, I have used the term "epiphany" to evoke this sense of givenness. For the so-called natural sphere, which for me concerns the Earth, and elemental being and beings, I employ the terms "disclosure" and "display" (one can think here of the later Husserl and St. Francis of Assisi, respectively). There are still other kinds of givenness too, kinds of givenness that I sketched out at the very beginning—those that pertain to the way in which cultural objects, things and the like, also "give" the sphere of the Holy. I reserve the term "manifestation" for this mode of vertical givenness. They have, each in their own way, their distinctive ways of giving and being given. I focus in this work on epiphany, and for this reason consider religious experience in the mode of epiphanic or personal givenness. It is in this way that I suggest epiphany *qua* religious experience is the foundation of religion.

For someone like Bergson, this means that mystical experiences take shape in, but are irreducible to, the symbolism and imagery of the static myth-making function.[54] For Scheler, this implies that religious knowledge is not given as ready-made prior to its liturgical and ritual expression; rather, ritual and cult is an essential *vehicle* of its unique kind of development. Religious experiences are only first complete and only first formed in and through ritual expression and the ritual exhibition of religious lived experience. Religious experience and concrete historical practices, for example in cult, are so mutually interdependent that we can say, along with Scheler, that those who pray kneeling have a different experience of God than those who pray standing. It is impossible, he writes, that the Roman, who covers his eyes in prayer and becomes submissive rather than expansive, has the same concrete experience and idea of God as does the Greek, who opens his eyes and arms wide to the Deity.[55]

We must not think, however, that there is a simple relationship between religious experience and religion; religion does not merely reflect religious awareness. Religion, with its ritual, cult, remembrances, and so forth, is also an institutional way of "working through" the impact of the Holy that each person carries with him or her as the "good-in-itself-for-me." The latter as over-full of meaning by its nature does not simply have an individually personal significance, but has a collectively personal meaning. Because it comes to us "before" we could choose it for ourselves, because its meaning is over-full, it has to be worked out individually, collectively, and historically. The cult of religion is one of those ways of working it out. Indeed, we could go so far as to say that even idolatry is a way of working through the experience of the Holy, but in a manner that has predominately negative, restrictive significance.

Religion can also have another significance, that is, ritual and liturgical practices can serve as "springboards" to possible experiences, functioning as pathways of disposing ourselves to this dimension of experience. One of the virtues of religion and its concrete types of practices, regulations of conduct, specific disciplines, and techniques of prayer is that it can dispose us more readily, more "directly" to religious experiences in a particular way. We do this integrated dynamic of religious experience/religion an injustice when we mistake the rituals and practices *tout court* for the religious experiences themselves, fixating on the former and deluding ourselves about the latter. Religious practices then can become all the more obfuscating regarding dynamic religious experiences.

This tension and interdependence cited here between religious experience and "established" religion gets embodied in the very lives of the mystics. For example, in the case of Rabbi Dov Baer, we witness a personal form of experience, an ecstatic or prophetic form of Kabbalah that at times is at odds both with theosophical-theurgical Kabbalah and with established Rabbinic tradition. Though himself a rabbi, immersed in Torah and Talmud, his personal experiences of Adonai led him beyond formalism to *hitlahavut,* or enthusiasm, to repentance and returning to the service of God. Coinciding with the will of God in the mode of *yechidah* is at the same time both the fulfillment of the "Law" and a transcending of the Law, instituting new or modified religious practices that for Jews deepen Judaism itself. Because these experiences are lived from the presence of the living God, they can come into conflict with past experiences of the same sort or with contemporary understandings that do not issue from the source of experience in the same ways.

This is especially evident in the experiences of St. Teresa of Avila. We need only recall how her "Book of Her Life" was sequestered by the Inquisitors. Her experiences (and the fact that she was a woman) challenged the familiar assumptions of the Christian tradition. Even more intimately, although she deferred the integrity of her experiences to Scripture in humility, it was ultimately the field of her own experiences of the Holy that initiated a personal transformation that became the final court of appeal: "Its [the soul's] thought becomes so accustomed to understanding what the real truth is that everything else seems to it to be child's play. It sometimes laughs to itself when it sees seriously religious and prayerful persons making a big issue out of some rules of etiquette which it has already trampled under foot."[56]

A similar tension is evident in the ecstatic experiences of those like Rūzbihān Baqlī (including Hallāj and Bisṭāmī). On the one hand, the Sufi lives in the recognition that Muhammad is the Messenger of God and seal of the prophets, but on the other hand, he or she experientially realizes that the *sunna* and *hadith* do not exhaust ways to be an exemplary Muslim. The direct and immediate teaching by the presence of God would seem to place the Sufi in the prophetic lineage; but to remain in accord with the tradition, they have to step back from such an assertion and rely on the distinction between the authority of the Prophet and God's revelation through him and on the open-ended divine inspiration that qualifies the friends of God or Sufi saints as such. At a minimum, the perfect imitation of the Prophet by the Sufi cannot be captured exhaustively by adhering to the revealed law or mere faith. The tension is no less evident, as we saw above, between the radical nature of ecstatic expressions ("I am the Truth") and the threat of being denounced a heretic.

These observations are not really new, and this tension is widely acknowledged. I recapitulate it here to underscore the irreducibility—not the separability—of religious experiences in relation to concrete practices of "religion," and to stress that the mere execution and amassing of ritual conduct can never exhaust the presence of God, since the latter founds the former. Measured by the standards of institutional religion and accustomed patterns of cult, mystical experiences as religious experiences will undoubtedly appear as "abnormal" and as in violation of "the norm." But the abnormality of vertical experiences in relation to the horizontality of institutional normality can also be, in reality, "hyper-normal," "optimal," to appeal yet again to Husserl's expressions, setting new standards of normality and instituting a transvaluation from *within* experience itself. Vertical epiphany might be experienced as an eruption in the "everyday," but the religiously informed life lives "from" this "eruption" and transforms the meaning of the everyday. This is why, as I mentioned at the beginning of this work, the individual mystics from different traditions at root often share more with each other than they do with others of their own religious tradition.

I mention this tension, finally, as a transition to the other facet of this kind of idolatry. If reducing religion merely to the historical form of life yields secularism in its various forms, then fixating on religion, "religious" conduct, and conceptual articulations of experience as if they passed for, are reducible to, and exhausted religious experiencing itself, yields what we know today as fundamentalism.

FUNDAMENTALISM AS A MODE OF IDOLATRY

It is commonplace to think of fundamentalism as a movement opposed to secularism. After all, secularism, it is held, puts its faith in reason or finds the ground for action in irrational, unconscious forces; it denies the involvement of a deity in worldly affairs or divorces historical human values from divine ones. On the other hand, fundamentalism, one rejoins, stresses faith in God, sees God as the cause for actions in the world, and asserts moral values as divine, eternal imperatives.

This opposition, however, is only an apparent one. Indeed, both secularism and fundamentalism have the same root, both historically and ontologically. To cite a popular source, Karen Armstrong, in her acclaimed work, *The Battle for God,* has shown that the fundamentalist movements in the Jewish, Christian, and Islamic faiths are not throwbacks to an out-moded past; both secularism and fundamentalism are "modern" responses to historical and personal exigencies.[57] For example, Armstrong locates the rise of secularism in the late-medieval/early-modern scientific ratio-nalism and in religious persecutions of other faiths that eventually yielded a visceral antipathy to all sorts of formal religion and its practices.[58] On the one hand, the universalism of science and rational principles did adjure a liberation from the "mystifications" of religious rites, rituals, and superstitions and thus provided a possibility of circumventing the basis for religious, sectarian, and ethnic violence. But extirpating what Armstrong calls *mythos* from our lives, and leaving only *logos,* eventu-ally created a religious vacuum, enabling the backlash we know today as fundamentalism.

Fundamentalism is a contemporary religious experiment (among other contemporary experiments) by those who attempt to fill the spiritual void left by modern scientific, secularist "progress," and who, as a result, find secular rationalism to be the worst kind of aggression. Fundamentalism and postmodernism are not that distinctive, insofar as both, each in their own way, are historical reactions to the insights of the modern.[59]

I do not want to belabor this point; the historical rise of fundamen-talism is well documented by Armstrong, among others, and I could do no more than repeat these lucid accounts.[60] But there is another relation between secularism and fundamentalism that is not merely historical but ontological: secularism and fundamentalism are both modes of idolatry. This may sound curious at first glance, since fundamentalists of various stripes are the ones known to accuse secularists as well as other religions of being idolatrous. Was it not the Taliban, for example, who destroyed the ancient statues of the Buddha, denouncing them as idols?

What is deeply curious about fundamentalism is that in its rejec-tion of scientific, rational (or irrational) secularism (in Armstrong's terms, *logos*), it presupposes the validity of the secular move: the uprooting of *mythos* in its ambiguous richness, symbolism, and evocative capacity, and the assertion of the one-sided validity of *logos.*[61] In attempting to return to so-called religious truths, fundamentalism takes with it the mind-set of the modern, scientific insights. Fundamentalism submits *mythos* to *logos,* demanding that Scripture be taken literally, expecting the myths and symbolism of Scripture to be equivalent to scientific explanations.

Certainly, this is an ambiguous claim. It is not at all clear that prior to the new science of history, Scripture was taken either as myth or "literally." What becomes clear, however, is that the new modern cosmology, among other things provoked a discrepancy between Scripture and "science" that brought into relief the "literal meaning of Scripture" and "figurative" meanings, provoking what Dupré alludes to as a "new literalism" peculiar to the Enlightenment.[62]

It is only now that Scripture and secular science can be placed on the same level precisely because they are both expected to correspond to the model of *exactitude* derived from the specifically modern epistemic demands. Only in this way could there be a so-called debate between "evolutionism" and "creationism." Scripture is read *as* a literal account, yielding precise, exclusive interpretations; it no longer functions evocatively, but provocatively, denoting "truth." Compare this with the Quran's assertion that no one knows the true interpretation of the Quran except God. Since the presence of God could not be exhausted in finite form, the Quran opened itself to, indeed demanded, a variety of interpretations, especially by the spiritually adept, on themes concerning the nature of God and the nature of humanity (Quran 3:7, 3:190).[63] As serious as this is, if this were *all* that fundamentalism amounted to, we could accuse it of nothing more than bad hermeneutics. Mere literalism is not fundamentalism, nor is it idolatry.

There is more. Fundamentalism has deeper personal implications that make it not only a historical or hermeneutic gesture but an ontological one as a mode of idolatry. At root, fundamentalism is the attempt to make God conform to our intentions and thereby to force others to conform to our intentions in the name of God. This gets expressed as the attempt to reduce the Holy to human understanding and to our imposition of meaning. It is to reduce the infinite to the finite in the name of God, but it does so in the Name of God. Fundamentalism might as well be secularism, but then it would lose its façade of religiosity. Precisely because it speaks within a "religious" context, fundamentalism becomes all the more an insidious form of idolatry. Fundamentalism, be it Christian, Jewish, or Islamic, is not religious in the specific sense we have been developing here. True, it uses religious discourse; it appeals to Scripture; it acts in the

Name of God. But the meaning of the actions is not religious in this more profound sense. Accordingly, Weil can write in a related context: "Even though they are monotheistic, they are idolatrous."[64]

The Holy as generative movement, as origin-originating, cannot be contained in a finite, historical structure, since by virtue of this very Personal, generative movement, it surpasses every determinate structure. Yet the Holy is given in the Abrahamic tradition fully, though not exhaustively, and experienced "only" in the historical forms of Islam, in Christianity, in Judaism ("only" in the sense of historically bound and not a-historically, not in the sense of "exclusively"). Fundamentalism as idolatry emerges the moment I say, "I've got it." Idolatry limits the ongoing "source" of history to and within that historically determined history, to "our world," to "me." God "in general" is in some sense impossible without the historical forms of religious practice; but religions and their historical emergence are likewise impossible without "God," who exceeds them. The latter movement is what fundamentalism as idolatry ignores to the extent that it no longer coincides with the generativity of the Holy. Instead of letting the Gift take its effect, asserts Buber, the one who seeks after God in a kind of "theo-mania" reflects on that which gives and misses both.[65]

This is not to say that fundamentalists are not well intentioned. What I am identifying, however, is the internal sense of the movement of fundamentalism, which is idolatrous. In fundamentalism as a mode of idolatry, I want to make God *my* witness, and please God as *I* see fit—which is ultimately another form of pride, measuring God by ourselves and not ourselves by God.[66] Let us recall that Aaron's two well-intentioned and on all accounts innocent sons were, according to the Torah, fatally struck down by a "strange" or "alien fire" (*esh zarah*), according to Leviticus 10:1–3, when they took it upon themselves to make an offering to God in a way that God had not enjoined upon them. What makes the fire alien, that is, alien to God, is not the kind of fire it was but the *manner* of "offering." It was imposed by the sons' will in an attempt to produce the presence of God on their time. The fire was not allowed to come forth of its own accord, announcing the presence of God as they had witnessed earlier; the fire was presented in advance, "offered" now so as to make God present.

One cannot possess the presence of God or have the presumption to make it manifest in a particular way. This is why in Bernanos's *Diary of a*

Country Priest, the priest does not produce the letter Madame la Comtesse had written him about the peace she finally found through their conversation; nor does he write an account of what transpired between her and him before she died in order to defend himself before the Church—even though he was accused, through rancorous presumption and rumor, of driving her to her death.[67] What the priest called the miracle of our empty hands—of giving to another what we ourselves do not possess—demands humble service in the face of mystery. Her letter or another's, it is no matter—one cannot conjure God to bear witness to epiphany in the everyday.

The so-called hermeneutic moment of fundamentalism is not merely hermeneutic. For the faithful, the Torah and the Quran are accepted as the revealed Word of God, and Jesus as the Word made Flesh; if God/God's Word is infinite, God could not be constrained by an exact interpretation, but instead—as I have mentioned above in relation to the mystics of these traditions—demands living interpretation, or perhaps more so, living struggle.[68] In fundamentalism, belief becomes the substitute for epiphany.

Mystical experience (religious experience understood in its most profound sense within the Abrahamic tradition) and the bondage to God *qua* spiritual freedom that accompanies it exist in tension with the letter of the law and with the literal sense of Scripture, inherently calling into question fundamentalism as its own style of idolatry.[69] Hallāj was well aware of this seeming paradox, one that he lived and died under: "May God veil you from the exterior of the religious law, and may he reveal to you the reality of infidelity. For the exterior of the religious law is a hidden idolatry, while the reality of infidelity is a manifest gnosis."[70]

Idolatry and Delimitation

Delimitation as a mode of idolatry can be summarized as an exclusive orientation to a particular thing, dimension of existence, or sphere of being such that it no longer is able to point beyond itself. Delimitation "limits" the experience so that it remains "horizontal" and does not point vertically. As Heschel writes, it is absurd to isolate the human situation, treating it on its own merely, and to divorce it from the movement of the Divine. This absurdity, which for him is exemplified in the self-defeating course of human history where the human being reigns supreme, is what we call idolatry.[71] Understood within the context of verticality, human history cannot be the only dimension to human history. To live it otherwise is idolatry. In pride, we live the self as self-grounding such that it does not open to the Holy; in secularism, the world only has eyes for itself; in fundamentalism, the "Word" is restricted to its denotative function, and the experience of God coming under our power of disposition is reduced to cult.

There is, of course, an internal temptation to stop short at different levels of experience, since each thing bears a value that is intrinsic to it, according to that sphere of being. A technician, for example, might focus on information technology because it is intrinsically useful. But when information technology is not accepted, for example, as a "gift," when it is not undertaken, as the mystics say, "for the glory and honor of God" or to serve others and God in humility, it becomes idolatry. Of course, simply saying that one does something for the glory and honor of God does not necessarily mitigate idolatry. For example, one does not tout the "Gospel of Prosperity," one does not "build bombs for God," or again, sell real estate (like "Divine Realty: Jesus Christ is our Lord"), reaping profits from others and pandering to the market, and then call it holiness.

The problem of idolatry arises when the delimitation or specific orientation of an act or way of life is not simultaneously realized as a de-limitation, when, for example, the technical life is restricted *to the technical sphere merely,* not allowing it to give beyond itself, opening itself, in a de-limiting manner, in the direction of the Holy. This de-limitation or in-direction *modifies the very experience itself and the orientation to that particular sphere of value.* Only with the integration of, say, technology and loving (verticality) is there the possibility of the redemption of the technical; only the integration of political history with loving (verticality) is there the possibility of humanity as the drama of redemption. Within verticality one cannot exploit others for God (even with "good intentions"); doing so deserves the name idolatry.

Idolatry applies to secularism and to fundamentalism alike as delimitations of verticality; they are not de-limitations that open up to the Holy. As infinite, the Holy is boundless, and within this vertical experience, we cannot arbitrarily limit this generative movement to a particular level of being. To do so would be to impose, arbitrarily, a restriction on experience. The arbitrary delimitation makes me the arbiter of the experience and issues in an insidious form of pride.

This is not to say that one should ignore things or look away from the world "to find God," or look intently at the world to find the world. These are both unjustified delimitations and abstractions. The point would be to give the world its proper due and yet not make things absolute or into gods (*shirk*); the point would be to allow things to be themselves and yet to manifest the infinite. Buber reflects: "'Here world, there God'—that is It-talk; and 'God in the world'—that is another form of It-talk." But, he continues, the perfect relationship consists in giving the world its due and truth, leaving nothing out, leaving nothing behind, comprehending everything, all the world in and through comprehending the You, having nothing besides God and associating nothing with God, grasping everything in God.[72]

The finite dimensions of existence are infinite insofar as they open up to the Holy. But within verticality, *the exclusive orientation* toward any particular sphere of being—say, the vital sphere or the sphere of use—closes us off to the level of spirit. If the vital or use values implicitly become the highest values, such an overvaluation of them indicates a disorder of the heart, and this disorder leaves us with a deep confusion about who we are.[73] Thus, writes, Simone Weil: "All these secondary kinds of beauty are of infinite value *as openings to* universal beauty. But, if we stop short at them, they are, on the contrary, veils; then they corrupt. They all have in them more or less of this temptation, but in very different degrees."[74] Human history, to go back to Heschel's observation, points beyond itself, is de-limiting, only to the extent that it is not taken as a fixed, self-subsistent horizontal fact and when it is taken up according to the power that gives it. What is *given* is *infinitely* richer than itself.

• • •

I mentioned in the Introduction to this work that idolatry is a creative, historical response to epiphany as a mode of vertical givenness. It is a manifest danger of idolatry that if we persist too deeply in it, we will become unable to discern verticality in our daily lives. In our distractions and spiritual down-turn, idolatry can characterize the general bearing of our lives as evil, only occasionally seasoned with good acts. Under the sway of idolatry, in whatever form, the dimension of the Holy—that which is most integral—seems to be what is most alien.

Our vocation as persons, however, points in another direction: it points vertically. In the face of pride, this vocation demands humility in service; in the face of secularism and fundamentalism, it calls for over-turning reversals and religious transformation; in the face of delimitation, it requires de-limitation.

Certainly, this could appear as just so much naïveté. There is no simple *saut* out of idolatry. To think so would be to sacrifice the serious to the spectacular in the name of religious romanticism and to forget that idola-try functions not only in explicit acts but as a diaphanous background whose curves are as difficult to detect as any politico-economic ideology. As Derrida writes with regard to the challenge of metaphysics, "The step 'outside philosophy' is much more difficult to conceive than is generally imagined by those who think they made it long ago with cavalier ease, and who in general are swallowed up in metaphysics in the entire body of discourse which they claim to have disengaged from it."[75] In this regard, Bruce Benson cautions that one must be ever vigilant, since idolatry can always return like a clever virus, and certain efforts to overcome idolatry can themselves transmogrify into new forms of idolatry.[76] Part of the difficulty here undoubtedly consists in the fact that we might become too attached precisely to *our efforts* of challenging idolatry such that, for example, pride returns more entrenched and insidious than before in confronting idolatry.

Ultimately, we have to go so far as to say that our orientation cannot be that of challenging idolatry, but of living vertically, which is thereby intrinsically a challenge to idolatry. For even in order to discern idolatry as a problem, there must be at least a "point," a "foothold" in vertical presence that allows idolatry to be confronted as such. Its confrontation has not only a religious, inter-Personal significance, but a moral, inter-personal one, since idolatry is not only an inter-Personal rupture, but an interpersonal disruption.

On the De-Limitation
of the Religious and the Moral

The philosophical task of this book has been to show that there are kinds of human experiencing that go beyond the presentation of empirical and ideal objects, and that although they do not conform to the way in which objects are presented, they are nonetheless modes of *human experience* that have their own modes of evidence and raise their own problems of evidence. Experience and evidence is decidedly more encompassing than the experience and evidence that occurs in the style of presentation. Evoking the peculiar non-presentational modes of givenness, I have referred to them as kinds of vertical presence or verticality. Through a phenomenological style of investigation, these vertical modes of givenness are susceptible to critical, philosophical analysis. I have focused in this work on epiphany, a vertical givenness that opens the religious dimension of experience. Religious experience is a quality of existence that is determined on its own level and in its own terms. By drawing on the descriptions of the selected mystics within the Abrahamic tradition, I have attempted to discern epiphany's unique evidential force, its own dynamic peculiar to the religious sphere, and its own special modalizations as it pertains to the inter-Personal sphere of experiencing.

The critical task has been to show that the difficulties we face today as persons are most profoundly to be characterized, not in terms of a crisis of understanding, a forgetfulness of Being, ideology, or drives, but as a de-spiritualization understood as idolatry. Idolatry as a problem is exposed through the clarification of verticality. Idolatry is the personal challenge to this vertical movement that gets played out in the field of human experience from the religious to the economic to the level of individual desires.

For St. Teresa of Avila, Rabbi Dov Baer, and Rūzbihān Baqlī, the *meaning* of the orientation to God opens itself to what they understand as humble service, love of neighbor, compassion, *tzedakah,* generosity. In the broadest sense, it is *prophetic*. This flows out of the religious experience itself. Epiphany is also a calling, a mission. It is, in fact, no coincidence that these mystics of the Abrahamic tradition all exhibit and share this prophetic dimension in one way or another. They live, work, and speak from the Holy toward others, and not from themselves, to and for themselves. This is not to reduce the social dimension of prophetic experience to the religious but to recognize that social criticism most profoundly cannot be *grounded* simply in the social; it is, rather, animated by the religious. This is how we can understand Gibbs's contention that the justification for speaking *to* others about their moral responsibilities *for* others requires the category of prophecy.[1]

We have seen in the chapter on individuation that the absolute uniqueness of the person means being irreducible to God and being irreducible to others. Only because of individuation in the sense of personal uniqueness is there opened a moral dimension of experience, for if one person were ultimately reducible to another, there would be no significance to *moral* action.

Although moral experience is phenomenologically distinct in relation to religious experience since it has a different meaning orientation or lived experiential quality, moral experience is realized most profoundly as pointing in a de-limiting manner toward the Holy. The moral dimension of experience is most fully what it is in its de-limiting openness, revealing the religious. This is much different from saying that one only loves others because of God, as if the other person had no intrinsic value of his or her own: "To love man *for God's sake*—that has so far been the noblest and most remote feeling attained among men. That the love of man is just one more stupidity and brutishness if there is no ulterior intent to sanctify it; that the inclination to such love of man must receive its measure, its subtlety, its grain of salt and dash of ambergris from some higher inclination—whoever the human being may have been who first felt and 'experienced' this, however much his tongue may have stumbled as it tried to express such *délicatesse,* let him remain holy and venerable for us for all time as the human being who has flown highest yet and gone astray most beautifully!"[2] Nietzsche understood the calamity of such a reduction.

From what we have gained from this exposition, we can say that, broadly speaking, ethics as it is usually understood today is a product of dissociation, or what I have termed here "delimitation." It delimits (in the restrictive sense) the moral simply to the human, and in this vertical disconnect it opens the door for all kinds of fragmented ethical theories that are as a result essentially severed "horizontally" from one another: communicative ethics, business ethics, engineering ethics, animal ethics, ecological ethics, computer ethics, advertising ethics, and so forth. It is not the areas designated by these ethics that are problematic; it is their very proliferation *as expressive* of a more profound uprootedness. It is not that one does not live morally in communication with others, with animals other than human, or in our service to others as we engineer buildings or automobiles. My point is rather that these relations have an utterly different meaning when there is a vertical resonance, a resonance that is not in evidence when regarding "ethics" in such a specialized and disconnected manner.

In the latter instance, we lose not only the vertical relation to the Holy in the moral; we sacrifice the vertical orientation of other persons as well as the vertical orientation inherent in cultural products.[3] Now the latter, in a mere "ethics," fails to give or "manifest" vertically in religious (Personal) or moral (personal) senses. We can build ethically according to "code" and not morally according to sustainable living for our neighbor. The orientation toward others has no personal basis. Products, in their turn, can become mystified objects, reified, and "absolute" in their own way, and thus idols to which we bow and which dominate us. These ethics, no matter how well intentioned, ultimately serve only to accommodate and fail to speak to us inter-*personally*. Capitalism is expressive of this flattening. It is evil in this sense.

The moral life inherently bears a religious quality. From this perspective, the other human person is not just another human being, another rational subject, the "other," the "alien," or a mere ward of the State, but "brother," "sister," "neighbor," "friend," enjoined collectively in the task of "perfecting" the world.[4]

GLOSSARY OF MAIN HEBREW AND ARABIC TERMS

HEBREW TERMS

avodah	service	*kelim*	vessels
ayin	nothingness, the "Primordial Point." *Ayin* is the name of the Hebrew letter, which is not pronounced	*kelipot*	shells
		keter	crown (the "head" *sefirah*)
		malchut	sovereignty, associated with the *shechinah* (one of the *sefirot*)
binah	understanding (one of the *sefirot*)	*metzarim*	מצרים limitations; see *mitzraim*
Chabad	a branch of Chassidic mysticism. Its name derives from the acrostic formed by *chochmah, binah,* and *daat*	*mitzraim*	מצרים Egypt; see *metzarim*
		mitzvah	good deed or commandment (pl. *mitzvot*)
chayyah	the second-highest level of natural and divine soul according to Dov Baer	*Mishnah*	earliest codification of Jewish Oral "Torah" by the third century CE
chesed	loving-kindness, mercy (one of the *sefirot*)	*navi*	prophet
chochmah	wisdom (one of the *sefirot*)	*nefesh*	the lowest level of natural and divine soul according to Dov Baer
daat	knowledge (one of the *sefirot,* depending upon the schema)	*neshamah*	the third in the ordering of natural and divine soul according to Dov Baer
devekut	cleaving to God		
en sof	the Infinite	*netzach*	lasting endurance, victory, associated with prophecy
gevurah	power, might, associated with *din* or judgment (one of the *sefirot*)		
		or en sof	Light of the Infinite One
hineni	"here I am"	*rachamim*	compassion, associated with *tiferet* or beauty
hitpaalut	ecstasy		
hod	splendor, Majesty, also associated with prophecy (one of the *sefirot*)	*ruach*	the second-lowest level of natural and divine soul according to Dov Baer
kavannah	sincere, focused, directed, concentration	*shechinah*	God's presence or Glory, often associated with God's feminine aspect

sefirah emanation (pl. *sefirot*)

shimacha hearing

shir ha-shirim
  "The Song of Songs"

sitra achra evil, "the other side"

Talmud midrash, or commentary on the *Mishnah;* a collection of books written between 200 and 600 CE, and next to the *Tanach,* one of the most important books in Judaism

Tanach (also *Tanakh*). The Hebrew Bible. "Tanach" is an acrostic formed by the first letter of Torah (the Five Books of Moses), Nevi'im (the Prophets), and Kethuvim (the Writings, i.e., Psalms, Proverbs, etc.)

teshuvah repentance, turning toward God

tikkun olam
  reparation of the world

Torah the "Five books of Moses" or the first five books of the Bible, the "Pentateuch." In a broader sense, the *Torah* is continuous "teaching" or "revelation" that includes the *Tanach* and the *Talmud*

tzedakah righteousness, charity, justice

tzaddik the "righteous" one, the holy one, or the saintly one

tzaddikim the community of righteous persons

tzimtzum contraction (of the Godhead)

yechidah the highest level of natural and divine soul, according to Dov Baer

yesod foundation

zarah foreign, alien, strange

ARABIC TERMS

Allāh literally, "al-Lāh" "the God"

asḥāb-i Suffa
  people of the Bench

'ayn essence

baqā subsistence or abiding

dhikr recollection or remembering God

du'ā supplication, prayer to God

fanā annihilation

faqr poverty

hal state, usually understood as the presence of God given beyond of efforts, grace. For Baqlī, however, state (*hal*) is used sometimes interchangeably with station (*maqām*)

ḥadīth a saying of the Prophet, Muhammad, contained in the collection of sayings constituting "the Hadith"

ḥayrat blessed perplexity

hijra Muhammad's emigration from Mecca to Medina in

	622 CE, also marking the beginning of the Islamic calendar
iltibās	clothed with divinity, one of the mystical stations in Baqlī
iḥsān	to act well or do what is beautiful
īmān	faith
'ishq	love
islām	built on the same root as "salām," or peace, meaning submission or self-surrender
ka'ba	The "House of God" (literally, "cube") in Mecca
kashf	unveiling
kibr	pride
maqām	station, traditionally it is associated with one's own striving, but for Baqlī it is more ambiguous and often used as the experience of God as beyond our efforts (pl. *maqāmāt*)
mūjahidā	striving
murīd	heir or aspirant
murshid	master or guide
nabī	prophet
Quran	The Holy Book of Islam, literally the "recitation" from Gabriel—given to Muhammad with the command "to recite" [*iqra'*]
riyadā	discipline
rasūl	messenger

ṣaḥw	ways of sobriety
shahādah	Witness or Testimony. The first statement of witnessing is that there is no god but the God: "lā ilāh illā Allāh." The second states that "Muhammad is God's messenger." "*Muhammadun rasūl Allāh.*"
sharī'a	revealed law
shaṭhiyyāt	ecstatic expressions
shirk	idolatry
sukr	intoxication (i.e., spiritual intoxication, rapture, ecstasy)
sunna	tradition, but more specifically the way of living exemplified by the Prophet
tashbih	anthropomorphism, the attempt to associate God to human likeness or to any created being
tajallī	manifestation
taṣawwuf	Sufism
ta'til	those of abstraction, God being removed from creation
tawḥīd	union or oneness
walī	friend (of God) or "saint" also (*walīallāh*; pl. *awliyā'-i allāh*)
wilāya	sainthood
wāridat	visitations

NOTES

INTRODUCTION

1. See Edmund Husserl, *Die Idee der Phänomenologie. Fünf Vorlesungen*, ed. Walter Biemel. Husserliana 2 (The Hague: Martinus Nijhoff, 1950, 2nd ed.). See also Jean-Luc Marion, *Étant donné: Essai d'une phénoménologie de la donation* (Paris: PUF, 1997).

2. See my *Home and Beyond: Generative Phenomenology after Husserl* (Evanston, Ill.: Northwestern University Press, 1995), esp. sec. 3.

3. "Der 'uninteressierte' Betrachter." See Edmund Husserl, *Die Krisis der europäschen Wissenschaften und die transzendentale Phänomenologie: Einleitung in die phänomenologische Philosophie*, ed. Walter Biemel, Husserliana 6 (The Hague: Martinus Nijhoff, 1954), 178; hereafter, *Krisis*.

4. Cf. *Home and Beyond*, esp. the "Introduction."

5. See the recent discussions by Dominique Janicaud in *Le tournant théologique de la phénoménologie française* (Combas: Éditions de l'Éclat, 1991).

6. Max Scheler, *Vom Ewigen im Menschen*, Gesammelte Werke, vol. 5, ed. Maria Scheler, 4th ed. (Bern: Francke, 1954), 250; Scheler's emphasis.

7. Emmanuel Levinas, *Totalité et infini* (The Hague: Martinus Nijhoff, 1961), 271. English: *Totality and Infinity*, trans. Alphonso Lingis (Pittsburgh: Duquesne University Press, 1969), 294.

8. Merleau-Ponty writes in *Phénoménologie de la perception* (Paris: Gallimard, 1945) [hereafter, *Phénoménologie*] that depth is the most existential dimension (296), and suggests in his *Le visible et l'invisible* (Paris: Gallimard, 1964) that depth is the very structure of Being (272); hereafter, *Le visible*. See my "Merleau-Ponty's Concept of Depth," *Philosophy Today* 31, no. 4 (1987): 336–51.

9. Husserl writes, for example: "Indeed, the call resounds as well with respect to the side that is already actually seen: 'Draw closer, closer still; now fix your eyes on me, changing your place, changing the position of your eyes, etc. You will get to see even more of me that is new, ever new partial colorings, etc. You will get to see structures of the wood that were not visible just a moment ago, and that formerly were only viewed indeterminately and generally,' etc." Edmund Husserl, *Analyses Concerning Passive and Active Synthesis: Lectures on Transcendental Logic,* trans. Anthony J. Steinbock (Boston: Kluwer Academic Publishers, 2001), 41–43; hereafter, *Analyses*.

10. See Husserl, *Analyses,* esp. Main Text, Part 2, Division 3, and Part 3. See also my "Affection and Attention: On the Phenomenology of Becoming Aware," in special issue, ed. Anthony J. Steinbock, *Continental Philosophy Review* 37, no. 1 (2004): 21–43.

11. What I have called, in a different work, "saturated intentionality." See my "Saturated Intentionality," in *The Body: Classic and Contemporary Readings,* ed., Donn Welton (Malden, Mass.: Blackwell Publishers, 1999), 178–99.

12. On a related point, see my "The Poor Phenomenon: Marion and the Problem of Givenness," in Bruce Benson and Norma Wirzba, forthcoming from Fordham University Press.

13. See my "Limit-Phenomena and the Liminality of Experience," *Alter: Revue de phénoménologie* 6 (1998): 275–96. To take a typical example, when one traditionally inquires into the constitution of the "Other" or the "Alien," the latter are often described in terms of a paradoxical mode of givenness: the Other is given as not being able to be given; the alien is accessible in the mode of inaccessibility and incomprehensibility. See, e.g., Edmund Husserl, *Zur Phänomenologie der Intersubjektivität. Texte aus dem Nachlaß*. Dritter Teil: 1929–1935, ed., Iso Kern, Husserliana 15 (The Hague: Martinus Nijhoff, 1973), 631.

Despite attempts to the contrary, there can be no moral relation on such an account because there is no presence of the person—or more precisely, no inter-Personal or interpersonal presence through which the moral sphere becomes expressed. For example, see what I now regard as my misguided attempt in chapter 12 of *Home and Beyond*.

14. Søren Kierkegaard, *Fear and Trembling*, ed. and trans. Howard V. Hong and Edna H. Hong (Princeton: Princeton University Press, 1983). The only exception to this might be Kierkegaard's *Works of Love*, in which loving is directed toward the neighbor as in accordance with the absolute character of the movement of love oriented toward God. Søren Kierkegaard, *Works of Love*, ed. and trans. Howard V. Hong and Edna H. Hong (Princeton: Princeton University Press, 1998). On Kierkegaard and his notion of love I am indebted to Christopher Nelson, "The Last Appropriation of Christ: Kierkegaard, Pseudonymity, and the Problem of Godman," unpublished manuscript.

15. This text is from 1916. Adolf Reinach, *Sämtliche Werke*, vol. 1, ed. Karl Schuhmann and Barry Smith (Munich: Philosophia, 1989), 593.

16. Jean Hering, *Phénoménologie et philosophie religieuse* (Paris: Felix Alcan, 1926). See esp. 87–140.

17. Kurt Stavenhagen, *Absolute Stellungnahmen: Eine ontologische Untersuchung über das Wesen der Religion* (Erlangen: Philosophischen Akademie, 1925). Gründler's work is a good example of the problematic attempt in early phenomenology simply to apply a phenomenology of presentation to "religious" phenomena. See Otto Gründler, *Elemente zu einer Religionsphilosophie auf phänomenologischer Grundlage* (Munich: Kösel and Pustet, 1922).

18. William James, *The Varieties of Religious Experience* (New York: Collier Books, 1961).

19. G. Van der Leeuw, *Phänomenologie der Religion*, 2nd ed. (Tübingen: J. C. B. Mohr/Paul Siebeck, 1956, [1933]).

20. Friedrich Heiler, *Erscheinungsformen und Wesen der Religion* (Stuttgart: W. Kohlhammer, 1961).

21. For example, Max Scheler, *Formalismus in der Ethik und die Materiale Wertethik*, Gesammelte Werke, vol. 2, ed. Maria Scheler (Bern: Francke, 1966); hereafter, *Formalismus*. Max Scheler, *Wesen und Formen der Sympathie*, Gesammelte Werke, vol. 7, ed. Manfred Frings (Bern: Francke, 1973); hereafter, *Wesen*. Scheler, *Vom Ewigen*.

22. Michel Henry, *L'essence de la manifestation*, 2nd ed. (Paris: PUF, 1990). See my "The Problem of Forgetfulness in the Phenomenology of Life," in *The Philosophy of Michel Henry*, ed. Anthony J. Steinbock, special issue *Continental Review* 32, no. 3 (1999): 271–302; hereafter, "Problem of Forgetfulness." And see

Henry's *C'est moi la vérité: Pour une philosophie du christianisme* (Paris: Seuil, 1996); hereafter, *C'est moi*.

23. After all, it is Levinas himself who writes that not every transcendent intention has the noesis–noema structure (*Totalité*, xvii/*Totality*, 29). See also xii/23, xvi/27–8. See my "Face and Revelation: Levinas on Teaching as Way-Faring," in *Addressing Levinas*, ed. Eric Nelson (Evanston, Ill.: Northwestern University Press, 2005), 119–37.

24. Jean-Luc Marion, *Dieu sans l'être* (Paris: PUF, 1991). See also his *Étant donné*. In many ways Derrida is much closer to this orientation with his "deconstructive strategy" in, for example, his *La voix et le phénomène*, or in essays from *L'écriture et la différence* and *De la grammatologie*, than he is when "religion" is his putative theme. See Jacques Derrida, "Foi et savoir: Les deux sources de la 'religion' aux limites de la simple raison," in *La religion*, ed. Jacques Derrida and Gianni Vattimo (Paris: Seuil, 1996), 9–86. See also Jacques Derrida, "On the Gift: A Discussion between Jacques Derrida and Jean-Luc Marion," in *God, the Gift, and Postmodernism*, ed., John D. Caputo and Michael J. Scanlon (Bloomington: Indiana University Press, 1999), 54–78. More specially, on Derrida, see John Caputo, *The Prayers and Tears of Jacques Derrida: Religion Without Religion* (Bloomington: Indiana University Press, 1997).

25. See Martin Buber, "Ich und Du," in *Das dialogische Prinzip* (Heidelberg: Lambert Schneider, 1965).

26. See my "Face and Revelation," esp. 120–24.

27. W. H. Auden, *Collected Poems* (New York: Vintage Books, 1991), 53.

28. Gaston Bachelard, *L'air et les songes: Essai sur l'imagination du mouvement* (Paris: José Corti, 1990), esp. 108; hereafter, "L'air."

29. Ibid., 17.

30. Ibid., 18–19.

31. See Erwin Strauss, *Vom Sinn der Sinne* (Berlin: Springer, 1956). See also Erwin W. Straus, *Phenomenological Psychology*, trans. Erling Eng (New York: Basic Books, 1966), esp. 137–46.

32. See Merleau-Ponty, *Le visible*, 280–81, 287–88.

33. Ibid., 237, 240.

34. Ibid., 325; English: *The Visible and the Invisible*, trans. Alphonso Lingis (Evanston, Ill.: Northwestern University Press, 1968), 271–72.

35. Merleau-Ponty, *Le visible*, 322; *The Visible*, 268.

36. In this sense, verticality suggests *eschaton* rather than *telos*, as Kearney intimates. See Richard Kearney, *The God Who May Be: The Hermeneutics of Religion* (Bloomington: Indiana University Press, 2001), 12ff.

37. See my "Totalitarianism, Homogeneity of Power, Depth: Towards a Socio-Political Ontology," *Tijdschrift voor Filosofie*, 51/4 (1989): 621–48.

38. Taking clues from Husserl's own work, I began a study of the Earth phenomenologically as Earth-ground and as a kind of aesthetic absolute in my *Home and Beyond*. See esp. 109–22.

39. See chapter 8.

40. See "Interview with Paul Schrader," in *Robert Bresson*, ed. James Quandt (Toronto: Toronto Center for Contemporary Art 1998), 489.

1. THE RELIGIOUS AND MYSTICAL SHAPE OF EXPERIENCE

1. Rudolf Otto, *The Idea of the Holy,* trans. John W. Harvey (New York: Oxford University Press, 1958), 10 (my emphasis).

2. Ibid., 11–23.

3. See Scheler, *Vom Ewigen,* 159ff. See Friedrich Nietzsche, *Zur Genealogie der Moral* in Sämtliche Werke, ed. Giorgio Colli and Mazzino Montinari, vol. 5 (Berlin: de Gruyter, 1980), esp. 268–69, 270–74, 281–83. See also Max Scheler, "Das Ressentiment im Aufbau der Moralen," in *Vom Umsturz der Werte,* Gesammelte Werke, vol. 3, ed. Maria Scheler (Bern: Francke, 1955), 33–147.

4. See Reinach, *Sämtliche Werke,* 598ff., 1:604–608.

5. See, for example, Caroline Franks Davis, *The Evidential Force of Religious Experience* (Oxford: Oxford University Press, 1989). Davis's work is aligned with this work to the extent that she recognizes a distinctive sphere of religious experience that bears its own quality of evidence. It diverges to the extent that she wants *to argue from* that evidential force rather than to clarify its nature (epiphany) in terms of the inter-Personal dimension of experience and to describe how it relates to a philosophical/mystical anthropology with its implications for a cultural critique in terms of idolatry.

6. *Popul Vol,* trans. Dennis Tedlock (New York: Simon and Schuster, 1985).

7. See especially chapter 5 on "Evidence." See also Scheler, *Vom Ewigen,* 244–46.

8. See Henri Bergson, *Les deux sources de la morale et de la religion* (Paris: PUF, 1984/1932); hereafter, *Les deux sources.*

9. Louis Bouyer, "Mysticism: An Essay on the History of the Word," in *Understanding Mysticism,* ed. Richard Woods, O.P. (New York: Image Books, 1980), 42–55.

10. See Michel de Certeau, *La fable mystique,* XVIe–XVIIe Siècle (Paris: Gallimard, 1982), 127ff. English: *The Mystic Fable,* vol. 1, trans. Michael B. Smith (Chicago: University of Chicago Press, 1992), 94ff.

11. Bernard McGinn, *The Foundations of Mysticism,* vol. 1 of *The Presence of God: A History of Western Christian Mysticism* (New York: Crossroad, 1999), xviii; hereafter, *Foundations.*

12. See Dorothee Soelle, *The Silent Cry: Mysticism and Resistance,* trans. Barbara and Martin Rumscheidt (Minneapolis: Fortress Press, 2001).

13. Ibid., 14.

14. Ibid., 15.

15. See chapter 6 below concerning the question of abandonment.

16. "Ich hoffe nur, daß ich nichts schrieb, was ich nicht selbst sah." Wilhelm Schapp, *Beiträge zur Phänomenologie der Wahrnehmung* (Wiesbaden: B. Heymann, 1976 [1910]), ix.

17. Cf. Husserl, *Krisis;* English: *The Crisis of European Sciences and Transcendental Phenomenology: An Introduction to Phenomenological Philosophy,* trans. David Carr (Evanston, Ill.: Northwestern University Press, 1970). Also Husserl, *Analyses,* esp. Part 1.

18. Was die Kirchen wollen, will ich auch: die Menschheit hinführen zur Aeternitas. Meine Aufgabe ist es, dies durch die Philosophie zu versuchen. Alles, was ich bis jetzt geschrieben habe, sind nur Vorarbeiten; es ist nur ein Aufstellen von Methoden. Leider kommt man im Verlauf eines Lebens gar nicht zum Kern, zum Westentlichen. Es ist so wichtig, daß die Philosophie aus dem Liberalismus und Rationalismus wieder zum Wesentlichen geführt wird, zu *Wahrheit*. Die Frage nach dem letzten Sein, nach Wahrheit, muß der Gegenstand jeder wahren Philosophie sein. Das ist mein Lebenswerk. (From Ms. E III 11, 1934, 3b: "Gespräche mit E. H. 1931–1938," Schwester Edelgundis.) Cited with the kind permission of Rudolf Bernet, Director, Husserl-Archief, Leuven, Belgium.

19. R. P. Augustin Poulan, *The Graces of Interior Prayer: A Treatise on Mystical Theology*, trans. Leonora L. Yorke Smith and corrected to accord with the 10th French edition (St. Louis: Herder, 1950), cf. xiii–xiv, and 539–49.

20. Gerda Walther, *Zur Phänomenologie der Mystik* (Halle: Niemeyer, 1923).

21. Nelson Pike, *Mystic Union: An Essay in the Phenomenology of Mysticism* (Ithaca, N.Y.: Cornell University Press, 1992), esp. 166–68.

22. For example, Carl Ernst in his works relating to Rūzbihān Baqlī. See Carl W. Ernst, *Rūzbihān Baqlī: Mysticism and the Rhetoric of Sainthood in Persian Sufism* (Richmond Surrey, GB: Curzon Press, 1996); and Carl W. Ernst, *Words of Ecstasy in Sufism* (New York: SUNY Press, 1985).

23. For example, Evelyn Underhill, *Mysticism: A Study in the Nature and Development of Man's Spiritual Consciousness* (New York: Penguin Books, 1974).

24. Leopold Bellak, M.D., in Hirsch L. Gordon, *The Maggid of Caro: The Mystic Life of the Eminent Codifier Joseph Caro as Revealed in his Secret Diary* (New York: Shoulson Press, 1949), 9.

25. George W. Henry, M.D., in Gordon, *Maggid of Caro*, 13–14.

26. Arthur J. Deikman, M.D., *The Observing Self: Mysticism and Psychotherapy* (Boston: Beacon Press, 1982).

27. For example, Harry T. Hunt, *Lives in Spirit: Precursors and Dilemmas of a Secular Western Mysticism* (Albany: SUNY Press, 2003).

28. Bergson, *Les deux sources*, 242–43.

29. Ibid., 253.

30. This is a work in progress whose features are sketched out in "Epiphanies in Joyce and Proust," his postface to *Traversing the Imaginary*, ed. Peter Gratton and John Panteleimon Manoussakis, Northwestern University Press, forthcoming.

31. Even Derrida—often taken to be a critic of phenomenology—shows that phenomenology is itself more than "phenomenology"—that is, if one reads a genetic phenomenology against a static one, or if one reads Husserl's phenomenological descriptions (which presuppose a peculiar phenomenological method) against his assertions.

32. Steinbock, *Home and Beyond*.

33. See, e.g., Kearney, *The God Who May Be*. See also Paul Ricoeur, *The Symbolism of Evil*, trans. Emerson Buchanan (Boston: Beacon Press, 1986); and Paul Ricoeur, *Time and Narrative*, vols. 1–3, trans. David Pellauer and Kathleen McLaughlin (Chicago: University of Chicago Press, 1990).

34. Cf. for example, Merleau-Ponty's treatment of psycho-physical normalities and abnormalities in the *Phénoménologie de la perception,* esp. 95ff.

35. See Husserl, *Analyses,* Introduction to Part 2.

36. An expression I take from Rebecca Comay, "Materialist Mutations of the *Bilderverbot,*" in *Walter Benjamin and Art,* ed., Andrew Benjamin (New York: Continuum, 2005).

37. See Eugene Gendlin, *Experiencing and the Creation of Meaning: A Philosophical and Psychological Approach to the Subjective* (Evanston, Ill.: Northwestern University Press, 1997).

38. On the discernment of spirits, see Ignatius of Loyola, *The Spiritual Exercises and Selected Works,* ed. and trans. George E. Ganss, S.J. et al. (Mahwah, N.J.: Paulist Press, 1991), 113–214.

39. In this vein, Levinas writes: "But can the hermeneutics of the religious do without thoughts that go off the deep end? And does not philosophy itself consist in treating 'crazy' ideas with wisdom or in bringing wisdom to love? Knowledge, the answer, the result . . . would be from a psychism still incapable of thoughts in which the word *God* takes on meaning." Emmanuel Levinas, *Entre Nous: On Thinking-of-the-Other,* trans. Michael B. Smith and Barbara Harshav (New York: Columbia University Press, 1998), 75.

40. See the classic texts by R. C. Zaehner, *Mysticism: Sacred and Profane* (New York: Oxford University Press, 1961), and Rudolf Otto, *Mysticism East and West: A Comparative Analysis of the Nature of Mysticism,* trans. Bertha L. Bracey and Richenda C. Payne (New York: Macmillan, 1970).

41. James, *Varieties of Religious Experience,* 40–43. He presupposes this because, given a plurality of possibilities, he thinks it impossible to discriminate between them. To prefer one possibility is only "arbitrary." But this is only the case because he unwittingly positions himself abstractly above them all and does not take lived experience seriously.

42. See my "Facticity and Insight as Problems of the Lifeworld: On Individuation," in *Continental Philosophy Review* 37, no. 2 (2004): 241–61.

43. In this regard, see Jacques Dupuis, *Toward a Christian Theology of Religious Pluralism* (Maryknoll, N.Y.: Orbis Books, 2002).

44. See my "Facticity and Insight."

45. See my *Home and Beyond,* esp. sec. 4.

46. Brainard's approach, which attempts to develop terminological tools applied across Eastern and Western traditions to help grasp mystical experience, unfortunately tends to border on the latter. See F. Samuel Brainard, *Reality and Mystical Experience* (University Park: Pennsylvania State University Press, 2000).

47. Hence, we read in Isaiah: "Listen to Me, you who pursue justice, / You who seek the Lord: / Look to the rock you were hewn from, / To the quarry you were dug from. / Look back to Abraham your father / And to Sarah who brought you forth. / For he was only one when I called him, / But I blessed him and made him many."

48. See, for example, an account of this in the Quran, 6:74, 21:51–73, 26:70–82.

49. For example, within the Christian tradition, the Greek and Russian Orthodox writings; within the Jewish tradition, the theosophical-theurgical

Kabbalah; within the Islamic tradition, the so-called "sober" Sufis—just to name a few. On the first, see Natalie Depraz, *Le corps glorieux: phénoménologie pratique de la Philocalie des Pères du désert et des Pères de l'Eglise* (forthcoming, Bibliothèque philosophique de Louvain).

2. ST. TERESA OF AVILA AND MYSTICISM OF PRAYER

1. McGinn, *Foundations,* 1:132.

2. See Athanasius, "The Life and Affairs of our Holy Father Anthony," in *Athanasius: The Life of Antony and the Letter to Marcellinus,* trans., Robert C. Gregg (New York: Paulist Press, 1980), 29–99.

3. Cf. McGinn, *Foundations,* 1:134.

4. Saint Pachomius, *The Rule or the Asketikon* (Willits, Calif.: Eastern Orthodox Books, 1976).

5. Saint Basil, *Ascetical Works,* trans. Sister M. Monique Wagner (Washington, D.C.: Catholic University of America Press, 1950). See also St. Basil, *Letters,* Vol. 1, trans. Sister Agnes Clare Way (Washington, D.C.: Catholic University of America Press, 1981), and Saint Basil, *Letters,* Vol. 2, trans. Sister Agnes Clare Way (New York: Fathers of the Church, 1955).

6. See, e.g., *The Rule of St. Benedict,* trans. Anthony C. Meisel and M. L. del Mastro (New York: Doubleday, 1975). See Bernard McGinn, *The Growth of Mysticism,* vol. 2 of *The Presence of God: A History of Western Christian Mysticism* (New York: Crossroad, 1999), 27. See also McGinn, *Foundations,* vol. 1, ch. 5. See also Anthony C. Meisel and M. L. del Mastro, "Introduction," *The Rule of St. Benedict,* 9–41.

In chapter 1 of his "Rule," St. Benedict distinguishes between four kinds of monks: the Sarabite, the worst kind of monk, who calls holy whatever he desires and unlawful whatever he dislikes; the gyratory monk, who wanders from monastery to monastery, yielding to the seduction of his will and appetite; the Cenobite, the monk living in organized communities under a rule and an abbot; and the Anchorite or hermit, who prepares his foundation in monasteries and, though he loves others and does not want to escape them, is still called to a different life. (A marvelous example of this is St. Meinrad, a Benedictine hermit who was said to love strangers to the point of his death at the hands of one.) In distinction to John Cassian (c. 360–c. 435), however, the cenobitical life was not just a holding-ground for the eremitical life; and even though the hermit could be considered the highest form of monk if this were his vocation, the Cenobites were regarded as "the best kind of monks." They were to hold everything in common, with no private property, and to live a life of simplicity, and to have regulated periods of both manual work and intellectual activity as well as communal and silent prayer. The three vows that marked this early Benedictine monastic life and that still mark a Benedictine monk today are obedience to another, namely, to the abbot (to do God's work and inculcate humility); stability (to combat pride by relying on the community of others as eternal beginners in life of prayer and service to God and thus to curb the itinerant ascetics); and conversion to the monastic way of life. I would also like to thank Fr. Edward Linton, O.S.B. for his kind and helpful instruction on Benedictine monasticism.

7. See Lowrie J. Daly, S.J., *Benedictine Monasticism: Its Formation and Development through the 12th Century* (New York: Sheed and Ward, 1965), esp. 142–47.

8. See Peter-Thomas Rohrbach, O.C.D., *Journey to Carith: The Story of the Carmelite Order* (New York: Doubleday, 1966), esp. 33ff., 45; hereafter *Journey*.

9. This is not the place to engage in christological interpretations and implications of this experience. See Bruce Vawter, *This Man Jesus: An Essay Toward a New Testament Christology* (Garden City, N.Y.: Image Books, 1973), 79ff. See also Edward Schillebeeckx, *Jesus: An Experiment in Christology,* trans. Hubert Hoskins (New York: Seabury Press, 1979), 519ff. See also Jean Daniélou, *Théologie du judéo-christianisme* (Tournai, Belgium: Desclée, 1958); English: *The Theology of Jewish Christianity: A History of Early Christian Doctrine Before the Council of Nicaea,* vol. 1, trans. John A. Baker (Philadelphia: Westminster Press, 1964). See, further, Jürgen Moltmann, *The Crucified God: The Cross of Christ as the Foundation and Criticism of Christian Theology* (New York: Harper and Row, 1974); Edward Schillebeeckx, *Christ: The Experience of Jesus as Lord,* trans. John Bowden (New York: Seabury Press, 1980); Karl Rahner, *Foundations of Christian Faith: An Introduction to the Idea of Christianity,* trans. William V. Dych (New York: Seabury Press, 1978).

10. Wolfhart Pannenberg, *Jesus-God and Man,* trans. Lewis L. Wilkins and Duane A. Priebe, 2nd ed. (Philadelphia: Westminster Press, 1977), 171.

11. See *A Select Library of Nicene and Post-Nicene Fathers of the Christian Church, Second Series.* Vol. 5, *Gregory of Nyssa,* ed. and trans. Philip Schaff and Henry Wace (Grand Rapids, Mich.: Eerdmans, 1954). See St. Gregory of Nazianzus, *On God and Christ: The Five Theological Orations and Two Letters to Cledonius,* trans. Frederick Williams and Lionel Wickham (Crestwood, N.Y.: St. Vladimir's Seminary Press, 2002); Basil of Caesarea, *The Treatise De Spiritu Sancto: The Nine Homilies of the Hexaemeron and the Letters of Saint Basil the Great, Archbishop of Caesarea,* trans. Blomfield Jackson (Oxford: James Parker and Co., 1895); and volume 4 of *The Philokalia,* compiled by St. Nikodimos of the Holy Mountain and St. Makarios of Corinth, ed., G. E. H. Palmer et al. (London: Farber and Farber, 1995), esp. 140, 217–18, 361–99.

12. In the Jewish celebration of Passover, a door is opened and a cup of wine is poured and left for Elijah. This symbolizes as well the fifth cup of wine that is not drunk. The first four correspond to things God promised and fulfilled in redeeming the Jews; the last one, which God has yet to fulfill: "And I will bring you into the land which I swore to give to Abraham, Isaac, and Jacob" (Exod. 6:8).

13. Rohrbach, *Journey,* 39.

14. Ibid., 37–38.

15. The insistence of the virgin birth concerns the fact that even though Jesus is human, he was not restricted by human nature, expressed in part by his radically different kind of origin or "birth." If we examine the gospel accounts from Matthew and Luke, we see that the virgin birth in the physiological sense was not the primary issue. Concerned with tracing Jesus to the Davidic messianic line (and hence the testimony to his messianic nature), Matthew, like Luke, traces Jesus to David *through Joseph* (Matt. 1:1–17; Luke 3:23–38; cf. Matt. 13:55). Accordingly,

even though Jesus was "born of a woman," he did not share in the sin of Adam. For the contemporary Catholic treatment, see, e.g., *The Documents of Vatican II*, ed. Austin P. Flannery, O.P. (New York: Pillar Books, 1975), esp. *Lumen Gentium*, 21, Nov. 1964, Ch. VIII, "Our Lady," 413–18.

16. Mary became for them their model, owner, and protector. See Rohrbach, *Journey*, 46–49.

17. Ibid., 42ff.

18. Ibid., 44.

19. On the Jewish background and the role of Spanish Kabbalism for St. Teresa of Avila, see Deirdre Green, *The Gold in the Crucible* (Longmead, UK: Element Books, 1989). On the personality of St. Teresa, see Victoria Lincoln, *Teresa: A Woman*, ed. Elias Rivers and Antonio T. de Nicolás (Albany: SUNY Press, 1984). See also Stephen Clissold, *St. Teresa of Avila* (London: Sheldon Press, 1979); William Thomas Walsh, *Saint Teresa of Ávila: A Biography* (Rockford, Ill.: Tan Books and Publishers, 1987); and Cathleen Medwick, *Teresa of Avila: The Progress of a Soul* (New York: Alfred A. Knopf, 2000).

20. See Kieran Kavanaugh, Introduction, in *The Collected Works of St. Teresa of Avila*, vol. 1, trans. Kieran Kavanaugh, O.C.D., and Otilio Rodriguez, O.C.D. (Washington, D.C.: ICS Publications, 1976), 6–9.

21. Santa Teresa de Jesus, *Obras Completas*, ed. Efren de La Madre de Dios, O.C.D. and Otger Steggink, O. Carm. (Madrid: Biblioteca de Autores Cristianos, 1997); hereafter, *Obras*. My citations of the English follow *The Collected Works of St. Teresa of Avila*, trans. Kieran Kavanaugh, O.C.D., and Otilio Rodriguez, O.C.D., vol. 1 (1976), vol. 2 (1980), and vol. 3 (1985); hereafter, *Collected Works*. For the Spanish citations, I give the page number. Because there are two different editions of the English Collected Works with different page numbers, I cite the chapter or section number, then the paragraph number, preceded by the specific volume number. I cite the Spanish and English editions differently because the two do not consistently share the same paragraph numbers. Finally, unless otherwise noted, Vol. 1 will refer to the "Book of Her Life," and Vol. 2 will refer to "The Interior Castle." See *Obras*, 121–22, 132, 149, 154–55; *Collected Works*, Vol. 1, 22.3, .6, .8, 24.2, 28.3, 29.1, .4.

22. *Obras*, 551–52; *Collected Works*, Vol. 2, VI:7.14.

23. Kavanaugh, *Collected Works*, 9.

24. Rohrbach, *Journey*, 137, 171.

25. In the strict sense, *discalced* means "without shoes," but it suggests more broadly a dedicated, austere form of life.

26. See Jodi Bilinkoff, *The Avila of Saint Teresa: Religious Reform in a Sixteenth-Century City* (Ithaca, N.Y.: Cornell University Press, 1989). See too, Sebastian V. Ramge, O.C.D., *An Introduction to the Writings of Saint Teresa* (Chicago: Henry Regnery, 1963).

27. See Walter T. Stace, *Mysticism and Philosophy* (Philadelphia: Lippincott, 1960).

28. For example, see *St. Ambrose: On the Sacraments and On the Mysteries*, trans. T. Thompson and J. H. Srawley (London: SPCK, 1950).

29. St. Augustine, *The Confessions*, trans. Maria Boulding, O.S.B. (Hyde Park,

N.Y.: New City Press, 1997); Pelagius, *Pelagius: Life and Letters,* ed. B. R. Rees (Woodbridge, UK: Boydell Press, 1991); *The Works of Saint Augustine: Answer to the Pelagians,* trans. Roland J. Teske, S.J., ed., John E. Rotelle, O.S.A. (Hyde Park, N.Y.: New City Press, 1997).

30. *Obras,* 179–80; *Collected Works,* Vol. 1, 33.5.

31. For example, on several occasions she implores that if her manuscript or parts of it are judged to be bad, they be destroyed (e.g., *Obras,* 229–30; *Collected Works,* Vol. 1, "Epiloge," .2–.3).

32. Farid ud-Din ʿAṭṭār, Mantiq al-tayr, *Conference of the Birds,* trans. Afkham Darbandi and Dick Davis (New York: Penguin Books, 1984); hereafter, *Conference.* For ʿAṭṭār, union (*tawḥīd*) is a penultimate stage, followed by *fanā,* or annihilation. I treat Baqlī below in chapter 4.

33. This emphasis on union is so ingrained that even someone like Pike privileges mystic union almost exclusively, even when treating St. Teresa of Avila. See Pike, *Mystic Union.*

34. "My intention is only to explain the different favors there are on this road, insofar as I understand them. Thus you will know, Sisters, their nature and their effects, lest we fancy that everything imagined is a vision" (*Obras,* 560; *Collected Works,*Vol. 2, VI:10.1). Or again: "For I never thought there could be any other way of hearing or understanding [than with bodily ears] until I saw this for myself. And so, as I said, the experience cost me much difficulty" (*Obras,* 134–35; *Collected Works,* Vol. 1, 25.1–4; *Obras,* 138–39, *Collected Works,* Vol. 1, 25.17–19).

35. Scheler, *Vom Ewigen,* 174.

36. *Obras,* 574; *Collected Works,* Vol. 2, VII: 2.11. Or again: "I shall have to make use of some comparison. . . . But these spiritual matters for anyone who like myself has not gone through studies are so difficult to explain. I shall have to find some mode of explaining myself, and it may be less often that I hit upon a good comparison. Seeing so much stupidity will provide some recreation for your Reverence" (*Obras,* 71; *Collected Works,* Vol. 1, 11.6).

37. On the parallels between Jewish mysticism and the imagery of the Interior Castle, see Green, *Gold in the Crucible,* 77ff. See also Gersham Gerhard Scholem, *Major Trends in Jewish Mysticism* (New York: Knopf Publishing Group, 1995).

38. She often returns to the metaphor of water in her descriptions in *Moradas* (e.g., *Obras,* 500ff.; *Collected Works,* Vol. 2, IV:2.4–9. It is also interesting to note that the favorite comparison for St. John of the Cross, a junior contemporary and confessor of St. Teresa, was also an element, namely, fire, especially the flame.

39. See *Obras,* 508; *Collected Works,* Vol. 2, IV:1.2; *Obras,* 517; *Collected Works,* Vol. 2, V:3.4; *Obras,* 524; *Collected Works,* Vol. 2, VI.1.2; *Obras,* 526; *Collected Works,* Vol. 2, VI:1.7; *Obras,* 81; *Collected Works,* Vol. 1, 13.13.

40. Let me give some examples. We read: "There is another kind of rapture—I call it flight of the spirit—which, though substantially the same as other raptures, is interiorly experienced very differently" (*Obras,* 540–41; *Collected Works,* Vol. 2, VI: 5.1). Or again, she writes: "What I know in this case is that the soul was never so awake to the things of God nor did it have such deep enlightenment and knowledge of His Majesty. This will seem impossible, for if the faculties are so absorbed that we can say they are dead, and likewise the senses, how can a soul know that it understands this secret? I don't know, nor perhaps does any creature but only the

Creator. And this goes for many other things that take place in this state—I mean in these two dwelling places, for there is no closed door between the one and the other. Because there are things in the last that are not revealed to those who have not yet reached it, I thought I should divide them" (*Obras*, 536–37; *Collected Works*, Vol. 2, VI:4.4). And again: "It may seem that this experience was nothing new since at other times the Lord had represented Himself to the soul in such a way. The experience was so different that it left her indeed stupefied and frightened." (*Obras*, 570–71; *Collected Works*, Vol. 2, VII:2.2).

41. "It causes the soul to go about like a person whose appetite is satisfied and who has no need to eat but feels that he has taken enough so that he wouldn't desire just any kind of food; yet he is not so filled that he wouldn't eagerly eat some if it were tempting to the appetite" (*Obras*, 97; *Collected Works*, Vol. 1, 17. 4; cf. *Obras*, 87–88; *Collected Works*, Vol. 1, 15.1; *Obras*, 493; *Collected Works*, Vol. 2, III:2.11; *Obras*, 101; *Collected Works*, Vol. 1, 18.9).

42. On the difference between acquired and infused prayer as it relates to the "self" and the prejudice of the modern worldview, see chapters 5 and 8.

43. *Obras*, 72–76; *Collected Works*, Vol. 1, 11.9–12. 4; *Obras*, 517ff.; *Collected Works*, Vol. 2, IV:3.4ff.; *Obras*, 576; *Collected Works*, Vol. 2, VII:3.10; *Obras*, 514; *Collected Works*, Vol. 2, V:2.10; *Obras*, 60–61; *Collected Works*, Vol. 1, 8.5.

44. *Obras*, 59–60; *Collected Works*, Vol. 1, 8.1; *Obras*, 629; *Collected Works*, Vol. 1, "Spiritual Testimonies," 59.25.

45. The prayer of recollection seems to be transitional because here the intellect is still working, though this must not be seen as our effort producing this prayer (*Obras*, 504–505; *Collected Works*, Vol. 2, IV:3.8).

46. *Obras*, 87–88; *Collected Works*, Vol. 1, 15.1–2; *Obras*, 625–26; "Spiritual Testimonies," *Collected Works*, Vol. 1, 59.1–7.

47. See *San Juan de la Cruz, Obras Completas*, ed., Licinio Ruano de la Iglesia (Madrid: Biblioteca de Autores Cristianos, 1982), 342, 345, 351, 362; hereafter, *Obras Completas*. English: *The Collected Works of Saint John of the Cross*, ed. Kieran Kavanaugh, O.C.D., and Otilio Rodriguez, O.C.D., rev. ed. (Washington, D.C.: ICS Publications, 1991), 382, 385, 392, 402.

48. This points, as we will see later, to the founding of the perceptual and epistemic spheres of existence in the emotional sphere of existence.

49. St. John of the Cross, *Obras Completas*, 340–41; *Collected Works*, 381.

50. St. Teresa, *Obras*, 74; *Collected Works*, Vol. 1, 11.14; cf. *Obras*, 78–9; *Collected Works*, Vol. 1, 13.4–5; and see *Obras*, 504; *Collected Works*, Vol. 2, IV:3.6.

51. See *Obras*, 100; *Collected Works*, Vol. 1, 18.3, my emphasis: ". . . en fin, vuestra, Señor mío, que dais *como* quien sois."

52. See *Obras*, 536; *Collected Works*, Vol. 2, VI:4.2; *Obras*, 510; *Collected Works*, Vol. 2, V:1.9; *Obras*, 520; *Collected Works*, Vol. 2, V:4.4.

3. RABBI DOV BAER AND MYSTICISM OF ECSTASY

1. Dobh Baer of Lubavitch, *Tract on Ecstasy*, 61, cf. 57; hereafter *Tract*. When citing this work, I use the transcription provided by Jacobs in his translation, "Dobh Baer." In the text I use the current form, "Dov Baer."

2. *Igeret Hakodesh,* sec. 27b in Rabbi Schneur Zalman of Liadi, *Likutei Amarim* (*Tanya*), Bilingual Edition (New York: Kehot Publication Society, 1984).

3. One of the reasons the internal workings of Jewish mysticism have remained relatively obscure and first-person testimonies relatively inaccessible concerns the tendency within certain developments of Jewish mysticism toward limiting practices to an isolated circle of adepts. The intention of this limitation, however, was not elitism but the protection of those who were not "perfect" from harm. See the *Chagigah,* 11b. *Talmud Bavli,* ed. Hersh Goldwurm, Schottensten ed. (Brooklyn, N.Y.: Mesorah Publications, 1990). And see *Chagigah,* 14b. Furthermore, the prophylactic measures with respect to the uninitiated, along with the unrelenting threats of persecution that Jews faced from outside of Judaism kept Jewish mystical practices particularly insular, and despite the vast printed literature, tended to confine it, along with its oral counterpart, to conventicles and intimate master/student relationships.

To these we can append the role that humility played in thwarting self-disclosure (Scholem, *Major Trends,* 120), along with the fact that in contrast to the Christian mystical tradition, women did not contribute directly to the wealth of Jewish mystical tradition and its literature. For the role of Jewish women in the Middle Ages based on the *Sefer Chasidim,* see Susanne Borchers, *Jüdisches Frauenleben im Mittelalter* (Frankfurt am Main: Peter Lang, 1998). See also Judith R. Baskin, "Jewish Women in the Middle Ages," in *Jewish Women in Historical Perspective* (Detroit, Mich.: Wayne State University Press, 1991), 94–114. See also S. A. Horodezky, *Leaders of Hassidism,* trans. Maria Horodezky-Magasanik (London: "Hasefer" Agency for Literature, 1928), 113–17.

4. Discerning these inexhaustible networks of deeper and deeper meanings demanded, for many of the Jewish mystics, rigorous spiritual practices, practices such as *gematria,* or the calculation of the numerical value of Hebrew words and their connection and conversion to other words having the same value; *notarikon,* the process of interpreting the letters of a word as abbreviations of sentences; and *temurah,* the process of interchanging Hebrew letters with others according to various rules. It also led to mystical practices like the meditation on the Holy Name and the permutation of the letters of the Name that elicited a direct experience of God—practices exemplified by the particular brand of ecstatic/prophetic Kabbalah practiced by Abraham Abulafia in the thirteenth century. See *The Path of the Names: Writings by Abraham ben Samuel Abulafia,* ed. David Meltzer, trans. Bruria Finke et al. (Berkeley, Calif.: Trigram, 1976). See also Moshe Idel, *Studies in Ecstatic Kabbalah,* (New York: SUNY Press, 1988). Moshe Idel, *The Mystical Experience in Abraham Abulafia,* trans. Jonathan Chipman (New York: SUNY Press, 1988). See also Elliot R. Wolfson, *Abraham Abulafia—Kabalist and Prophet: Hermeneutics, Theosophy and Theurgy* (Los Angeles: Cherub Press, 2000).

See, e.g., *The Bahir,* English and Hebrew text, trans. Aryeh Kaplan (York Beach, Maine: Samuel Weiser, Inc., 1989), esp. pars. 14–61. The authorship of the Bahir is generally attributed to Rabbi Nehuniah ben HaKana; it was first published about 1176, but its oral teachings were handed down for centuries prior to its written appearance. See also Marc-Alain Ouaknin, *Tsimtsoum: Introduction à la méditation hébraïque* (Paris: Albin Michel, 1992).

5. Cf. Scholem, *Major Trends,* 19ff.

6. The *Zohar* is a mystical midrash or commentary, primarily on the Torah, but it includes commentaries, mystical descriptions, and discussions. Making up about sixteen large volumes, and written in Aramaic and Hebrew, it was composed by the Spanish Kabbalist Moses b. Shem Tov de Leon but was originally attributed to Simeon b. Yohai, a second-century sage who lived in a cave for thirteen years to escape the Romans after they killed Rabbi Akiba. On the composition and authorship of the *Zohar,* see Scholem, *Kabbalah* (New York: Meridian, 1978), 213ff. See the five-volume English edition, *The Zohar,* trans. Harry Sperling, Maurice Simon, and Dr. Paul P. Leverthoff (New York: Soncino Press, 1984, 2nd ed.).

7. Theosophy, as Scholem notes, originally meant a doctrine claiming that it is possible for one to be able to perceive the mysterious workings of the Divine and to become absorbed in its contemplation, whereby the mysteries of creation reflect the movement of divine life. See Scholem, *Major Trends,* 56, 206. Originally an ancient Egyptian-Platonic system of magic, theurgy was the practice of producing wondrous effects through the assistance of spirits. It can therefore be closely associated with magic. Although this is rather simplistic, one finds in the theosophical-theurgical mysticism, expressive of Merkabah or Chariot mysticism, an emphasis on power and sublimity rather than love and mercy, like we find in the ecstatic-prophetic Kabbalah.

8. Sabbatai Zevi (1625–1676) proclaimed himself the Messiah, engaged in antinomian acts, and became apostate, converting to Islam. His following, especially through the promotion by Nathan of Gaza (1644–1680), sadly tended to glorify antinomianism and apostasy as a mystery of the Messiah, and led to a kind of religious nihilism.

9. Jacob Frank (1726–1791) was a charismatic, power-seeking, and resolute apostate with messianic aspirations, who eventually embraced Catholicism.

10. See, for example, *In Praise of The Baal Shem Tov: The Earliest Collection of Legends about the Founder of Hasidism,* ed. and trans. Dan Ben-Amos and Jerome R. Mintz (Bloomington: Indiana University Press, 1970). See also Martin Buber, *The Tales of Rabbi Nachman,* trans. Maurice Friedman (New York: Horizon Press, 1956); and Nahman of Bratslav, *Rabbi Nachman's Stories,* trans. Rabbi Aryeh Kaplan (New York: HaNachal Press of the Breslov Research Institute, 1983). Rabbi Zalman, *Likutei Amarim (Tanya).*

11. Briefly, according to the symbolism of Rabbi Isaac Luria (the Ari), the sixteenth-century Safed mystic, the Light of the Infinite One (*or en sof*) gives itself in various degrees or emanations that are called the ten *sefirot.* These emanations are said to be various kinds of "screenings" or "contractions" of the *or en sof,* described further in terms of *kelim,* "vessels," that once harbored the light. When the vessels broke, they shattered and dispersed so that the Divine Indwelling Presence, the *shechinah,* is now in exile. The parts of the broken vessels that could not be assimilated formed the four *kelipot,* or shells, to which a spark of holiness is attached, three of which are impure, and the other, the *kelipat nogah,* which immediately covers the spark of holiness and which is somewhere between absolute goodness and absolute evil. The task of the human being is to extricate the divine sparks and to restore them to their source, thus participating in the restoration, or

tikkun of the Divine, or redemption. This is acting in the service of God, the process of raising evil to holiness, and sanctifying all of creation.

12. See Abraham J. Heschel, "The Mystical Element in Judaism," in *The Jews: Their History, Culture, and Religion,* ed. Louis Finkelstein (Philadelphia: Jewish Publication Society of America, 1949), 615; hereafter, "Mystical Element."

13. Simone Weil, *Attente de Dieu* (Paris: La Colombe, 1963), 101; hereafter, *Attente.* English: *Waiting for God,* trans. Emma Craufurd (New York: Perennial Classics, 2001), 85; hereafter, *Waiting.*

14. See Schneur Zalman, *Igeret Hakodesh,* sec. 3.

15. Ibid., secs. 6 and 4; see sec. 7.

16. Ibid., *Likutei Amarim,* chs. 32, 33.

17. Ibid., *Igeret Hakodesh,* sec., 23.

18. Ibid., *Igeret Hakodesh,* secs. 5 and 16. See also secs. 10, 11, 12, 13. As it is said, violate one Sabbath for another person that this individual may observe many Sabbaths.

19. It is said that the *tzaddikim,* or the community of holy persons, shield the world, and without their prayers, the world could not endure. See ibid., Sec. 27 b.

20. Schneur Zalman, *Likutei Amarim,* chs. 10, 13.

21. See Martin Buber, *Tales of the Hasidim,* trans. Olga Marx (New York: Schocken Books, 1991), 132.

22. Schneur Zalman, *Likutei Amarim,* chs. 1, 14; see also *Shaar Hayichud,* "Chinuch Katan."

23. Schneur Zalman, *Likutei Amarim,* ch. 43; *Igeret Hakodesh,* sec. 2; see also Daniel 4:32.

24. Note also that *ayin* is the name of a Hebrew letter, which is not pronounced.

25. Heschel, "Mystical Element," 604.

26. See Rabbi Jacob Immanuel Schochet, "Mystical Concepts in Chassidism," in *Likutei Amarim,* 872–956.

27. Examples of such communities of mystics can be found throughout the history of the Kabbalah. Most notable, perhaps, is the city of Safed (located in Northern Galilee) in the sixteenth century. Occupied by mystics from all walks of life—scholars, artisans, merchants—Safed took its inspiration from the commune structure of existence and was host to such great mystical figures as Joseph Caro (see R. Joseph Caro, *Code of Hebrew Law* [*Shulchan 'Aruk Choshen HaMishpat*]), trans. Rabbi Dr. Chaim N. Denburg [Montreal: Jurisprudence Press, 1954]); Moses Cordovero (see Ira Robinson, *Moses Cordovero's Introduction to Kabbalah: An Annotated Translation of His* Or Ne'erav (New York: Michael Scharf Publication Trust, 1994]); Solomon Alkabez, composer of the mystical prayer, Leha Dodi, used as part of liturgical Shabbat services; Chayyim Vital (see Chayyim Vital, "Book of Visions" in *Jewish Mystical Autobiographies,* trans. and ed. Morris M. Faierstein [New York: Paulist Press, 1999], 43–263); and of course the Rabbi Isaac Luria, the Ari, whose Kabbalistic system made such a profound impact on the likes of the Besht and Rabbi Zalman (see Solomon Schechter, "Safed in the Sixteenth Century," in *Studies in Judaism,* Second Series [Piscataway, N.J.: Gorgias Press, 2003 (1908)], 202–306).

28. Dov Baer Schneersohn, *Kuntres ha-hitpa'alut* (Warsaw, Poland, 1876). Dobh Baer of Lubavitch, *Tract on Ecstasy,* trans. Louis Jacobs (London: Vallentine, Mitchell, 1963), 57, 150, 175; hereafter cited in the text as *Tract.*

There are no essential reasons why there could not have been a fully developed line of women mystics in Judaism, especially in the Chassidic mystical tradition. The difficulty in writing on Dov Baer is that here are no indications of this possibility (a difficulty which is not peculiar to him alone). Rather than make Dov Baer into someone he is not, I sometimes use just the masculine pronoun when explicating his thought.

29. See Idel, "Preface," xviii in *Jewish Mystical Autobiographies.*

30. Louis Jacob reports of Dov Baer that he was often witnessed caught up in prayer, standing without making the slightest movement for up to three hours at a time, with his hat and shirt saturated with perspiration (see Jacobs, "Introduction," 12, and 49 n. 34).

31. For Dov Baer and for some mystics within the Jewish tradition, the divine soul is specific to Israel. This cannot be rooted in a biological or vitalistic orientation since one can convert to Judaism, as Dov Baer remarks concerning one of the mystical dimensions of ecstasy. Rather, it concerns a spiritual vocation (which in principle must be open to all), one in which the Jewish person takes on the given, awe-filled responsibility, expressed by the covenant, for the return of all God's people to him and establishing God's exiled presence in human history.

32. See above, n. 4.

33. See Chart 1 above.

34. Hence it can also be understood as "spirit" in the sense of breath. See Genesis 2:7: "He [the Lord God] blew in his nostrils the breath [*neshamah*] of life, and man became a living being."

35. See *The Bahir,* par. 79. See also Kaplan's commentary, 144.

36. *Tract,* 80 and fn. 6: "Es is der inyan weit zehr fun ihm; es gehört tzu ihm nit shayyach klal tzu ihm."

37. *Tract,* 83: "acrop fall bei sich zehr stark un die welt wert zehr arop gefallen."

38. *Tract,* 82: "er hat der hört gut zehr be-mahashavah."

39. Schneur Zalman, *Likutei Amarim,* ch. 42; and see *Igeret Hakodesh,* Sec. 1.

40. Of the 613 commandments given to Moses, which are symbolized by the 613 knots on the fringes of the *tallit* or prayer shawl, the 248 positive ones are said to be founded in love of God (comprised by the commandment, "I am the Lord your God . . ."), and the 365 negative ones are said to be founded in the fearsome awe of God (comprised by the commandment, "You shall not make for yourself . . ."). For the mystic, the commandments or *mitzvot* are not performed for their own sake, but are expressive of the love and fearsome awe of God *qua chesed* (loving-kindness) and *gevurah* (power, might).

41. It may appear that the fourth and fifth modes of natural ecstasy are also without effort, since they are said to be spontaneous, and thus do not require (the same kind of) effort. Still, Dov Baer regards even the fourth and fifth, too, as in concealment because they are modes of ecstasy that are separate from the Essence of that which is comprehended, that is, of some thing that is still apart from the

Divine. In this respect, they are not true modes of divine ecstasy. See Dobh Baer, *Tract*, 104–105.

42. One could interpret the garments donned by Adam and Eve, not in a mundane way as a result of a Sartrean shame of our bodies under the gaze of the other accompanying a loss of innocence, but rather, as a cloak of "naturalness" that covers over divinity (due to our faults, i.e., not taking responsibility in the presence of God and before one another). Here donning garments in the myth of Adam and Eve would express the deeper spiritual dimension of our distance from Divinity, namely, we shield ourselves as divine from the Divine. To dispose ourselves to God in our "nakedness," or to be naked before another—as the philosopher Emmanuel Levinas might say—then, would be the process of cleaving to God.

43. See Schneur Zalman, *Likutei Amarim*, chs. 16 and 44. Love and fearsome awe are further characterized as two "wings" for children (chs. 40 and 41) that are born of the Divine *chochmah* (wisdom).

44. If one did have a "choice," suggests Dov Baer, being separate from the Holy would be worse than losing one's life.

45. See Schneur Zalman, *Likutei Amarim*, chs. 6, 19.

46. The *Shema* reads שמע ישראל יהוה אלהנו יהוה אחד.

47. It is said of Rabbi Akiba that he thought he was finally able to fulfill this commandant—to love God absolutely—when, in his nineties, even as he was being tortured and executed by the Romans, his skin flayed, he was able to recite the *Shema* at sunrise.

48. Schneur Zalman, *Likutei Amarim*, chs. 26–27. According to Zalman and Dov Baer, the divine soul is possessed by all of Israel. Those who work for themselves alone, as if to insist, "Give me, give me" or "Feed me," are called "gentiles." Gentiles are those who love themselves to the extent of removing themselves from God, ostensibly becoming like independent entities, or what Zalman, like Dov Baer, would define as "dead."

See Schneur Zalman, *Likutei Amarim*, chs. 19, 24; and see *Igeret Hakodesh*, ch. 11. Cf. Dov Baer, *Tract*, 62 and passim.

49. See Schneur Zalman, *Likutei Amarim*, chs. 10, 11, 16, 26, 28, 39, 40; and *Shaar Hayichud*, "Chinuch Katan."

50. Schneur Zalman, *Likutei Amarim*, ch. 31. The traditional form of the confession of sins in the Jewish tradition is the collective recitation of the *Al-chet* directly to God during the High Holy Days. This is in contrast to the Catholic tradition of individual confessions meditated by a priest.

51. See Schneur Zalman, *Likutei Amarim*, ch. 43, and *Likutei Amarim*, "Chinuch Katan." And see *Igeret Hakodesh*, sec. 18.

52. Dobh Baer, following the Jewish medieval philosophers, refers to the Greek term *hyle*, in the sense of the most basic matter. Cf. ibid., and 108, nn. 2 and 4.

53. Moreover, it is called the "simple" or "essential song." As such, it is distinguished from "duplicated song," a melody without words, or the song of Moses peculiar to the fourth stage (the ecstasy of the mind). This, in turn, is distinguished from the ecstasy of the heart, to which words are attached, or the song of the Levites (131–33).

4. RŪZBIHĀN BAQLĪ AND MYSTICISM OF UNVEILING

1. References to Rūzbihān Baqlī, *Unveiling of Secrets: Diary of a Sufi Master,* trans. Carl W. Ernst (Chapel Hill, N.C.: Parvardigar Press, 1997) are cited in the text itself according to the section headings supplied by Ernst.

I acknowledge my gratitude to Lucian Stone for his assistance in citing the Persian and Arabic script and the respective diacritical marks for the transliterations.

2. See Karen Armstrong, *Muhammad: A Biography of the Prophet* (New York: HarperCollins, 1993), cf. 69ff.; hereafter, *Muhammad.*

3. See Carl W. Ernst, *The Shambhala Guide to Sufism* (Boston: Shambhala, 1997), esp. xi–xx; hereafter, *Shambhala.* See also Reynold A. Nicholson, *The Mystics of Islam* (New York: Penguin Books, 1989/1914).

4. See, e.g., Annemarie Schimmel, *Mystical Dimensions of Islam* (Chapel Hill: University of North Carolina Press, 1975), 25ff., 33ff.; hereafter, *Mystical Dimensions.*

5. I cite from the following bi-lingual edition of the Quran, *Quran: The Meaning of The Holy Quran,* trans. ʿAbullah Yusuf ʿAli (Beltsville, Md.: Amana Publications, 1420 AH/1999 CE).

6. To the best of my knowledge, the first part of the *shahādah* is not given word for word in the Quran, though there are similar expressions given in Quran, for example: "There is nothing / Whatever like unto Him, / And He is the One / That hears and sees (all things)" (42:11). And: 112:1–4:

> Say: He is Allah
> The One and Only;
> Allah, the Eternal, Absolute;
> He begetteth not,
> Nor is He begotten;
> And there is none
> Like unto Him.

7. Or 124,000 prophets and 124,000 Friends of God. See Henry Corbin, *En Islam iranien: Aspects spirituals et philosophiques* (Paris: Gallimard, 1972), 3:36, n. 22. See also Sachiko Murata and William C. Chittick, *The Vision of Islam* (St. Paul, Minn.: Paragon House, 1994), 134ff; hereafter, *Vision.*

8. Murata and Chittick, *Vision,* 134.

9. It was on the 20th of Ramadan, in the eighth year of hijra (that is, after Muhammad and his companions migrated from Mecca to Medina in the year 622 CE), that Muhammad is said to have stood before the Gate of the Kaʿba and proclaimed that there is no god but Allah alone. See, for example, Abdul Hameed Siddiqui, *Life of Muhammad* (Chicago: Kazi Publications, 1983), 249.

10. All dates are given either according to the Islamic hijri calendar followed by the corresponding date in the Gregorian Christian calendar or the calendar of the "common era" (CE), or simply according to the Muslim calendar, AH (after hijra).

11. See al-Qushayrī, *Principles of Sufism,* trans. B. R. von Schlegell (Berkeley, Calif.: Mizan Press, 1990), esp. 301–302. See also Ernst, *Sufism,* 19–22; and Schimmel, *Mystical Dimensions,* 14.

12. Cited by al-Qushayrī, *Principles,* 306.

13. See Murata and Chittick, *Vision,* 238ff. However, this is a point contested by philosophers who are also mystics, e.g., Mulla Sadra. See Seyyed Hossein Nasr, *Knowledge and the Sacred* (Albany: SUNY Press, 1989), and Seyyed Husayn Nasr, *Sadr al-Dīn Shīrāzī [Mullā Sadrā] and his Transcendental Theosophy* (Tehran: Imperial Iranian Academy of Philosophy, 1978). See also Javad Nurbakhsh, "The Key Features of Sufism in the Early Islamic Period," xvii–xi, and S. H. Nasr, "The Rise and Development of Persian Sufism," 13–16, both in *The Heritage of Sufism,* vol. 1, ed. Leonard Lewisohn (Oxford: Oneworld Press, 1999). I express my appreciation to Lucian Stone for references on this topic.

14. See Ernst, *Words of Ecstasy,* 4ff.

15. See J. Spencer, Trimingham, *The Sufi Orders in Islam* (New York: Oxford University Press, 1971), esp. 1–30; and Schimmel, *Mystical Dimensions,* 231ff.

16. See Ernst, *Rūzbihān Baqlī,* 111. In fact, according to the Sunan Abū Dāwūd (202–275 AH), Muhammad is said to have promulgated, on the subject of prayer, that monasticism was not a prescription for submitting to God (Sunan Abū Dāwūd, Bk. 4, Number 4886).

17. Murata and Chittick, *Vision,* 246.

18. Cf. for example, Ernst, *Sufism,* 58–68.

19. Ernst, *Sufism,* 154–61.

20. Armstrong, *Muhammad,* 61.

21. Ernst, *Sufism,* 85.

22. Schimmel, *Mystical Dimensions,* 298.

23. See Quran 2:195, 28:77. See also Murata and Chittick, *Vision,* esp. 265ff.

24. See Margaret Smith, *Rabiʿa the Mystic and Her Fellow-Saints in Islam* (Cambridge: Cambridge University Press, 1984).

25. On Ḥallāj, see Louis Massignon, *La passion de Husayn ibn Mansur ḥallāj, martyr mystique de l'Islam execute à Baghdad le 26 mars 922. Étude d'histoire religieuse,* 2nd ed., 4 vols. (Paris: Gallimard, 1975).

26. Michael A. Sells, trans. and ed., *Early Islamic Mysticism: Sufi, Qur'an, Miʿraj, Poetic and Theological Writings* (New York: Paulist Press, 1996), 17–26.

27. See, e.g., Ernst, *Words of Ecstasy,* 49ff.; Schimmel, *Mystical Dimensions,* 58ff.

28. See Triminghan, *Sufi Orders,* esp. 3–5.

29. Sells, *Early Islamic Mysticism,* 23ff.

30. Ernst, *Rūzbihān Baqlī,* 2ff.

31. Ernst, *Rūzbihān Baqlī,* 2–3.

32. Murata and Chittick, *Vision,* 295.

33. See Ernst, *Rūzbihān Baqlī,* 17, 35ff.

34. See Corbin, *En Islam iranien,* 30ff. See also Ernst, *Rūzbihān Baqlī,* 36.

35. For example, Rûzbihân Baqlî Sîrâzî, *Le jasmin des fidèles d'amour* (Kitâb-e ʿAbbar al-ʿâshiqîn)/ *[The Jasmine of the Lovers],* ch. 1, trans. Henry Corbin (Paris: Verdier, 1991); hereafter, *Le jasmin.*

36. See also Ernst, *Rūzbihān Baqlī*, 5.

37. "Before this visitation I was concerned about some utterances of members of my assembly, when I heard some nonsense of sayings that understand God in human terms" (§197). See also: "Glory be to him who transcends the reference of everyone who reduces God to abstractions and the expression of all who see him in human terms" (§91, cf. §157).

38. From Ernst, *Rūzbihān Baqlī*, 34.

39. See also Ernst, *Rūzbihān Baqlī*, 40–1. See also Corbin, *En Islam iranien*, 87.

40. Baqlî, *Le jasmin*, ch. 30, §271 (my translation from the French). Cf. Corbin, *En Islam iranien*, 79. See also (§191): "I saw God from every atom, though he transcends incarnation and human forms."

41. Corbin, *En Islam iranien*, 88.

42. To thwart some of these possible misreadings, Rūzbihān will often preface these and other descriptions with an "as though" or "as if," alerting the reader that the presence of God is given in some way, and the best way he can describe these epiphanies or evoke the experience is with an image that will stir the reader.

43. See Ernst, *Words of Ecstasy*.

44. Henry Corbin edited Baqlī's work under the title, *Sharh-e Shathîyât* (*Commentaire sur les paradoxes des Soufis*), or as Ernst renders it, *Commentary on Ecstatic Expressions* (Paris: Librairie d'Amerique et d'Orient Adrien—Maisonneuve, 1966).

45. See Ernst, *Words of Ecstasy*, esp. 32ff.

46. Sells, *Early Islamic Mysticism*, 102–103.

47. Schimmel, *Mystical Dimensions*, 100. For Sarrāj, for example, we move from the stations of repentance (*tawba*), to watchfulness (*warā*), to renunciation (*zuhd*), to poverty (*faqr*), to patience (*sabr*), to trust (*tawakkul*), to acceptance (*ridā*). See Sells, *Early Islamic Mysticism*, 199–211.

48. See Carl W. Ernst, "Stages of Love in Early Persian Sufism from Rābi'a to Rūzbihān," in *Classical Persian Sufism: From Its Origins to Rumi*, ed. Leonard Lewisohn (New York: Khaniqahi Nimatullahi Publications, 1993); hereafter, "Stages of Love." See also Ernst, *Shambhala*, 102–103. And see Seyyed Hossein Nasr, *Sufi Essasys* (New York: Schocken Books, 1977), 71ff. Regarding 'Aṭṭār, see Lucian Stone, "Blessed Perplexity: The Topos of Ḥayrat in Farid al-Din 'Aṭṭār's Mantiq al-tayr" (unpublished manuscript), chapter 1.

49. For the purposes of this study, I explicate Baqlī's *Unveiling of Secrets*. Another work by Baqlī describes 1001 stages or stations (*maqāmāt*) of the spiritual path, "*Mashrab al-Arwāḥ*" [*The Spirits' Font*]. According to Ernst, it begins with the pre-creational experiences of spirits, traces the movement through the various classes of the spiritual traveler, culminating in the experience of divine lordship and the knowledge of universal names of God. See Ernst, *Words of Ecstasy*, 92ff.

Furthermore, in his *Le jasmin/The Jasmine of the Lovers* (chs. 16–32), Baqlī describes twelve stages of mystical ascent to the ultimate stage of perfect love, ranging from servanthood (ch. 20) to longing or ardent desire (ch. 31), and finally to universal love as the perfection of love (ch. 32). See also Ernst, "Stages of Love," esp. 450–53.

50. Cf. §164. Rūzbihān writes: "One night I was confronted with psychic

imaginings, trivial imaginings, and spiritual imaginings. . . . I said, 'My God! What are these likenesses in which I have been veiled before witnessing.' He said, 'This is for one who seeks me in the first unveilings of my majesty, until he knows me through these veils, and this is the station of knowledge; one who only knows me through them is not a [true] knower of me. This is the station of striving for the people of witnessing' (§180)." Similarly, in a visitation God appears to Rūzbihān ("I looked at the beauty of his transcendent face with the eye of the heart") and says: "'How can they reach me by strivings and disciplines, if my noble face remains veiled to them.'"

51. Although the dominant term used by Baqlī in this diary is "station," it is nonetheless replete with an expression that verges on being synonymous with the latter. In another terminological shift, Baqlī tends to press the term "ocean" into service in the same manner that he does "station." He accordingly writes both of an "ocean of oneness" (§152) like he does a "station of oneness" (§136), of an "ocean of astonishment" (§142) like he does a "station of astonishment" (§144), or again, "oceans of nearness" (§104) like he does a "state of nearness" (§103), the oceans of ecstasy and the spiritual state of ecstasy (cf. §§83, 117, 143, 156, 161, 184).

This is not to say that Rūzbihān does not also use the term "ocean" in a more general sense (cf. §§99, 123), where it might imply something like vastness (§179). But it is also clear from other expressions like "oceans of magnificence" (§36), "oceans of mystical knowledge" (§79), "oceans of ecstasy" (§156 passim), "ocean of astonishment" (§142), or "oceans of pure remembrance of God's names" (§185) that he is using this term as a synonym for station.

52. Thus, we read the record of these kinds of appeals: "I said, 'My God, I am not satisfied with that.' And it was as though I saw him and did not see him, for I was in a kind of blindness. Then he took the veil off that blindness, and I saw him in the inner world of the hidden, but still I did not see him as I wished. So I implored him; I saw him in the outer world of the hidden, and I did not recognize the reality of union with him. I became angry and pained and said, 'It is right that your servants turn away from your door and face inward to themselves as their direction of prayer. What is this distress?' I remained for a while, and saw the Most High, and he appeared in the outer world of the angelic realm. I saw him in the form of majesty and beauty, and he drew me near and I approached, and it was as I wished, but I could not bear the extreme ecstasy, spiritual state, cries, sighs, and disturbance from his overwhelming loveliness and beauty, and the sweetness of union with him. I remained in that state for a time" (§150).

"The Truth (glory be to him) appeared to me in the station of intimacy, with a lovely quality and graceful beauty. He seized my heart with his beauty, and I was overwhelmed by cries, sobs, tears, clapping, ecstasy, intimacy, longing, passion, raving, affection, and love. Then he hid, and I abased myself, begging to meet with the Generous One. Then he appeared to me in a quality that is foremost in the symbolic verses; then he hid from me" (§129).

53. See an earlier expression of this in Bāyazid, cited by Ernst, *Words of Ecstasy*, 26–27.

54. Baqlī, *Sharh-e Shathîyât* (*Commentaire sur les paradoxes des Soufis*) [*The Commentary on Ecstatic Expressions*], 549, cited by Ernst in *Rūzbihān*, 33.

55. Literally, a finding, namely, a finding of God. It also has the same root as *wujud* (existence, or being). On the latter point, see Murata and Chittick, *Vision*, 248.

56. See Baqlī, *Sharh-e Shathîyât* (*Commentaire sur les paradoxes des Soufis*) [*The Commentary on Ecstatic Expressions*], 558, 617; cited by Ernst in *Rūzbihān*, 34.

57. See other instances in §§97, 107, 117, 123. But also see the passage in which he does one time associate intimacy with there being "no between" (§138).

58. Rūzbihān explicitly contrasts annihilation with witnessing God in the form of the cloak of divinity. We read the entreaty from Rūzbihān: "He said, 'And what do you want?' I said, 'I want my annihilation in the wrath of eternity, for I am not content with the vision of the cloak of divinity'" (§58).

59. See Schimmel, *Mystical Dimensions*, 55.

60. See Schimmel, *Mystical Dimensions*, 58–59, 144, passim.

61. See Aṭṭār, *Conference*. See also Stone, "Blessed Perplexity."

62. I follow Lucian Stone's translation of this passage. For the sake of consistency, however, I use "subsistence" for *baqā* rather than his suggested "permanence."

63. Baqlī, *Sharh-e Shathîyât* (*Commentaire sur les paradoxes des Soufis*) [*Commentary on Ecstatic Expressions*], 554, cited by Ernst, *Rūzbihān*, 35.

64. Cited by Ernst, *Words of Ecstasy*, 33.

65. Corbin, *En Islam iranien*, 131. As Schimmel also notes, it is really only the enthusiastic expressions of unity that lead many an outsider to conjecture that the mystical journey culminates in a pantheism or a reduction. See *Mystical Dimensions*, 147.

66. In a different work by Baqlī cited by Ernst, Rūzbihān gives a different ordering, namely, the station of unification (*ittihād*), of which the beginning is annihilation (*fanā*), the middle subsistence (*baqā*), and the end, essential union (*'ayn al-jam*). "Annihilation is the veil of subsistence, and subsistence is the veil of annihilation, but essential union is pure unification. The appearance of God [*zuhūr al-ḥaqq*] from this (station) is by the quality of essential manifestation . . . which, in the experience of *tawḥīd*, is the infidelity of reality. That is the greatest veil in gnosis, and the sixty-ninth veil" (Rūzbihān Baqlī, *Sharh al-Hujub wa al-Astar fi Maqamat Ahl al-Anwar wa al-Asrar*, Ailsilah-I Isha'at al-'Ulum, No. 41, Hyderabad, 1333, p. 21; cited by Ernst, *Words of Ecstasy*, 94).

67. Corbin, *En Islam iranien*, 131.

5. MATTERS OF EVIDENCE IN RELIGIOUS EXPERIENCE

1. It is itself a great favor from God, she continues, if the person receiving the favor recognizes it, and it is a very great one if he or she does not abandon his or her path (*Obras*, 501; *Collected Works*, Vol. 2, IV:2.8).

2. See St. John of the Cross, Prologue to "The Ascent of Mt. Carmel," *Obras Completas*, 89; *Collected Works*, 115.

3. See *Obras*, 91, 137–38; *Collected Works*, Vol. 1, 15.11–12, 25.14; *Obras*, 691; *Collected Works*, Vol. 3, "Foundations," 5.12.

4. See *Obras*, 548–49, 558–59, 551–52; *Collected Works*, Vol. 2, VI:7.5, VI:9.13, VI:7.14; *Obras*, 155; *Collected Works*, Vol. 1, 29.4–5.

5. "On another day the Lord told me this: 'Do you think, daughter, that merit lies in enjoyment? No, rather it lies in working and suffering and loving'" (*Obras*, 606; *Collected Works*, Vol. 1, "Spiritual Testimonies," 32.

6. See St. John of the Cross, *Obras Completas*, 51; *Collected Works*, 93.

7. See, e.g., *Obras*, 82, 89–90, 100–103, 108–109, passim; *Collected Works*, Vol. 1, 13.17–19, 14.6–8, 18.4–15, 20.1–4, passim. See "Fundaciones"/"Foundations," passim.

8. He writes further that each one should know oneself and be attentive to possible delusion, because one should not excuse oneself out of self-conceit, valuing the self over all else. Out of humility, one should not strive after what is too great, being propelled into self-doubt and the like, nor should one reflect on the evils of others, nor be envious of one's neighbor's superiority and goodness.

9. *Sitra achra* is known as "the other side," that is, the side that negates holiness. Anything that attempts to separate one from God is said to belong to the *sitra achra*. For some mystics this root of evil gets characterized as a personal force (like *ha-satan*, the Evil One), for others, it is treated as an impersonal force.

10. See Schneur Zalman, *Likutei Amarim*, ch. 40.

11. Ibid., chs. 17, 31.

12. Schneur Zalman, *Igeret Hakodesh*, Sec. 10. Hence, it is said that nothing can stand in the way of repentance; if one has transgressed but repents, one is forgiven on the spot. See Schneur Zalman, *Likutei Amarim*, chs. 25 and 26.

13. Dobh Baer, *Tract*, 149–50. "But upon my soul, the great ones need it more than the small." See also Schneur Zalman, *Igeret Hakodesh*, Sec. 2.

14. God descended from his majesty in the heavens, His power embracing all, and He said: "Rūzbihān the leader [*makhdum*]! . . . Do you have any remaining doubt that I have unveiled this to you, and that I have chosen you for this station?" (§73). Other times he experiences sighs and tears in the spiritual state of ecstasy (§83), or as a loving and maddened son (§99). As God's face, transcending the indication of thought, was unveiled to him, and from this manifestation came "the sweetness of longing, the melting of spirit, the agitation of the inner consciousness, the shattering of the heart, the annihilation of the intellect; he was sighing, weeping, turning, and sobbing (§124). Given as a stranger (§176) among other strangers (§120). Constant experience of sighs, tears, of the conscience being reckless, the intellect baffled, the heart and self annihilated (§184 passim). God ravishes him and sits him down like a lover (§198), and makes him his essence (§148).

15. There are other evocative images as well, e.g., of God eating, consuming, ingesting the prophets, messengers, saints, etc. (§57). "I said, 'God, you transcend eating and drinking. When I cried from regret, the angels drank my tears. What will they do with my weeping from longing and intimacy in witnessing? He (glory be to him) said, 'That is my wine'" (§146).

16. See, e.g., §§41, 44, 54, 68, 75, 83, 84, 103, 127, 136, 162, 171.

17. The text continues: "I saw wonders of seclusion from him. When he manifested himself in the form of splendor and happiness, he was manifesting to me the qualities of the attributes, until he plundered my heart more than he had ever plundered it before in my entire life, with that seclusion and that unveiling and witnessing. Then the fields of glory, the sublimities of eternity, the lights of divine pres-

ence, and the oceans of greatness became clear to me. God hid after that in the veils of the hidden. I remained there in the form of astonishment with the pleasure of ecstasy, spiritual states, tears, and sighs, until I returned to the first state. This unveiling was one of the rarities of the unknown sciences; creatures do not know its realities because their sciences are incomplete and their intellects defective" (§201).

18. And: "The Truth drew me from the wombs of the hidden power and I approached him, taking the form of an arrow shot by a powerful bow, or a speeding gear" (§137).

19. This is a topic to be treated in another work. See Anthony J. Steinbock, "Interpersonal Attention through Exemplarity," *Journal of Consciousness Studies: Beyond Ourselves,* ed., Evan Thompson (2001): 179–96.

20. See Sigmund Freud, *Three Case Histories,* ed. Philip Rieff (New York: Colllier Books, 1963), esp. 103ff.

21. See Daniel Paul Schreber, *Memoirs of My Nervous Illness,* trans. Ida Macalpine et al. (New York: New York Review of Books, 2000).

22. See Freud, *Three Case Histories,* esp. 133ff.

23. Ibid., 117, 114.

24. Ibid., 133.

25. See my *Home and Beyond,* esp. Sec. 3.

26. See the concern Talmudic rabbis express when relating the fates of four great Jewish sages who embarked on a mystical ascent to God. Rabbi Ben Azai, who so longed for God, immediately looked and died in his prime; Ben Abuyah, who remained intellectually confused, saw two gods instead of the One God and became an apostate; Ben Zoma, who had not reconciled ordinary life with his mystical experiences, gazed and went insane; only Rabbi Akiba, who was perfectly balanced in the order of his heart and mind, entered *pardeis,* left the garden an enlightened saint, and later died a martyr at the hands of the Romans at the age of 90. See Talmud, *Chagigah,* 14b.

27. See Emmanuel Levinas, *De Dieu qui vient à l'idée* (Paris: Vrin, 1982), 154; English: *Of God Who Comes to Mind,* trans. Bettina Bergo (Stanford, Calif.: Stanford University Press, 1998), 97.

28. For example, in Tarkovsky's *Nostalghia,* Dominico (a mystic?) had held his family hostage in their house for seven years "to protect his family." We learn later that Dominico sequestered his family to save them from the sickness (spiritual sickness) of the world. "I was selfish; I wanted to save *my* family." On the basis of a later experience, he realizes his own misinterpretation, namely, that instead his calling was for everyone to be saved.

His mystical experiences are further suggested as mystical in the context of (1) various experiences and insights (e.g., the drops of water returning to their source, "1+1=1," i.e., mystical union); (2) the authority of other mystics and saints (e.g., the others bathing in the pool of St. Catherine's forget what God said to St. Catherine, namely, "You are she who is not, but I am who is." The task is to forget the self, while the "lovers" in the waters are doing everything to cling to the self); and (3) Dominico's final social address:

"That's why I can't be just one person. I can feel myself countless things at once. There are no great masters left. That's the real evil of our time. The heart's path is covered in shadow. We must listen to the voices that seem useless. In brains full of long sewer pipes, of school wall, tarmac, and welfare papers, the buzzing of insects must enter. We must fill the eyes and ears of all of us with things that are the beginning of a great dream. Someone must shout that we'll build the pyramids. It doesn't matter if we don't! We must fuel that wish and stretch the corners of the soul like an endless sheet.

"If you want the world to go forward, we must hold hands. We must mix the so-called healthy with the so-called sick. You healthy ones! What does your health mean? The eyes of all mankind are looking at the pit into which we are plunging. Freedom is useless if you don't have the courage to look us in the eye, to eat, drink, and sleep with us! It is the so-called healthy who have brought the world to the verge of ruin. . . . Where am I when I am not in reality or in my imagination?

"Here's my new pact: It must be sunny at night and snowy in August. Great things end, small things endure. Society must become united again instead of so disjointed. . . . Just look at nature and you'll see that life is simple. We must go back to where we were to the point where you took the wrong turn. We must go back to the main foundations of life without dirtying the water. What kind of a world is this if a madman tells you that you must be ashamed of yourselves!"

29. See Claude Lefort, *Élements d'une critique de la bureaucratie* (Paris: Gallimard, 1979); *L'invention démocratique* (Paris: Fayard, 1981); and *Le formes de l'histoire* (Paris: Gallimard, 1978).

30. See Claude Lefort, *Le travail de l'oeuvre Machiavel* (Paris: Gallimard, 1986).

31. This is the theme of another work on the inter-personal sphere of verticality.

32. This is why St. Teresa will insist on several occasions that God is not only present in special, isolated instances or extraordinary events, as if God only punc-tuated our existence, but is always already persistently in "there" or "here" (*Obras*, 125; *Collected Works*, Vol. 1, 22.15; *Obras*, 510–11; Vol. 2, V:1.10). Hence, she writes in her "Foundations" as cited above: "Well, come now, my daughters, don't be sad when obedience draws you to involvement in exterior matters. Know that if it is in the kitchen, the Lord walks among the pots and pans, helping you both interiorly and exteriorly" (*Obras*, 690; *Collected Works*, Vol. 3, "Foundations," 5.8).

33. Even though experiences peculiar to this initial degree of prayer are said to be acquired through our own efforts, in the final analysis they are linked to the movement of God: "For it must be understood, in whatever I say, that without Him we can do nothing" (*Obras*, 495–96; *Collected Works*, Vol. 2, IV:1.4; *Obras*, 72; *Collected Works*, Vol. 1, 11.9).

34. Dobh Baer, *Tract*, 96.

6. EPIPHANY AND WITHDRAWAL

1. "Le bonté du Bien—du Bien qui ne dort, ni ne somnole—incline le mouve-ment qu'elle appelle pour l'écarter du Bien et l'orienter vers autrui et ainsi seule-ment vers le Bien." "Dieu et la philosophie," in *De Dieu qui vient à l'idée* (Paris: Vrin, 1982), 114. English translation by Alphonso Lingis, "God and Philosophy" in *Collected Philosophical Papers* (The Hague: Martinus Nijhoff, 1987), 165.

2. Annie Dillard's extraordinary work, *For the Time Being* (New York: Vintage Books, 1999), raises these key experiential issues.

3. See, e.g., Martin Heidegger, *Phänomenologie des religiösen Lebens.* Gesamtausgabe. II. Abteilung, vol. 60 (Frankfurt am Main: Klostermann, 1995); Martin Heidegger, *Phänomenologie und Theologie* (Frankfurt am Main: Klostermann, 1970); John D. Caputo, *The Mystical Element in Heidegger's Thought* (New York: Fordham University Press, 1986, reprint). See also George Kovacs, *The Question of God in Heidegger's Phenomenology* (Evanston, Ill: Northwestern University Press, 1990).

4. Certainly, one can find related notions in religious traditions prior to Heidegger, for example, the earlier Jewish Kabbalism of Isaac Luria (the Ari), and his doctrine of *tzimtzum* whereby God withdraws into a point. See, e.g., Scholem, *Major Trends*, 260–65; and see Quaknin, *Tsimtsoum.*

Where contemporary work is concerned, one can see Heidegger's formulation assumed, *mutatis mutandis,* in the Christian tradition in the work of Michel Henry. See my "The Problem of Forgetfulness in the Phenomenology of Life," *The Philosophy of Michel Henry,* ed. Anthony J. Steinbock, special issue, *Continental Philosophy Review,* 32, no. 3 (1999): 271–302.

5. Martin Heidegger, *Sein und Zeit* (Tübingen: Niemeyer, 1979).

6. Ibid., 187–88.

7. See Martin Heidegger, *Identität und Differenz* (Tübingen: Neske, 1982), 16–17.

8. Ibid., 18–19.

9. "*Die Seinsvergessenheit ist die Vergessenheit des Unterschiedes des Seins zum Seiendem.*" See Martin Heidegger, *Holzwege* (Frankfurt am Main: Klostermann, 1980), 360.

10. Martin Heidegger, "Das Ding," in *Vorträge und Aufsätze* (Tübingen: Neske, 1954), 180.

11. Martin Heidegger, *Zur Sache des Denkens* (Tübingen: Niemeyer, 1976), 2ff., 25; hereafter, *Sache.*

12. Martin Heidegger, *Gelassenheit* (Tübingen: Neske, 1982), 47: "Eine rätselhafte Gegend, wo es nichts zu verantworten gibt."

13. Heidegger, *Sache,* 8.

14. Ibid., 23: "Das jetzt Genannte: *Ansichhalten, Verweigerung, Vorenthalt,* zeigt dergleichen wie ein Sichentziehen, kurz gesagt: *den Entzug.* Sofern aber die durch ihn bestimmten *Weisen des Gebens,* das Schicken und das Reichen, im Ereignen beruhen, muß der *Entzug zum Eigentümlichen des Ereignisses gehören*" (my emphasis). English: *On Time and Being,* trans. Joan Stambaugh (New York: Harper and Row, 1972), 22.

15. Heidegger, *Identität und Differenz,* 56.

16. Ibid., 40–41.

17. See Arthur R. Luther, "Original Emergence in Heidegger and Nishida," in *Philosophy Today* 26, no. 4/4 (1982): 345–56.

18. Heidegger, *Identität und Differenz,* 59–60.

19. Ibid., 65.

20. Heidegger, *Gelassenheit,* 31–34, 57.

21. Ibid., 34.

22. Heidegger, *Identität und Differenz,* 65.

23. See Marion, *Dieu sans l'être*. Jean-Luc Marion, *Réduction et donation: Recherches sur Husserl, Heidegger et la phénoménologie* (Paris: PUF, 1989). See also, Marion, *Étant donné*, and Jean-Luc Marion, *De surcroît: Études sur les phénomènes saturés* (Paris: PUF, 2001).

24. Heidegger, *Holzwege*, 59–61.

25. Heidegger, in ". . . dichterisch wohnet der Mensch . . . ," *Vorträge und Aufsätze*, 197.

26. Martin Heidegger, *Beiträge zur Philosophie (Vom Ereignis)* GA 65 (Frankfurt am Main: Klostermann, 1989), 8, 14ff., 396. See also Klaus Held, "Fundamental Moods and Heidegger's Critique of Culture," trans. Anthony J. Steinbock, in *Reading Heidegger: Commemorations,* ed. John Sallis (Bloomington: Indiana University Press, 1993), 286–303.

27. A point, for example, that Scheler also makes. See Max Scheler, "Ordo Amoris," in *Schriften aus dem Nachlaß*, Vol. 1 [*Gesammelte Werke*, Vol. 10], ed. Maria Scheler (Bern: Francke, 1957), 362–65. See also Scheler, *Formalismus*, 82–84. English: *Formalism in Ethics and Non-Formal Ethics of Value*, trans. Manfred S. Frings and Roger L. Funk (Evanston, Ill.: Northwestern University Press, 1973), 63–65; hereafter, *Formalism*.

28. Scheler, *Wesen*, 164, 191.

29. Ibid., 151, 161ff.

30. Ibid., 156.

31. As does Scheler. See, e.g., his *Formalismus*, 382; *Formalism*, 382.

32. Hence, Luther calls person an intrinsic coherence of dynamic orientation. See A. R. Luther, *Persons in Love: A Study of Max Scheler's Wesen und Formen der Sympathie* (The Hague: Martinus Nijhoff, 1972); hereafter, *Persons*.

33. Luther, *Persons*, 47.

34. See the Introduction, p. 15. This sense of person as absolute is behind the Jewish insight that when you save a person, you save a world.

35. Buber, "Ich und Du," 134.

36. Ibid., 135.

37. Scheler, *Vom Ewigen*, 331ff.

38. Or as Scheler would say, from "revelation": "Wenn dieser Gedanke eines Gottes, der sich selbst—sein Dasein selbst—verschwiege, so selten klar und rein gedacht worden ist, so ist der Grund dafür nur, daß Gott das, was er vermag und kann—als absolute freie, souveräne, unendliche und vollkommene Person—, schon vermöge seiner *Idee* gleichzeitig wesennotwendig *nicht* kann, da er diese seine Freiheit, es zu können, vermöge seiner *Allleibe* und *Allgüte*, desgleichen seiner *Wahrhaftigkeit* wesenmäßig nicht anwenden kann. Nur weil *Leibe als höchster* Aktwert ebenso wesennotwendig zur Idee Gottes gehört als die Personalität; ja weil Liebe es ist, die in allen möglichen Gesitern Wollen und Erkennen, in Gott aber—wie gezeigt—Schöpfung und Weisheit gleichzeitig fundiert, enthüllt sich uns die Idee eines sich selbst verbergenden und schweigenden, ja sich selbst und selbst sein Dasein verschweigenden Gottes als das, was sie its: als Idee eines furchtbaren Gespenstes, das Dasein nicht haben *kann*, da Widersinniges auch nicht da sein kann" (*Vom Ewigen*, 332–33). And see ibid., 339.

39. Scheler makes a similar point in *Vom Ewigen*, 330–32.

40. Weil, *Attente,* 84; *Waiting,* 70.

41. Weil, *Attente,* 84 passim; *Waiting,* 70 passim.

42. Based on a report from Barbara Bradley Hagerty, "Mother Teresa Beatified," NPR, October 14, 2003. See also Mother Teresa, *A Simple Path,* ed. Lucinda Vardey (New York: Ballantine Books, 1995), 65.

43. Again, a point made implicitly in Dillard's *For the Time Being.*

44. A topic to be taken up in a later work.

7. ON INDIVIDUATION

1. Husserl, *Analyses,* Appendix 8. Although I am taking this example from Husserl, he did come to see birth and death as "phenomena," that is, as constitutive problems within the context of generativity. See my *Home and Beyond,* and "From Phenomenological Immortality to Phenomenological Natality," in *Rethinking Facticity,* ed. Eric Nelson and Francois Raffoul (Albany: SUNY Press, 2007).

2. St. John of the Cross, *Obras Completas,* 446; "The Spiritual Canticle," in *Collected Works,* 485.

3. See Dobh Baer, *Tract,* 76, 129.

4. Dobh Baer, *Tract,* 128 and 77; my emphasis.

5. See, e.g., Dan Zahavi, *Self-Awareness and Alterity: A Phenomenological Investigation* (Evanston, Ill.: Northwestern University Press, 1999). The loss of self as an explicit theme does not exclude an implicit non-conscious dimension of (self)-awareness. See also Merleau-Ponty, *Phénoménologie;* and Aron Gurwitsch, *Das Bewußtseinsfeld* (Berlin: de Gruyter, 1974).

6. Dan Zahavi, *Subjectivity and Selfhood: Investigating the First Person Perspective* (Cambridge: MIT, 2005).

7. Zahavi, *Subjectivity and Selfhood,* 124–26.

8. Ibid., 127.

9. Ibid., 122–23; cf. 106–20. We are now at the most resilient and most remedial sense of self, what Zahavi calls the "minimal" or "core self." Having an experiential reality that is neither a social construct (i.e., a mere narrative self) nor a mere precondition of the unity of experiences like we might find in Kant, it is a function of the givenness of phenomenal objects or the stream of experiences; it is linked to the first-personal givenness of the experiential phenomena in such a way that even if others experience the same object(s) as I do, this self of experiential life in which the experiences are mine, this mineness, is irreducible to the mineness of others. So while what the object is like for the subject, or how the object appears, may be the same for me as it is for others, what the experience of the object is like for the subject, or how my experiences of the object are given to me, are distinctive.

10. See Gordon, *The Maggid of Caro,* esp. 9–14.

11. See Eugène Minkowski, *Lived Time: Phenomenological and Psychopathological Studies,* trans. Nancy Metzel (Evanston, Ill.: Northwestern University Press, 1970), 328–29. See also what Zahavi refers to as pre-psychotic stages relating to self-disorders in *Subjectivity and Selfhood,* 132ff.

12. Zahavi gives only the briefest allusion to Metzinger and the latter's treatment of Buddhism. See *Subjectivity and Selfhood,* 101–103.

13. See the discussion of Dennett in Zahavi, *Subjectivity and Selfhood,* 110ff.

14. See my *Home and Beyond,* Section 3. See also Georges Canguilhem, *Le normal et le pathologique* (Paris: PUF, 1966).

15. See my *Home and Beyond,* sec. 3.

16. See Stace, *Mysticism and Philosophy,* 86, 94, 161, 178.

17. Zahavi, *Subjectivity and Selfhood,* 106.

18. For example, see my *Home and* Beyond on the co-relational/co-foundational and asymmetrical character of the home and alien.

19. On this point, see Zaehner, *Mysticism,* and Otto, *Mysticism East and West.*

20. In his reply to the bonze during his stay in a Zen Temple in 1978, he writes: "As for Zen, it seems that all the techniques linked to spirituality are, conversely, tending to attenuate the individual. Zen and Christian mysticism are two things you can't compare, whereas the technique of Christian spirituality and that of Zen are comparable. And, here, there exists a great opposition. In Christian mysticism, even when it preaches the union of God and the individual, there is something that is individual; because it is a question of the relations of love between God and the individual. The one is he who loves and the other is he who is loved. In a word, Christian mysticism concentrates on individualization" (Michel Foucault, *Religion and Culture,* ed. Jeremy R. Carrette [New York: Routledge, 1999], 112).

21. See Soelle, *The Silent Cry.* See also the point developed in Pike, *Mystic Union,* esp. ch. 5. See Stace, *Mysticism and Philosophy;* Walter T. Stace, *The Teachings of the Mystics* (New York: New American Library, 1960), 156; and see Ninian Smart, "Interpretation and Mystical Experience," *Religious Studies* 1 (1965): 75–87.

22. Zahavi, *Subjectivity and Selfhood,* Zahavi writes: "Owing to the first-personal givenness of experience, our experiential life is inherently individuated. However, it is a purely formal kind of individuation. In contrast, a more concrete kind of individuality manifests itself in my personal history, in my moral and intellectual convictions and decisions. It is through such acts that I define myself; they have a character-shaping effect. I remain the same as long as I adhere to my convictions" (129).

23. Zahavi, *Subjectivity and Selfhood,* 130.

24. Ibid.; my emphasis.

25. Max Scheler, "Die Stellung des Menschen im Kosmos," in *Gesammelte Werke,* Vol. 9, ed. Manfred S. Frings (München: Francke Verlag, 1976), 35ff.; hereafter, "Stellung."

26. See also Arthur R. Luther, "The Articulated Unity of Being in Scheler's Phenomenology," in *Max Scheler (1874–1928) Centennial Essays,* ed. Manfred S. Frings (The Hague: Martinus Nijhoff, 1974), 6–7; hereafter, "Articulated Unity."

27. Edmund Husserl, *Die Bernauer Manuskripte über das Zeitbewußtsein (1917/18),* Husserliana 33, ed. Rudolf Bernet and Dieter Lohmar (Dordrecht: Kluwer, 2001); 297, 316–17, 321; cited as Hua 33.

28. Edmund Husserl, *Logische Untersuchungen,* Vol. II: *Elemente einer phänomenologischen Aufklärung der Erkenntnis,* Part 2 (Tübingen: Niemeyer, 1968), 129, 135–36; hereafter *Logische Untersuchungen,* II/2.

29. Furthermore, this particular instance (or instances) through which an essence is given need not be "real." An imaginary individual can also yield eidetic

insight and function as a conveyor of the essence. It is just that the act of imagination is given as a "quasi-perception"; the object has "quasi-being" since it is given in the mode of "as if" it were real; it is "quasi-temporal" since it is given as "as if" it were temporally determined, e.g., as present (cf. Hua 33, 341–42, 349–50). How is the temporality of essential objects different from empirical objects, and can the former even be predicated of temporality? If we identify temporality with the temporality of individual objects, then it would make perfect sense to assert that the essence is not extended in time, since it does not diminish or come into being like a sensuous object; it is given in time, but time does not belong to the nature of the essence itself (Hua 33, 311). If, for example, duration is a stretch of time with individual determinate temporal positions, then duration cannot be a determination of the essential object (Hua 33, 321–22; 316).

30. Time-consciousness is the primordial source for the constitution of unity of any individual object. If we stay with the bare form of time, which is explicated in terms of its temporal modes of present, retention, protention, coexistence, and succession, we are able to treat the necessary individualizing temporal form of all singular objects and pluralities of objects. "But," writes Husserl, "what gives unity to the particular object with respect to content, what makes up the differences between each of them with respect to content . . . the analysis of time alone cannot tell us, for it abstracts precisely from content. Thus, it does not give us any idea of the necessary synthetic structures of the streaming present and of the unitary stream of the presents—which in some way concerns the particularity of content" (*Analyses,* 174).

31. Husserl, *Analyses,* 178.

32. The individualized-particularized entity may be prominent for itself and exercise an affective allure in going from one present to the next, or red and/or triangle may only become prominent after the two are linked up in uniformity or similarity. See Husserl, *Analyses,* 174–89.

33. See Edmund Husserl, *Ideen zu einer reinen Phänomenologie und phänomenologische Philosophie. Zweites Buch,* ed. Marly Biemel (The Hague: Martinus Nijhoff, 1952); and Scheler, "Stellung," 12.

34. Scheler, "Stellung," 42, 15.

35. Ibid., 13–16.

36. See my *Home and Beyond,* Section 2. See Luther, "Articulated Unity," 9.

37. Scheler, "Stellung," 18.

38. See Husserl, *Analyses,* especially Division 3, Part 2. See also my "Translator's Introduction."

39. Scheler, "Stellung," 25.

40. Ibid., 27–28.

41. Luther, "Articulated Unity," 11.

42. See Merleau-Ponty, *Phénoménologie,* 191ff. See also Merleau-Ponty, *Le visible,* 172ff.

43. See Scheler, *Formalismus,* 382ff.

44. Scheler, "Stellung," 39; *Formalismus,* 385ff.

45. Scheler, "Stellung," 40.

46. See also Luther, "Articulated Unity," 16.

47. See my "Facticity and Insight as Problems of the Lifeworld: On Individuation," *Continental Philosophy Review* 37, no. 2 (2004): 241–61.

48. Simone Weil, *Le pesanteur et la grâce* (Paris: Librairie Plon: 1988), 44. English: *Gravity and Grace,* trans. Emma Crawford and Mario von der Ruhr (New York: Routledge, 2002), 33ff. See Scheler, "Stellung," 44.

49. Scheler, "Stellung," 44, cf. 70.

50. See Luther, "Articulated Unity," 20–23.

51. Scheler, "Stellung," 49, 54. Max Scheler, *Vom Ewigen,* 198.

52. See Luther, "Articulated Unity," 20ff.

53. Luther, *Persons,* 64.

54. See Scheler, "Stellung," 30.

55. See Merleau-Ponty, *Le visible.*

56. See my *Home and Beyond,* Section 4.

57. Scheler, *Formalismus,* 482; 490; *Formalism,* 490. Buber writes: "Zu bewähren vermag den empfangenen Sinn jeder nur mit der Einzigkeit seines Wesens and in der Einzigkeit seines Lebens" ("Ich und Du," 112).

58. Cf. Scheler, "Ordo Amoris," 354.

59. Franz Kafka, "Vor dem Gesetzt," in *Franz Kafka: Erzählungen,* ed. Martin Pfeifer (Stuttgart: Ernst Klett, 1986), 24–26.

60. Weil, *Attente,* 55; *Waiting,* 40, my insertion.

61. The religious but also the moral, political, and economic implications of this are reserved for another work.

62. See Luther, *Persons,* 48.

63. See, e.g., Brainard's equation, though only made in passing in his *Reality and Mystical Experience,* 1ff.

64. See Scheler, *Formalismus,* 382ff; *Formalism,* 382ff.

65. Dogen writes, for example: "'Emancipation' means that in birth you are emancipated from birth, in death you are emancipated from death. Thus, there is detachment from birth-and-death and penetrating birth-and-death. Such is the complete practice of the great way. There is letting go of birth-and-death and vitalizing birth-and-death. Such is the thorough practice of the great way.

"'Realization' is birth, birth is realization. At the time of realization there is nothing but birth totally actualized, nothing but death totally actualized" (*Moon in a Dewdrop: Writings of Zen Master Dogen,* ed. Kazuaki Tanahashi [New York: North Point Press, 1998], 84).

66. I realize there are other doctrines, even experiences of the "after-life," such as reincarnation, even within the Abrahamic tradition. (See, e.g., Vital, "Book of Visions," esp. 43–263.) The evidence I have been developing here does not point in this direction, however, and my intention in this work has been to follow out the clues presented by these mystics. At the very least the existence of these other experiences should throw us back on ourselves (or others back on themselves) in a critical examination of what we accept as the mystery of being.

67. Baqlî, *Sharh-e Shathîyât (Commentaire sur les paradoxes des Soufis)* [*Commentary on Ecstatic Expressions*], 554, cited by Ernst, Rūzbihān, 35.

68. Cited by Ernst, *Words of Ecstasy,* 33.

69. See my "Problem of Forgetfulness."

70. Henry, *C'est moi,* 263.

71. Ibid., 212–15; my emphasis.

72. Cf. Luther, *Persons,* 127.

73. Ibid. See also Leo Baeck, "Judaism in the Church," in *The Pharisees and Other Essays,* translated from the German (New York: Schocken Books, 1966).

74. Cf. Zaehner, *Mysticism: Sacred and Profane,* esp. 153–97.

75. See also Scheler, *Vom Ewigen,* 191–92.

76. Ibid., 202.

77. See also Max Scheler, *Schriften aus dem Nachlass,* Vol. 4 of *Philosophie und Geschichte,* ed. Manfred S. Frings (Bonn: Bouvier, 1990), 89, n. 1.

78. Mother Teresa, *Mother Teresa: In My Own Words,* ed., José Luis González-Balado (New York: Gramercy Books, 1996), 99.

79. See Luther, "Articulated Unity," 28.

80. Ibid., 28–29.

81. Buber, "Ich und Du," 92.

82. Cf. my *Home and Beyond,* ch. 14.

83. This is the perspective developed, from a Christian faith, in Jacques Dupuis's *Toward a Christian Theology of Religious Pluralism* (2002).

8. IDOLATRY

1. See *Autour de l'idolâtrie: Figures actuelles de pouvoir et de domination,* ed. Bernard von Meenen (Bruxelles: Publications des Facultés universitaires Saint-Louis, 2003).

2. Jean-Luc Marion, *L'idole et la distance* (Paris: Bernard Grasset, 1977). Marion, *Dieu sans l'être.* Marion, *Étant donné.*

3. Bruce Ellis Benson, *Graven Ideologies: Nietzsche, Derrida and Marion on Modern Idolatry* (Downers Grove, Ill.: InterVarsity Press, 2002).

4. Robert Gibbs, personal conversation. See also his *Correlations in Rosenzweig and Levinas* (Princeton, N.J.: Princeton University Press, 1992); hereafter, *Correlations.* And see his *Why Ethics? Signs of Responsibilities* (Princeton, N.J.: Princeton University Press, 2000).

5. Scheler, "Ordo Amoris," 353–54.

6. We could also say that in self-love, one is given as God's image of me with and for others, not the image I merely fashion of and for myself.

7. Max Scheler, "Die Demut," in *Vom Umsturz der Werte,* Gesammelte Werke, vol. 3, ed. Maria Scheler (Bern: Francke, 1955), 18–19.

8. Ibid., 19–20.

9. St. John of the Cross, *Obras Completas,* 305; *Collected Works,* 338.

10. See *Early Islamic Mysticism,* 171–95.

11. See Baeck, "Judaism in the Church," 71–90.

12. See Alighieri Dante, *The Divine Comedy: I. Inferno,* trans. John D. Sinclair (New York: Oxford University Press, 1961), Canto xxxiv; and *II. Purgatorio,* Canto xx–xii.

13. For the Chabad mystic, in particular, it is through our *avodah,* or service of *tzedakah* that God's countenance, or the *shechinah* radiates with us in and through

our co-participation. Understanding oneself as self-grounding is a different kind of service, an *avodah zarah:* the service of other gods, the service of foreign, alien, strange things—not service toward other persons, but service to what is made separate, disconnected, etc. From the standpoint of Divine service, it is a strange service, an estranged service: to stand before God as if self-grounding. See Schneur Zalman, *Likutei Amarim,* chs. 19, 24; and see *Igeret Hakodesh,* ch. 11. Cf. Dov Baer *Tract,* 62 and passim, and Schneur Zalman, *Igeret Hakodesh,* sec. 3

14. Georges Bernanos, *The Diary of a Country Priest,* trans. Pamela Morris (New York: Carroll and Graf Publishers, 1965), 249. Cf. St. John of the Cross, *Obras Completas,* 323; *Collected Works,* 364: "Sometimes they minimize their faults, and at other times they become discouraged by them, since they felt they were already saints, and they become impatient and angry with themselves, which is yet another fault."

15. See Scheler, "Ressentiment," 81–82. See Nietzsche, *Zur Genealogie der Moral,* esp. 268–69, 270–74, 281–83.

16. See the point made by Scheler in "De Demut," 21–22.

17. *Obras,* 501; *Collected Works,* Vol. 2, IV:2.9.

18. Dov Baer, *Tract,* 163–64.

19. Schneur Zalman, *Likutei Amarim,* chs. 26–27.

20. Weil, *Attente,* 152; *Waiting,* 132.

21. Weil, *Le pesanteur et la grâce,* 9; *Gravity and Grace,* 3.

22. Weil, *Le pesanteur et la grâce,* 35; *Gravity and Grace,* 26. See also, Weil, *Attente,* 84–5; *Waiting,* 70–1.

23. St. John of the Cross, *Obras Completas,* 326; *Collected Works,* 366.

24. I do not use it in his later understanding of the world as horizon, which cannot be given as a being. See my *Home and Beyond,* ch. 7.

25. See Edmund Husserl, *Erste Philosophie (1923/24),* ed. R. Boehm, Husserliana 7 (The Hague: Martinus Nijhoff, 1956), 252, 276.

26. See Husserl, *Krisis,* 148, 155.

27. Scheler, *Vom Ewigen,* 263.

28. Ibid., 261–62; see also 292–93.

29. See, e.g., St. John of the Cross, *Obras Completas,* 117–18, 258–59, 299–300, 307, 325–26; *Collected Works,* 143, 290, 333, 340, 366.

30. St. John of the Cross, *Obras Completas,* 117–18; and see 325–26; *Collected Works,* 143; and see 366. He notes further: "And they should never assure themselves that, since their attachment is small, they will break away from it in the future even if they do not do so immediately. If they do not have the courage to uproot it when it is small and in its first stages, how do they think and presume they will have the ability to do so when it becomes greater and more deeply rooted?" (*Obras Completas,* 269; *Collected Works,* 301). "Nothing but what belongs to the service of God should be the object of our joy" (*Obras Completas,* 265; *Collected Works,* 297).

31. A point that is missed for the most part by some contemporary contributions to the problem of addiction in *High Culture: Reflections on Addiction and Modernity,* ed. Anna Alexander and Mark S. Roberts (New York: SUNY Press, 2003). Bruce Wilshire, in his "Possession, Addiction, Fragmentation," included in

this collection, however, verges on seeing the spiritual dimension to addiction (see 297–307).

32. Weil, *Attente,* 130; *Waiting,* 111.

33. Margaret R. Miles, *Fullness of Life: Historical Foundations for a New Asceticism* (Philadelphia: Westminster Press, 1981); hereafter, *Fullness.*

34. Ibid., 163.

35. Cf. Scheler, "Ressentiment," 128–31.

36. See Miles, *Fullness,* 157ff.

37. "Je veux délivrer mon univers de ses fantômes et le peupler seulement des vérités de chair dont je ne peux nier la présence." Albert Camus, *Le mythe de Sisyphe: Essai sur l'absurde* (Paris: Gallimard, 1942), 139; hereafter, *Le mythe;* English: *The Myth of Sisyphus,* trans. Justin O'Brien (New York: Vintage Books, 1983), 102; hereafter, *Myth.*

38. Camus, *Le mythe,* 100–1, 109; *Myth,* 72, 79.

39. Weil, *Attente,* 130; *Waiting,* 110.

40. Scheler writes in this regard that one cannot choose between having and not having a good valued as absolute: "You can only choose whether your absolute sphere will be inhabited by God . . . or by an idol." See Scheler, *Vom Ewigen,* 263.

41. Martin Buber, "Ich und Du," 7ff.

42. Ibid., 65.

43. Ibid., 107.

44. Cf. Husserl, *Crisis.* See my *Home and Beyond,* sec. 3.

45. It should be noted, however, that it is possible not to live in the naturalistic attitude (the former sense of world as objectivistic), but still live in a secular manner. For example, just because I do not take color to be definable in terms of light waves, just because I do not regard spirit as objectively determinable according to intelligence quotients, or just because I do not regard objects in my surroundings in terms of measurable exactitude or causal laws, does not mean that I no longer live from the world. Indeed, I can presuppose the world in my work-a-day activities as the ground of meaning already there, ready-made. In short, I can still live in the world, from the world, and transform the world according to it—merely.

46. Henry, *C'est moi,* esp. 212–15, 295–317.

47. See, e.g., Foucault, *Religion and Culture,* 106ff.

48. Bergson, *Les deux sources,* esp. 222ff.

49. Émile Durkheim, *Les formes élémentaires de la vie religieuse,* 5th ed. (Paris: PUF, 1968).

50. See, e.g., Max Sorre, *Les fondements biologiques de las géographie humaine: Essai dé une écologie de l'homme* (Paris: Colin, 1943).

51. See also Max Scheler's discussion of Rudolf Eucken's "Der Wahrheitsgehalt der Religion," in *Gesammelte Werke: Frühe Schriften,* Vol. 1, ed., Maria Scheler and Manfred Frings (Bern: Francke, 1971), 343–53. See Rudolf Eucken, *Der Wahrheitsgehalt der Religion,* 2nd ed. (Leipzig: Von Veit and Co., 1905).

52. Bergson, *Les deux sources,* 101.

53. Ibid., 223.

54. Ibid., 285.

55. Scheler, *Vom Ewigen,* 260.

56. *Obras,* 119; *Collected Works,* Vol. 1, 21.9. And see: *Obras,* 145; *Collected Works,* Vol. 1, 27.9.

57. Karen Armstrong, *The Battle for God* (New York: Ballantine Books, 2001).

58. Husserl is an interesting figure in this regard. While Husserl identified the forgetfulness of the lifeworld as a betrayal of Reason through practices of scientific exactitude and quantification, his commitment to Reason would still have to be seen as a kind of secularism. His movement is clearly Modern, seeing the roots of transcendence in immanence. Put in the broader context of his life's work, this can be seen as merely a prelude to the religious. See chapter 1, above.

59. See Thomas P. Brockelman, *The Frame and the Mirror: On Collage and the Postmodern* (Evanston, Ill.: Northwestern University Press, 2001).

60. See, for example, Thomas Meyer, *Fundamentalismus: Aufstand gegen die Moderne* (Reinbek bei Hamburg: Rowohlt Taschenbuch Verlag, 1989); and Hans Küng and Jürgen Moltmann, eds., *Fundamentalism as an Ecumenical Challenge* (London: SCM Press, 1992). See also Martin E. Marty and R. Scott Appleby, eds., *Fundamentalism Observed* (Chicago: University of Chicago Press, 1994); Gabriel A. Almond et al., eds., *Strong Religion: The Rise of Fundamentalisms around the World* (Chicago: University of Chicago Press, 2003); Martin E. Marty and R. Scott Appleby, eds., *Fundamentalisms Comprehended* (Chicago: University of Chicago Press, 2004).

61. See also Erazim Kohák, *The Embers and the Stars: A Philosophical Inquiry into the Moral Sense of Nature* (Chicago: University of Chicago Press, 1984), 55ff.

62. Louis Dupré, *The Enlightenment and the Intellectual Foundations of Modern Culture* (New Haven, Conn.: Yale University Press, 2004), 229ff.

63. See also Ernst, *Sufism,* 37.

64. Weil, *Attente,* 106; *Waiting,* 89.

65. Buber, "Ich und Du," 117.

66. St. John of the Cross, *Obras Completas,* 304–5, 334; *Collected Works,* 338, 374.

67. Bernanos, *Diary,* see esp. 146–86.

68. This is one of the probable meanings of "Israel." After Jacob fought with the Angel, who revealed itself as God, Jacob was renamed *yisrael:* he who struggles with God (Genesis 33:29; 35:10).

69. Ernst, *Ecstatic Sayings,* 2.

70. Cited by Ernst, *Ecstatic Sayings,* 3; see also 88, 91.

71. Abraham J. Heschel, *The Prophets* (New York: Harper and Row, 1962), 1:190.

72. Buber, "Ich und Du," 80.

73. See Scheler, "Ressentiment," 131–35, 145–47.

74. Weil, *Attente,* 123; *Waiting,* 104, my emphasis.

75. Jacques Derrida, *L'ecriture et la différance,* 416; English: *Writing and Difference,* trans. Alan Bass (Chicago: University of Chicago Press, 1978), 284.

76. Cf. Benson, *Graven Ideologies,* 13.

EPILOGUE

1. Gibbs, *Correlations,* 257.

2. Friedrich Nietzsche, *Jenseits von Gut und Böse,* in *Sämtliche Werke,* Vol. 5, ed. Giorgio Colli and Mazzino Montinari (Berlin: de Gruyter, 1980), 79. English: *Beyond Good and Evil,* trans. Walter Kaufmann (New York: Vintage Books, 1966), 72.

3. See Robert Gibbs, "Height and Nearness: Jewish Dimensions of Radical Ethics," in *Ethics as First Philosophy,* ed. Adriaan T. Peperzak (New York: Routledge, 1995), 13–23.

4. It will be the task of another work to distinguish, on the one hand, a dissociative, delimited ethics, for which I reserve the term "ethics," from a religiously founded ethics, for which I reserve the term "moral." Whereas the sphere of religious experiencing has a single mode of evidence, a mode of givenness I termed "epiphany" (though highly articulated within this mode of givenness), the moral sphere of experience admits of two modes of evidence or givenness: "revelation" for the vertical givenness of the human person to other persons and how persons reveal vertically in the manner of exemplarity, and "manifestation" for the givenness of things and the way they "point back" vertically to human persons and Person. As vertical modes of givenness, each of them is beset in its own way by threats of moral idolatry unique to them. The expression for moral idolatry is evil.

BIBLIOGRAPHY

Abulafia, Samuel. *The Path of the Names: Writings by Abraham ben Samuel Abulafia.* Ed. David Meltzer. Trans. Bruria Finkel et al. Berkeley, Calif.: Trigram, 1976.

Al-Balkhi, Shaqiq. *Trois oeuvres inédites de mystiques musulmans.* Ed. Paul Nwyia. Bayrūt: Dār al-Mashriq, 1973.

Al-Kalabadhi, Muhammed ibn Ibrahim. *The Doctrine of the Sufis: Kitab Al-ta'arruf Li-madhhabahl Al-tasawwuf.* Cambridge: Cambridge University Press, 1977.

Al-Qushayrī. *Principles of Sufism.* Trans. B. R. von Schlegell. Berkeley, Calif.: Mizan Press, 1990.

Alexander, Anna, and Mark S. Roberts, eds. *High Culture: Reflections on Addiction and Modernity.* New York: SUNY Press, 2003.

Almond, Gabriel A., et al., eds. *Strong Religion: The Rise of Fundamentalisms around the World.* Chicago: University of Chicago Press, 2003.

Ambrose, Saint. *St. Ambrose: On the Sacraments and On the Mysteries.* Trans. T. Thompson and J. H. Srawley. London: SPCK, 1950.

Armstrong, Karen. *The Battle for God.* New York: Ballantine Books, 2001.

———. *Muhammad: A Biography of the Prophet.* New York: HarperCollins, 1993.

Athanasius. *Athanasius: The Life of Antony and the Letter to Marcellinus.* Trans. Robert C. Gregg. New York: Paulist Press, 1980.

'Aṭṭār, Farid ud-Din. *The Conference of the Birds.* Trans. Afkham Darbandi and Dick Davis. New York: Penguin Books, 1984.

Auden, W. H. *Collected Poems.* New York: Vintage Books, 1991.

Augustine, Saint. *The Confessions.* Trans. Maria Boulding, O.S.B. Hyde Park, N.Y.: New City Press, 1997.

———. *De Natura Boni.* Trans. A. Anthony Moon. Washington, D.C.: Catholic University of America Press. 1955.

———. *On the Trinity: Books 8–15.* Ed. Gareth B. Matthews. Trans. Stephen McKenna. Cambridge: Cambridge University Press, 2002.

———. *Treatises on Various Subjects.* Trans. Mary Sarah Muldowney. Washington, D.C.: Catholic University of America Press, 1965.

———. *The Works of Saint Augustine: Answer to the Pelagians.* Trans. Roland J. Teske, S.J. Ed. John E. Rotelle, O.S.A. Hyde Park, N.Y.: New City Press, 1997.

Ba'al Shem Tov. "The Mystical Epistle of the Ba'al Shem Tov." In *The Schocken Book of Jewish Mystical Testimonies,* ed. Louis Jacobs, 182–91. New York: Schocken Books, 1996.

Bachelard, Gaston. *L'air et les songes: Essai sur l'imagination du mouvement.* Paris: José Corti, 1990.

Baeck, Leo. "Judaism in the Church." In *The Pharisees and Other Essays,* trans. from the German. New York: Schocken Books, 1966.

Baer, Yitzhak. *A History of the Jews in Christian Spain,* vols. 1 and 2. Trans. Louis Schoffman. Philadelphia: Jewish Publication Society of America, 1978.

The Bahir. English and Hebrew text. Trans. Aryeh Kaplan. York Beach, Maine: Samuel Weiser, 1989.

Baillie, John. *The Idea of Revelation in Recent Thought.* New York: Columbia University Press, 1964.

Baqlî Sîrâzî, Rûzbihân. *Sharh-e Shathîyât (Commentaire sur les paradoxes des Soufis).* Ed. Henry Corbin. Paris: Librairie d'Amerique et d'Orient Adrien—Maisonneuve, 1966.

———. *Le jasmin des fidèles d'amour* (Kitâb-e 'Abbar al-'âshiqîn)/ [*The Jasmine of the Lovers*]. Trans. Henry Corbin. Paris: Verdier, 1991.

Baqli, Ruzbihan. *Unveiling of Secrets: Diary of a Sufi Master.* Trans. Carl W. Ernst. Chapel Hill, N.C.: Parvardigar Press, 1997.

Basil of Caesarea. *The Treatise De Spiritu Sancto: The Nine Homilies of the Hexaemeron and the Letters of Saint Basil the Great, Archbishop of Caesarea.* Trans. Blomfield Jackson. Oxford: James Parker and Co., 1895.

Basil, Saint. *Ascetical Works.* Trans. Sister M. Monique Wagner. Washington, D.C.: Catholic University of America Press, 1950.

———. *Letters,* Vol. 1. Trans. Sister Agnes Clare Way. Washington, D.C.: Catholic University of America Press, 1981.

———. *Letters.* Vol. 2. Trans. Sister Agnes Clare Way. New York: Fathers of the Church, 1955.

Baskin, Judith R. "Jewish Women in the Middle Ages." In *Jewish Women in Historical Perspective,* 94–114. Detroit, Mich.: Wayne State University Press, 1991.

Ben-Amos, Dan, and Jerome R. Mintz, eds. *In Praise of The Baal Shem Tov: The Earliest Collection of Legends about the Founder of Hasidism.* Bloomington: Indiana University Press, 1970.

Benedict, Saint. *The Rule of St. Benedict.* Trans. Anthony C. Meisel and M. L. del Mastro. New York: Doubleday, 1975.

Benson, Bruce Ellis. *Graven Ideologies: Nietzsche, Derrida and Marion on Modern Idolatry.* Downers Grove, Ill.: InterVarsity Press, 2002.

Bergson, Henri. *Les deux sources de la morale et de la religion.* Paris: PUF, 1984/1932.

Bernanos, Georges. *The Diary of a Country Priest.* Trans. Pamela Morris. New York: Carroll and Graf, 1965.

Bilinkoff, Jodi. *The Avila of Saint Teresa: Religious Reform in a Sixteenth-Century City.* Ithaca, N.Y.: Cornell University Press, 1989.

Boccaccini, Gabriele. *Beyond the Essene Hypothesis: the Parting of the Ways Between Qumran and Enochic Judaism.* Grand Rapids, Mich.: William B. Eerdmans, 1998.

Bogue, Robert H. *The Dawn of Christianity: The Essene Heritage.* New York: Vantage Press, 1986.

Bokser, Ben Zion. *From the World of the Cabbalah: The Philosophy of Rabbi Judah Loew of Prague*. London: Vision Press, 1957.

Borchers, Susanne. *Jüdisches Frauenleben im Mittelalter*. Frankfurt am Main: Peter Lang, 1998.

Bouyer, Louis. "Mysticism: An Essay on the History of the Word." In *Understanding Mysticism*, ed. Richard Woods, O.P., 42–55. New York: Image Books, 1980.

Brainard, F. Samuel. *Reality and Mystical Experience*. University Park: Pennsylvania State University Press, 2000.

Brockelman, Thomas P. *The Frame and the Mirror: On Collage and the Postmodern*. Evanston, Ill.: Northwestern University Press, 2001.

Buber, Martin. "Ich und Du." In *Das dialogische Prinzip*. Heidelberg: Lambert Schneider, 1965.

———. *Jewish Mysticism and the Legends of Baalshem*. Trans. Lucy Cohen. London: M. Dent and Sons, 1931.

———. *The Origin and Meaning of Hasidism*. Ed. and trans. Maurice Friedman. New York: Horizon Press, 1960.

———. *Tales of Rabbi Nachman*. Trans. Maurice Friedman. New York: Horizon Press, 1956.

———. *Tales of the Hasidim*. Trans. Olga Marx. New York: Schocken Books, 1991.

———. *Ten Rungs: Hasidic Sayings*. Trans. Olga Marx. New York: Schocken Books, 1968.

Camus, Albert. *Le mythe de Sisyphe: Essai sur l'absurde*. Paris: Gallimard, 1942.

———. *The Myth of Sisyphus*. Trans. Justin O'Brien. New York: Vintage Books, 1983.

Canguilhem, Georges. *Le normal et le pathologique*. Paris: PUF, 1966.

Caputo, John D. *The Mystical Element in Heidegger's Thought*. Reprint. New York: Fordham University Press, 1985.

———. *The Prayers and Tears of Jacques Derrida: Religion Without Religion*. Bloomington: Indiana University Press, 1997.

Caro, Joseph ben Ephraim. *Code of Hebrew Law [Shulchan 'Aruk Choshen HaMishpat]*. Trans. Chaim N. Denburg. Montreal: Jurisprudence Press, 1954.

Cassian, John. *Conferences*. Trans. Colm Luibheid. New York: Paulist Press, 1985.

———. *The Institutes*. Trans. Boniface Ramsey. New York: Newman Press, 2000.

Certeau, Michel de. *La Fable Mystique: XVIe–XVIIe Siècle*. Paris: Gallimard, 1982.

———. *The Mystic Fable*. Vol. 1. Trans. Michael B. Smith. Chicago: University of Chicago Press, 1992.

Chagigah. Talmud Bavli. Ed. Hersh Goldwurm. The Schottenstein Edition. Brooklyn, N.Y.: Mesorah Publications, 1990.

Clissold, Stephen. *St. Teresa of Avila*. New York: Seabury Press, 1982.

Cohn, Haim. *The Trial and Death of Jesus*. New York: KTAV Publishing House, 1967.

Corbin, Henry. *En Islam iranien: Aspects spirituals et philosophiques.* Vol. 3. Paris: Gallimard, 1972.

———. *The Man of Light in Iranian Sufism.* Trans. Nancy Pearson. New Lebanon, N.Y.: Omega Publications, 1994.

Cordovero, Moses. *The Palm Tree of Deborah.* Trans. Louis Jacobs. New York: Hermon Press, 1974.

Cross, Frank Moore. *The Ancient Library of Qumran and Modern Biblical Studies.* New York: Anchor Books, 1961.

Daly, Lowrie J. *Benedictine Monasticism: Its Formation and Development Through the 12th Century.* New York: Sheed and Ward, 1965.

Daniélou, Jean. *Théologie du judéo-christianisme.* Tournai, Belgium: Desclée, 1958.

———. *The Theology of Jewish Christianity: A History of Early Christian Doctrine Before the Council of Nicaea.* Vol. 1. Trans. John A. Baker. Philadelphia: Westminster Press, 1964.

Dante, Alighieri. *The Divine Comedy: I. Inferno.* Trans. John D. Sinclair. New York: Oxford University Press, 1961.

———. *The Divine Comedy: II. Purgatorio.* Trans. John D. Sinclair. New York: Oxford University Press, 1961.

Davis, Caroline Franks. *The Evidential Force of Religious Experience.* Oxford: Oxford University Press, 1989.

The Dead Sea Scriptures, 3rd ed. Ed. Theodor H. Gaster. Garden City, N.Y.: Anchor Books, 1976.

Deikman, Arthur. *The Observing Self: Mysticism and Psychotherapy.* Boston, Mass.: Beacon Press, 1982.

Depraz, Natalie. *Le corps glorieux: phénoménologie pratique de la Philocalie des Pères du désert et des Pères de l'Eglise.* Forthcoming, Bibliothèque philosophique de Louvain.

Derrida, Jacques. *De la grammatologie.* Paris: Les Éditions de Minuit, 1967.

———. *L'écriture et la difference.* Paris. Éditions du Seuil, 1967.

———. "Foi et savoir: Les deux sources de la 'religion' aux limites de la simple raison." In *La religion,* ed. Jacques Derrida and Gianni Vattimo, 9–86. Paris: Seuil, 1996.

———. "On the Gift: A Discussion between Jacques Derrida and Jean-Luc Marion." In *God, The Gift, and Postmodernism,* ed. John D. Caputo and Michael J. Scanlon, 54–78. Bloomington: Indiana University Press, 1999.

———. *La voix et le phénomène.* Paris: PUF, 1967.

———. *Writing and Difference.* Trans. Alan Bass. Chicago: University of Chicago Press, 1978.

Deutsch, Nathaniel. *The Gnostic Imagination: Gnosticism, Mandaeism, and Merkabah Mysticism.* Brill: Leiden, 1995.

Dicken, E. W. Trueman. *The Crucible of Love: A Study of the Mysticism of St. Teresa of Jesus and St. John of the Cross.* New York: Sheed and Ward, 1963.

Dillard, Annie. *For the Time Being.* New York: Vintage Books, 1999.

Dobh Baer of Lubavitch. *Tract on Ecstasy.* Trans. Louis Jacobs. London, Vallentine, Mitchell, 1963.

The Documents of Vatican II. Ed. Austin P. Flannery, O.P. New York: Pillar Books, 1975.

Dogen. *Moon in a Dewdrop: Writings of Zen Master Dogen.* Ed. Kazuaki Tanahashi. New York: North Point Press, 1998.

Dov Baer ben Samuel, of Linits. *In Praise of the Baal Shem Tov [Shivhei ha-Besht]: The Earliest Collection of Legends about the Founder of Hasidism,* ed. and trans. Dan Ben-Amos and Jerome R. Mintz. Bloomington: Indiana University Press, 1970.

Dov Baer Schneersohn. *Kuntres ha-hitpa'alut.* Warsaw, Poland, 1876.

Dresner, Samuel H. *The Zaddik: The Doctrine of the Zaddik According to the Writings of Rabbi Yaakov Yosef of Polnoy.* New York: Schocken Books, 1974.

Drouilly, Jean. *La Pensée Politique et Religieuse de F. M. Dostoievski.* Paris: Librairie des Cinq Continents, 1971.

Duméry, Henry. *Phenomenology and Religion: Structures of the Christian Institution.* Berkeley: University of California Press, 1975.

Dupré, Louis. *The Enlightenment and the Intellectual Foundations of Modern Culture.* New Haven, Conn.: Yale University Press, 2004.

Dupuis, Jacques. *Toward a Christian Theology of Religious Pluralism.* Maryknoll, N.Y.: Orbis Books, 2002.

Durkheim, Émile. *Les formes élémentaires de la vie religieuse,* 5th ed. Paris: PUF, 1968.

Eckhart, Meister. *Meister Eckhart: The Essential Sermons, Commentaries, Treatises, and Defense.* Trans. Edmund Colledge and Bernard McGinn. New York: Paulist Press, 1981.

Epstein, Perle. *The Kabbalah: The Way of the Jewish Mystic.* Boston: Shambhala, 2001.

Ernst, Carl W. *Ruzbihan Baqlī: Mysticism and the Rhetoric of Sainthood in Persian Sufism.* Richmond Surrey, GB: Curzon Press, 1996.

———. *The Shambhala Guide to Sufism.* Boston: Shambhala, 1997.

———. "Stages of Love in Early Persian Sufism from Rābia to Rūzbihān." In *Classical Persian Sufism: From Its Origins to Rumi,* ed. Leonard Lewisohn. New York: Khaniqahi Nimatullahi Publications, 1993.

———. "The Symbolism of Birds and Flight in the Writings of Ruzbihan Baqlī." In *The Heritage of Sufism.* Vol. 2, *The Legacy of Medieval Persian Sufism (1150–1500),* ed. Leonard Lewisohn. Oxford: Oneworld, 1999.

———. *Words of Ecstasy in Sufism.* New York: SUNY Press, 1985.

Eucken, Rudolf. *Der Wahrheitsgehalt der Religion,* 2nd ed. Leipzig: Von Veit and Co., 1905.

Ewing, Upton Clary. *The Prophet of the Dead Sea Scrolls.* New York: Philosophical Library, 1963.

Fine, Lawrence. *Essential Papers on Kabbalah*. New York: New York University Press, 1995.

Finkelstein, Louis. *The Jews*. New York: Schocken Books, 1971.

———. *The Pharisees: The Sociological Background of Their Faith*. Philadelphia: Jewish Publication Society of America, 1946.

Foucault, Michel. *Religion and Culture*. Ed. Jeremy R. Carrette. New York: Routledge, 1999.

Freud, Sigmund. *Three Case Histories*. Ed. Philip Rieff. New York: Collier Books, 1963.

Gendlin, Eugene. *Experiencing and the Creation of Meaning: A Philosophical and Psychological Approach to the Subjective*. Evanston, Ill.: Northwestern University Press, 1997.

Gibbs, Robert. *Correlations in Rosenzweig and Levinas*. Princeton, N.J.: Princeton University Press, 1992.

———. "Height and Nearness: Jewish Dimensions of Radical Ethics." In *Ethics as First Philosophy*, ed. Adriaan T. Peperzak, 13–23. New York: Routledge, 1995.

———. *Why Ethics? Signs of Responsibilities*. Princeton, N.J.: Princeton University Press, 2000.

Ginsburg, Christian D. *The Essenes: Their History and Doctrines*. New York: Macmillan, 1956.

The Gnostic Scriptures: A New Translation with Annotations and Introductions. Trans. Bentley Layton. New York: Doubleday, 1995.

Gordon, Hirsch L. *The Maggid of Caro: The Mystic Life of the Eminent Codifier Joseph Caro as Revealed in His Secret Diary*. New York: Shoulson Press, 1949.

Green, Deirdre. *The Gold in the Crucible*. Longmead, UK: Element Books, 1989.

Gregory of Nazianzus, Saint. *On God and Christ: The Five Theological Orations and Two Letters to Cledonius*. Trans. Frederick Williams and Lionel Wickham. Crestwood, N.Y.: St. Vladimir's Seminary Press, 2002.

Gregory of Nyssa. *A Select Library of Nicene and Post-Nicene Fathers of the Christian Church. Second Series. Gregory of Nyssa*. Vol. 5. Ed. and Trans. Philip Schaff and Henry Wace. Grand Rapids, Mich.: Wm. B. Eerdmans, 1954.

Gründler, Otto. *Elemente zu einer Religionsphilosophie auf phänomenologischer Grundlage*. Munich: Kösel and Pustet, 1922.

Gurwitsch, Aron. *Das Bewußtseinsfeld*. Berlin: de Gruyter, 1974.

Heidegger, Martin. *Beiträge zur Philosophie (Vom Ereignis)*. Gesamt Ausgabe. Frankfurt am Main: Klostermann, 1989.

———. "Das Ding." In *Vorträge und Aufsätze*. Tübingen: Neske, 1954.

———. *Gelassenheit*. Tübingen: Neske, 1982.

———. *Holzwege*. Frankfurt am Main: Klostermann, 1980.

———. *Identität und Differenz*. Tübingen: Neske, 1982.

———. *On Time and Being*. Trans. Joan Stambaugh. New York: Harper and Row, 1972.

————. *Phänomenologie des religiösen Lebens*. Gesamtausgabe. II. Abteilung, vol. 60. Frankfurt am Main: Klostermann, 1995.

————. *Phänomenologie und Theologie*. Frankfurt am Main: Klostermann. 1970.

————. *Sein und Zeit*. Tübingen: Niemeyer, 1979.

————. *Zur Sache des Denkens*. Tübingen, Niemeyer, 1976.

Heiler, Friedrich. *Erscheinungsformen und Wesen der Religion*. Stuttgart: W. Kohlhammer, 1961.

Held, Klaus. "Fundamental Moods and Heidegger's Critique of Culture." Trans. Anthony J. Steinbock. In *Reading Heidegger: Commemorations,* ed. John Sallis, 286–303. Bloomington: Indiana University Press, 1993.

Henry, Michel. *C'est moi la vérité: Pour une philosophie du christianisme*. Paris: Seuil, 1996.

————. *L'essence de la manifestation,* 2nd ed. Paris: PUF, 1990.

————. *Philosophy and Phenomenology of the Body*. Trans. Girard Etzkorn. The Hague: Martinus Nijhoff, 1975.

Hering, Jean. *Phénoménologie et philosophie religieuse*. Paris, Felix Alcan, 1926.

Heschel, Abraham Joshua. *The Circle of the Baal Shem Tov: Studies in Hasidism*. Ed. Samuel H. Dresner. Chicago: University of Chicago Press, 1985.

————. "The Mystical Element in Judaism." In *The Jews: Their History, Culture, and Religion,* ed. Louis Finkelstein, 602–623. Philadelphia: Jewish Publication Society of America, 1949.

————. *The Prophets,* Vol. 1. New York: Harper and Row, 1962.

Hollywood, Amy. *Sensible Ecstasy: Mysticism, Sexual Difference, and the Demands of History*. Chicago: University of Chicago Press, 2001.

Hopkins, Jasper. *Nicholas of Cusa's Dialectical Mysticism: Text, Translation and Interpretive Study of De Visione Dei*. Minneapolis: A. U. Banning Press, 1988.

Horodezky, S. A. *Leaders of Hassidism*. Trans. Maria Horodezky-Magasanik. London: "Hasefer" Agency for Literature, 1928.

Horkheimer, Max, and Theodor W. Adorno. *Dialektik der Aufklärung*. Frankfurt am Main: Fischer, 1988.

Hunt, Harry T. *Lives in Spirit: Precursors and Dilemmas of a Secular Western Mysticism*. Albany: SUNY Press, 2003.

Husserl, Edmund. *Analyses Concerning Passive and Active Synthesis: Lectures on Transcendental Logic*. Trans. Anthony J. Steinbock. Boston: Kluwer Academic Publishers, 2001.

————. *Die Bernauer Manuskripte über das Zeitbewußtsein (1917/18)*. Ed. Rudolf Bernet and Dieter Lohmar. Husserliana 33. Dordrecht: Kluwer Academic Publishers, 2001.

————. *The Crisis of European Sciences and Transcendental Phenomenology: An Introduction to Phenomenological Philosophy*. Trans. David Carr. Evanston, Ill.: Northwestern University Press, 1970.

————. *Erste Philosophie (1923/24)*. Ed. R. Boehm. Husserliana 7. The Hague: Martinus Nijhoff, 1956.

————. *Die Idee der Phänomenologie. Fünf Vorlesungen,* 2nd ed. Ed. Walter Biemel. Husserliana 2. The Hague: Martinus Nijhoff, 1950.

————. *Ideen zu einer reinen Phänomenologie und phänomenologische Philosophie. Zweites Buch.* Ed. Marly Biemel. The Hague: Martinus Nijhoff, 1952.

————. *Die Krisis der europäschen Wissenschaften und die transzendentale Phänomenologie: Einleitung in die phänomenologische Philosophie.* Ed. Walter Biemel. Husserliana 6. The Hague: Martinus Nijhoff, 1954.

————. *Logische Untersuchungen.* Vol. II: *Elemente einer hänomenologischen Aufklärung der Erkenntnis, Part II.* Tübingen: Niemeyer, 1968.

————. Ms. E III 11, 1934, 3b: "Gespräche mit E. H." 1931–1938, Schwester Edelgundis 1934.

————. *Zur Phänomenologie der Intersubjektivität. Texte aus dem Nachlaß.* Dritter Teil: 1929–1935. Ed. Iso Kern. Husserliana 15. The Hague: Martinus Nijhoff, 1973.

Ibn Daud, Abraham. *A Critical Edition with a Translation and Notes of the Book of Tradition (Sefer ha-Qabbalah).* Trans. Gerson D. Cohen. London: Routledge and K. Paul, 1969.

Idel, Moshe. "Enoch Is Metatron," *Immanuel* 24/25 (1990): 220–40.

————. *Hasidism: Between Ecstasy and Magic.* Albany: SUNY Press, 1995.

————. *Kabbalah: New Perspectives.* New Haven, Conn.: Yale University Press, 1988.

————. *Language, Torah, and Hermeneutics in Abraham Abulafia.* Albany: SUNY Press, 1988.

————. *Messianic Mystics.* New Haven, Conn.: Yale University Press, 1998.

————. *The Mystical Experience in Abraham Abulafia.* Trans. Jonathan Chipman. New York: SUNY Press, 1988.

————. "Preface." In *Jewish Mystical Autobiographies,* trans. and ed. Morris M. Faierstein. New York: Paulist Press, 1999.

————. *Studies in Ecstatic Kabbalah.* New York: SUNY Press, 1988.

Idel, Moshe, and Bernard McGinn, eds. *Mystical Union in Judaism, Christianity, and Islam: An Ecumenical Dialogue.* New York: Continuum, 1999.

Ignatius of Loyola. *The Spiritual Exercises and Selected Works.* Ed. and trans. George E. Ganss, S.J., et al. Mahwah, N.J.: Paulist Press, 1991.

Jacobs, Louis. *The Schocken Book of Jewish Mystical Testimonies.* New York: Schocken Books, 1996.

James, William. *Essays in Religion and Morality.* Cambridge, Mass.: Harvard University Press, 1982.

————. *The Varieties of Religious Experience.* New York: Collier Books, 1961.

Janicaud, Dominique. *Une généalogie du spiritualisme française: Aux sources du Bergsonisme: Ravaisson et la métaphysique.* La Haye: M. Nijhoff, 1969.

————. *Le tournant théologique de la phénoménologie française.* Combas: Éditions de l'Éclat, 1991.

Jerome, Saint. *Select Letters of St. Jerome.* Trans. F. A. Wright. Cambridge, Mass.: Harvard University Press, 1980.

Jewish Mystical Autobiographies. Ed. and trans. Morris M. Faierstein. New York: Paulist Press, 1999.

John of the Cross, Saint. *The Collected Works of Saint John of the Cross.* Revised edition. Trans. Kieran Kavanaugh, O.C.D. and Otilio Rodriguez, O.C.D. Washington, D.C.: ICS Publications, 1991.

Jonas, Hans. *Gnosis und Spätantiker Geist.* Göttingen: Vandenhoeck and Ruprecht, 1993.

Josephus, Flavius. *The Complete Works of Josephus.* Trans. William Whiston. Grand Rapids, Mich.: Kregel Publications, 1999.

Juan de la Cruz, San. *Obras Completas.* Ed. *Licinio Ruano de la Iglesia.* Madrid: Biblioteca de Autores Cristianos, 1982.

Kafka, Franz. "Vor dem Gesetzt." In *Franz Kafka: Erzählungen,* ed. Martin Pfeifer. Stuttgart: Ernst Klett, 1986.

Kearney, Richard. *The God Who May Be: The Hermeneutics of Religion.* Bloomington: Indiana University Press, 2001.

―――. *Traversing the Imaginary.* Ed. Peter Gratton and John Panteleimon. Evanston, Ill.: Northwestern University Press, forthcoming.

Kierkegaard, Søren. *Fear and Trembling.* Ed. and trans. Howard V. Hong and Edna H. Hong. Princeton, N.J.: Princeton University Press, 1983.

―――. *Works of Love.* Ed. and trans. Howard V. Hong and Edna H. Hong. Princeton, N.J.: Princeton University Press, 1998.

Kohák, Erazim. *The Embers and the Stars: A Philosophical Inquiry into the Moral Sense of Nature.* Chicago: University of Chicago Press, 1984.

Kovacs, George. *The Question of God in Heidegger's Phenomenology.* Evanston, Ill.: Northwestern University Press, 1990.

Küng, Hans, and Jürgen Moltmann, eds. *Fundamentalism as an Ecumenical Challenge.* London: SCM Press, 1992.

Laski, Marghanita. *Ecstasy: A Study of Some Secular and Religious Experiences.* New York: Greenwood Press, 1968.

Lefort, Claude. *Élements d'une critique de la bureaucratie.* Paris: Gallimard, 1979.

―――. *Le formes de l'histoire.* Paris: Gallimard, 1978.

―――. *L'invention démocratique.* Paris: Fayard, 1981.

―――. *Le travail de l'oeuvre Machiavel.* Paris: Gallimard, 1986.

Lenowitz, Harris. *The Jewish Messiahs: From the Galilee to Crown Heights.* New York: Oxford University Press, 1998.

Levinas, Emmanuel. *De Dieu qui vient à l'idée.* Paris: Vrin, 1982.

―――. *Entre Nous: On Thinking-of-the-Other.* Trans. Michael B. Smith and Barbara Harshav. New York: Columbia University Press, 1998.

―――. "God and Philosophy." In *Collected Philosophical Papers,* trans. Alphonso Lingis. The Hague: Martinus Nijhoff, 1987.

———. *Of God Who Comes to Mind*. Trans. Bettina Bergo. Stanford, Calif.: Stanford University Press, 1998.

———. *Totalité et infini*. The Hague: Martinus Nijhoff, 1961.

———. *Totality and Infinity*. Trans. Alphonso Lingis. Pittsburgh, Pa.: Duquesne University Press, 1969.

Lichtmann, Maria R. *The Contemplative Poetry of Gerard Manley Hopkins*. Princeton, N.J.: Princeton University Press. 1989.

Lincoln, Victoria. *Teresa: A Woman*. Eds. Elias Rivers and Antonio T. de Nicolás. Albany: SUNY Press, 1984.

Lindhagen, Curt. *The Servant Motif in the Old Testament: A Preliminary Study to the 'Ebed-Yahweh Problem' in Deutero-Isaiah*. Uppsala: Lundequistaska Bokhandeln, 1950.

Lossky, Vladimir. *In the Image and Likeness of God*, ed. John H. Erickson and Thomas E. Bird. Crestwook, N.Y.: St. Vladimir's Seminary Press, 1985.

———. *The Mystical Theology of the Eastern Church*. Translated by members of the Fellowship of St. Alban and St. Sergius. Crestwood, N.Y.: St. Vladimir's Seminary Press, 1976.

Luther, Arthur R. "The Articulated Unity of Being in Scheler's Phenomenology." In *Max Scheler (1874–1928) Centennial Essays*, ed. Manfred S. Frings. The Hague: Martinus Nijhoff, 1974.

———. "Original Emergence in Heidegger and Nishida." *Philosophy Today* 26, no. 4/4 (1982): 345–56.

———. *Persons in Love: A Study of Max Scheler's Wesen und Formen der Sympathie*. The Hague: Martinus Nijhoff, 1972.

Marion, Jean-Luc. *Dieu sans l'être*. Paris: PUF, 1991.

———. *Étant donné: Essai d'une phénoménologie de la donation*. Paris: PUF, 1997.

———. *L'idole et la distance*. Paris: Bernard Grasset, 1977.

———. *Réduction et donation: Recherches sur Husserl, Heidegger et la phénoménologie*. Paris: PUF, 1989.

———. *De surcroît: Études sur les phénomènes saturés*. Paris: PUF, 2001.

Marty, Martin E., and R. Scott Appleby, eds. *Fundamentalisms Comprehended*. Chicago: University of Chicago Press, 2004.

———. *Fundamentalism Observed*. Chicago: University of Chicago Press, 1994.

Massignon, Louis. *La passion de Husayn ibn Mansur Hallaj, martyr mystique de l'Islam executé à Baghdad le 26 mars 922. Étude d'histoire religieuse*, 2nd ed. 4 Vols. Paris: Gallimard, 1975. Second edition.

McGinn, Bernard. *The Foundations of Mysticism*. Vol. 1 of *The Presence of God: A History of Western Christian Mysticism*. New York: Crossroad, 1999.

———. *The Growth of Mysticism*. Vol. 2 of *The Presence of God: A History of Western Christian Mysticism*. New York: Crossroad, 1999.

Medwick, Cathleen. *Teresa of Avila: The Progress of a Soul*. New York: Alfred A. Knopf, 2000.

Meisel, Anthony C., and M. L. del Mastro. "Introduction." In *The Rule of St. Benedict,* trans. Anthony C. Meisel and M. L. del Mastro. New York: Image Books, 1975.

Merleau-Ponty, Maurice. *Phénoménologie de la perception.* Paris: Gallimard, 1945.

———. *Le visible et l'invisible.* Paris: Gallimard, 1964.

———. *The Visible and the Invisible.* Trans. Alphonso Lingis. Evanston, Ill.: Northwestern University Press, 1968.

Meyer, Thomas. *Fundamentalismus: Aufstand gegen die Moderne.* Reinbek bei Hamburg: Rowohlt Taschenbuch Verlag, 1989.

Milbank, John, Catherine Pickstock, and Graham Ward, eds. *Radical Orthodoxy: A New Theology.* New York: Routledge, 1999.

Miles, Margaret R. *Fullness of Life: Historical Foundations for a New Asceticism.* Philadelphia: Westminster Press, 1981.

Minkowski, Eugène. *Lived Time: Phenomenological and Psychopathological Studies.* Trans. Nancy Metzel. Evanston, Ill.: Northwestern University Press, 1970.

Moltmann, Jürgen. *The Crucified God: The Cross of Christ as the Foundation and Criticism of Christian Theology.* New York: Harper and Row, 1974.

Moffatt, James. *The Theology of the Gospels.* New York: Scribner, 1920.

Müller, Ludolf. *Das Religionsphilosophische System Vladimir Solovjevs.* Berlin: Evangelische Verlagsanstalt, 1956.

Murata, Sachiko, and William C. Chittick. *The Vision of Islam.* St. Paul, Minn.: Paragon House, 1994.

Myer, Isaac. *Qabbalah: The Philosophical Writings of Solomon Ben Yehudah Ibn Gebirol or Avicebron, and Their Connection with the Hebrew Qabbalah and Sepher Ha-Zohar.* New York: Ktav Publishing House, 1970.

Mykoff, Moshe. *The Empty Chair: Finding Hope and Joy: Timeless Wisdom From a Hasidic Master, Rebbe Nachman of Breslov.* Woodstock, Vt.: Jewish Lights Publishing, 1994.

Nahman of Bratslav. *Rabbi Nachman's Stories: The Stories of Rabbi Nachman of Breslov.* Trans. Aryeh Kaplan. Brooklyn, N.Y.: Breslov Research Institute, 1983.

Nasr, Seyyed Hossein, ed. *Islamic Spirituality: Manifestations.* New York: Crossroad, 1991.

———. *Knowledge and the Sacred.* Albany: SUNY Press, 1989.

———. "The Rise and Development of Persian Sufism." In *The Heritage of Sufism,* Vol. 1, ed. Leonard Lewisohn. Oxford: Oneworld Press, 1999.

———. *'Sadr al-Dīn Shīrāzī [Mullā Sadrā] and his Transcendental Theosophy.* Tehran: Imperial Iranian Academy of Philosophy, 1978.

———. *Sufi Essays.* New York: Schocken Books, 1977.

Nelson, Christopher. "The Last Appropriation of Christ: Kierkegaard, Pseudonymity, and the Problem of Godman." Unpublished manuscript.

Newman, Louis I. *Hasidic Anthology: Tales and Teachings of the Hasidism.* Trans. Louis I. Newman and Samuel Spitz. New York: Schocken Books, 1987.

Nicholson, Reynold A. *The Mystics of Islam*. New York: Penguin Books, 1989/1914.

———. *Studies in Islamic Mysticism*. Cambridge: Cambridge University Press, 1978.

Nietzsche, Friedrich. *Beyond Good and Evil*. Trans. Walter Kaufmann. New York: Vintage Books, 1966.

———. *Jenseits von Gut und Böse*. In Sämtliche Werke, Vol. 5, ed. Giorgio Colli and Mazzino Montinari. Berlin: de Gruyter, 1980.

———. *Zur Genealogie der Moral*. In Sämtliche Werke, Vol. 5, ed. Giorgio Colli and Mazzino Montinari. Berlin: de Gruyter, 1980.

North, Christopher R. *The Suffering Servant in Deutero-Isaiah: An Historical and Critical Study*. Oxford: Oxford University Press, 1956.

Nurbakhsh, Javad. "The Key Features of Sufism in the Early Islamic Period." In *The Heritage of Sufism*, Vol. 1, ed. Leonard Lewisohn. Oxford: Oneworld Press, 1999.

Origen. *Prayer: Exhortation to Martyrdom*. Trans. John J. O'Meara. New York: Newman Press, 1954.

Otto, Rudolf. *The Idea of the Holy*. Trans. John W. Harvey. New York: Oxford University Press, 1958.

———. *Mysticism East and West: A Comparative Analysis of the Nature of Mysticism*. Trans. Bertha L. Bracey and Richenda C. Payne. New York: Macmillan, 1970.

———. *Naturalism and Religion*. Trans. J. Arthur Thomson and Margaret R. Thomson. Ed. Rev. W. D. Morrison. New York: G. P. Putnam's Sons, 1913.

Ouaknin, Marc-Alain. *Tsimtsoum: Introduction à la méditation hébraïque*. Paris: Albin Michel, 1992.

Pachomius, Saint. *The Rule or the Asketikon*. Willits, Calif.: Eastern Orthodox Books, 1976.

Pannenberg, Wolfhart. *Jesus-God and Man*. Trans. Lewis L. Wilkins and Duane A. Priebe, 2nd ed. Philadelphia: Westminster Press, 1977.

Peers, E. Allison. *Handbook to the Life and Times of St. Teresa and St. John of the Cross*. Westminster, Md.: Newman Press, 1954.

Pelagius. *Pelagius: Life and Letters*. Ed. B. R. Rees. Woodbridge, UK: The Boydell Press, 1991.

Philo of Alexandria. "Every Good Man Is Free." Trans. F. H. Colson and G. H. Whitaker. Vol. 9, Loeb Edition. Cambridge, Mass.: Harvard University Press, 1954.

———. "Hypothetica." Trans. F. H. Colson and G. H. Whitaker. Vol. 9, Loeb Edition. Cambridge, Mass.: Harvard University Press, 1954.

The Philokalia. Compiled by St. Nikodimos of the Holy Mountain and St. Makarios of Corinth. Ed. G. E. H. Palmer et al. Vol. 4. London: Farber and Farber, 1995.

Pike, Nelson. *Mystic Union: An Essay in the Phenomenology of Mysticism*. Ithaca, N.Y.: Cornell University Press, 1992.

The Pilgram's Tale. Ed. Aleksei Pentkovsky. Trans. T. Allan Smith. New York: Paulist Press, 1999.

Pliny. *Natural History*. Trans. H. Rackham. Loeb Edition. Vol. II. Cambridge, Mass.: Harvard University Press, 1989.

Popul Vol. Trans. Dennis Tedlock. New York: Simon and Schuster, 1985.

Poulan, R. P. Augustin. *The Graces of Interior Prayer: A Treatise on Mystical Theology*. Trans. Leonora L. Yorke Smith. Corrected to accord with the 10th French Edition. St. Louis: Herder, 1950.

Pseudo-Dionysius, the Areopagite. *Pseudo-Dionysius: The Complete Works*. Trans. Colm Luibheid. New York: Paulist Press, 1987.

Quran: The Meaning of The Holy Quran. Bi-Lingual edition. Trans. 'Abullah Yusuf 'Ali. Beltsville, Md.: Amana Publications, 1420 AH/1999.

Rabinowicz, Harry M. *World of Hasidism*. Hartford: Hartmore House, 1970.

Rahner, Hugo. "Das mystische Tau." *Zeitschrift für katholosche Theologie* 75 (1953): 385–410.

Rahner, Karl. *Foundations of Christian Faith: An Introduction to the Idea of Christianity*. Trans. William V. Dych. New York: Seabury Press, 1978.

———. *Theological Investigations*. Trans. Cornelius Ernst. Baltimore, Md.: Helicon Press, 1979.

Ramge, Sebastian. *An Introduction to the Writings of Saint Teresa*. Chicago: Henry Regnery, 1963.

Reinach, Adolf. *Sämtliche Werke: Textkritische Ausgabe in 2 Bänden*, Vols. 1 and 2. Ed. Karl Schuhmann und Barry Smith. München: Philosophia, 1989.

Ricoeur, Paul. *The Symbolism of Evil*. Trans. Emerson Buchanan. Boston: Beacon Press, 1986.

———. *Time and Narrative*. Vols. 1, 2, 3. Trans. David Pellauer and Kathleen McLaughlin. Chicago: University of Chicago Press, 1990.

Robinson, Henry Wheeler. *The Cross of the Servant: A Study in Deutero-Isaiah, The Cross in the Old Testament*. Philadelphia Westminster Press, 1956.

Robinson, Ira. *Moses Cordovero's Introduction to Kabbalah: An Annotated Translation of His Or Ne'erav*. New York: Michael Scharf Publication Trust, 1994.

Rohrbach, Peter-Thomas, O.C.D. *Journey to Carith: The Story of the Carmelite Order*. New York: Doubleday, 1966.

Rosman, Murray Jay. *Founder of Hasidism: A Quest for the Historical Ba'al Shem Tov*. Berkeley: University of California Press, 1996.

Safran, Bezalel, ed. *Hasidism: Continuity or Innovation?* Cambridge, Mass.: Harvard University Center for Jewish Studies, 1988.

Saudreau, Auguste. *The Degrees of the Spiritual Life: A Method of Directing Souls According to Their Progress in Virtue*. Trans. Dom Bede Camm, O.S.B. London: Burns Oates and Washbourne, 1926.

———. *The Mystical State, Its Nature and Phases*, Trans. D.M.B. London: Burns Oates and Washbourne, 1924.

The Sayings of the Desert Fathers. Trans. Benedicta Ward. London: A. R. Mowbray, 1975.

Schapp, Wilhelm. *Beiträge zur Phänomenologie der Wahrnehmung*. Wiesbaden: B. Heymann, 1976/1910.

Schechter, Solomon. "Safed in the Sixteenth Century." *Studies in Judaism*, Second Series, 202–306. Piscataway, N.J.: Gorgias Press, 2003.

Scheler, Max. "Die Demut." In *Vom Umsturz der Werte*. Gesammelte Werke, Vol. 3, 17–26, ed. Maria Scheler. Bern: Francke, 1955.

———. *Formalism in Ethics and Non-Formal Ethics of Value*. Trans. Manfred S. Frings and Roger L. Funk. Evanston, Ill.: Northwestern University Press, 1973.

———. *Formalismus in der Ethik und die Materiale Wertethik*. Gesammelte Werke, Vol. 2. Ed. Maria Scheler. Bern: Francke, 1966.

———. "Kultur und Religion." (Eine Besprechung zu Rudolf Eucken's 'Der Wahrheitsgehalt der Religion'). In *Gesammelte Werke: Frühe Schriften*, Vol. 1, 343–53, ed. Maria Scheler and Manfred Frings. Bern: Francke, 1971.

———. "Ordo Amoris." In *Schriften aus dem Nachlaß*, Vol. 1. Gesammelte Werke, Vol. 10, 345–76, ed. Maria Scheler. Bern: Francke, 1957.

———. "Das Ressentiment im Aufbau der Moralen." In *Vom Umsturz der Werte*. Gesammelte Werke, Vol. 3, 33–147, ed. Maria Scheler. Bern: Francke, 1955.

———. *Schriften aus dem Nachlass*. Vol. 4 of *Philosophie und Geschicte*. Ed. Manfred S. Frings. Bonn: Bouvier, 1990.

———. "Die Stellung des Menschung im Kosmos." Gesammelte Werke, Vol. 9. Ed. Manfred S. Frings. München: Francke Verlag, 1976.

———. *Vom Ewigen im Menschen*. Gesammelte Werke, Vol. 5. Ed. Maria Scheler. Bern: Francke, 1954.

———. *Wesen und Formen der Sympathie*. Gesammelte Werke, Vol. 7. Ed. Manfred Frings. Bern: Francke, 1973.

Schillebeeckx, Edward. *Christ: The Experience of Jesus as Lord*. Trans. John Bowden. New York: Seabury Press, 1980.

———. *Jesus: An Experiment in Christology*. Trans. Hubert Hoskins. New York: Seabury Press, 1979.

Schimmel, Annemarie. *Mystical Dimensions of Islam*. Chapel Hill: University of North Carolina Press, 1975.

———. *Deciphering the Signs of God: A Phenomenological Approach to Islam*. Albany: SUNY Press, 1994.

Schochet, Rabbi Jacob Immanuel. "Mystical Concepts in Chassidism." In Rabbi Schneur Zalman of Liadi, *Likutei Amarim (Tanya)*, 872–956. Bi-Lingual edition. New York: Kehot Publication Society, 1984.

Scholem, Gershom Gerhard. *Les grands courants de la mystique Juive: La Merkaba, la Gnose, la Kabbale, le Zohar, le Sabbatianisme, le Hassidisme*, Trans. M. M. Davy. Paris: Payot, 1950.

———. *Kabbalah*. New York: Meridian, 1978.

———. *Major Trends in Jewish Mysticism*. New York: Knopf Publishing Group, 1995.

———. *On the Mystical Shape of the Godhead: Basic Concepts in the Kabbalah*. New York: Schocken Books, 1991.

Schrader, Paul. "Interview with Paul Schrader." In *Robert Bresson*, ed. James Quandt. Toronto: Toronto Center for Contemporary Art, 1998.

Schreber, Daniel Paul. *Memoirs of My Nervous Illness*. Trans. Ida Macalpine et al. New York: New York Review of Books, 2000.

Schürmann, Reiner. *Meister Eckhart, Mystic and Philosopher: Translations with Commentary*. Bloomington: Indiana University Press, 1977.

Sells, Michael A., ed. and trans. *Early Islamic Mysticism: Sufi, Quran, Mi'raj, Poetic and Theological Writings*. New York: Paulist Press, 1996.

Shaner, David Edward. *The Bodymind Experience in Japanese Buddhism: A Phenomenological Perspective of Kukai and Dogen*. Albany: SUNY Press, 1985.

Siddiqui, Abdul Hameed. *Life of Muhammad*. Chicago: Kazi Publications, 1983.

Singer, Isaac Bashevis. *Reaches of Heaven: A Story of the Baal Shem Tov*. New York: Farrar, Straus, Giroux, 1980.

Smart, Ninian. "Interpretation and Mystical Experience." *Religious Studies* 1 (1965): 75–87.

Smith, Margaret. *Rabi'a the Mystic and Her Fellow-Saints in Islam*. Cambridge: Cambridge University Press, 1984.

Soelle, Dorothee. *The Silent Cry: Mysticism and Resistance*. Trans. Barbara and Martin Rumscheidt. Minneapolis: Fortress Press, 2001.

Sorre, Max. *Les fondements biologiques de las géographie humaine: Essai dé une écologie de l'homme*. Paris: Colin, 1943.

Stace, Walter T. *Mysticism and Philosophy*. Philadelphia: Lippincott, 1960.

———. *The Teachings of the Mystics*. New York: New American Library, 1960.

Stavenhagen, Kurt. *Absolute Stellungnahmen: Eine ontologische Untersuchung über das Wesen der Religion*. Erlangen: Philosophischen Akademie, 1925.

Stegemann, Hartmut. *The Library of Qumran, on the Essenes, Qumran, John the Baptist, and Jesus*. Grand Rapids, Mich.: William B. Eerdmans, 1998.

Steinbock, Anthony J. "Affection and Attention: On the Phenomenology of Becoming Aware." In *Continental Philosophy Review*, Special Issue. Ed. Anthony J. Steinbock. Vol. 37, no. 1 (2004): 21–43.

———. "Face and Revelation: Levinas on Teaching as Way-Faring." In *Addressing Levinas*, ed. Eric Nelson et al., 119–37. Evanston, Ill.: Northwestern University Press, 2005.

———. "Facticity and Insight as Problems of the Lifeworld: On Individuation." *Continental Philosophy Review* 37, no. 2 (2004): 241–61.

———. "From Phenomenological Immortality to Phenomenological Natality." In *Rethinking Facticity*, ed. Eric Nelson and Francois Raffoul. Albany: SUNY Press, 2007.

———. *Home and Beyond: Generativity after Husserl*. Evanston, Ill.: Northwestern University Press, 1995.

————. "Interpersonal Attention through Exemplarity." *Journal of Consciousness Studies: Beyond Ourselves,* ed. Evan Thompson (2001): 179–196.

————. "Limit-Phenomena and the Liminality of Experience." *Alter: Revue de phenomenology* 6 (1998): 275–96.

————. "The Problem of Forgetfulness in the Phenomenology of Life." *Continental Philosophy Review. The Philosophy of Michel Henry,* ed. Anthony J. Steinbock. Vol. 32, no. 3 (1999): 271–302.

————. "Saturated Intentionality." In *The Body: Classic and Contemporary Readings,* ed. Donn Welton, 178–99. Malden, Mass.: Blackwell, 1999.

————. "Totalitarianism, Homogeneity of Power, Depth: Towards a Socio-Political Ontology." *Tijdschrift voor Filosofie,* 51/4 (1989): 621–48.

Stone, Lucian. "Blessed Perplexity: The Topos of Ḥayrat in Farid al-Din ʿAṭṭār's Mantiq al-tayr." Unpublished manuscript.

Strauss, Erwin. *Phenomenological Psychology.* Trans. Erling Eng. New York: Basic Books, 1966.

———— *Vom Sinn der Sinne.* Berlin: Springer, 1956.

Stroumsa, Gedaliahu G. "Form(s) of God: Some Notes on Metatron and Christ." *Harvard Theological Review* 76 (1983): 269–88.

Tao-Yüan, Shih. *The Transmission of the Lamp: Early Masters.* Trans. Sohaku Ogata. Wolfeboro, N.H.: Longwood Academic, 1990.

Teresa of Avila, Saint. *The Collected Works of St. Teresa of Avila,* Vol. 1. Trans. Kieran Kavanaugh, O.C.D., and Otilio Rodriguez, O.C.D. Washington, D.C.: ICS Publications, 1976.

————. *The Collected Works of St. Teresa of Avila,* Vol. 2. Trans. Kieran Kavanaugh, O.C.D., and Otilio Rodriguez, O.C.D. Washington, D.C.: ICS Publications, 1980.

————. *The Collected Works of St. Teresa of Avila,* Vol. 3. Trans. Kieran Kavanaugh, O.C.D., and Otilio Rodriguez, O.C.D. Washington, D.C.: ICS Publications, 1985.

———— [Teresa de Jesús]. *Obras Completas.* Ed. Efren de La Madre de Dios, O.C.D., and Otger Steggink, O. Carm. Madrid: Biblioteca de Autores Cristianos, 1997.

Teresa, Mother. *Mother Teresa: In My Own Words.* Ed. José Luis González-Balado. New York: Gramercy Books, 1996.

————. *A Simple Path.* Ed. Lucinda Vardey. New York: Ballantine Books, 1995.

Tobin, Frank. *Meister Eckhart, Thought and Language.* Philadelphia: University of Pennsylvania Press, 1986.

Trimingham, J. Spencer. *The Sufi Orders in Islam.* New York: Oxford University Press, 1971.

Underhill, Evelyn. *Mysticism: A Study in the Nature and Development of Man's Spiritual Consciousness.* New York: Penguin Books, 1974.

Usener, Hermann. *Kleine Schriften.* Leipzig: B. G. Teubner, 1912.

————. *Götternamen, Versuch einer Lehre von der Religiösen Begriffsbildung.* Frankfurt/Main: Verlag G. Schulte-Bulmke, 1948.

Van der Leeuw, G. *Phänomenologie der Religion*. Tübingen: J. C. B. Mohr/Paul Siebeck, 1933. Second edition. 1956.

Vawter, Bruce. *This Man Jesus: An Essay Toward a New Testament Christology: An Essay Toward a New Testament Christology*. Garden City, N.Y.: Image Books, 1973.

Vital, Chayyim. "Book of Visions." In *Jewish Mystical Autobiographies*, trans. and ed. Morris M. Faierstein, 43–263. New York: Paulist Press, 1999.

Walsh, William Thomas. *Saint Teresa of Ávila: A Biography*. Rockford, Ill.: Tan Books and Publishers, 1987.

Walther, Gerda. *Zur Phänomenologie der Mystik*. Halle: Niemeyer, 1923.

Weber, Alison. *Teresa of Avila and the Rhetoric of Femininity*. Princeton, N.J.: Princeton University Press, 1996.

Weil, Simone. *Attente de Dieu*. Paris: La Colombe, 1963.

———. *Gravity and Grace*. Trans. Emma Crawford and Mario von der Ruhr. New York: Routledge, 2002.

———. *Le pesanteur et la grâce*. Paris: Librairie Plon, 1988.

———. *Waiting for God*. Trans. Emma Craufurd. New York: Perennial Classics, 2001.

Werblowsky, R. J. Zwi. *Joseph Karo: Lawyer and Mystic*. Philadelphia: Jewish Publication Society of America, 1980.

Wilshire, Bruce. "Possession, Addiction, Fragmentation." In *High Culture: Reflections on Addiction and Modernity*, ed. Anna Alexander and Mark S. Roberts. New York: SUNY Press, 2003.

Windelband, Wilhelm. *Das Heilige: Skizze zur Religionsphilosophie*. Tübingen: J.C.B. Mohr, 1916.

Wolfson, Elliot R. *Abraham Abulafia—Kabalist and Prophet: Hermeneutics, Theosophy and Theurgy*. Los Angeles: Cherub Press, 2000.

Wolfson, Harry Austryn. *Philo: Foundations of Religious Philosophy in Judaism, Christianity, and Islam*, Vol. 1. Cambridge, Mass.: Harvard University Press, 1968.

Woods, Richard, ed. *Understanding Mysticism*. Garden City, N.Y.: Image Books, 1980.

Zaehner, R. C. *Mysticism: Sacred and Profane*. New York: Oxford University Press, 1961.

Zahavi, Dan. *Self-Awareness and Alterity: A Phenomenological Investigation*. Evanston, Ill.: Northwestern University Press, 1999.

———. *Subjectivity and Selfhood: Investigating the First Person Perspective*. Cambridge, Mass.: MIT Press, 2005.

Zalman, Rabbi Schneur, of Liadi. *Likutei Amarim (Tanya)*. Bilingual edition. New York: Kehot Publication Society, 1984.

Zohar, The. Trans. Harry Sperling, Maurice Simon, and Dr. Paul P. Leverthoff. 2nd ed. New York: Soncino Press, 1984.

INDEX

Italicized page number refers to illustration.

ANTHONY J. STEINBOCK is Professor of Philosophy at Southern Illinois University, Carbondale. He is author of *Home and Beyond: Generative Phenomenology after Husserl* and editor-in-chief of *Continental Philosophy Review*.